Proceedings of the
Danish Institute at Athens

Proceedings of the
Danish Institute at Athens · III

Edited by Signe Isager and Inge Nielsen

The publication was sponsored by:
The Danish Research Council for the Humanities.
Consul General Gösta Enbom's Foundation.
Konsul Georg Jorck og hustru Emma Jorck's Fond.

Proceedings of the Danish Institute at Athens

General Editors: *Signe Isager and Inge Nielsen*
Graphic design and Production by: *Freddy Pedersen*

Printed in Denmark on permanent paper

ISBN 87 7288 723 0

Distributed by:
AARHUS UNIVERSITY PRESS
Langelandsgade 177
DK-8200 Århus N
Fax (+45) 8942 5380

73 Lime Walk
Headington, Oxford OX3 7AD
Fax (+44) 865 750 079

Box 511
Oakvill, Conn. 06779
Fax (+1) 203 945 94 9468

The cover illustration depicts the theatre of Delphi.
Photo by R. Frederiksen, see p. 135, Fig. 1.

Contents

Preface

"Proceedings of the Danish Institute at Athens (PDIA)" is a periodical appearing every second year. Its aim is to publish the results of the archaeological activities of the Institute as well as articles by scholars, Danish or foreign, in the fields of Greek archaeology, history, philology, and literature. Articles submitted should follow the guidelines or PDIA and preferably be in English, though contributions in German, French and Italian will also be accepted. Scholars who wish to contribute to the journal should get in touch with:

The Director
The Danish Institute at Athens
Herefondos 14
GR-105 58 GREECE

The present volume was sponsored by The Danish Research Council for the Humanities, Consul General Gösta Enbom's Foundation and Konsul Georg Jorck and hustru Emma Jorck's Fond. We are very grateful to all of them for their generous contributions.

Athens, February 2000

Signe Isager and Inge Nielsen

Prehistoric Tumuli at Portes in Achaea. First Preliminary Report*

"SOMETIMES REMEMBER BUT SOMETIMES FORGET"

Ioannis Moschos

Our information concerning the prehistoric tumuli of Achaea (Fig. 1) is fragmentary, obscure and, in part, debatable.[1] Until now we knew of three MH tumuli at Aravonitsa[2] and another two at Mirali,[3] while a LH tumulus also exists in Agr(i)apidia, Chalandritsa.[4] These tumuli, though, cannot be properly studied, because our knowledge is restricted by the limited or even non-existent excavation reports, so that the sparse data that is available cannot be used in a fruitful manner. It is worth noting that Pelon in his catalogue refers only to the tumuli from Mirali. Thus, although in Achaean funerary customs tumuli do exist, their study has hardly anything to present. In archaeological literature Achaea is often ignored, so that it appears to be lagging behind regions such as Messenia, or Attica.[5] The situation is somewhat similar in neighbouring Korinthia,[6] in Aitoloakarnania,[7] across the channel, in Kephallenia,[8] the largest of the Ionian islands and in Elis,[9] regions with little or no evidence at all.

During the LH period at least, the existence of only one tumulus in Achaea can be attributed to the restricted Mycenaean presence in the region during the early and middle stages of the period,[10] and the almost unique use of chamber tombs at a later stage.[11]

Recent research of three tumuli at Portes, Achaea, which date from, or at least

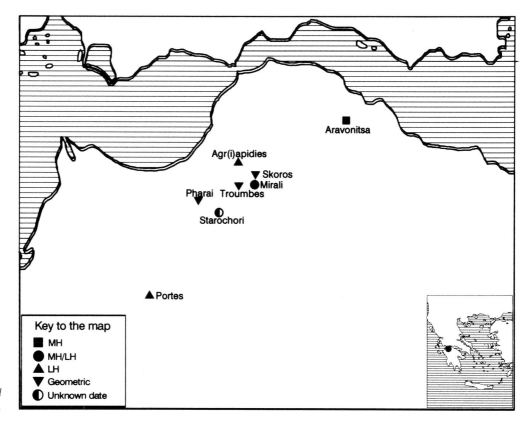

Fig. 1. Prehistoric and Geometric tumuli in Achaea.

Aravonitsa

Agr(i)apidies

Skoros
Mirali

Pharai Troumbes

Starochori

▲Portes

Key to the map
■ MH
● MH/LH
▲ LH
▼ Geometric
◑ Unknown date

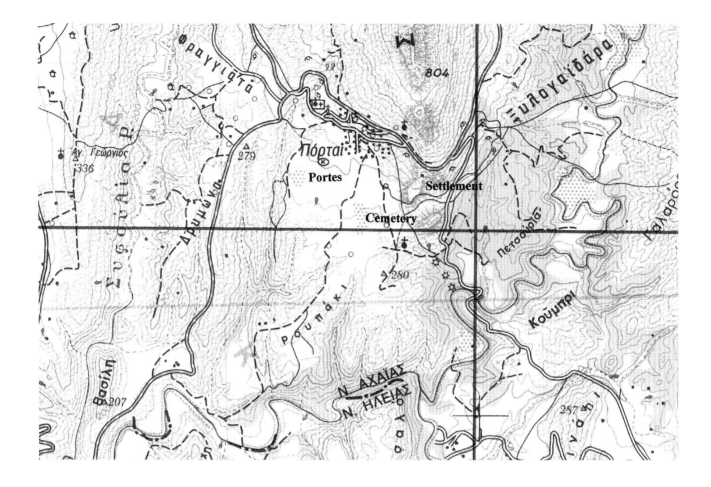

continued to be in use during the Early and Middle Mycenaean times, might drastically change our picture about the use of tumuli in Achaea and its wider region. To start with, we can now be certain about the presence of a population that was using family tumuli as a matter of custom. These tumuli continue the MH tradition, which is known in Achaea from Aravonitsa and Mirali. Furthermore, our knowledge concerning the graves and the funerary practices in the region is advanced, while at the same time obtaining comparative data in relation to the rest of the Mycenaean world.

The mountainous village of Portes is situated in SW Achaea, near the border with Elis (Fig. 2). The village[12], in existence at least since 1697, occupies the terraced steep SW foot of Mt. Skollis[13] (modern Santamerianiko, Santameriotiko, Santameri), which is called Portaiko in this part. During the Middle Ages it was situated a little higher in the mountain,

surrounded by a fortification wall, which was guarded in 1391 by Saint Jacob of Cyprus. The name of that village was also Portes (*Les Portes*). The area is mountainous, there are however some fertile upland fields and pastures.[14]

The most prominent geomorphologic feature of the region is Skollis, a three-peaked rocky massif reaching an altitude of 1016 m. Its summit, unobscured by other mountains, can be seen from the whole west Achaea, as well as coastal Aitolia.[15] Those travelling in the Ionian Sea lose sight of Skollis only after they have sailed for a considerable distance. Thus, the region of Portes can be easily traced and Mt. Skollis must have been a reference point in antiquity, especially for sailors.

Indeed, the geomorphologic features of the region are such that the name Portes (=passing of a gateway) at least since the Middle Ages, indicates the characteristics mentioned by name.[16] The strategic importance of the region for the control

Fig. 2. Portes. General plan of the area.

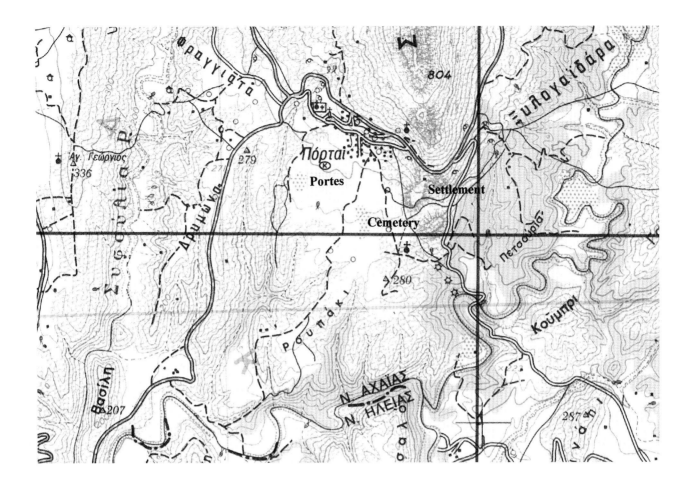

of the passage must have been recognised since prehistoric times. It is worth noting the reference of a French chronicle to Mt. Santameri as "Escuel de la montagne des Aventures". It would be most interesting to clarify whether the name Portaiko was prior to the village-name.[17] It is, though difficult to avoid comparing this region to its northern namesake Elian Pylos.[18] The worship of Hades, unique in antiquity, which is implied in Homer[19] and clearly stated by Pausanias,[20] reflects an older tradition connecting Elian Pylos with the Gates of the Underworld and the kingdom of death.[21] This tradition could very well be combined with the caves of Portaiko, namely the Neraidotrypa (or Kalogerotrypa) and the Korakofolia, to name a few, among several, caves occupied by hermits during Byzantine times.

The prehistoric cemetery occupies a low hill about 1500 m to the east of the village of Portes and close to a water-spring called Kefalovryso.[22] To the north

of the spring and the cemetery, in an area known as Porta Petra[23] or simply Porta, a survey has located the ancient settlement. Sherds from all periods of the Bronze Age were collected, while its occupation continued in the Hellenistic period. In the past, E. Mastrokostas had found Neolithic remains in the nearby cave of Korakopholia.[24]

The prehistoric settlement (Fig. 3) is situated on the summit plateau of a low hill, but later spread towards its slopes reaching Kefalovryso. The foundations of houses, though badly damaged, are still preserved on these slopes, while on the summit of the hill a considerable accumulation of deposits covers the remains. The excavation of the specific site would be of great interest to the region, since the depth of stratigraphical layers to be expected would solve many problems.

On the summit terrace of the cemetery three tumuli (A, 'B', C) were partly excavated.[25] The excavation was carried out

under particular conditions, for the tumuli had been repeatedly looted in the past and were partly destroyed. This intervention must have started during the Mycenaean period, when, due to the presence in the area of suitable rock formations, the common practice of inhumations in chamber tombs was followed. In the process of organising the cemetery of chamber tombs within the existing one, many of the tumuli graves were destroyed and their building material was re-used[26] for walling up the entrances[27] of the chamber tombs and for lining parts of the sides of the dromoi, where the rock was friable. Twelve chamber tombs have been excavated so far, spanning a use-period from the LH IIIA to the LH IIIC. Although the evidence is not available yet, it is possible that the cemetery was first used during the LH IIB, as is the case in many of the cemeteries in Achaea. Chamber tomb 3 lies

beneath tumulus C and could be characterised as an under-tumulus monument.[28] Among the other finds the tomb contained an intact burial of an early LH IIIC warrior/official.[29]

The tumuli were part of a large cemetery,[30] whose full extent will be appreciated in due course, after the excavation of the most vulnerable chamber tombs have been completed.

Tumulus A

It is situated on the central part of the hill (Fig. 4). It was formed by the accumulation of brown – dark brown earth (Munsell 7,5 YR, 4/4) mixed with fine gravel and held in place by a stone ring (*peribolos*) that was partly uncovered in the east. This ring was made of medium sized stones, which are abundant in the area, and is preserved in places up to a height

Fig. 4. General view of Tumulus A as seen from the east. The excavated part of the peribolos is visible.

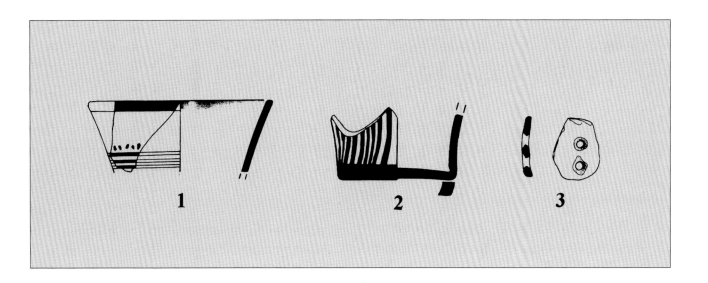

Fig. 5. Finds from tumulus A. 1-2: sherds of Vapheio cups (LH IIA). 3: pendant (?).

of three rows. The earth accumulation had an average thickness of 0.40 m and was only preserved on the tumulus' eastern side. The small part of the deposit that has been removed was gradually becoming thinner towards the stone ring and gave no characteristic pottery. The tumulus included five tombs.[31] To the north there are three, cut in the bedrock (A1, A2, A3),[32] all of them plundered. Tomb A1 is architecturally intact. It is a rectangular built chamber tomb with horizontal roof,[33] using one of the short sides as a *stomion*. Small slabs were used for its construction, built in horizontal rows, while three large and heavy slabs were used as a cover. Its long sides slant gradually upwards. A bronze ring was recovered from the tomb's disturbed deposit. Tombs A2 and A3 were partly destroyed. Architecturally, they are similar to A1, their main difference being that their short sides have the form of an entrance with pilars,[34] closed by a dry-stone wall. They must have been covered in a similar way, although none of the covering slabs were found in the vicinity. This could be an indication that they were removed in antiquity. The possibility that they were shaft-graves roofed with wooden planks and other perishable materials is not likely, due to the fact that the tombs were found at a shallow depth and were definitely covered by the small deposits that had accumulated over their lip. It should be noted that there is no evidence of a tomb with a stomion roofed with perishable materials,[35] since such an arrangement would be meaningless. As seen in the tombs in Argos,[36] the replacement of perishable roofs by slabs was made as a matter of convenience, first in shaft graves, before or during the appearance of the built chamber tombs. Instructive is the case of tomb *P* in Mycenae which is covered with an apsidal roof and had replaced a shaft-grave.[37] Thus, tombs A2 and A3 belong to the type of rectangular built chamber tombs with horizontal roof. In the eastern part of the tumulus the remains were found of a fourth destroyed cist tomb (A4). Its sides are constructed with upright slabs[38] and another, horizontal, slab was used for the floor.[39] Although it was found uncovered, amidst a deposit of black-earth and probably partly disturbed by tomb-robbers, the flexed lower limbs of a primary burial were preserved, accompanied by a small golden leaf decorated with linked argonauts and a steatite sealstone,[40] dating to the LH IIIA:2-B period. A similar, almost completely destroyed tomb, A5, was found at the southern part of the tumulus.

A few finds were recovered from the disturbed deposit covering the tumulus, which cannot, however, be associated with any of the tombs A1, A2, or A3. Among them were sherds of Vapheio cups of LH IIA date[41] (Fig. 5.1-2), the neck of a burnished LH I stamnos with vertical handles and pale-reddish slip,[42] as well as a small oval sherd (Fig. 5.3) with a pair of perforations that was probably used as a pendant.[43]

Cist graves were built during the Late Mycenaean period, as manifested by the tombs A4 and A5. This practice, which was rather rare, yet not unknown to the rest of the Mycenaean world,[44] was attributed by Deilaki to the "perpetuation of family traditions".[45] At this point, it should be stressed that we expect the forthcoming discovery of an under-tumulus chamber tomb.

'Tumulus B

It lies at the northern end of the plateau and is covered by an accumulation of earth, the upper layer of which is black (Fig. 6). Even though the observed accumulation is not clearly associated with this construction,[46] it covers a neatly built stone ring (peribolos), as in the case of the tumulus in Aphidna.[47] The peribolos is constructed of small stones arranged in horizontal rows. It was unearthed by chance during the excavation and its southern section had tumbled down. Considering the fact that the peribolos is a well-built, double-faced construction, one could argue that we are dealing with a possible grave circle.[48] It has an average thickness of 0.40 m while in height it goes beyond 1.30 m. The current research was confined to the summit of the tumulus,[49] where three plundered cist graves had been located (B1, B2?, B3). Grave B1 was inserted in the east section of the peribolos, which was dismantled down to the level of the grave floor. The long sides of the grave were lined with large, vertically placed slabs, while the remaining parts of the peribolos served as short sides and were rebuilt with small stones. The grave was initially covered with large slabs, a number of which lay scattered in the surrounding area – including the one removed by tomb robbers, while two slabs had fallen in the interior. With the exception of a few bones recovered from the fill

of the grave, there were no other finds in the interior. From the destroyed grave B2? only a few small slabs had survived that lay in alignment at the top of the fill. A fragmentary goblet (FS 264) of the LH I-IIA period and the shoulder of a small piriform jar dating to LH IIIA were either recovered from the immediate vicinity, or from the grave itself. Grave B3 had been better preserved. It was constructed of small upright slabs that were filled in with small, dry-stone built walls of horizontal rows.[50] The covering slabs had either been removed, or had fallen towards the interior. A small handless jar was recovered from the inside of the grave, while another example was found in the immediate vicinity. Both specimens (FS 77) are monochrome, like a few examples from Elis[51] and from Achaea,[52] unlike the usual dotted variety. They date to the LH IIIA period.

The better-preserved graves B1 and B3 exhibit a notable difference in construction to the ones in Tumulus A.[53] Of course, as in the case of A4 and A5, they too attest the use of cist-graves during the Late Mycenaean period, contemporary with that of an organised chamber tombs cemetery in the same locality. However, it should be stressed that these graves do not relate to the period of construction and first use of 'Tumulus' B, whose investigation should continue deeper.

Tumulus C

It is situated at the eastern part of the plateau and is severely damaged (Fig. 7). There are no surface signs to indicate the existence of a tumulus, with the exception of a few traces of a ring-wall (peribolos) consisting of a row of slabs, at the eastern and northern sides. What has remained of the tumulus' fill is a number of small piles of earth produced by tomb-robbers, consisting of mainly black deposits that have been greatly disturbed. The disturbance, however, dates to the LH I phase and continued during the Late Mycenaean period, as will be shown in due course. The extensive damage inflicted upon the fill

Fig. 6. General view of 'tumulus' B as seen from the east. Notice below the cist grave B1, founded on the peribolos.

and the recurrent nature of these disturbances, have not made possible the study of the site's stratigraphy. Three rectangular built chamber tombs came to light, all of them badly damaged. Tomb C1 (Fig. 8) occupies the centre of the tumulus and has very large dimensions[54] (8 × 1.60 m). In the process of laying down the foundations, tombs C2 and C3 were destroyed, thus C1 is the latest in date of the three. Some of the material from the dismantling of the tombs must have been used in the construction of this monumental tomb, which is made of small slabs in horizontal rows and has a stomion with pilasters at one of its short sides. The eastern of its long sides has been almost entirely dismantled, apart from a few foundation stones. Its building material, including many stones of the other sides, was removed during the Late Mycenaean period together with the covering slabs, which were not detected in the vicinity.[55] The

small slabs were reused in the dry masonry of the chamber tombs, or in the linings of their dromoi. At the rear part of the floor, below a pile of small slabs that lay in disorder (only in that part of the tomb), a few decayed bones were piled up, as if they were intentionally but carelessly covered up, either for protection or in showing respect, even though there was no apparent evidence of ancestral worship. The remains of the burial layer produced a piriform jar[56] (Fig. 9.1), a hight-based cup[57] (Fig. 9.2), six one-handled small jugs (Fig. 9.3), a jug with cut-away neck, six two-handled kantharoi (Fig. 9.4-5), two clay whorls and a bronze one-edged knife, dating from the LH IA to the LH II period. Tomb C2 lies directly to the east of C1. Little has remained of the tomb's construction: one of the long sides, consisting of flat stones laid in horizontal rows, is preserved at a low height, in addition to part of the stomion of one of the short

Chamber tomb 3

C3

C1

C2

Fig. 7. General view of the destroyed tumulus C, as seen from the east. Notice on the right side the peribolos made of a simple row of stones.

sides that was covered with a pile of stones; the possible remains of the dry-wall. A pile of decayed bones was found on the floor of the tomb, among with five one-handled jugs, a tall straight-sided cup[58] (Fig. 9.6), a double-handled amphoriskos with a tall base and a clay whorl, all dating to the LH IA period. Tomb C3 lies directly to the north of C1, it was of similar construction and its short side was destroyed. The tomb was found empty of its contents.

The recovery of grey Minyan ware, which is represented by a jug[59] discovered in tomb C1 and by a double-handled amphoriskos[60] and two jugs from the earlier tomb C2, is of considerable importance. It is characterised by the presence of both light-grey and dark-grey fabrics, as well as by the absence of well-smoothed surfaces, perhaps a local characteristic of the ware's late appearance. Matt painted pottery has not been recorded[61] so far.

However, survivals of MH shapes, mostly of matt painted ware and of Minyan ware (to a lesser extent) are evident in the pottery finds (rim-handled jugs, jug with cutaway neck, straight-sided cup, kantharoi), while only two vases belong to the characteristic Mycenaean repertoire (FS 27, 212). The life span of this advanced phase of MH ware covers chronologically the entire LH IA period and part of LH IB. Compared to the early wares of Samiko and Makrysia 'tumuli' in Elis,[62] the LH I ceramics from Portes exhibit a higher degree of conservatism.[63] That in itself is indicative of a smooth transition to the LH period, even though evidence on the MH period is still lacking. In dating the kantharoi of tomb C1 to the LH IA (-B) period and not earlier,[64] apart from comparative finds, the material of the destroyed tomb C2 is important, serving as a *terminus ante quem*.

The excavation of this particular tumu-

Fig. 8. The monumental built chamber tomb C1. Note the preserved height of one of the long sides near the stomion, which supported the adjacent dromos of CT3. Judging by that piece of evidence, we deduce that the destruction of the tumuli began in the Late Mycenaean period.

lus can by no means be considered complete. However, two of its tombs (C1, C2) allow some insight into its use, at least during the LH period. As far as tomb C1 is concerned, we can place its construction in the LH IA phase with relative certainty. Unfortunately, we cannot determine whether it had replaced some other construction at the centre of the tumulus,[65] and probably never will. That is because the foundations of this monumental tomb lay deeper than the floors of the pre-existing tombs C2 and C3, thus resulting in the destruction of the entire central part of the tumulus.

Conclusions

In this section, it will not be attempted to give a detailed account of all known tumuli[66] on the mainland in order to determine similarities and differences, however crucial that may be to the

present study. However, one should mention the striking similarities with the tumuli at Marathon, on which Dickinson[67] notes that they "... are notable for their structures rather than their goods, and seem rather special". The tumulus at Agr(i)apidia in Chalandritsa also seems similar, while the MH tumuli at Mirali and, possibly at Aravonitsa are different. In the region of Elis, many similarities are noticed with the tumuli at Samiko,[68] so as to make us speculate that we are dealing with a relevant group. In this way, we place certain regional characteristics of funerary architecture and burial practices in western Greece to the beginning of LH period. Naturally, we should not look very far for the place of origin of these particular burial practices. Gimbutas's and Hammond's theory,[69] according to which the bearers of these funerary practices in tumuli are associated with the *Kurgan* civilization, which spread southwards from coastal Albania and the Ionian islands to Attica and the SW Peloponnese, has received a lot of criticism. This is because of the great lapse of time between the tumuli that were discussed, and because of their differences in burial practices.[70] The above argument was also questioned because it relied exclusively on the presence of tumuli, considering their mere existence crucial to the theory,[71] while it is not.

Worth noting are the rectangular built chamber tombs A1-A3 and C1-C3. Such tombs can be found in various parts of the Mycenaean world, yet they do not belong to a deeply rooted tradition.[72] Their appearance is roughly contemporary to tholos tombs (e.g. late MH) and as the latter, antedate the introduction of the chamber tombs.[73] They have been found within the limits of tumuli (e.g. Argos, Vrana, Samikon, Portes) and cist cemeteries (e.g. Eleusis, Psara, Iolkos?), but they are more commonly found in small groups of two or three, or even isolated. In some cases they have been inserted in earlier constructed tumuli (e.g. Vrana, Samikon, Portes?), just like pits, cists and pithoi. One example (Tzannata) is referred to as an "ossuary" of the nearby tholos tomb. Several variations on construction, which are mainly related with dromoi, entrances and roofs, appear to be of no significance concerning their chronology. They might, however, be useful as evidence of relations and influences, or otherwise only reflect local peculiarities. There also exist circular, oval and apsidal built chamber tombs (see below), which are clearly predominant in Messenia and Laconia and probably assoiate their origin with tumuli and tholos tombs.

The best known rectangular built chamber tombs are those from the area of Argos.[74] Examples from Krokees[75] in Laconia, Medeon of Phocis,[76] Thebes[77] in Boeotia, Pharsala[78] and Pefkakia[79] in Thessaly, the tumuli I, II and IV at Vrana Marathon,[80] Eleusis,[81] Delos,[82] Archontiki on Psara,[83] Lazarides on Aigina,[84] Koukounaries on Paros,[85] Lygaridia on Naxos,[86] a few tombs from the tumuli at Samiko[87] and a single specimen from Babes[88] in Elis, are

included in the short catalogue of known sites. The "ossuary" near the royal tholos tomb at Tzannata in Poros, Kephallenia[89] is the sole example known from the Ionian Islands, yet of considerable significance. To the built chamber type belongs the grandest of all examples, tomb *P* of Grave Circle B.[90] According to Choremis, tomb 2 Niketopoulou at Karpophora is another example of built chamber tomb.[91] Besides, the use of a stomion is also found in the cist graves T.188 and T.198 at Nea Ionia in Volos[92]. However, one should not fail to mention the tombs with a side entrance (Gamma type (*type I*) at the Eleusis cemetery,[93] at Medeon in Phokis,[94] at Lefkandi in Euboea,[95] grave 1 of tumulus B at Dendra,[96] tombs I and II at Thorikos,[97] in addition to two tombs at Ayios Antonios at Pharsala.[98] Characteristic, though of different construction, is the built side-chamber with a horizontal roof of the "Treasury of Minyas",[99] as well as the small built niche in the tholos tomb at Vasiliko in Messenia.[100]

As far as construction is concerned, the tombs in question exhibit similarities with the built apsidal – horse-shoe shaped type.[101] L. Parlama[102] has already associated the Messenian apsidal tombs with MH apsidal houses and has regarded the type as clearly Messenian, nevertheless, leaving open the issue of Cretan influence,[103] if any. The well-known Cretan monumental examples, on one hand those at Maleme,[104] at Damania and tomb B at Praisos,[105] and on the other hand the A and B examples at Mouliana and the tomb at Vourlia,[106] have led Choremis[107] to the conclusion that the tomb at Karpophora "faintly recalls the monumental built chambers of Crete".

Turning to the issue of origin and appearance of the built chamber tomb on the Greek mainland, this requires thorough study[108] and lies beyond the scope of the present paper. It should be noted that their appearance could be explained if viewed as part of a general scheme of experimentation that led to the formulation of the typical Mycenaean tombs. These changes in mortuary practic-

18

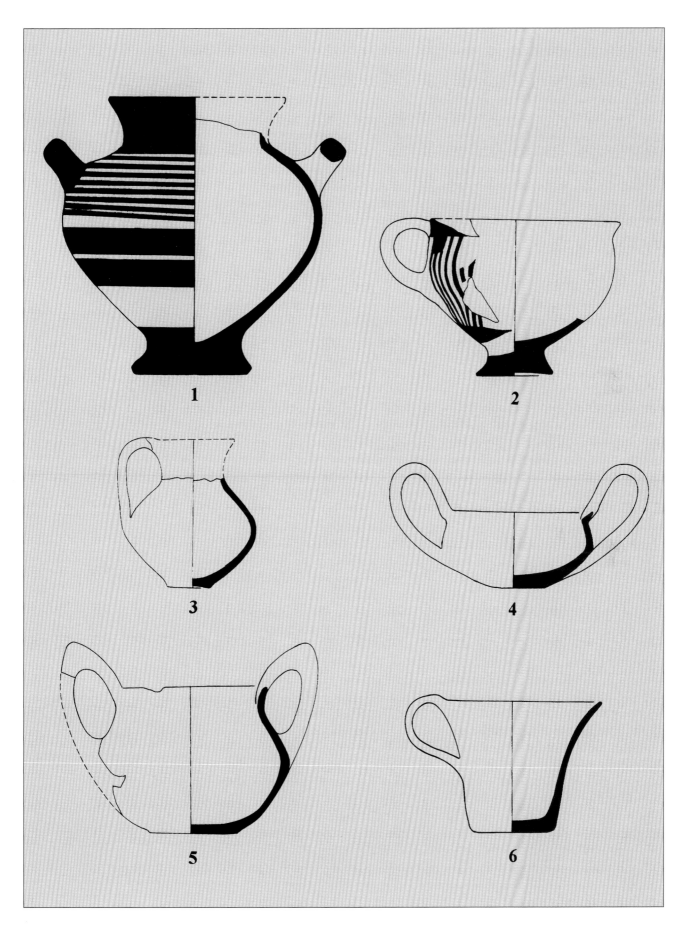

1

2

3

4

5

6

es had already appeared in MH III. Also, the presence of a stomion is clearly related to the practice of multiple burials and family sepulchres,[109] which was gradually adopted since the late MH period. In certain cases, they have served as an alternative solution to chamber tombs, when suitable rock for cutting was lacking.[110] But this is not the rule as there are cases where chamber tombs and built chamber tombs exists at the same cemetery. However, as Dickinson has argued on their origin, they seem to have much in common with the simple built cist graves.[111] E. Sapouna – Sakellaraki[112] also regards "the tomb at Lefkandi as linking the shaft grave with the built cist types …". As a conclusion, built chamber tombs probably form an advanced stage of cist and (probably) shaft graves and as the latter, they were never used intramurally.

Similarities in construction are also to be found with the tholos tombs.[113] Certain tombs on the Greek mainland belong to a formative stage between a tholos tomb and a built chamber monument and sometimes are referred to as "pseudo-tholoi" or "tholos-like structures", which are free-standing or in complex tumuli. The majority of these tombs date to the LH IIIA-B period and examples are known from Alea[114] in Arcadia; Arkines[115] and Analipsi[116] in Laconia; Vlachopoulo[117], Fourtsovrysi[118] and Gouvalari[119] in Messenia; Keri[120] in Zakynthos; Velousia[121] and Oxylithos[122] in Euboea; Medeon,[123] Sesklo,[124] Larisa,[125] Spilia,[126] Rachmani[127] and Anavra[128] in Thessaly, and possibly in Kephallenia.[129] Therefore, it should be noted that the built chamber tombs were linked to the tholos tombs and the apsidal tombs through a system of mutual-borrowing, as far as conception and construction is concerned.

The formative period of the rectangular built chamber type seems to have been of short duration and should be placed in the latest phase of the MH period, as we can see from tumulus I at Marathon and probably in the recently excavated tumuli at Samiko. The present deduction is of great significance, since at precisely the same period, the first beehive tholos tombs monuments appear, for which a mainland, and more specifically a Messenian, origin has been argued.[130] Thus, the construction of the built chamber tombs should be associated with the Mycenaean period and be regarded as a new and innovative construction that can hardly be associated with the late MH period, as is the case with tholos tombs. In this respect, finds of MH tradition that may have derived from rectangular built chamber tombs could belong to the Myceneaen period, instead.[131]

The evolution of the built chamber type is evident in the construction of tomb *P*, at Grave Circle B in Mycenae, which was reconstructed as the above type, with a saddle-shaped roof, and for which a Syrian and Cypriot origin was sought. Even though the largest rectangular built chamber tomb known so far, Tomb C1, reveals dependency on pre-existing practices, total ignorance of the beehive tholos tombs monuments or lack of technical knowledge,[132] it was built on a monumental scale, equivalent to that of the tholos tombs. Is this an indication of social power and richness? Evidence concerning the cemetery in the early and middle period is still lacking, so as to safely reach such a conclusion.

Furthermore, the large dimensions indicate the transition from the custom of burying family members in groups of family sepulchres (cist and pits, tumuli) to the innovation of using a single family tomb (tholos tomb, chamber tomb), a Mycenaean custom that originated in the MHIII.

In the Geometric period, the built chamber tombs survive in several variations, even in northern Greece where they were known in prehistoric times.[133] In Achaea, we are aware of two tombs associated with geometric finds: at Skoros in Chalandritsa[134] and at the tumuli in the valley of Pharai.[135] It is possible that in the latter area there exist three more tombs of the Geometric period.[136]

★ ★ ★

Taking into account the comparative data and the pottery finds (however fragmentary they may be), the period of construction and use of the rectangular built chamber tombs at Portes should be placed within LH IA-IIA (-B?), and not earlier. However, the above dating does not necessarily apply to the construction of the tumuli, a topic to which we will return in due course, when the excavation of the deepest layers has been completed.

Summing up our discussion, we may state that the earliest phase of use of the tumuli at Portes, but not necessarily that of their construction, is placed within LH IA period (tumuli A and C) and is characterised by the construction of rectangular built chamber tombs (A1-A3, C1-C3). Built cist graves are inserted in tumuli A and B during the LH IIIA-B period (A3,A4,B1,B2?,B3) and may be regarded as simple individual tombs, while there is no evidence, so far, for the continuous use of built chamber tombs until that time.[137] During the Late Mycenaean period, the practice of burying the dead in chamber tombs predominates, as attested by the presence of a chamber tomb cemetery in the same area.

The completion of the excavation is bound to lead to "safer" conclusions. Until then, all of the above should be regarded as mere speculations that lie within one's judgement.

General Abbreviations

EH   Early Helladic
FM   Furumark Motif
FS   Furumark Shape
LH   Late Helladic
MH   Middle Helladic

Notes

★ I warmly thank the ex-director of the 6th Ephorate of Prehistoric and Classical Antiquities and now general director of antiquities, Dr. Lazaros Kolonas, who has entrusted me with the supervision of the excavation. His help during the past years has been invaluable. He has attended closely all stages of the excavation and has contributed in a number of ways, from raising funds, to organizing and conducting the excavation, making decisions at crucial moments. Discussing with him and exchanging views, not only during the excavation but also in the process of compiling the present paper, has been extremely valuable to me. The undivided support of the ex-director of antiquities, Dr. I. Tzedakis and that of the ex-secretary general of the Greek Ministry of Culture, Mr. G. Thomas, who ensured, out of personal interest, sufficient raising of funds for the 1997 rescue excavation, is hereby greatly acknowledged. On matters of chronology, I have discussed the dating of the material with S. Dietz and J. Maran. L. Kolonas, prof. Th. I. Papadopoulos and prof. G. S. Korres offered constructive suggestions and made necessary alterations to the text; I am greatly indebted for their time and consideration. The archaeologists M. Gazis and K. Soura have participated in the excavation. My warmest thanks are also due to the well-experienced excavation technicians D. Evangeliou, S. Pittas, S. Tsamis, A. Anastasopoulos, E. Konstantinopoulos and K. Antonopoulos, devoted and tireless associates. The map of Fig.1 was laid out by the topographer Ch. Marinopoulos; K. Iliogamvrou has scetched the vases of Figs. 5 and 9. M. Logodoti has offered invaluable help in the Archaeological Library at Athens University. The translation of the Greek text was undertaken by M. Kamoulakou and M. Gazis, while the revision of the English text was done by C. Barton.

NOTE 1

Those reported at Pavlokastro – Tsaplanéika as four-sided tumuli by Protonotariou – Deilaki *1980*, 224 and by Syriopoulos 1964, 483, are not tumuli, as also shown by Kyparissis 1935, 70. Cf. Triantafyllou 1995, col. 2114; Syriopoulos 1964, 542, wrongly reports a tumulus at Tsoukaléika; The presence of Geometric tumuli or tholos tombs is reported in the hillocks of Troumbes Chalandritsa, see Kyparissis 1928, 110-111. Kyparissis 1929, 89-91, Figs. 4-7. Kyparissis 1930, 83. Cf. Vermeule 1960, 14, 17. Ålin 1962, 64. Åström 1964, 101. Syriopoulos 1964, 106, 482. Papadopoulos 1978-79, 29 (no. 24), Fig. 19. Hope Simpson & Dickinson 1979, 89 (B 50). Schachermeyr 1980, 256, 257. Dakoronia 1987, 53. Zavadil 1995, 22-23. Gadolou 1998, 31, 84, 203-205. French 1971, 180 reports a LH IIIA animal figurine from Troumbes; At the location Lalikosta of Pharai, a Geometric tumulus was excavated, see Zapheiropoulos 1957, 117. Zapheiropoulos 1957α, 69-70. Cf. Syriopoulos 1964, 481ff. Åström 1964, 104. Protonotariou – Deilaki 1980, 224. Schachermeyr 1980, 257. Lewartowski 1989, 62. Zavadil 1995. Papadopoulos does not refute Mycenaean presence in the region, see Papadopoulos 1978-79, 30 (no. 31); Zavadil 1995, 21 (A1) includes to her catalogue a LH (?) tumulus from Kamares – Paliomylos, according to Neratzoulis (Neologos Patron, 21.10.1930) and Thomopoulos (Thomopoulos 1950, 122, note 1). But the evidence is striking; cf. Åström 1964, 106, 109. Hope Simpson & Dickinson 1979, 86 (B41). My colleague M. Petropoulos informs me that he is excavating a tumulus at Starochori (Aghios Ioannis). It probably dates to prehistoric times. Geometric tumuli are also reported from Skoros Chalandritsa, see Yialouris 1960, 138. Mastrokostas 1961/2, 129, pl. 153β. Cf. Daux 1961, 682. Snodgrass 1971, 171, 211. Zavadil 1995, 21-22. A Late Geometric tumulus at Katarraktis (Lopesi), see Zapheiropoulos 1956, 197ff. Cf. Papadopoulos 1978-79, 31 (no 35).

NOTE 2

My colleague A. Vordhos has recently located three prehistoric tumuli, see Vordhos 1995, in print. A number of MH Minyan vases, found at the same site in the past, were either left behind by robbers or peasants, or belong to an old, forgotten excavation (as it is even now clear from an open trench), conducted in one of the tumuli by Zapheiropoulos, see Daux 1956, 291. Schachermeyer 1957, 94. Åström 1964, 100. Syriopoulos 1964, 80, 344, 378. Papadopoulos 1978-79, 34 (no. 56), 50. Hope Simpson & Dickinson 1979, 86 (B40). Zavadil 1995, 21 (A2). Triantafyllou 1995, col. 231. Cavanagh & Mee 1998, 36. A few unpublished vases from a chamber tomb at Aravonitsa (?), dating to the early LH IIIC period, kept in the storerooms of the museum at Aigion, belong to another, probably contemporary, excavation, see Kolonas 1995, 486.

NOTE 3

Tumuli A and B, see Zapheiropoulos 1952, 398-400, figs. 4,8. Cf. Vermeule 1960, 4 (no. 12a). Åström 1964, 106. Syriopoulos 1964, 80, 342, 344, 378. Howell 1974, 76. Wardle 1972, 40. Pelon 1976, 79 (7A,7B), fig. 1. Cavanagh 1977, 65. Dickinson 1977, 94. Papadopoulos 1978-79, 30 (no. 32), 50. Hope Simpson & Dickinson 1979, 90 (B 55). Protonotariou – Deilaki 1980, 224. Dakoronia 1987, 55. Müller 1989, 23, 37, fig. 10. Zavadil 1995, 25-26 (A7), 113-114. Cavanagh & Mee 1998, 30, 38. I think that they probably belong to the transitional period, rather than to MH.

NOTE 4

It contains "τάφους παλαιοτάτους", see Kyparissis 1930, 85, fig. 10. Cf. Åström 1964, 101. Syriopoulos 1964, 482. Hammond 1976, 151, map 25. Hope Simpson & Dickinson 1979, 89 (B50). Dakoronia 1987, 52. As justly noted by Papadopoulos, the finds belong to the LHI-II period and not to the Dark Ages, see Papadopoulos 1978-79, 29 (no. 25) 59, 95, fig. 19. Cf. Maran 1988, 341ff. Rutter 1993, 789. Papazoglou-Manioudaki 1994a, 272, note 25. Papadopoulos 1995, 203-204. Zavadil 1995, 23-24 (A5), 140ff., wrongly dates it to LH IIIC-Dark Ages?. Cf. Desborough

1972, 92, 395. It is not mentioned by Pelon. Its omission by Müller 1989 and Cavanagh & Mee 1998, is also characteristic. During a recent survey that was conducted in the region, I noticed other tumuli. The site is known to local inhabitants as Agrapidia, Agrapidia/Agrapidies, Agrapidoula, Agrapiditsa.

NOTE 5
Especially see Pelon 1976, passim. *MESSENIA*: Marinatos 1953, 250. Marinatos 1954, 311-316. Marinatos 1955, 254-255, pl. 97ß. Marinatos 1960, 112 ff. Marinatos 1964a, 92-93, pl. 85ß-γ. Marinatos 1966, 121-128, pls. 100-105, 110-111. Parlama 1972, 262-264, plan 3, pls. 198-199. McDonald & Rapp 1972, 266-267 (no. 14). Korres 1975, passim. Parlama 1976, 253-256. Korres 1980a, 311-343. Korres 1980b, passim. Korres 1980c. Korres 1980e, 456ff. Korres 1980f, 658-659. Korres 1980/83, 232, 234ff. Korres 1984, 11-79, figs.1-6. Korres 1984α, passim. Korres 1987, passim. Korres 1988, 224ff. Korres 1989, passim. Korres 1990, passim. Korres 1996, in print. Also see the excavation reports of G.S. Korres in Praktika and Ergon since 1974 ff. Cf. Syriopoulos 1964, 413-414. Wardle 1972, 39-40. Schachermeyr 1976a, 52ff. Protonotariou – Deilaki 1980-81, 226-229. Voutsaki 1985, passim. Müller 1989, passim. Voutsaki 1992, 73. Zavadil 1995, 49ff. Kilian – Dirlmeier 1997, 97ff. Cavanagh & Mee 1998, passim. Voutsaki 1998, 50, fig. 3.2. Boyd 1999, passim. ATTICA: Aphidna, see Wide 1896, 388-402. Cf. Tsountas & Manatt 1897, 385-386. Ålin 1962, 111. Syriopoulos 1968, 80. Blackburn 1970, 193-195. Pelon 1976, 80. Dickinson 1977, 34, 95, 97. Hope Simpson & Dickinson 1979, 197, 220 (F54). Brea 1985, 49. Cavanagh & Mee 1998, 30, 39; Athens, see Skias 1902, 123-130. Cf. Syriopoulos 1968, 316. Immerwahr 1971, 52-53. Pantelidou 1976, 166. Pelon 1976, 79-80. Hope Simpson & Dickinson 1979, 200 (F1). Cavanagh & Mee 1998, 39; Vrana (Marathon), see Marinatos 1970, 7-11. Marinatos 1970a, 68. Marinatos 1970b, 158-163. Marinatos 1970c, 351-357. Marinatos 1970d, 9-18. Marinatos 1970e, 109-117, fig. 3, pl. II. Marinatos 1972, 184-190. Marinatos 1974, 107-113. Cf. Wardle 1972, 39. Themelis 1974, 242-244. Pelon 1976, 82. Schachermeyr 1976, 246-250, figs. 66, 67, pl. 39. Schachermeyr 1976a, 35, 96, fig. 16. Dickinson 1977, 96. Hope Simpson & Dickinson 1979, 218 (F49). Protonotariou – Deilaki 1980, 231. Korres 1980g, 720-721. Maran 1992, 319ff. Kilian – Dirlmeier 1997, 91ff, figs. 52-56. Cavanagh & Mee 1998, 30, 39, 44, 58, 80, 91,

98; Thorikos, see Servais – Soyez 1972/76, 61-67. Müller 1989, 22. Müller 1994. Müller 1995, passim. Müller 1997, 82ff. Cf. Schachermeyr 1976a, 37, fig. 2. Dickinson 1977, 60, 62-64, 81, 96. Hope Simpson & Dickinson 1979, 209 (F25). Kilian – Dirlmeier 1997, 88ff, figs. 49-51. Cavanagh & Mee 1998, 39.

NOTE 6
No certain tumulus. Protonotariou – Deilaki 1980, 223 speculates on the existence of a tumulus in Aghioi Theodoroi and Dakoronia 1987, 56 in Galataki. For a possible tumulus at Corinth (North Cemetery), see Rutter 1990, 455-458; cf. Blegen et al. 1964, 1. Lambropoulou 1997, 138-143.

NOTE 7
Years ago, a tumulus was excavated near Stratos. Today, it is covered by the waters of the Stratos dam, see Sotiriadis 1908, 100. Cf. Wace & Thompson 1912, 229. Hope Simpson 1965, 92-93 (no 315). Syriopoulos 1968, 111. Wardle 1977, 161-162. Soueref 1986, 145. Wardle 1972, 40, 96, claims that it was "apparently similar to those in Lefkas". A pebble filled tumulus at Loutraki Katouna, is contemporary with the grave circles R on Lefkas. Most probably there are more tumuli, see Kolonas 1988, 173. Kolonas 1990, 140-141. Kolonas 1995c, 111. Kolonas 1997, 60-62, fig. 26. Kolonas 1998b, 15-16, fig. on p. 14 (not included in Cavanagh & Mee 1998 catalogue). Possibly in Chalkis (K. Vasiliki), see Moschos 2000, in this volume. Recently, a depas amphikypellon, together with a few MH and Mycenaean sherds, were discovered at Thyrreion. The presence of a cemetery there is considered possible, yet we cannot be certain, unless an excavation is conducted. However, the above vessels are normally for burial ceremonies; see Korres 1984, 55-58. Korres 1989, 235. Similar ones have come from the neighbouring burial circles R10 and R27 on Lefkas, see Dörpfeld 1927, 230, 248, 302-303, pls. 64,7 and 66,2a-3. Cf. Hammond 1974a, 138, fig. 3d. Also, at Paliki in Kephallenia, see Marinatos 1932, 13, fig. 14γ. Recently at Kalamaki, Achaea; see Vasilogamvrou 1995, 375, fig. 29. Dakoronia 1987, 52, includes to her catalogue a tumulus at Ag. Ilias, Mesologgi.

NOTE 8
Possibly at the locality "Sta Oikopeda" in Paliki, see Marinatos 1932, 10 ff., figs. 12-16; cf. Wardle 1972, 40, 111. Dickinson 1977, 60. Hope Simpson & Dickinson 1979, 191 (E33). Souyoudzoglou – Hay-

wood 1986, 59, note 2. Souyoudzoglou – Haywood 1990, 138-139. Sotiriou 1997, in print. Cavanagh & Mee 1998, 62-63, 80. A tumulus (?) at Same, see Marinatos 1964, 26-27, fig. 4, pl. 5:3-5; cf. Hammond 1974, 191. Hope Simpson & Dickinson 1979, 190 (E30). Possibly at the location Litharia in Poros, if we are not dealing with a tholos tomb, or a well-type tomb, see Sotiriou 1991, 168. Kolonas 1995b, in print. Blackman 1997, 44. Kalligas claimed that there was a tumulus above the MH graves at Kokkolata, see Kalligas 1977, 116-125. Kalligas 1983, 83, note 15. Cf. Wardle 1972, 111. Protonotariou – Deilaki 1980, 234. Dakaronia 1987, 55. Müller 1989, 26 (note 124), 39. On the contrary, Korres has convincingly argued against the above view and has shown that we are simply dealing with a MH cemetery, see Korres 1991, 191-199. Cf. Korres 1979, 421, note 22.

NOTE 9
The existence of the old excavated tumuli at Samiko and Makrysia has been doubted, see below note 48. Samiko: see Yialouris 1965, 6-40, 185-186, pls. 5-25, plan 1-2. Papakonstantinou 1981, 148-149. Papakonstantinou 1982, 133-134. Papakonstantinou 1983, 109-110. Papakonstantinou 1983a, 287-306. Cf. Daux 1956, 290. Schachermeyer 1957, 94. McDonald & Hope Simpson 1961, 23. Andronikos 1961/2, note 93. Ålin 1962, 79. Syriopoulos 1964, 479. Hammond 1967, 90, note 6. Schachermeyer 1971, 409, pl. 90. McDonald & Rapp 1972, 302-303, pls. 5-1, 7-3. Wardle 1972, 40. Blegen et al. 1973, 72, 153, 154. Parlama 1974, 55. Hammond 1974, 191. Howell 1974, 76. Korres 1975, 363. Pelon 1976, 77-78 (T. 5). Hooker 1976, 55-57, 235, pl. 4. Dickinson 1977, 60. Hope Simpson & Dickinson 1979, 101 (B92). Papahatzis 1979, 206-210. Liagouras 1980, 261-268. Protonotariou – Deilaki 1980, 224-225. Korres 1980b, 444. Korres 1980e, 458. Dietz 1980, 73. Sakellariou 1980, 90ff. Polychronopoulou 1980, 90. Korres 1981, 79-80. Hope Simpson 1981, 95 (D68). Iakovidis 1981, 21, note 21. Hiller 1982, 202ff. Hood 1986, 54ff. Korres 1987, 737-738. Lolos 1987, 216-217a, figs. 490-511. Dakoronia 1987, 50, 51, notes 18, 31. Syriopoulos 1987, 232. Herrmann 1987, pl. 112. Müller 1989, 22, 24, 37, fig. 10. Korres 1990, 10-11. Korres 1991, 194-195. Zavadil 1995. Papadopoulos 1995, 203. Cavanagh & Mee 1998, 30, 38, 44, 58, 62, 80. Boyd 1999, 678-691 Makrysia: see Themelis 1968, 126-127. Themelis 1968α, 284-288, pls. 121-128, plan 1. Cf. Blegen et al. 1973, 153. Korres 1975, 363. Pelon 1976, 78 (T.

6). Schachermeyr 1976a, 57. Dickinson 1977, 34, 60. Hope Simpson & Dickinson 1979, 99 (B86). Protonotariou – Deilaki 1980, op. cit. Korres 1980e, op. cit. Hope Simpson 1981, 95 (D 64). Lolos 1987, 218-219a, figs. 512-627. Dakoronia 1987, 51. Müller 1989, 22, 37, fig. 10. Zavadil 1995. Cavanagh & Mee 1998, 44, 57. Boyd 1999, 705-708. Agrapidochori: see Themelis 1965, 216-217, plan 2, pls. 244γ-248. Hammond 1974, 192. Dietz 1980, 74. Hope Simpson & Dickinson 1979, 93 (B66), 386. Olympia (Pelopio), see Syriopoulos 1968, 322-323. Protonotariou – Deilaki 1978, 229-234. Syriopoulos 1987, 232, 233. Kyrieleis 1988, 23-24, pls. V, VI. Kyrieleis 1990, 184, fig. 10. Tumuli are also reported from Mageira, Aghios Ilias, Olympia (Altis), Aghiorghitika, Kavkania, Ladhiko, Bouchioti, Tsaléika, see Hope Simpson & Dickinson 1979, passim. Müller 1989, 37. Zavadil 1995, 28-48, 105, 114-115, 123-127, 142-143. Boyd 1999, passim.

NOTE 10
Wace 1946, 631. Papadopoulos 1978-79, 183. Cf. Papadopoulos 1976, 407. Hope Simpson & Dickinson 1979, 75. Papadopoulos 1991, 32. The picture gained by the article of Vermeule was misleading, see Vermeule 1960, 1-20. Cf. Ålin 1962, 63-68. Desborough 1964, 97-101. Dickinson 1977, 95. It is now more clear that the coastal and inland Achaea was of interest to the Mycenaeans from the beginning. To the sites of the Early and/or Middle Mycenaean period should be now included Vounteni, see Kolonas 1998, vol. II, 607-612. Kato Sychaina, near Vounteni, see Stavropoulou – Gatsi 1994, 221-222. Pagona, within the limits of Patras, see Kotsaki 1987, 137. Kotsaki 1988, 149. Stavropoulou – Gatsi 1989, 121-122. Stavropoulou – Gatsi 1995, 514ff. Alexopoulou & Stavropoulou – Gatsi 1996, in print. Stavropoulou – Gatsi 1998, in print. Petroto, see Petropoulos 1989, 132. Petropoulos 1990, 499-504, plans 1-2. Petropoulos 1991, 249ff. Cf. Papazoglou – Manioudaki 1994, 200. Kontorli – Papadopoulou 1995, 114, fig 8. The cemetery at Kallithea (Laganidia) near Patras, see Papadopoulos 1987a, 89ff, fig. 103. Papadopoulos 1987b, 69ff, pls. 58-63. Papadopoulos 1988, 24ff. Papadopoulos 1988a, 32ff. Papadopoulos 1989, 23ff. Papadopoulos 1996, 7. Papadopoulos 1999, 270, pl. LVIId. Cf. Papazoglou – Manioudaki 1994, 200. Kontorli – Papadopoulou 1995, 113, fig. 6. Cavanagh & Mee 1998, 58. Katarrachia at Riolo (Lappa) see Petritaki 1988, 166. Vasilogamvrou 1998, in print. Aigion, see Papazoglou 1982, 149. Petropoulos 1990a,

137. Papazoglou – Manioudaki 1998. The cave-site at Kastria, see Sampson 1997, 309-310, 327-328, 336-337, pl. 10, plans 81.792, 84.799. The cemetery at Nikoleika in Aigion, see Petropoulos 1991a, 156. Petropoulos 1995, in print. I believe that the early phase of the building at Katarraktis (Drakotrypa) should be dated to the Early Mycenaean period, rather than to the MH, see Zapheiropoulos 1957, 115. Zapheiropoulos 1958, 167. Cf. Dickinson 1977, 23. Papadopoulos 1978-79, 30 (no. 33), 45-46. Hope Simpson & Dickinson 1979, 89 (B51). Concerning other new sites, see Rizakis 1992, passim. Kolonas 1995, 468ff. Papazoglou – Manioudaki 1994a, 269ff. Papazoglou – Manioudaki 1998. See also note 44.

NOTE 11
Papadopoulos 1978-79, 62, 127ff. Papadopoulos 1991, 31.

NOTE 12
On the history of the region, see Triantafyllou 1995, col. 1699-1700, 1861-1864, 2291-2292. Cf. Thomopoulos 1950, 314 (note 1), 330.

NOTE 13
See Philippson-Kirsten 1959, 197.

NOTE 14
The animal species and the vegetation of the region are notable. The general area of Mt. Erymanthos was well-forested in antiquity. Characteristic is the following reference taken from Homer's Odyssey (ς 102-104):

Οἵη δ' Ἄρτεμις εἶσι κατ' οὔρεα ἰοχέαιρα,
ἢ κατὰ Τηΰγετον περιμήκετον ἢ Ἐρύμανθον,
τερπομένη κάπροισι καὶ ὠκείησ' ἐλάφοισι·

NOTE 15
Kolonas 1995α, in print.

NOTE 16
The term Porta-Portes is Latin in origin and denotes the passing of a gateway. It is probably connected with the Venetian occupation in this region. In Achaea the place-name is also known at Skoura and at Zarouchléika – Patras, where it has the meaning of entrance to the city, see Triantafyllou 1995, 1699. The place-name is widely attested in Greece, see Ηπειρωτικά Χρονικά, Α', 90 and Θ', 200. Concerning the site Portes with a small ancient fortification, near the outlet of river Acheloös,

see Mastrokostas 1963, 213. About a passage in Fthiotidha with the place-name Porta, see Afroudakis 1990, 367 (no. 2565). On Portes, Portitses in the Argolid, see Vagiakakos 1986, 343. Portes in the area of the Bay of Navarino, see McDonald & Rapp 1972, 264-265 (no 3). Porta or Portes in a narrow passage outside Kozani, see Karamitrou – Mentesidi 1993, 380-381. Variations are also known: as Bara (= doorway), at the narrow passage before Siatista, as Pyli or Porta Panaghia, at the narrow passage before Koziaka at Trikala, see Ioannidaki 1983, 215. On the site Pori (= passage) with chamber tombs near Agr(i)apidhia in Chalandritsa, see Kyparissis 1930, 87 Syriopoulos 1964, 106. Triantafyllou 1995, 2228. In literature it appears with 'ω' (Πωρί), and relates to the type of rock. In my opinion, more accurate is the term Pori written with 'o' (Πορί), denoting a narrow passage towards Kantalo. Several place-names Pori/Poria are attested at Lygies in Achaea.

NOTE 17
A similar case known in Achaea is that of Alyssos/Alis(s)os, a term applied to a hill's crest prior to the foundation of the village. For its identification with Homeric Alision, see Sakellariou 1958-59, 34, note 4. A recent discovery in the area is that of a Mycenaean cemetery of chamber tombs, see Petropoulos 1990b, 135, 136.

NOTE 18
Pausanias, 4.36.1, 5.3.1, 5.18.6, 6.22.5, 6.25.2. Strabo, 8. 3.24-29. Sakellariou 1958-59, 44. Marinatos 1968, 173. For comparison to neighbouring Armatova, see Themeliš 1965, 215. Cf. Papandreou 1924, 97. Meyer, v.s. Pylos, RE, col. 2133-2134. Sperling 1942, 79. Daux 1968, 832 ff. Der Kleine Pauly, vol. 4, col. 1249-1251. Papahatzis 1979, 388ff., note 1. Korres 1982a, 114. Themelis 1965, 218, note 9, relates the word Pylos to the place-name Portes. The association of Portes with Elian Pylos has been suggested first by Kolonas, see Kolonas 1996, in print. Kolonas 1998α, in print. Judging by the finds of the chamber tomb cemetery, the region lies within Achaean domain. That is not against the suggested identification with Elian Pylos as Strabo (8. 3.10) reports that Mt. Skollis was "ὄρος πετρῶδες κοινὸν Δυμαίων τε καὶ Τριταιέων καὶ Ἠλείων" (a mountain common to Dyme, Tritaia and Elis). Besides, in Late Mycenaean times the regions of west Achaea and north Elis were one and the same.

NOTE 19
"ἐν Πύλῳ ἐν νεκύεσσι", *Iliad*, E 397.

NOTE 20
6. 25. 2-3.

NOTE 21
Sakellariou 1958-59, 44, note 4, for the relevant bibliography. Cf. Syriopoulos 1983, 68-69. Syriopoulos 1987, 230, 233. Kolonas 1998α, in print.

NOTE 22
For the type of spring see Kiskyras 1983, 180, 182. Seven more springs in Achaea belong to same category.

NOTE 23
Triantafyllou 1995, op.cit. The place-name is perhaps not irrelevant to what Homer referred to as "πέτρη τ' Ὠλενίη" (*Iliad*, B 617, Λ 757), which Strabo (8. 7.5) finally identifies with Skollis: "τοῦτο δ' οἱ μὲν Σκόλλιν καλοῦσιν, Ὅμηρος δὲ πέτρην Ὠλενίην.". And in Hesiod (74) : "ὤικεε δ' Ὠλενίην πέτρην ποταμοῖο παρ' ὄχθας εὐρεῖος Πείροιο", cf. Pausanias 6.20.16. Sakellariou 1958-59, passim. Pausanias, 5.20.16. Cf. Sakellariou 1958-59, passim. Xydis 1971, 149. The rendering of the village's name in plural, since at least 1391, denotes "extent" (Portes) rather than "place" (Porta), i.e. the wider area, the region around this place (Porta). Cf. Delopoulos 1990, 195 ff. Thus, the survival of the place-name Porta at the very spot where the ancient settlement lies, which coincides with the most strategic crossing of the mountain, is quite significant, and gives weight to the identification with Elian Pylos.

NOTE 24
Mastrokostas 1967, 216. Mastrokostas 1968, 138. Cf. Schachermeyr 1976, 79.

NOTE 25
The results of the excavation are briefly discussed below. We are very cautious in stating any far-reaching conclusions, as the investigation of the site is still in progress and this may lead to future reconsiderations and reshaping of views. The author is in the process of completing a Ph.D. diss. on the present topic.

NOTE 26
For a similar case at Dendra, see Protonotariou – Deilaki 1980, "poster" and Protonotariou – Deilaki 1990, 95. Cf. Protonotariou – Deilaki 1990a, 69. At Prosymna, see Blegen 1937, passim. Similar problems

exist at Kalamaki in Achaea, where the Mycenaean cemetery of chamber tombs has developed within the boundaries of a pre-existing EH cemetery, see Vasilogamvrou 1995, 367, fig. 1. Vasilogamvrou 1995a, in print. There are other cases of tumuli that were disturbed by the construction of tholos tombs within their limits, e.g. at Voidokoilia, see Korres 1984, 67-68. Korres 1989, 237. At Tourliditsa, see Marinatos 1966, 129-132, pls. 106-109, 112-114. At Loutraki in Katouna, see supra note 7.

NOTE 27
Characteristic is also the case of chamber tomb 1, see Kolonas & Moschos 1994, 231.

NOTE 28
The choice of site probably indicates that the authority exercised by the specific family group was a matter of family tradition, handed down from previous generations. See also the discussion in Mee & Cavanagh 1990, 227-228. Of course, no evidence of ancestral worship is attested at the Portes' tumuli.

NOTE 29
See Kolonas 1995, 474-475, fig. 2. Kolonas 1995α, in print. Kolonas & Moschos 1995, in print. Kolonas 1996, in print. Kolonas 1996a, 7, figs. on p.7. Moschos 1996, in print. Tomlinson 1996, 15. Touchais 1996, 1170-1171. Papazoglou – Manioudaki 1998. Papadopoulos 1999, 268, 271-272, pl. LIXa,b. For a LM IIIC stirrup jar from this tomb, see Moschos 1996, in print and Kanta 1998, 44-45.

NOTE 30
Moschos 1996, in print. For isolated tumuli and tumulus cemeteries see Cavanagh & Mee 1998, 25. It is the fourth tumulus cemetery in Achaea after Aravonitsa, Mirali and Agr(i)apidia.

NOTE 31
Kolonas & Moschos 1994, 230. See also supra notes 29, 30.

NOTE 32
Cavanagh & Mee 1998, 26 claims that "…on hard rock, built graves might be preferred".

NOTE 33
The term is first employed by D. Theocharis in order to describe a variation tholos tomb ("pseudo-tholos") that exhibits similarities to the chamber tombs, see Theocharis 1964, 261. Theocharis 1966, 253. Also, Choremis 1973, 28. Dickinson 1977,

60. Protonotariou – Deilaki 1980, 152, note 138. Verdelis describes the built tombs, of similar construction, at Pharsala as "θαλαμοειδείς τετράγωνους τάφους" (square chamber tombs), see Verdelis 1952, 197. "- Built graves" in Hope Simpson & Dickinson 1979, 427. Cf. Vatin 1969, 44. Pelon 1987, 107-115, pls. XXVI-XXVIII. Dickinson 1989, 133-134. Hiller 1989, 137-144. Müller 1989, 4, note 11. "Built chamber tombs" and "built tombs" in Cavanagh & Mee 1998. Dickinson 1983, 57 and Dickinson 1994, 223 prefers the terms "rectangular built tombs" and "stone-built tombs", in the latter including the well constructed built tombs without a *stomion*. Müller 1994, 224ff, insists on the distinction of this certain type to built chamber tombs (e.g. tombs of square plan and corbelled ceiling) and stone-built tombs (e.g. side approach, Gamma type graves, absence of corbelling). However, the most important and most distinctive characteristic of the two categories suggested is no other than the one-side entrance and this is why the term built chamber tomb should be exclusively given preference. Useful for the variations that appear are the terms rectangular, oval, apsidal, circular, Gamma type, according to the shape of the built chamber tomb and the position of the *stomion* or the dromos in relation to the tomb axis. In fact, the same applies to the terminology of chamber tombs, where the shape of chamber, the form of roof and other structural details are just defining elements of this certain type. Moreover, the local or other peculiarities of tholos tombs have never led to a different terminology. The presence or not of dromos at the built chamber tombs, the corbelled ceiling and other peculiarities are of no special significance and simply reflect local architectural characteristics, solution to constructive and static problems or a different aproach of this certain tomb type; issues not relevant to the present study. In fact, the presence of certain characteristics in tomb groups (e.g. Medeon, Vrana, Portes), confirms what is mentioned above and does not form the motive of further research, exept for the drafting and research of local peculiarities, perhaps also of chronological differences, that are more easily determined within the necropolis.

NOTE 34
A similar tomb of the Late Geometric period at Skoros in Chalandritsa, see Mastrokostas 1961/2, 129, pl. 153β. Cf. Gadolou 1998, 31-32 (no. 23), 205.

NOTE 35

The large opening of the first tomb at Pharsala (2,50m. wide) seems extremely difficult to cover with slabs, see Verdelis 1952, 197. Most likely, it had an arched roof, as the second tomb probably had, see Verdelis 1953, 129. The side chamber of the 'Treasury of Minyas', which is of comparable width, has been roofed with slabs, but this was a different construction, see note 99. The "built-like tomb" ("κτιστοειδής τάφος") at Skoura in Achaea also has a large opening (2m.), see note 44. For a possible wooden roof at Paliki ("Sta Oikopeda"), see Marinatos 1932, 11, fig. 12. Even so, this is highly unlikely. Protonotariou – Deilaki 1990a, 78, fig. 6, describes a grave near the hospital area in Argos as a "shaft grave with a side entrance", which is rather unlikely; the term "shaft grave" is probably used instead of the term "built chamber tomb". Note also the grave on Skopelos (Cape Staphylos) where the stone slabs were laid on wooden beams, see Platon 1949, 534ff.

NOTE 36

Protonotariou – Deilaki 1980, passim.

NOTE 37

Mylonas 1972-73, 211-222, fig. 25, pls. 192-196. Somewhat similar is the case of tomb Iπ1 at Eleusis, which was originally a large cist, see Mylonas 1975, 102ff, plan 114, pls. 141-143a. cf. Blackburn 1970, 216. Similar suggestion for the tomb S2 at Medeon, see Müller 1994, 226, note 10.

NOTE 38

Cavanagh & Mee 1998, passim. These tombs are known since the EH III period. The type is frequent in the MH period, found mainly in central Greece, see Blackburn 1970, 14 (no 1), 284-285, fig. 3. Cf. Blegen & Wace 1931, 28ff. Mylonas 1951, 64ff. Dickinson 1983, passim. Dakoronia 1987, 61-62, notes 5-10. Nordquist 1987, 91ff, 97. See also Mylonas 1975, 205ff. Polychronopoulou 1980, 19-20, 59ff. Of a similar type are tombs II and XI at the tumulus at Aphidna in Attica, see Wide 1896, 388-402. Cf. Pelon 1976, 80-82 (T. 9), pl. XXI:1-2. At the tumulus at Asine, see Dietz 1980, passim; cf. Dietz 1975, 157ff. At the tumuli Γ and ΣT at Argos, their use continued during the LH IA-IIIA period, see Protonotariou – Deilaki 1980, 31-59, 191. Similar tombs are also known from the rest of the Mycenaean world, as for example at Nea Ionia in Volos, see below notes 44 and 50. Also, notice the tombs at the later tumuli at Pogoni and other sites in Epirus, see Andreou 1979,

239. Andreou 1980, 303-307, plan 2, pls. 145δ-147. Andreou 1981, 271-273, pl. 163δ. Andreou 1982, 259, pl. 161. Andreou 1982a, 54-60. Andreou 1983, 229-230, pl. 95γ. Andreou 1994, 233ff. Andreou & Andreou 1994, 82ff, Figs. 22, 23, 31, 32, 34, 40, 41, 45. Cf. Papadopoulos 1987, 141. Cist graves in the A grave circle at Antrona, see Papakonstantinou 1994, 171ff.

NOTE 39

Holmberg 1944, 25, fig. 26 (of MH times). Verdelis 1952, 191. Theocharis D-M. 1970, 201. Chantziagelakis 1982, 226. Chantziagelakis 1983, 195 (T. 172). Cf. Baziou-Eustathiou 1985, 18 (T40). At Mazaraki and Elaphotopos in Epirus, see Vokotopoulou 1969, 179-181, 191; cf. Papadopoulos 1976α, 278. At Kefalovryso in Nafpaktos, as my colleague H. Kolia informs me. At chamber P of Grave Circle B, see Mylonas 1972-73, 217. Also known from the floor of tholos tombs, e.g. in the case of Kakovatos (B), see Pelon 1976, 220-221 (Th. 28B), pl. CII:1. At Karpofora, see Choremis 1973, 46, 62-65, 70, 72. In chamber tomb Λ at Kallithea in Patras, see Papadopoulos 1978, 123, pl. 101α. At Vrohitsa in Elis, see Vikatou 1996-97, 309. From the floor of rectangular built chamber tombs at Karfi – Crete, see Pendlebury et al. 1937-38, 100ff.

NOTE 40

CMS, V, Suppl. III, forthcoming.

NOTE 41

FS 224, FM 64:5, 78:3. Mountjoy 1986, 33-34, fig. 34.

NOTE 42

Mylonas 1972-73, 55 (Γ-20), pl. 43γ. Cf. Dietz 1991, 192, fig. 58 (AI-3).

NOTE 43

For similar amulets, see Protonotariou – Deilaki 1980, 83-84, note 181, pl. Γ53,1-2. For similar perforated rhomboidal finds of ivory of non-reported use, see Mylonas 1972-73, pl. 22α,6. Clearly, we are not dealing merely with a perforated vase sherd.

NOTE 44

The existence of a tomb at Skoura in Achaea has been known for years, see Mastrokostas 1960, 144. Cf. Åström 1964, 107. Papadopoulos 1978-79, 33 (no. 52). Hope Simpson & Dickinson 1979, 106. Cavanagh & Mee 1998, 80. Mastrokostas has described it as «κτιστοειδή» ("built-like"), perhaps in order to point out that it is not a cist grave, as has prevailed in literature. Unfortunately the exact place of the tomb

is ignored. Also note a pit grave at Drimaleika in Krini, with one side built, see Petropoulos 1985, 135; cf. Cavanagh & Mee 1998, 80. Pit graves and cist tombs of the LH IIIA-B period are reported from Arnouga (Kantalos) in Kalavryta, see Sampson 1997, 361. Intramural burial (LH IIIB) at Katarraktis (Ag. Athanasios), see Zapheiropoulos 1958, 172. Cf. Papadopoulos 1978-79, 59-60. Cavanagh & Mee 1998, 36. Intramural burial in a cist grave at Aigion, see Papazoglou 1982, 149. Also, a child burial of sub-Mycenaean or Geometric times, see Papazoglou 1984, 95. Earlier cist graves are also known in the region, as in the case of two graves in Thea (Rodista), which are not sub-Mycenaean as originally thought, but belong to the MH/LH I period, see Dekoulakou 1973-74, 381-382, Fig. 247. Cf. Papazoglou – Manioudaki 1994, 200, note 181. Papazoglou – Manioudaki 1994a, 272, Figs. 14-19. Five MH tombs have been discovered in Patras, see Papakosta 1980, 193 and Petropoulos 1990, 495, 514-515, note 3. An intramural cist at Pagona, see Stavropoulou – Gatsi 1995, 518, plan 2, Fig. 7. At Aigion, pit graves and cist tombs of MH/LH period within and outside a peribolos, see Petropoulos 1990, 508 and Petropoulos 1990a, 137. A MH tomb at Krathio in Aigialeia, from which a Minyan kantharos was derived, see Papadopoulos 1978-79, 36-37 (no. 67-68), 50. Recently, also at Nikoleika in Aigion, see Petropoulos 1996, in print. A MH intramural pit or cist at Teichos Dymaion, see Mastrokostas 1966, 159; cf. Cavanagh & Mee 1998, 37. For the distribution of cist graves, see relevant bibliography in Dickinson 1977, 59-60, 65. Cf. Snodgrass 1971, 180-182. Desborough 1964, 33. Protonotariou – Deilaki 1980, 139ff. Dickinson 1983, 62 and notes 41-45. Syriopoulos 1983a, 393. Mee & Cavanagh 1984, passim. Dakoronia 1987, 61ff. Vanschoonwinkel 1991, 184, 187-188. Cavanagh & Mee 1998, passim. Also add: Nea Ionia in Volos, see Injesiloglou 1981, 252, pl. 151δ-γ. Chantziagelakis 1982, 225-226. Baziou-Eustathiou 1984, 140, 142, pl. 44δ. Cf. Baziou-Eustathiou 1985, 17ff., plans 1-17, pls. 13-30. Baziou-Eustathiou 1991, 1183. Baziou-Eustathiou 1993, 59-60. Kynos, see Dakoronia 1993, 218. Athens, see Alexandri 1976, 26 (T. I, II), pl. 31δ-γ. Karagiorga – Stathakopoulou 1979, 16-17 (T. I - VIII). Vravrona, see Kakavogianni 1984, 45. Epirus, see Tartaron & Zachos 1994, 63ff, table 1 and Andreou 1976, 202. Cf. Soueref 1986, 113-115. Papadopoulos 1987, 137ff., pl. XXXVa-b. Papadopoulos 1987c, 361. Andreou 1994, 233ff. Also in Albania, see Bejko 1994, 110-111.

NOTE 45
See Protonotariou – Deilaki 1966, 246 and note 22. According to Dickinson 1983, 62 it was mainly attributed to the continuity of Mycenaean tradition. Cf. Desborough 1964, 37-40, 70. Styrenius 1967, 161-162. Vokotopoulou 1969, passim. Snodgrass 1971, 173, 177-184. Papadopoulos 1976a, 278. Dakoronia 1987, 65-66. Mee & Cavanagh 1990, 242.

NOTE 46
Before the completion of the excavation, it would be difficult to decide whether the accumulation of earth was intended to create a tumulus, or whether it simply served the purpose of concealing a pre-existing structure (perhaps a grave circle?) which served to define and set apart the burial ground. It should be noted that with the creation of this fill the regular access to the cemetery of chamber tombs was restored. Anyway, this fill was already there at LH IIIA period, when cist graves were inserted in the mound (see the text below). It might even be the case of a well-shaped tomb or of a damaged above ground tholos tomb (like Cretan and early examples from Messenia) of the early-middle Mycenaean period, or even earlier. Such a case would be of particular interest to the region of Achaea.

NOTE 47
Supra note 5. According to Andronikos, the covering of the peribolos in the case of Aphidna, reveals that "… το νόημα της κρηπίδος είναι αναμφιβόλως συμβολικόν Σημαίνει το θεμέλιον, το οποίον θα στηρίξει το 'μνημείον'…", see Andronikos 1961/2, 173.

NOTE 48
For the distinction between grave circles and tumuli see Korres 1991, 191ff. He describes the 'tumulus' at Samiko as a Grave circle and the 'tumulus' at Makrysia, which is of comparable construction to 'tumulus' B at Portes, as a tholos tomb, see ibid., 194-195. Korres 1975, 363. Korres 1980b, 444. Korres 1981, 79. Cf. Korres 1980e, 458. Korres 1987, 737-738. On the contrary, Dickinson 1977, 60 and 1983, 61 regards them as tumuli, while he mentions the different view expressed by Iakovidis. Cf. Iakovidis 1981, 21, note 21. Other authors, too, believe that they are tumuli, see Dietz 1980, 73. Müller 1989, 22, 37. Papadopoulos 1995, 203. Cavanagh & Mee 1998, 44. See also Dakoronia 1987, 51, 58-59 (notes 18, 31). Papakonstantinou in Korres 1990, 11 regards the burial structure

at Samiko as a well-shaped tomb and compares it to tumulus III from the same region.

NOTE 49
Kolonas & Moschos 1994, 230-231. See also supra notes 29, 30.

NOTE 50
Tsountas 1898, 142 (Early Cycladic). At Paliokklisi in Farsala (MH), see Toufexis 1991, 222. At Lerna (MH, LH), see Blackburn 1970, 13. At Iolkos, see Theocharis D.-M. 1970, 200, plan 1; cf. Schachermeyr 1976a, 60-61, fig. 10. Batziou-Eustathiou 1985, 23, pl. 16α (T. 49); 24, pl. 17α (T.50); 29, pl. 19ϐ (T. 166); 33, pl. 21ϐ (T. 188); 42, pl. 25α (T. 189); 50, pl. 30ϐ (T198). At Lefkandi, see Sapouna – Sakellaraki 1993, 196 (tomb B). At Eleusis, see Pahygianni-Kaloudi 1979, 39-40 (T.1). At Pavlopetri Laconia, see Harding, Cadogan & Howell 1969, 123. At Marmara, see Dakoronia 1987, 39-40 (T. E4), 45-46 (T. Θ3), 61. The shaft grave at Englianos had a vertical slab at one narrow side; this is probably an indication of a stomion (rectangular chamber tomb?), see Blegen & Rawson 1996, pls. 229-231; cf. Boyd 1999, 503-504, 510, 528-529. Cavanagh & Mee 1998, 27 claims that "… there seems to be no significance, beyond convenience – a balance between the effort of building the wall and the inconvenience of hauling a slab some distance". But, in Portes, the quarring area is less than 20 m from this particular '-tumulus'. So, the material (slabs and small stones) might have come from other nearby destroyed tombs.

NOTE 51
Yialouris 1966, 171, pl. 182ε. Papathanasopoulos 1969, 149, pl.147ε. Parlama 1974, 40, pl. 31οτ. Cf. Mountjoy 1999, 378, fig. 131:31. Unpublished material from Chelidoni and Ag. Triadha.

NOTE 52
Papadopoulos 1978-79, 84 (group A). Kolonas 1998, vol. II, 511-512; vol. III2, pls. 179.501, 180.503, 182.513. Cf. Mountjoy 1999, 407, fig. 142:14.

NOTE 53
For this variation see the discussion in Dietz 1991, 277; Cavanagh & Mee 1998, passim.

NOTE 54
It is the largest, up to date, rectangurar built chamber tomb. Of similar scale is the triple-grave at the later tumulus IV at Marathon (supra note 5) and the tomb at

Thebes (see note 77). Comparative is also the domed like a tholos oval built tomb at Thorikos (9 × 3 m) and the rectangular F structure at Lefkas; Dörpfeld 1927, 213ff.

NOTE 55
It seems probable they were used in the construction of an elusive, as yet, tholos tomb.

NOTE 56
FS 27, FM 76:3. Cf. Marinatos 1953, 248, fig. 9. Yialouris 1965, 23-24, pls. 14ζ-η, 15α (no 48-50). Pantelidou 1976, 62-64, 177, pl. 9α-ϐ. Protonotariou – Deilaki 1980, pl. 39:5. Lolos 1987, 286ff.

NOTE 57
FS 212, FM 67:3 or 78. This shape is not as popular as FS 211. Of course, it`s the first among the published material from Achaea. For the shape see Blegen 1937, pl. 195:496. Mylonas 1972-73, 67 (Γ-55), pl. 52ε. For a similar decoration in a FS 211 cup, see Blegen 1937, fig. 105:407. Also in an ephyrian gobblet (FS 270) from Athens, see Pantelidou 1976, 83 (no 13), 86, 185, pl. 24ζ.

NOTE 58
Mylonas 1972-73, 66 (Γ-53), pl. 52α. Cf. Dietz 1991, 160, fig. 48:AB-10(2), note 371 (with the revelant bibliography). Spyropoulos 1973, 265-266, pl. 218ϐ. Yalouris 1965, pl. 14a. Cf. Lolos 1987, 233ff. Mountjoy 1999, 374:10, fig. 128:10.

NOTE 59
Cf. Dietz 1991, 200, 204, fig. 61(BE-2,3). It dates to the LH IA period, in accordance with other vessels from the same grave. In Achaea, parallels are known from Vrysari, Thea (Rodista) and Chalandritsa, see Papazoglou – Manioudaki 1994a, 271-273, figs. 12,13,15,16, where one finds the relevant bibliography. Also, at Petroto, as my colleague M. Petropoulos informs me. Cf. Papazoglou – Manioudaki 1998. Minyan ware was recently recovered from the acropolis at Vounteni, see Kolonas 1998, vol. II, 608.5. At Pagona, see Stavropoulou – Gatsi 1995, 520-521. At Xirokambos in Starochori, see Petritaki 1988a, 164. At Kastria in Kalavryta, see Sampson 1997, 308. A three-handled piriform jar (FS 48) of LH IIIB:1, from chamber tomb 5 at Portes (exc. no. 1997.CT5.19), exhibits a smooth (burnished) grey surface.

NOTE 60
It belongs to early LH IA and is reminiscent of Argive Minyan ware. A similarly shaped vessel from Samiko has been dated to the

LH IIIA(?) period, see Yialouris 1965, 33 (no. 100), pl. 22:στ. Yet, it belongs to LH I, see Lolos 1987, 217, 369, fig. 504b. Argive Minyan ware is known in Achaea, see Zapheiropoulos 1958, 173-174, pl. 135α,β. Cf. Papadopoulos 1978-79, 64 (a). Also, at Xirokambos in Starochori, see Petritaki 1988a, 164. Possibly from other sites, the material of which remains unpublished.

NOTE 61
Most of the vases are worn off. The straight-sided cup might have been decorated in matt paint.

NOTE 62
Yialouris 1965, 36; Themelis 1968α, 284-285.

NOTE 63
This view may have been formed because of the probably short period of use of the early tomb C2, on one hand, and of the possibly circumstantial use of tomb C1, during the LH IA/B-LH II period, on the other. Most likely, the same family group used tombs in other tumuli at the same time, since only tomb C1 continued in use in the particular tumulus. Comparable is the case of the tholos tombs that are found in pairs, see Mylonas 1948, 74. Cf. Korres 1984a. For the continuity of local tradition of MH ware, see the discussion in Dickinson 1989, 134; cf. Mountjoy 1999, 19.

NOTE 64
All kantharoi have a small body, a trait which is characteristic of that period. Most important of them all is a kantharos with pointed handles of the late LH IA or LH IB period (Fig. 9.5). The shape is extremely rare and happens to be the second complete specimen known in Achaea, see Zapheiropoulos 1958, pl. 135. Cf. Papadopoulos 1978-79, 65, fig. 48d. Sherds of similar vessels have come from excavations in Aigion (L.Papazoglou-Manioudhaki and A. Vordhos personal communication), see Papazoglou – Manioudaki 1998. On similar vessels, see Romaios 1916, 185, fig. 8 (Thermos). Dörpfeld 1927, pl. 72:6 (Skara Lefkas). Mylonas 1972-73, 191(O-192), pls. 170ζ, 235 (Mycenae); cf. Dietz 1991, 214 (GA-2), 215, fig. 67. A single specimen from an early grave in the inner tumulus at Vodhinë (Albania), see Hammond 1971, 234, pl. 35,17. An almost similar example from the tumulus at Mikromilia-Kourou in Drama, see Koukouli – Chrysanthaki 1976, 304, pl. 245α. On the vessel's shape, see Dor et al. 1960, 91, 133 (no. 53a,b), pl. L:53 and Maran 1992, 108, pl. XVI:2, 108:4, pl. 19:3

(2CIV). The shape of the body is very common in south Albania. Cf. Matan 1998, pl. 49. Maran and Dietz are in favour of a Thessalian origin.

NOTE 65
E.g. Mirali, Drachmani, Lefkas, Pazhok, Thorikos and Papoulia; see Cavanagh & Mee 1998, 30.

NOTE 66
See Pelon 1976, 99-115. Protonotariou – Deilaki 1980, 133-138. Dietz 1980, 73ff. Dakoronia 1987, 48-60. Müller 1989. Cavanagh & Mee 1998, passim.

NOTE 67
Dickinson 1977, 60. Cf. Wardle 1972, 39: "They are still, however, an exceptional form of burial in Mycenaean times, when tholos and chamber tombs are the normal practice".

NOTE 68
Papakonstantinou 1981, 148-149 (T. XI of tumulus 2 and T.VII of tumulus 3). Papakonstantinou 1982, 133 (T. IV of tumulus 2).

NOTE 69
Gimbutas 1961, 193ff. Gimbutas 1974, 133. Gimbutas 1979, 113ff.; Hammond 1967, 96ff. Hammond 1972, 243ff. Hammond 1974, 191, fig. 17.2. Hammond 1976, 118; Sakellariou 1980, 90ff.

NOTE 70
See Mylonas 1972-73, 249-254.

NOTE 71
Häusler 1981, 59ff. Cf. Wardle 1972, 38ff., 40. Schachermeyr 1976, 276. Dickinson 1977, 34. Dietz 1980, 71,73-74. Korres 1980e, 458. Korres 1988, 227-228. Cavanagh & Mee 1998, 29, note 91.

NOTE 72
According to Dickinson 1983, 57, "They are commoner than is often suggested", but he includes in that category the well-constructed cist graves without a stomion. Cf. Müller 1994, 224. See also supra note 33.

NOTE 73
Built chamber tombs are clearly a separate tomb type and they are not "stone versions of chamber tombs" as Dickinson 1994, 225 suggests. Cf. Müller 1994, 229.

NOTE 74
Protonotariou – Deilaki 1966, 239-247, pls. XL-XLIV. Deshayes 1966, 104 (T 26), pls. XI,2 and XCVII,8. Cf. BCH 83, 1959, 774;

Protonotariou – Deilaki 1980, 54-59. Cf. Protonotariou – Deilaki 1990a, 78, fig. 7. Also, at Perseus or Alexander the Great side-street, see Banaka – Dimaki 1991, 96 (tomb 164).

NOTE 75
Waterhouse & Hope Simpson 1960, 103. Hope Simpson & Dickinson 1979, 112 (C 14). Boyd 1999, 777.

NOTE 76
Sotiriadis 1907, 111. EFA & Constantinou 1964, 223. Vatin 1969, 27, 44-45. Müller 1994, 223ff. Müller 1995. Müller 1997, 82ff. Cf. Dickinson 1977, 60, 65. Hope Simpson & Dickinson 1979, 255 (G 51). Korres 1980h, 240-241.

NOTE 77
Christopoulou 1986, 388. Cf. Dickinson 1989, 134. Faraklas 1996, 223.

NOTE 78
Verdelis 1951, 156, plan III. Verdelis 1952, 197ff., fig. 13. Verdelis 1953, 128-131, pl. II, fig. 9. Hope Simpson & Dickinson 1979, 290 (H48). Voutsaki 1992, 101.

NOTE 79
Wolters 1889, 262-269. Hope Simpson & Dickinson 1979, 274 (H 2). Voutsaki 1992, 101.

NOTE 80
See supra note 5.

NOTE 81
Mylonas 1932, 53-57, figs. 32-33. Mylonas 1975, 205ff; cf. Blackburn 1970, 216.

NOTE 82
Gallet de Santerre 1958, 93-94. Syriopoulos 1983a, 377 (LXXXIII).

NOTE 83
Karelli et al. 1983, 6-11. Karelli et al. 1984, 2-5. An additional tomb from the excavations of 1985, see Achilara 1991, 1351-1353 (Tomb B). Cf. Achilara 1986, 10-11. Catling 1988, 61. Tsaravopoulos & Zafiriou 1995, 2, 5, fig. on p. 2; On older reports, see Charitonidis 1961/2, 266, pl.321γ-ζ. Daux 1962, 878. Hope Simpson & Dickinson 1979, 371. Dickinson 1983, 62.

NOTE 84
Eustratiou 1979, 70-71.

NOTE 85
Skilardi 1987, 113.

NOTE 86
Zapheiropoulos 1965, 505-506, pl. 640β.
Hope Simpson & Dickinson 1979, 333.
Syriopoulos 1983a, 380 (LXXXVII:9).
Vlachopoulos 1995, 10, 283, 636.

NOTE 87
See supra note 68. Other tombs probably
exist, which, however, are not mentioned.
The tombs possibly belong to the LH period and not to MH III, in which last period
the tumulus' construction should in all
likelihood be sought.

NOTE 88
Daux 1959, 658. *Atti e memoria del primo
congresso internazionale di micenologia,* vol. I,
1968, 177. Dickinson 1977, 65. McDonald
& Hope Simpson 1969, 130. Hope Simpson & Dickinson 1979, 99 (B88).

NOTE 89
Kolonas 1993, 150. Kolonas 1994, 21.
Kolonas 1997a, 28.

NOTE 90
See note 37. The tombs at Ras – Shamra
(Ugarit), one example at Enkomi (Cyprus),
but also Egyptian tombs are believed to
have been the prototypes of tomb *P*. Cf.
Iakovidis 1991, 1042. Cavanagh & Mee
1998, 47. Also, note the subterranean shrine
at Hattuša (Boğhazköy); see Belli 1991,
1384 ff., figs. 1,2. Of great importance is
the recently recovered Mycenaean sword
from this region, see Ünal, Ertekin & Ediz
1990-91, 46-52. Neve 1993, 648-652, pls.
27-28. Cf. Hansen 1994, 213-215. But, this
foreign inspiration looks rather unique in
Mycenaean burial customs, so, Dickinson's
opinion for "another reminder of the
diversity of tomb-types in early Mycenaean
times", might be correct; see Dickinson
1977, 64. For Medeon tombs Müller 1994,
229ff, who also finds influences from Near
East.

NOTE 91
See Choremis 1973, 28-30, fig. 3, pl. 6α.
Parlama justly claims that it is apsidal, see
Parlama 1976, 253.

NOTE 92
Baziou-Eustathiou 1985, 60.

NOTE 93
Mylonas 1966, 89, fig. 110. Mylonas 1975,
passim. Cf. Blackburn 1970, 216. Schachermeyr 1976a, 94-95, fig. 15. Hope Simpson
& Dickinson 1979, 197, 203-204 (F9).

NOTE 94
Müller 1994, 227-228 (T. 264), figs. 11-13.

NOTE 95
Sapouna – Sakellaraki 1993, 195-196. *AR*
1993-94, 38. Sapouna – Sakellaraki 1995,
41ff, figs. 2-4, pl. 5. Cavanagh & Mee 1998,
39 (as Beta? type). This tomb is of great
importance, having a roofed *stomion* as tholos tombs. Its might be later than it is
suggested (early Late Helladic?).

NOTE 96
Protonotariou – Deilaki 1980, 198, g. plan
18, pl. Dendra 5,3. Protonotariou – Deilaki
1990, 94, fig. 4, 6a-b.

NOTE 97
Mussche et al. 1963, 29-46, plan III.

NOTE 98
Theocharis 1964, 261. Theocharis 1966,
253-254, pl. 245α. Cf. Hope Simpson &
Dickinson 1979, 292 (H 57).

NOTE 99
Schliemann 1881, 17-39. Tsountas and
Manatt 1897, 126-129. Bulle 1907, 85-87.
Orlandos 1915, 51-53. Pelon 1976, 233-
237 (Th. 33), pls. CX-CXV. Hope Simpson
& Dickinson 1979, 236-7 (G1).

NOTE 100
Valmin 1927-28, 190-201, 214-216, pls. IX,
X:1. McDonald & Hope Simpson 1961,
234. Pelon 1976, 217-219 (Th. 27), pl.
XCIX. Hope Simpson & Dickinson 1979,
173 (D 220). Boyd 1999, 658-662.

NOTE 101
Waterhouse & Hope Simpson 1961, 131,
132. Marinatos 1955, pl. 97δ. Marinatos
1966, 121-128, fig. 2, pls. 100-105, 110-
111. Korres 1974, 142-143. Korres 1975,
349. Korres 1975a, 478-482, pl. 317δ.
Korres 1978, 326-332, note 2, fig. 1, pls.
197-198. Korres 1980d, 132-137, 149-150,
pls. 105α, 106α, 115-116. Korres 1991, 195-
196 and notes 10-12α. Harding, Cadogan
& Howell 1969, 123 (C.G. 14), fig. 8. Parlama 1972, 262-264, plan 3, pls. 198-200.
Also, note the "circular" tomb at the location "Sta Oikopeda" in Paliki, for which a
wooden roof is being suggested, see Marinatos 1932, 11, fig. 12.

NOTE 102
Parlama 1976, 255-256.

NOTE 103
The typical built chamber tombs are also
known from LM Crete, cf. Syriopoulos

1983a, 383ff. See also one example of LM
IIIA at Ag. Triadha in Blackman 1998, 111,
fig. 151. Recently at Pantanassa Amariou of
Late SM – Early Iron Age, see Tegou 1999,
forthcoming.

NOTE 104
Davaras 1966, 185ff., pls. 155-161. Pini
1968, 46, fig. 94. On Cretan examples, see
Papadimitriou 1954, 253-257; Mylonas
1972-73, 221, note 2. Cf. Davaras 1985,
625, figs. 1-5.

NOTE 105
Pini 1968, 47, figs. 92, 95.

NOTE 106
Xanthoudidis 1904, 22ff. Desborough
1952, 269-270. Desborough 1964, 177. Pini
1968, 48.

NOTE 107
Choremis 1973, 30. Similar suggestion for
the tomb at Lefkandi, see Sapouna – Sakellaraki 1995, 46.

NOTE 108
The imperfectly formed and blocked
entrance, leading to the *periboloi* of the EH
cists (lined with upright slabs) at Tsepi in
Marathon, is remarkable, see Marinatos
1970b, 281, fig. 4. Pantelidou – Gofa 1997,
19-22, figs. 7-11. Pantelidou – Gofa 1998,
18-23, figs. 4-11. Cf. Travlos 1988, 225-6,
figs. 273, 274. Blackman 1998, 14, fig. 22;
Papachristodoulou 1971, 140ff. Tsountas
1899, 74, 79-84. Cf. Barber 1981, 167-179.
Barber 1994, 79, 82. Mylonas 1959, 64ff.
Cf. Cavanagh & Mee 1998, 16; Belmont &
Renfrew 1964, 397-398. Doumas 1963,
279. Cf. Renfrew 1972, 179, 514. Doumas
1977, 44-46 (type B1, B2), 47 (type E),
128, figs. 29-31. Doumas 1988, 25. Coleman 1977, 47-48, 58 (T. 7), 62 (T. 14), 105,
pls. 13, 15, 19, 20, 59, 60g,h. Overbeck
1977, 120, 129-130. Dummler 1886, 21.
Klon 1908, 116. Pelon 1987, 113, 114, pls.
XXVI-XXVIII. Cf. Vermeule 1964, 80.
Mylonas 1966, 89-90. Hiller 1989, 138,
142. Dickinson 1989, 135. Dickinson 1994,
222-223. Cavanagh & Mee 1998, 16, 29,
46-48, 54, 64.

NOTE 109
Cavanagh & Mee 1998, 29.

NOTE 110
Cf. Mastrokostas 1960, 144. Waterhouse &
Hope Simpson 1961, 134-135. Theocharis
1964, 261. Dickinson 1977, 61. Dickinson
1983, 62. Cavanagh & Mee 1998, 46.

NOTE 111
Dickinson 1983, 57. But on p. 64 notes that the "shaft grave and rectangular built tomb derive from cist and pit"; cf. Dickinson 1977, 51. Dickinson 1989, 133. Dickinson 1994, 222-223. See also Vermeule 1964, 80. Mylonas 1966, 89-90. Pelon 1987, 112-115. Müller 1994, 228. Cavanagh & Mee 1998, 29.

NOTE 112
Sapouna – Sakellaraki 1995, 46.

NOTE 113
See, also, Cavanagh 1971, passim. Cavanagh & Mee 1998, 46: "We believe that they formed a link between tumuli and tholoi and consequently merit careful analysis".

NOTE 114
Waterhouse & Hope Simpson 1961, 130. Hope Simpson & Dickinson 1979, 77-78 (B8).

NOTE 115
McDonald & Hope Simpson 1961, 130. Hope Simpson & Dickinson 1979, 110-111 (C 9).

NOTE 116
Romaios 1956, 185-186. Romaios 1957, 110-111. Hope Simpson & Dickinson 1979, 123-124 (C58). Boyd 1999, 718ff.

NOTE 117
Marinatos 1964a, 89ff. Marinatos 1965, 204-205. McDonald & Hope Simpson 1969, 152. Hope Simpson & Dickinson 1979, 136 (D 25).

NOTE 118
McDonald & Hope Simpson 1964, 233. Korres 1975b, 137ff. Hope Simpson & Dickinson 1979, 139 (D 34).

NOTE 119
Marinatos 1954, 311. Marinatos 1958, 187. Marinatos 1959, 174. Marinatos 1960, 115. Marinatos 1960a, 195. Marinatos 1961, 174. Marinatos 1963, 114. Korres 1974, 139. Korres 1975, passim. Korres 1975a, 431-484. Hope Simpson & Dickinson 1979, 139 (D 35). Boyd 1999, 313ff.

NOTE 120
Dontas 1966, 325, pl. 334ε. Agallopoulou 1972, 65. Agallopoulou 1973, pls. 113-114. Hope Simpson & Dickinson 1979, 193 (E 39).

NOTE 121
Papavasileiou 1907, 114ff. Papavasileiou 1910, 42. Sackett et al. 1966, 69, fig. 11. Hope Simpson & Dickinson 1979, 231 (F 89).

NOTE 122
Papavasileiou 1907, 114ff. Papavasileiou 1910, 24, 29. Sackett et al. 1966, 73, 74, fig. 13. Hope Simpson & Dickinson 1979, 232 (F 93, 94).

NOTE 123
See supra note 76.

NOTE 124
Thessalika 1, 74. Hunter 1953, 142, 151. Hope Simpson & Dickinson 1979, 275 (H4).

NOTE 125
Megaw 1962-3, 24. Hope Simpson & Dickinson 1979, 281 (H 22).

NOTE 126
Theocharis 1969, 165ff. Theocharis 1969α, 223. Hope Simpson & Dickinson 1979, 284 (H 31).

NOTE 127
Wace & Thompson 1912, 25. Hunter 1953, 12, 41, 182, 198. Hope Simpson & Dickinson 1979, 284 (H 32).

NOTE 128
Seferiadou 1896, 247. Wace & Thompson 1912, 208. Hunter 1953, 16, 232. Ålin 1962, 145. Hope Simpson & Dickinson 1979, 294 (H 63).

NOTE 129
At the location "Sta Oikopeda" in Paliki, at Litharia on Poros and at Kokkolata, see supra note 8.

NOTE 130
Korres 1975, passim. Korres 1982, 143, 145ff. Korres 1984, 69ff. Korres 1988, 225-228. Korres 1989, 237. Korres 1996, in print. Cf. Dickinson 1977, 61. Dickinson 1983, 60, 64. Hiller 1989, 143. Voutsaki 1998, 42ff. G.S. Korres has suggested a con-nection between tholos tomb and MH tumulus, see Korres 1989, 236; cf. Howell 1992, 37.

NOTE 131
Perhaps many of the tombs at Eleusis should be dated to the LH I period, instead of the final MH. Cf. Dickinson 1983, 60-61, note 32. The same is applied to T.164 at Argos and maybe at Lefkandi. In view of the recent discoveries at Portes, perhaps the dating of the new Samiko tumuli should be reconsidered.

NOTE 132
Müller 1994, 229 claimes that the presence of built chamber tombs at Medeon «ανέβαλε για λίγο ζ …».

NOTE 133
Choremis 1973, 70-74. Koukouli – Chrisanthaki 1992, B, 369ff., plan 68. See also similar tombs in 9th c. B.C tumuli at Roussa (Evros); Skarlatidou 1980, 432, pl. 253δ.

NOTE 134
Mastrokostas 1961/2, 129, pl. 153δ. Subgeometric lekythoi were recovered from the interior. The tomb is not illustrated.

NOTE 135
Zapheiropoulos 1957, 117. Zapheiropoulos 1957a, 69-70. Syriopoulos 1964, 481ff. Papadopoulos 1978-79, 30 (no. 31). Lewartowski 1989, 62. Zavadil 1995, 27 (A8). The sole find reported among the skeletal material was a loom weight. The tomb is not illustrated.

NOTE 136
Zapheiropoulos 1952, 400ff.

NOTE 137
E.g. in Attica, Boetia, Phokis and Thessaly where a few continued in use or were constructed in LH IIIA-B. In all likelihood tomb A1 continued in use, since it was not destroyed in late Mycenaean times. Unfortunately, its recent looting inhibits the drawing of any safe conclusions, although a seated female figurine of LH IIIA:1 date was handed over as a find from this tomb. Note that figurines were common at Lazarides and in Eleusis LHIII graves of Gamma type.

Bibliographical Abbreviations

AA   Archäologischer Anzeiger
AAA   Athens Annals of Archae-
          ology
          (Αρχαιολογικά Ανάλεκτα εξ
          Αθηνών)
ADelt   Αρχαιολογικόν Δελτίον
AE   Αρχαιολογική Εφημερίς
Aegaeum   Annales d'archéologie égéenne
          de l'Université de Liège
AJA   American Journal of Archae-
          ology
AkorrBl   Archäologisches Korrespon-
          denzblatt
AM   Mitteilungen des Deutschen
          Archäologischen Instituts:
          Athenische Abteilung
AR   Archaeological Reports
Archaeologia
          Αρχαιολογία
          Τριμηνιαίο περιοδικό,
          Αθήνα
ASAG   Archives Suisses d' Anthropo-
          logie Générale, Genève
BCH   Bulletin de Correspondance
          Hellénique
BSA   Annual of the British School
          at Athens

BullLund Bulletin de la Société Royale
          des Letters de Lund
CMS   Corpus der Minoischen und
          Mykenischen Siegel
Dodoni   Επιστημονική Επετηρίς της
          Φιλοσοφικής Σχολής του
          Πανεπιστημίου Ιωαννίνων
EAZ   Ethographisch –
          Archäologische Zeitung
EEFSPA
          Επιστημονική Επετηρίς της
          Φιλοσοφικής Σχολής του
          Πανεπιστημίου Αθηνών
Ergon   Το Έργον της Αρχαιολογικής
          Εταιρείας
JHS   Journal of Hellenic Studies
JMAA   Journal of Mediterranean
          Anthropology and Archaeo-
          logy
IAB   Institute of Archaeology Bul-
          letin, University College
          London
Kr. Chron.
          Κρητικά Χρονικά

MeditArch
          Mediterranean Archaeology
OJA   Oxford Journal of Archaeo-
          logy
OpAth   Opuscula Atheniensia
PAA   Πρακτικά Ακαδημίας Αθηνών
ΠΛΑΤ ΟΝ
          Δελτιο της Εταιρείας
          Ελλήνων Φιλολόγων, Εν
          Αθήναις
Prakt   Πρακτικά της εν Αθήναις
          Αρχαιολογικής Εταιρείας
Πυρφόρος
          Δικηνιαία Έκδοση Εθνικού
          Μετσόβιου Πολυτεχνείου
RE   Pauly – Wissowa, Real-
          Encyclopädie der klassischen
          Altertumswissenschaft
SIMA   Studies in Mediterranean
          Archaeology
Thessalika
          Αρχαιολογικόν Περιοδικόν
          Δημοσίευμα, Volos
TUAS   Temple University Aegean
          Symposium

Bibliography

Achilara, L. 1986
Tα Ψαρά 67-68-69, 10-11.

Achilara, L. 1991
Mycenaean events from Psara, in:
Atti e Memorie del Secondo Congresso Internazionale di Micenologia, Roma
- Napoli 14-20 Ottobre 1991
(Roma 1996), vol. III, 1349-1353.

Afroudakis, A. 1990
Τοπωνυμικό υλικό από την επαρχία Φθιώτιδας, in: *Acts of the First Congress of Fthiotian Search*, Loutra Ipatis April 1990 (Lamia 1993), 361-372.

Agallopoulou, P. 1972
Ανασκαφή μυκηναϊκών τάφων παρά το Καμπί δυτικής Ζακύνθου,
AAA V 1, 63-66.

Agallopoulou, P. 1973
Μυκηναϊκόν νεκροταφείον παρά το Καμπί Ζακύνθου, *ADelt* 28, A, 198-214.

Alexandri, O. 1976
Αθήνα. Οδός Αιόλου 72, *ADelt* 31, B1 Chron, 26-27.

Alexopoulou, G. & Stavropoulou-Gatsi M. 1996
Το έργο των σωστικών ανασκαφών στην πόλη των Πατρών και στην ευρύτερη περιοχή της, in: *Acts of the First Archaeological Congress of South and West Greece*, Patras 1996, in print.

Ålin, P. 1962
Das Ende der Mykenischen Fundstätten auf dem Griechischen Festland, SIMA I. Lund.

Andreou, E. 1976
Νομός Ιωαννίνων. Κάτω Πεδινά, *ADelt* 31, B2 Chron., 202.

Andreou, E. 1979
Πωγώνι, *ADelt* 34, B2 Chron., 239-240.

Andreou, E. 1980
Μερόπη και Παληόπυργος Πωγωνίου, *ADelt* 35, B1 Chron., 303-307.

Andreou, E. 1981
Πωγώνι. Ανασκαφή τύμβων, *ADelt* 36, B2 Chron., 271-273.

Andreou, E. 1982
Μερόπη – Παλιόπυργος Πωγωνίου, *ADelt* 37, B2 Chron., 259.

Andreou, E. 1982a
Οι τύμβοι Πωγωνίου Μερόπης, *Archaeologia* 3, 54-60.

Andreou, E. 1983
Τύμβος Κάτω Μερόπης, *ADelt* 38, B2 Chron., 229-230.

Andreou, E. 1994
Νέες προϊστορικές θέσεις στην Ήπειρο, in: *ΦΗΓΟΣ, Volume in Honor of prof. S. Dakaris, Ioannina*, 233-265.

Andreou, E. & I. Andreou 1994
Η κοιλάδα του Γορμού στο Πωγώνι της Ηπείρου, κέντρο ζωής και ανάπτυξης κατά την Πρώιμη εποχή του Σιδήρου, in: *The Regions of the Mycenaean World. First International Interdisciplinary Symposium*, Lamia 25-29/9/1994 (1999), 77-90.

Andronikos, M. 1961/2
Ελληνικά επιτάφια μνημεία, *ADelt* 17, A, 152-210.

Åström, P. 1964
Mycenaean pottery from the region of Aigion, with a list of prehistoric sites in Achaia, *OpAth* 5, 89-110.

Banaka – Dimaki, A. 1991
Άργος. Πάροδος Περσέως ή Μεγάλου Αλεξάνδρου (οικόπεδο Δημ. Τρίκκα – Ανδρομάχης Κουτσαχείλη), *ADelt* 46, B1 Chron., 95-96.

Barber, R.N.L. 1981
A tomb at Ayios Loukas Syros: Some thoughts on Early - Middle Cycladic chronology, *JMAA* 1:2, 167-179.

Barber, R.N.L. 1994
Οι Κυκλάδες στην Εποχή του Χαλκού. Athens.

Baziou – Eustathiou, A. 1984
Νέα Ιωνία, *ADelt* 39, B Chron., 141-142.

Baziou – Eustathiou, A. 1985
Μυκηναϊκά από τη Νέα Ιωνία
Βόλου, *ADelt* 40, A, 17-70.

Baziou – Eustathiou, A. 1991
Νέα στοιχεία για τις μυκηναϊκές
θέσεις στην περιοχή του Βόλου, in:
*Atti e Memorie del secondo Congresso
Internazionale di Micenologia,* Roma
- Napoli 14-20 Ottobre 1991
(Roma 1996), 1175-1187.

Baziou – Eustathiou, A. 1993
Αποτελέσματα των πρόσφατων
ανασκαφικών ερευνών στη Ν.
Ιωνία και στην περιοχή
Πευκακίων, in: *New evidence from
the research concerning Ancient Iolkos.
Acts of the scientific meeting, Volos,*
May 1993 (Volos 1994), 59-70.

Bejko, L. 1994
Some problems of the Middle and
Late Bronze Age in southern Alba-
nia, *IAB* 31, 105-125.

Belli, P. 1991
Architetture per le acque nel mon-
do Egeo ed in quello Ittita, in: *Atti
e Memorie del secondo Congresso Internazionale di Micenologia,* Roma -
Napoli 14-20 Ottobre 1991 (Roma
1996), vol. III, 1381-1390.

Belmont & C. Renfrew 1964
Two prehistoric sites on Mykonos,
AJA 68.

Blackburn, E.T. 1970
*Middle Helladic Graves and Burial
Customs with Special Reference to Lerna in the Argolid,* PhD Thesis, University of Cincinnati (Ann Arbor
1977).

Blackman, D. 1997
Archaeology in Greece 1996-97:
Kephallenia, *AR* 43, 44.

Blackman, D. 1998
Archaeology in Greece 1997-98:
Marathon Tsepi & Agia Triada, *AR*
44, 14 & 111-112.

Blegen, C.W. 1921
*Korakou. A Prehistoric Settlement near
Corinth.* Boston.

Blegen, C.W. 1937
*Prosymna. The Helladic Settlement
Preceding the Argive Heraeum.* Cam-
bridge.

Blegen, C.W. & A.J.B., Wace 1931
Middle Helladic tombs, *Symbolae
Osloenses* 9, 28-37.

Blegen, C.W. et al. 1964
Blegen C.W., Palmer H. & Young
R.S., *Corinth XIII: The North Ceme-
tery.* Princeton.

Blegen C.W. & Rawson M. 1966
*The Palace of Nestor at Pylos in
Western Messenia,* vol. I. Princeton.

Blegen, C.W. et al. 1973
Blegen, C.W., Rawson, M., Taylour,
W. & Donovan, W.P., *The Palace of
Nestor at Pylos in Western Messenia,*
vol. III. Princeton.

Boyd, M.J. 1999
*Middle Helladic and Early Mycenaean
Mortuary Customs in the Southern
and Western Peloponnese,* vols. I-II,
PhD Thesis, University of Edin-
burgh.

Brea, L.B. 1985
*Gli Eoli e l' inizio dell' età del Bronzo
nelle Isole Eolie e nell' Italia Meridionale. Archeologia e Leggende.* Napoli.

Bulle, H. 1907
*Orchomenos I. Die älteren Ansied-
lungsschichten.* Munich.

Catling, H.W. 1988
Archaeology in Greece 1987-88:
Psara, *AR* 34, 61.

Cavanagh, W. 1971
*Mycenaean Tholos Tombs and Related
Tombs,* MA Thesis, Edinburgh.

Cavanagh, W. 1976
*Attic Burial Customs ca. 2000-700
B.C.* (unpublished PhD Thesis,
London).

Cavanagh, W. & Mee C. 1998
*A Private Place: Death in Prehistoric
Greece* SIMA CXXXV, Jonsered.

Chantziagelakis, L.P. 1982
Μείζων περιοχή Βόλου, *ADelt* 37,
B2 Chron., 225-226.

Chantziagelakis, L.P. 1983
Έργο αποχέτευσης μείζονος
περιοχής Βόλου, *ADelt* 38, B1
Chron., 197.

Charitonidis, S. 1961/2
Ψαρά, *ADelt* 17, B Chron., 266.

Choremis, A. 1973
Μυκηναϊκοί και πρωτογεωμετρικοί
τάφοι εις Καρποφόραν Μεσσηνίας,
AE, 25-74.

Christopoulou, A. 1986
Two Early Mycenaean burials at
Thebes (summary), in: *First Interna-
tional Congress of Boeotian Studies,*
Thebes 10-14 September 1986, in:
*Annual of the Society of Boeotian
Studies,* vol. A1, Athens 1988, 388.

Coleman, J.E. 1977
Keos I. Kephala. Princeton, New
Jersey.

Dakoronia, F. 1987
Μάρμαρα. Τα Υπομυκηναϊκά Νεκροταφεία των Τύμβων. Athens.

Dakoronia, F. 1993
Κύνος, *ADelt* 48, B1 Chron., 218-219.

Daux, G. 1956
Samikon. Aigion. Chronique des fouilles en 1955, *BCH* 80, 290, 291.

Daux, G. 1959
Babés. Chronique des fouilles en 1958, *BCH* 83, 656-658.

Daux, G. 1961
Skoros. Chronique des fouilles en 1960, *BCH* 85, 682.

Daux, G. 1962
Psara. Chronique des fouilles 1961, *BCH* 86, 878.

Daux, G. 1968
Armatova (Élide). Chronique des fouilles 1967, *BCH* 92, 832-834.

Davaras, C. 1966
Ανασκαφή θολωτού τάφου Μάλεμε, *Prakt*, 185-188.

Davaras, C. 1985
Une tombe à voûte en Crète orientale (note complémentaire), *BCH* 109, 625-628.

Dekoulakou, I. 1973-74
Θέα Πατρών, *ADelt* 29, B2 Chron., 381-382.

Delopoulos, G.D. 1990
Τοπωνύμια της **Φθιώτιδας** σε ενικό / πληθυντικό, in: *Acts of the First Congress of Fthiotian Search,* Loutra Ipatis April 1990 (Lamia 1993), 195-212.

Desborough, V.R.d'A. 1952
Protogeometric Pottery. Oxford.

Desborough, V.R.d'A. 1964
The Last Mycenaeans and their Successors. Oxford.

Desborough, V R.d'A. 1972
The Greek Dark Ages. London.

Deshayes, J. 1966
Argos. Les Fouilles de la Deiras, *Etudes Péloponnésiennes* IV, Paris.

Dickinson, O.T.P.K. 1977
The Origins of Mycenaean Civilisation, SIMA XLIX. Göteborg.

Dickinson, O.T.P.K. 1983
Cist graves and chamber tombs, *BSA* 78, 55-67.

Dickinson, O.T.P.K. 1989
"The Origins of Mycenaean Civilisation" revisited, in: *TRANSITION. Le monde égéen du Bronze moyen au Bronze récent,* R. Laffineur, ed. Aegaeum 3, 131-136.

Dickinson, O.T.P.K. 1994
The Aegean Bronze Age. Cambridge.

Dietz, S. 1975
A Bronze Age tumuli cemetery in Asine, southern Greece, *Archaeology* 28, 157-163.

Dietz, S. 1980
Asine II.2: Results of the Excavations East of the Acropolis 1970-74. The Middle Helladic Cemetery. The Middle Helladic and Early Mycenaean Deposits. Acta Atheniensia 4, 24:2, Stockholm.

Dietz, S. 1991
The Argolid at the Transition to the Mycenaean Age. Studies in the Chronology and Cultural Development in the Shaft Grave Period. Copenhagen.

Dontas, G. 1966
Ζάκυνθος, *ADelt* 21, B2 Chron., 325.

Dor, L. et al. 1960
Dor L., Jannoray J., van Effenterre H & M., *Kirrha, Étude de Préhistoire Phocidienne*. Paris.

Dörpfeld, W. 1927
Alt-Ithaka, Ein Beitrag zur Homer Frage. Studien und Ausgrabungen auf der Insel Leukas – Ithaka, vols. I-II. Munich.

Doumas, C. 1963
Νάξος. Λιώνας, *ADelt* 18, B2 Chron., 279.

Doumas, C. 1977
Early Bronze Age Burial Habits in the Cyclades. SIMA XLVIII, Göteborg.

Doumas, C. 1988
EBA in the Cyclades: Continuity or Discontinuity?, in: *Problems in Greek Prehistory,* 21-29.

Dummler, F. 1886
Mittheilungen von den griechischen Inseln, *AM* 11, 15-46.

EFA & Constantinou J. 1964
Fouilles a Médéon, *ADelt* 19, B2 Chron., 223-225.

Eustratiou, Kl. 1979
Αίγινα. Λαζάρηδες, *ADelt* 34, B1 Chron., 70-71.

Faraklas, N. 1996
Θηβαϊκά, ΑΕ.

French, E. 1971
The development of Mycenaean terracotta figurines, *BSA* 66, 101-187.

Gadolou, A. 1998
Η Αχαΐα στους Πρώιμους Ιστορικούς Χρόνους. Κεραμεική Παραγωγή και Έθιμα Ταφής, vols. I–II (unpublished PhD Thesis, University of Athens).

Gallet de Santerre, H. 1958
Délos Primitive et Archaïque. Paris.

Gimbutas, M. 1961
Notes on the chronology and Expansion of the Pit-Grave Culture, Académie Tchécoslovaque des Sciences. L' Europe à la fin de l' âge de la pierre. in: *Actes du Symposium Consacré aux Problèmes du Néolithique Européen,* Prague – Liblice – Brno, 5-12 October 1959, Praga 1961, 193-200.

Gimbutas, M. 1974
The destruction of Aegean and East Mediterranean urban civilization around 2300B.C., in: *Bronze Age Migrations in the Aegean,* R.A Crossland & A. Birchall, eds., Park Ridge, New Jersey, 129-139.

Gimbutas, M. 1979
The three waves of the Kurgan people into Old Europe, 4500-2500 B.C., *ASAG* 43/2, 113-137.

Hammond, N.G.L. 1967
Tumulus-burial in Albania, the grave circles of Mycenae, and the Indo-europeans, *BSA* 62, 77-105.

Hammond, N.G.L. 1971
The dating of some burials in tumuli in south Albania, *BSA* 66, 229-241.

Hammond, N.G.L. 1972
A History of Macedonia, vol. I. Oxford.

Hammond, N.G.L. 1974
Grave circles in Albania and Macedonia, in: *Bronze Age Migrations in the Aegean,* R.A Crossland & A. Birchall, eds., Park Ridge, New Jersey, 189-195.

Hammond, N.G.L. 1974a
The tumulus – burials of Leucas and their connections in the Balkans and northern Greece, *BSA* 69, 129-144.

Hammond, N.G.L. 1976
Migrations and Invasions in Greece and Adjacent Areas. Park Ridge, New Jersey.

Hansen, O. 1994
A mycenaean sword from Boğasköy – Hattuša found in 1991, *BSA* 89, 231-215.

Harding, A., G. Cadogan & R. Howell 1969
Pavlopetri, an underwater Bronze Age town in Laconia, *BSA* 64, 113-142.

Häusler, A. 1981
Die Indoeuropäisierung Griechenlands nach Aussage der Grab- und Bestattungssitten, *Slovenska Archeológia* XXIX-1, 59-66.

Herrmann, H.-V. 1987
Prähistorisches Olympia, in: *Ägäische Bronzezeit,* H.-G. Buchholz, ed., 426-436.

Hiller, S. 1982
Zum archäologischen Evidenz der Indoeuropäisierung Griechenlands, in: *Symposia Tracica,* Xanthi October 1981 (1982), A, 183-210.

Hiller, S. 1989
On the origins of the Shaft Graves, in: *TRANSITION. Le monde égéen du Bronze moyen au Bronze récent,* R. Laffineur, ed., (Aegaeum 3), 137-144.

Holmberg, E.J. 1944
The Swedish Excavations at Asea in Arcadia. Lund.

Hood, M.S.F. 1986
Evidence for invasions in the Aegean area at the end of the Early Bronze Age, in: *The End of the Early Bronze Age in the Aegean,* G. Gadogan, ed., 31-68.

Hooker, J. 1976
Mycenaean Greece. London.

Hope Simpson, R. 1965
A Gazetteer and Atlas of Mycenaean Sites. London.

Hope Simpson, R. 1981
Mycenaean Greece. Park Ridge.

Hope Simpson, R. & Dickinson O.T.P.K. 1979
A Gazetteer of Aegean Civilisation in the Bronze Age, vol. I : The Mainland and the Islands. SIMA LII, Göteborg.

Howell, R.J. 1974
The origins of the Middle Helladic culture, in: *Bronze Age Migrations in the Aegean,* R.A Crossland & A. Birchall, eds., Park Ridge, New Jersey, 73-106.

Howell, R.J. 1992
The Middle Helladic settlement: pottery, in Excavations at Nichoria in Southwestern Greece. II, in: *The Bronze Age Occupation,* W.A. McDonald & N.C. Wilkie, eds., Minneapolis, 43-204.

Hunter, A. 1953
The Bronze Age in Thessaly and its Environs, with Special Reference to Mycenaean Culture (unpublished B. Litt. Thesis, Oxford University).

Iakovidis, S. 1981
Royal Shaft Graves outside Mycenae, *TUAS* 6, 17-23.

Iakovidis, S. 1991
Mycenae in the light of recent discoveries, in: *Atti e Memorie del Secondo Congresso Internazionale di Micenologia,* Roma - Napoli 14-20 Ottobre 1991 (Roma 1996), 1039-1049.

Immerwahr, S.A. 1971
The Athenian Agora: Results of excavations conducted by the American School of Classical Studies at Athens, vol. XIII. The Neolithic and Bronze Ages. Princeton, New Jersey.

Intzesiloglou, A. 1981
Νέα Ιωνία Βόλου. Έργο αποχέτευσης Δήμου, *ADelt* 36, B2 Chron., 252.

Ioannidaki, E. 1983
Πύλη, *ADelt* 38, B1 Chron., 215.

Kakavogianni, O. 1984
Βραυρώνα, *ADelt* 39, B Chron., 45.

Kalligas, P.G. 1977
Κεφαλληνιακά Γ' (Από την προϊστορική Κεφαλλονιά), *AAA* X 1, 116-125.

Kalligas, P.G. 1983
Η Μυκηναϊκή Κράνη της Κεφαλλονιάς, *Archaeologia* 1, 77-83.

Kanta, A. 1998
Relations between Crete, the Aegean and the Near East in the Late Bronze Age, An overview, in: *Eastern Mediterranean, Cyprus – Dodecanese – Crete, 16th – 6th cent. B.C.,* Heraklion, 30-67.

Karagiorga – Stathakopoulou, Th. 1979
Αθήνα. Οδός Θ. Ρέντη 8, *ADelt* 34, B1 Chron., 16-17.

Karamitrou – Mentesidi, G. 1993
Ξηρολίμνη, ADelt 48, B2 Chron, 380-381.

Karelli, N. et al. 1983
N. Karelli, N. Ζafiriou, St. Moschouris, A. Tsaravopoulos, *Τα Ψαρά* 37-38-39, 6-11.

Karelli, N. et al. 1984
N. Karelli, N. Ζafiriou, St. Moschouris, A. Tsaravopoulos, *Τα Ψαρά* 49-50-51, 2-5.

Kilian – Dirlmeier, I. 1997
Das Mittelbronzezeitliche Schachtgrab von Ägina, *VPhZ,* Mainz.

Kiskiras, D. 1983
Ο υδάτινος πλούτος του Νομού Αχαΐας, in: *Acts of the Second Local Congress of Achaean Studies,* Kalavryta June 1983 (Athens 1986), 177-186.

Klon, S. 1908
Ανασκαφικαί εργασίαι εν Νάξω, *Prakt,* 114-117.

Kolonas, L. 1988
Θέση Αμπάρια, *ADelt* 43, B1 Chron., 173.

Kolonas, L. 1990
Μόσχοβη Λουτρακίου Κατούνας, *ADelt* 45, B1 Chron., 140-141.

Kolonas, L. 1993
Τζαννάτα, *ADelt* 48, B1 Chron., 149-150.

Kolonas, L. 1994
Πόρος Κεφαλονιάς. Patras.

Kolonas, L. 1995
Νεώτερη μυκηναϊκή τοπογραφία της Αχαΐας, in: *Acts of the Fifth International Congress of Peloponnesian Studies, Argos – Nauplio* 1995 (Athens 1998), 468-496.

Kolonas, L. 1995a
Μυκηναϊκές εγκαταστάσεις στην ορεινή Δυμαία Χώρα, in: *Acts of International Congress. Dymaia – Vouprasio, Kato Achaia* June 1995, in print.

Kolonas, L. 1995b
Πόρος, *ADelt* 50, B Chron., in print.

Kolonas, L. 1995c
Ανασκαφές στην Αιτωλοακαρνανία, in: *Η Ελλάδα μέσα από τις πρόσφατες αρχαιολογικές ανασκαφές, Πρακτικά Επιμορφωτικού Σεμιναρίου Ξεναγών,* Αθήνα, 109-113.

Kolonas, L. 1996
Το έργο της ΣΤ ΕΠΚΑ, in: *Acts of the First Archaeological Congress of South and West Greece,* Patras 1996, in print.

Kolonas, L. 1996a
Τα ευρήματα στη Βούντενη, in: *Οι Ανασκαφές στην Πελοπόννησο, ΕΠΤΑ ΗΜΕΡΕΣ* (leaflet of Kathimerini newspaper), 28.01.1996, 6-7.

Kolonas, L. 1997
Τα μνημεία της Αιτωλοακαρνανίας κατά την υλοποίηση της Προγραμματικής Σύμβασης Αμβρακικού, *Πυρφόρος* 27, Jan.-Feb. 1997, 49-83.

Kolonas, L. 1997a
Ανασκαφές στην Κεφαλονιά, in: *Ανασκαφές στα Επτάνησα, ΕΠΤΑ ΗΜΕΡΕΣ* (leaflet of Kathimerini newspaper), 26.01.1997, 27-29.

Kolonas, L. 1998
Βούντενη. Ένα Σημαντικό Μυκηναϊκό Κέντρο της Αχαΐας, vols. I-III (unpublished PhD Thesis, University of Rethymno).

Kolonas, L. 1998a
Ηλειακή Πύλος, in: *Forschungen in der Peloponnes. 1898-1998: 100 Jahre des Österreichisches Instituts Athen,* Athens 5-7 March 1998, in print.

Kolonas, L. 1998b
Μνημεία και ανασκαφές, in: *Μνημεία της Αιτωλοακαρνανίας, ΕΠΤΑ ΗΜΕΡΕΣ* (leaflet of Kathimerini newspaper), 27.09.1998, 14-17.

Kolonas, L. & Moschos I. 1994
Πόρτες, *ADelt* 49, B Chron., 230-231.

Kolonas, L. & Moschos I. 1995
Κεφαλόβρυσο Πορτών, *ADelt* 50, B Chron., in print

Kontorli – Papadopoulou, L. 1995
Mycenaean tholos tombs: Some thoughts on burial customs and rites, Klados, in: *Essays in Honor of J. N. Coldstream,* C. Morris, ed., London, 111-122.

Korres, G.S. 1974
Ανασκαφαί Πύλου, *Prakt,* 139-162.

Korres, G.S. 1975
Τύμβοι, θόλοι και ταφικοί κύκλοι της Μεσσηνίας, in: *Acts of the First International Congress of Peloponnesian Studies,* Sparta 1975, vol. II, (Athens 1976-78), 337-369.

Korres, G.S. 1975a
Ανασκαφαί Πύλου, *Prakt,* 428-514.

Korres, G.S. 1975b
Μεσσηνία. Κουκουνάρα – Κρεμμύδια, *Ergon,* 132-140.

Korres, G.S. 1978
Ανασκαφαί Πύλου, *Prakt,* 323-360.

Korres, G.S. 1979
Η Προϊστορία της Βοϊδοκοιλιάς, in: *"Mneme" of George I. Kourmoulis,* Athens.

Korres, G.S. 1980a
Η Προϊστορία της Βοϊδοκοιλιάς Μεσσηνίας κατά τας ερεύνας των ετών 1956, 1975-79, Επετηρίδα της Παντείου Ανωτάτης Σχολής Πολιτικών Επιστημών.

Korres, G.S. 1980b
Η προβληματική διά την μεταγενεστέραν χρήσιν των Μυκηναϊκών τάφων Μεσσηνίας, in: *Acts of the Second International Congress of Peloponnesian Studies,* Patras 1980, vol. II (Athens 1981-82), 363-450.

Korres, G.S 1980c
Οι Μεσοελλαδικοί τύμβοι της Μεσσηνίας. Εθνολογικά προβλήματα και συμπεράσματα, in: *Proceedings of the 1st International Mycenaeological Congress: Pre-Mycenaean and Mycenaean Pylos,* Athens December 1980, in print.

Korres, G.S. 1980d
Ανασκαφαί ανά την Πυλίαν, *Prakt,* 120-187.

Korres, G.S. 1980e
s.v. *Μεσσηνία, Μεγάλη Σοβιετική Εγκυκλοπαίδεια* 21 (Greek edition 1980), Athens, 456-464.

Korres, G.S 1980f
s.v. *Βοϊδοκοιλιά, Μεγάλη Σοβιετική Εγκυκλοπαίδεια* 5 (Greek edition 1980), Athens, 658-659.

Korres, G.S. 1980g
s.v. *Μαραθών, Μεγάλη Σοβιετική Εγκυκλοπαίδεια* 20 (Greek edition 1980), Athens, 718-721.

Korres, G.S. 1980h
s.v. *Μεδεών, Μεγάλη Σοβιετική Εγκυκλοπαίδεια* 21 (Greek edition 1980), Athens, 240-241.

Korres, G.S. 1981
s. v. *Σαμικόν, Μεγάλη Σοβιετική Εγκυκλοπαίδεια* 30 (Greek edition 1981), Athens, 79-80.

Korres, G.S. 1982
The Relations between Crete and Messenia in the Late Middle Helladic and Early Late Halladic Period, in: *The Minoan Thalassocracy. Myth and Reality, Proceedings of the Third International Symposium at the Swedish Institute in Athens,* 31 May – 5 June 1982, R. Hägg & N. Marinatos, eds., Stockholm 1984, 141-152.

Korres, G.S. 1982a
s.v. *Πύλος(Ηλειακή), Μεγάλη Σοβιετική Εγκυκλοπαίδεια* 29 (Greek edition 1982), Athens, 114.

Korres, G.S. 1980/83
Archaeological investigations at Voïdokoiliá, near Pylos, Greece, *National Geographic Society, Research Reports,* vol. 21, 231-237.

Korres, G.S. 1984
Το Χρονικόν των ανασκαφών της Βοϊδοκοιλιάς, Αρχαιολογικαί Διατριβαί επί θεμάτων της Εποχής του Χαλκού (Σειρά Διατριβών και Μελετημάτων 21, 1979). Athens 1984, 11-41, 97-99.

Korres, G.S. 1984a
LH IIIB burial customs and rites in Messenia, paper read in: *Pylos Comes Alive, Industry & Administration in a Mycenaean Palace,* New York Symposium, May 1984.

Korres, G.S. 1987
Neue Ausgrabungen im Gebiet von Pylos, *EAZ* 28, 711-743.

Korres, G.S. 1988
Αρχαιολογικαί ειδήσεις. Το Διεθνές Αρχαιολογικόν - Γλωσσολογικόν Συμπόσιον in: *Pylos Comes Alive – Industry and Administration in a Mycenaean Palace,* Fordam University New York (Lincoln Center), 4-5 May 1984. ΠΛΑΤΩΝ 40/79-80, 221-237.

Korres, G.S. 1989
Messenia and its commercial connections in the Bronze Age, in: *Wace and Blegen: Pottery as Evidence for Trade in the Aegaean Bronze Age, 1939-1989. Proceedings of the International Conference held at the American School of Classical Studies at Athens,* 2-3/12/1989, C.A. Zerner, P. Zerner & J. Winder, eds. (Amsterdam 1993), 231-248.

Korres, G.S. 1990
Excavations in the region of Pylos, in: *Ευμουσία, Ceramic and Iconographic Studies in Honour of Alex. Cambitoglou* (MeditArch-Suppl. 1), J.-P. Desoeudres, ed., Sydney, 1-11.

Korres, G.S. 1991
Ο λεγόμενος τύμβος των Κοκκολάτων Κεφαλληνίας, *EEFSPA* 29, 191-199.

Korres, G.S. 1996
Οι τύμβοι της Εποχής του Χαλκού στην Μεσσηνία και συναφή εθνολογικά συμπεράσματα, in: *Acts of the First Archaeological Congress of South and West Greece,* Patras 1996, in print.

Kotsaki, M. 1987
Πάτρα. Οδός Παγώνας 41, *ADelt* 42, B1 Chron., 137.

Kotsaki, M. 1988
Πάτρα. Αρχαία Πόλη. Οδός Χρυσοβιτσίου 11, *ADelt* 43, B1 Chron., 149.

Koukouli – Chrysanthaki, C. 1976
Ποταμοί. Διασταύρωση δασικής οδού Μικρομηλιάς – Κουρού, *ADelt* 31, B2 Chron., 304.

Koukouli – Chrysanthaki, C. 1992
Πρωτοϊστορική Θάσος, vol. A-C. Athens.

Kyparissis, N. 1928
Ανασκαφή μυκηναϊκού νεκροταφείου εν Αγ. Βασιλείω Χαλανδρίτσης Αχαΐας, *Prakt,* 110-119.

Kyparissis, N. 1929
Ανασκαφή μυκηναϊκών νεκροταφείων Δήμου Φαρών Αχαΐας, εν Αγ. Βασιλείω Χαλανδρίτσης και Μητοπόλει, *Prakt,* 86-91.

Kyparissis, N. 1930
Ανασκαφαί μυκηναϊκών νεκροταφείων της Αχαΐας, *Prakt,* 81-88.

Kyparissis, N. 1935
Ανασκαφαί εν τη Αχαΐα, *Prakt,* 70-71.

Kyrieleis, H. 1988
Neue Ausgrabungen in Olympia, in: *Proceedings of an International Symposium on the Olympic Games,* W. Coulson & H. Kyrieleis, eds., 5-9 September 1988 (Athens 1992), 19-24.

Kyrieleis, H. 1990
Neue Ausgrabungen in Olympia, *Antike Welt* 21, 177-188.

Lambropoulou, A. 1997
The Middle Helladic Period in the Corinthia and the Argolid: An Archaeological Survey, PhD Thesis Bryn Mawr College 1991, UMI, Ann Arbor.

Lewartowski, K. 1989
The Decline of the Mycenaean Civilization. An Archaeological Study of Events in the Greek Mainland. Breslau – Warschau – Krakau – Danzig – Lodz.

Liagouras, A. 1980
Αρήνη, in: *Acts of the First Congress of Elian Studies,* Athens 1980.

Lolos, Y. 1987
The LH I Pottery of the SW Peloponnesos and its Local Characteristics, vols. 1-2. (SIMA pocketbook 50), Göteborg.

Maran, J. 1988
Zur Zeitstellung der Grabhügel von Marmara, *AKorrBl* 18, 341-355.

Maran, J. 1992
Die mittlere Bronzezeit. Die Deutschen Ausgrabungen auf der Pevkakia-Magula in Thessalien III, vol. I-II. Bonn.

Maran, J. 1998
Kulturwandel auf dem griechischen Festland und den Kykladen im späten 3. Jahrtausend v. Chr., vols. I-II. Bonn.

Marinatos, S. 1932
Αι ανασκαφαί Goekoop εν Κεφαλληνία, *AE,* 1-47.

Marinatos, S. 1953
Ανασκαφαί εν Πύλω, *Prakt,* 238-250.

Marinatos, S. 1954
Ανασκαφαί εν Πύλω, *Prakt,* 299-316.

Marinatos, S. 1955
Ανασκαφαί εν Πύλω, *Prakt,* 245-255.

Marinatos, S. 1958
Ανασκαφαί εν Πύλω, *Prakt,* 184-193.

Marinatos, S. 1959
Ανασκαφαί εν Πύλω, *Prakt,* 174-179.

Marinatos, S. 1960
Ανασκαφαί Πύλου (1952-1960), *ADelt* 16, B Chron., 112-119.

Marinatos, S. 1960a
Ανασκαφαί εν Πύλω, *Prakt,* 195-209.

Marinatos, S. 1961
Ανασκαφαί εν Πύλω, *Prakt,* 169-176.

Marinatos, S. 1963
Ανασκαφαί εν Πύλω, *Prakt,* 114-121.

Marinatos, S. 1964
Έρευναι εν Σάμη της Κεφαλληνίας, *AE,* 15-27.

Marinatos, S. 1964a
Ανασκαφαί εν Πύλω, *Prakt,* 78-95.

Marinatos, S. 1965
Ανασκαφαί εν Πύλω. 2. Βλαχόπουλον, *ADelt* 20, B Chron., 204-205.

Marinatos, S. 1966
Ανασκαφαί εν Πύλω, *Prakt,* 119-132.

Marinatos, S. 1968
Die Eulengöttin von Pylos, *AM* 83, 167-174.

Marinatos, S. 1970
Μαραθών, *Ergon,* 5-13.

Marinatos, S. 1970a
From the silent earth, *AAA* III 1, 61-68.

Marinatos, S. 1970b
Further news from Marathon, *AAA* III 2, 153-166.

Marinatos, S. 1970c
Further discoveries at Marathon, *AAA* III 3, 349-366.

Marinatos, S. 1970d
Ανασκαφαί Μαραθώνος, *Prakt,* 5-28.

Marinatos, S. 1970e
Μαραθών, *PAA* 45, 109-117.

Marinatos, S. 1972
Prehellenic and Protohellenic discoveries at Marathon, in: *Acts of the 2nd International Colloquium on Aegean Prehistory,* Athens April 1971 (Athens 1972), 184-190.

Marinatos, S. 1974
The first 'Mycenaeans' in Greece, in: *Bronze Age Migrations in the Aegean,* R.A Crossland & A. Birchall, eds., Park Ridge, New Jersey, 107-113.

Mastrokostas, E. 1960
Περιοχή Αχαΐας, *ADelt* 16, Chron., 144-145.

Mastrokostas, E. 1961/2
Περιοχή Αχαΐας, *ADelt* 17, B Chron., 129.

Mastrokostas, E. 1963
Ανασκαφή Αγίου Ηλία Μεσολογγίου – Ιθωρίας, *Prakt,* 203-217.

Mastrokostas, E. 1966
Τείχος Δυμαίων, *Ergon,* 156-165.

Mastrokostas, E. 1967
Ήλις. Σπήλαιον Πορτών επί της Σκόλλιος, *ADelt* 22, B1 Chron., 216.

Mastrokostas, E. 1968
Ειδήσεις εξ Αχαΐας, *AAA* I 2, 136-138.

McDonald, W.A. & Hope Simpson, R. 1961
Prehistoric habitation in the southwestern Peloponnese, *AJA* 65, 221-260.

McDonald, W.A. & Hope Simpson, R. 1964
Further explorations in southwestern Peloponnese 1962-63, *AJA* 68, 229-245.

McDonald, W.A & Hope Simpson, R. 1969
Further explorations in the southwestern Peloponnese 1964-68, *AJA* 73, 123-178.

McDonald, W.A. & Rapp, G. (eds.) 1972
The Minnesota Messenia Expedition: Reconstructing a Bronze Age Regional Environment. Minneapolis.

Mee, C.B. & Cavanagh, W.G. 1984
Mycenaean tombs as evidence for social and political organisation, *OJA* 3:3, 45-64.

Mee, C.B. & Cavanagh, W.G. 1990
The spatial distribution of Mycenaean tombs, *BSA* 85, 225-243.

Megaw, A.H.S. 1962-63
Archaeology in Greece, 1962-63:
Larissa, *AR,* 24.

Moschos, I. 1996
Το προϊστορικό νεκροταφείο των
τύμβων στις Πόρτες Αχαΐας, in:
Acts of the First Archaeological Congress of South and West Greece, Patras
1996, in print.

Moschos, I. 2000
The ancient cemetery of Chalkis.
Recent rescue excavation, *in this
volume.*

Mountjoy, P. 1986
*Mycenaean Decorated Pottery. A Guide
to Identification.* SIMA LXXIII,
Göteborg.

Mountjoy, P. 1999
Regional Mycenaean Decorated Pottery, vols. I-II. VML-Rahden/
Westf.: Leidorf.

Müller, S. 1989
Les tumuli helladiques: Où? quand?
comment?, *BCH* 113, 1-42.

Müller, S. 1994
Ιδιομορφίες στην ταφική
Αρχιτεκτονική του Μεδεώνα
Φωκίδας, in: *The Regions of the
Mycenaean World. First International
Interdisciplinary Symposium,* Lamia
25-29/9/1994 (1999), 223-234.

Müller, S. 1995
*Les Tombes Mycéniennes de Médéon de
Phocide: Architecture et Mobilier*
(unpublished PhD Thesis).

Müller, S. 1997
Les tombes de Médéon de Phocide, *Dossiers d'Archéologie* 222, 82-
85.

Mussche, H.F. et al. 1963
H.F. Mussche, J. Bingen,
J. Servais, R. Paepe & T. Hackens,
*Thoricos 1963, I, Rapport préliminaire
sur la premiere campagne de fouilles.*
Brussels 1968.

Mylonas, G.E. 1932
Προϊστορικύ Ελευσίς, in:
Κουρουνιώτη, Ελευσινιακά, Α,
Athens, 1-172.

Mylonas, G.E. 1948
Homeric and Mycenaean burial
customs, *AJA* 52, 56-81.

Mylonas, G.E. 1951
The cult of the dead in Helladic
times, in: *Studies presented to David
Moore Robinson* 1, G.E. Mylonas &
D. Raymond, eds., Saint Louis, 64-
105.

Mylonas, G.E. 1959
*Ayios Kosmas. An Early Bronze Age
Settlement and Cemetery in Attica.*
Princeton.

Mylonas, G.E. 1966
Mycenae and the Mycenaean Age.
Princeton.

Mylonas, G.E. 1972-73
Ο Ταφικός Κύκλος Β των Μυκηνών,
vols. A-B. Athens.

Mylonas, G.E. 1975
*Το Δυτικόν Νεκροταφείον της
Ελευσίνος,* vols. I-III. Athens.

Neve, P. 1993
Die Ausgrabungen in Boğasköy-
Hattuša, *AA,* 621-652.

Nordquist, G.C. 1987
*A Middle Helladic Village. Asine in the
Argolid. Acta Univ. Ups. Boreas.*
Uppsala Studies in Ancient Mediterranean and Near Eastern Civilizations 16, Uppsala.

Orlandos, A. 1915
Περί των αναστηλωτικών εργασιών
εν Ορχομενώ της Βοιωτίας, *ADelt*
1, Suppl., 51-53.

Overbeck, G.F. 1977
*Graves and Burial Customs at Ayia
Irini, Kea,* Dis. univ. of New York at
Albany 1974 (Ann Arbor 1977).

Pahygianni- Kaloudi, F. 1979
Ελευσίνα. Χώρος εργοστασίου
ΒΟΤΡΥΣ, *ADelt* 34, B1 Chron.,
37-40.

Pantelidou, M. 1976
Αι Προϊστορικαί Αθήναι. Athens.

Pantelidou – Gofa, M. 1997
Μαραθών. Τσέπι, *Ergon,* 19-22.

Pantelidou – Gofa, M. 1998
Μαραθών. Τσέπι, *Ergon,* 18-23.

Papachristodoulou, I. 1971
Ειδήσεις εκ της Β' Αρχαιολογικής
Περιφερείας, *AAA* IV 2, 140-146.

Papadimitriou, I. 1954
Ανασκαφαί εν Μυκήναις, *Prakt,*
242-269.

Papadopoulos, T.J. 1976
Μυκηναϊκή Αχαΐα και Κρήτη, in:
Acts of the Fourth International Cretological Congress, Iraklio 29/8 - 3/9
1976, vol. A2 (Athens 1981), 407-
415.

Papadopoulos, T.J. 1976α
Η Εποχή του Χαλκού στην Ήπειρο.
Dodoni 5, 271-338.

Papadopoulos, T.J. 1978
Ανασκαφή Καλλιθέας Πατρών,
Prakt, 122-124.

Papadopoulos, T.J. 1978-79
Mycenaean Achaea, vols. 1-2. SIMA
LV:1-2, Göteborg.

Papadopoulos, T.J. 1987
Tombs and burial customs in Late
Bronze Age Epirus, in: *THANA-
TOS. Les coutumes funéraires en Egée
à l'âge du Bronze,* R. Laffineur, ed.
Aegaeum 1, 137-143.

Papadopoulos, T.J. 1987a
Καλλιθέα Πατρών, *Ergon,* 89-91.

Papadopoulos, T.J. 1987b
Ανασκαφή Καλλιθέας Πατρών,
Prakt, 69-72.

Papadopoulos, T.J. 1987c
Zum Stand der Bronzezeitforsch-
ung in Epeiros, in: *Ägäische Bronzezeit,* H.-G. Buchholz, ed., 359-
378.

Papadopoulos, T.J. 1988
Καλλιθέα Πατρών, *Ergon,* 24-26.

Papadopoulos, T.J. 1988a
Ανασκαφή Καλλιθέας – Κλάους
Πατρών, *Prakt,* 32-36.

Papadopoulos, T.J. 1989
Καλλιθέα – Κλάους Πατρών,
Ergon, 23-25.

Papadopoulos, T.J. 1991
Achaea's role in the Mycenaean
World, in: *Achaia und Elis in der
Antike,* A.D. Rizakis, ed. (Meletem-
ata 13, Athens 1991), 31-37.

Papadopoulos, T.J. 1995
A Late Mycenaean koine in west-
ern Greece and the adjacent Ionian
islands, Klados, in: *Essays in Honor of
J. N. Coldstream,* C. Morris, ed.,
London, 201-208.

Papadopoulos, T.J. 1996
Η προϊστορική Αχαΐα, in: *Οι
Ανασκαφές στην Πελοπόννησο, ΕΠΤΑ
ΗΜΕΡΕΣ* (leaflet of Kathimerini
newspaper), 28.01.1996, 3-5.

Papadopoulos, T.J. 1999
Warrior–graves in Achaean Myce-
naean Cemeteries, in: *POLEMOS.
Le contexte guerrier en Egée à l'âge du
Bronze,* R. Laffineur, ed. Aegaeum
19, 267-274.

Papahatzis, N. 1979
*Παυσανίου Ελλάδος Περιήγησις.
Βιβλία 4., 5. και 6. Μεσσηνιακά και
Ηλειακά.* Athens.

Papakonstantinou, E. 1981
Κάτω Σαμικό, *ADelt* 36, Β1
Chron., 148-149.

Papakonstantinou, E. 1982
Κάτω Σαμικό, *ADelt* 37, Β1
Chron., 133-134.

Papakonstantinou, E. 1983
Κάτω Σαμικό, *ADelt* 38, Β1
Chron., 109-110.

Papakonstantinou, E. 1983a
*Περιοχή Σαμικού. Αρχαιολογικές
ενδείξεις κατοικήσεως στα ιστορικά
χρόνια.* Annual of Elian Studies
Society, vol. B, Athens.

Papakonstantinou, E.-M. 1994
Ο ταφικός κύκλος Α της Αντρώνας.
Πρώτη παρουσίαση, in: *The Regions
of the Mycenaean World. First International Interdisciplinary Symposium,*
Lamia 25-29/9/1994 (1999), 171-
180.

Papakosta, L. 1980
Νότιο Νεκροταφείο. Οδός
Σμύρνης 145 και Λασκάρεως, *ADelt*
35, Β1 Chron., 193.

Papandreou, G. 1924
Η Ηλεία διά μέσου των Αιώνων. Athens.

Papathanasopoulos, G. 1969
Επισήμανσις αρχαίων. Αρχαία
Ολυμπία, *ADelt* 24, Β1 Chron., 149.

Papavasileiou, G.A. 1907
Ανασκαφαί εν Ευβοία, *Prakt,* 114-
119.

Papavasileiou, G.A. 1910
Περί των εν Ευβοία Αρχαίων Τάφων.
Athens.

Papazoglou, L. 1982
Αίγιο. Οδός Πολυχρονιάδου 8,
ADelt 37, Β1 Chron., 149.

Papazoglou, L. 1984
Αίγιο. Οδός Αριστείδου 2
(οικόπεδο Βασ. Τσινούκα), *ADelt*
39, Β Chron., 94-95.

Papazoglou – Manioudaki, L. 1994
A Mycenaean warrior's tomb at
Krini near Patras, *BSA* 89, 171-
200.

Papazoglou – Manioudaki, L. 1994a
Πήλινα και χάλκινα της Πρώιμης
Μυκηναϊκής Εποχής από την
Αχαΐα, in: *The Regions of the Mycenaean World. First International Interdisciplinary Symposium,* Lamia 25-
29/9/1994 (1999), 269-283.

Papazoglou – Manioudaki, L. 1998
*Ο Μυκηναϊκός Οικισμός του Αιγίου και
η Πρώιμη Μυκηναϊκή Εποχή στην
Αχαΐα* (unpublished PhD Thesis,
University of Athens).

Parlama, L. 1972
Καρποφόρα, *ADelt* 27, Β1 Chron.,
262-264.

Parlama, L. 1974
Μυκηναϊκά Ηλείας, *ADelt* 29, A, 25-58.

Parlama, L. 1976
Αψιδωτοί Μυκηναϊκοί τάφοι στη Μεσσηνία, *AAA* IX 2, 252-257.

Pelon, O. 1976
Tholoi, tumuli et circles funéraires. Recherches sur les Monuments Funéraires a Plan circulaire dans l' Egee de l'âge du Bronze (IIIe et IIe millenaires av. J.-C.). Paris – Athens.

Pelon, O. 1987
L' architecture funéraire de Grèce Continentale á la transition du Bronze Moyen et du Bronze Récent, in: *THANATOS. Les coutumes funéraires en Egée à l'âge du Bronze,* R. Laffineur, ed. Aegaeum 1, 107-115.

Pendlebury, J.D.S. et al. 1937-38
Karphi; A city of refuge of the Early Iron Age in Crete, *BSA* 1937-38, 57-145.

Petritaki, M. 1988
Ριόλο. Θέση Καταρράχια, *ADelt* 43, B1 Chron., 164-166.

Petritaki, M. 1988a
Σταροχώρι. Θέση Ξηρόκαμπος, *ADelt* 43, B1 Chron., 164.

Petropoulos, M. 1985
Κρήνη. Θέση Δριμαλέικα, *ADelt* 40, B Chron., 135 -136.

Petropoulos, M. 1989
Πετρωτό. Θέση Γούπατα, *ADelt* 44, B1 Chron., 132.

Petropoulos, M. 1990
Αρχαιολογικές έρευνες στην Αχαΐα, in: *Volume in Honor of K. N. Triantafyllou,* vol. A, Patras.

Petropoulos, M. 1990a
Αίγιο. Οδός Πλαστήρα 7 (οικόπεδο Ασύλου Ανιάτων – Γηροκομείο), *ADelt* 45, B1 Chron., 137.

Petropoulos, M. 1990b
Αλισσός. Καμενίτσα Αλισσού, *ADelt* 45, B1 Chron., 135, 136.

Petropoulos, M. 1991
Τοπογραφικά της χώρας των Πατρέων, in: *Achaia und Elis in der Antike,* A.D. Rizakis, ed. (Meletemata 13, Athens 1991), 249-258.

Petropoulos, M. 1991a
Κερύνεια. Θέση Άγιος Γεώργιος, *ADelt* 46, B Chron., 156.

Petropoulos, M. 1995
Νικολέικα, *ADelt* 50, B Chron., in print.

Petropoulos, M. 1996
Ρακίτα. Νικολέικα. Ελίκη. Σαλμενίκο, in: *Acts of the First Archaeological Congress of South and West Greece,* Patras 1996, in print.

Philippson, A. – Kirsten, E. 1959
Die Griechischen Landschaften, Eine Landeskunde, Band III, Der Peloponnes. Teil I, Der Osten und Norden der Halbinsel. Frankfurt am Main.

Pini, I. 1968
Beiträge zur Minoischen Graberkunde. Wiesbaden.

Platon, N. 1949
Ο τάφος του Σταφύλλου και ο Μινωικός αποικισμός της Πεπαρήθου, *Kr. Chron.* 3, 534-573.

Polychronopoulou, O. 1980
Les Coutumes Funeraires au Bronze Moyen en Grèce Continentale (unpublished. University of Paris Sorbonne).

Protonotariou – Deilaki, E. 1966
Μυκηναϊκός τάφος εξ Άργους, in: *Χαριστήριον εις Αναστάσιον Κ. Ορλάνδον,* vol.. B, Athens, 238-247.

Protonotariou – Deilaki, E. 1978
Ο προϊστορικός τύμβος υπό το Πελόπιον της Ολυμπίας, in: *Acts of the First Congress of Elean Studies,* November 1978 (Athens 1980), 229-234.

Protonotariou – Deilaki, E. 1980
Οι Τύμβοι του Άργους, PhD Thesis, Athens.

Protonotariou – Deilaki, E. 1980-81
Τύμβοι Αργολίδος και Μεσσηνίας, *Peloponnesiaka* 14, 222-231.

Protonotariou – Deilaki, E. 1990
The tumuli of Mycenae and Dendra, in: *Celebrations of Death and Divinity in the Bronze Age Argolid,* R. Hägg & G. Nordquist, eds., Stockholm, 85-102.

Protonotariou – Deilaki, E. 1990a
Burial customs and funerary rites in the prehistoric Argolid, in: *Celebrations of Death and Divinity in the Bronze Age Argolid,* R. Hägg & G. Nordquist, eds., Stockholm, 69-83.

Renfrew, C. 1972
The Emergence of Civilisation: The Cyclades and the Aegean in the Third Millennium B.C. London.

Rizakis, A.D. (ed.) 1992
R. Dalongeville, M. Lakakis & A.D. Rizakis, *Paysages d' Achaie I, Le Bassin du Peiros et la Plaine Occidentale* (Meletemata 15). Athens.

Romaios, K.A. 1916
Έρευναι εν Θέρμω, *ADelt* 2, 179-189.

Romaios, K.A. 1956
Ανασκαφική έρευνα κατά την Ανάληψιν της Κυνουρίας, *Prakt,* 185-186.

Romaios, K.A. 1957
Ανασκαφική έρευνα κατά την Ανάληψιν της Κυνουρίας, *Prakt,* 110-111.

Rutter, J.B. 1990
Pottery groups from Tsoungiza of the end of the Middle Bronze Age. Appendix: The north cemetery at Corinth, *Hesperia* 59, 375-458.

Rutter, J.B. 1993
Review of Aegean prehistory II: The Prepalatial Bronze Age of the southern and central Greek mainland, *AJA* 97, 745-794.

Sackett, L.H. et al. 1966
Sackett L.H., V. Hankey, R.J. Howell, T.W. Jacobsen & M.R. Popham, Prehistoric Euboea: Contributions towards a survey, *BSA* 61, 33-112.

Sakellariou, M.V. 1958-59
Ένα πρόβλημα της ομηρικής γεωγραφίας: Τα όρια της χώρας των Επειών, *Peloponnesiaka* 3-4, 17-46.

Sakellariou, M.V. 1980
Les Proto-Grecs. Athens.

Sampson, A. 1997
Το Σπήλαιο των Λιμνών στα Καστριά Καλαβρύτων. Athens.

Sapouna – Sakellaraki, E. 1993
Λευκαντί, *ADelt* 48, B1 Chron., 195-196.

Sapouna – Sakellaraki, E. 1995
A Middle Helladic tomb complex at Xeropolis (Lefkandi), *BSA* 90, 41-54.

Schachermeyr, F. 1957
Der Forschungsbericht. Die ägäische Frühzeit (Kreta und Mykenai). III. Bericht, die Jahre von 1953 bis 1956 umfassend, *Anzeiger für die Altertumswissenschaft* X, col. 65-126.

Schachermeyr, F. 1971
Forschungsbericht zur ägäischen Frühzeit: Frühe Bronzezeit, *AA,* 387-419.

Schachermeyr, F. 1976
Die Ägäische Frühzeit I. Die vormykenischen Perioden des griechischen Festlandes und der Kykladen. Vienna.

Schachermeyr, F. 1976a
Die Ägäische Frühzeit II. Die mykenischen Zeit und die Gesittung von Thera. Vienna.

Schachermeyr, F. 1980
Die Ägäische Frühzeit IV. Griechenland im Zeitalter der Wanderungen vom Ende der Mykenischen Ära *bis auf die Dorier.* Vienna.

Schliemann, H. 1881
Orchomenos. Bericht über meine Ausgrabungen im Böotischen Orchomenos. Leipzig.

Seferiadou, E. 1896
Funde, *AM* 21, 246-261.

Servais – Soyez, J. & B. 1972/76
La "tholos" oblongue (tombe IV) et le tumulus (tombe V) sur le Vélatouri, in: *Thorikos VIII: rapport preliminaire sur les 9ème, 10ème, 11ème et 12ème campagnes de fouille,* Mussche H.F., J. Bingen, J. Servais & P. Spitaels, eds., Gent, Comité des fouilles belges en Grèce, 14-71.

Skarlatidou, E. 1980
Ρούσσα, *ADelt* 35, B2 Chron., 432.

Skias, A.N. 1902
Τύμβος προϊστορικός υπό την Ακρόπολιν, *AE,* 123-130.

Skilardi, D. 1987
Κουκουναριές Πάρου, *Ergon,* 109-113.

Snodgrass, A.M. 1971
The Dark Age of Greece. Edinburgh.

Sotiriadis, G. 1907
Ανασκαφαί εν Χαιρωνεία παρά τον Ορχομενόν και εν Φωκίδι (Αντίκυρα), *Prakt,* 111-112.

Sotiriadis, G. 1908
Ανασκαφαί εν Αιτωλία και Ακαρνανία, *Prakt,* 95-100.

Sotiriou, A. 1991
Κοινότητα Πόρου, *ADelt* 46, B Chron., 168.

Sotiriou, A. 1997
Οικόπεδα, *ADelt* 52, B Chron., in print.

Soueref, K.I. 1986
Μυκηναϊκές μαρτυρίες από την Ήπειρο, PhD Thesis, University of Thessaloniki.

Souyoudzoglou – Haywood, C. 1986
Mycenaean refuges and the Kefalonian cemeteries, in: *Acts of the 5th International Panionian Congress,* Argostoli – Lixouri 17-21 May 1986 (Argostoli 1991), 59-67.

Souyoudzoglou – Haywood, C. 1991
The Ionian Islands in the Bronze Age (unpublished PhD Thesis, University of Liverpool).

Sperling, J. 1942
Explorations in Elis 1939, *AJA* 46,
77-89.

Spyropoulos, T. 1973
Παραλίμνη, *ADelt* 28, B1 Chron.,
265-266.

Stavropoulou – Gatsi, M. 1989
Πάτρα. Δημόσια κτίρια και
κατοικίες. Οδός Ανθ/γού
Λιακόπουλου 6 (Παγώνα) –
Πάροδος ΖΔ 50 (πλάτωμα
Παγώνας) – Οδός Παγώνας
(αποχετευτικό έργο Δήμου) –
Πάροδος Άνθιμου Γαζή
(Αναπηρικά), *ADelt* 44, B Chron.,
121-122.

Stavropoulou – Gatsi, M. 1994
Πάτρα. Κάτω Συχαινά, ανώνυμη
δημοτική οδός, *ADelt* 49, B
Chron., 221-222.

Stavropoulou – Gatsi, M. 1995
Οικισμός της Εποχής του Χαλκού
στην "Παγώνα" της Πάτρας, in:
*Acts of the Fifth International Congress
of Peloponnesian Studies, Argos –
Nauplio* 1995 (Athens 1998), 514-
533.

Stavropoulou – Gatsi, M. 1998
Οικισμός της Εποχής του Χαλκού
στην Παγώνα Πάτρας, in: *Forschungen in der Peloponnes. 1898-1998:
100 Jahre des Österreichisches Instituts
Athen,* Athens 5-7 March 1998, in
print.

Styrenius, C.-G. 1967
Submycenaean Studies (Acta Instituti
Atheniensis Regni Sueciae, VII).
Lund.

Syriopoulos, K. 1964
Η Προϊστορία της Πελοποννήσου.
Athens.

Syriopoulos, K. 1968
Η Προϊστορία της Στερεάς Ελλάδος.
Athens.

Syriopoulos, K. 1983
Η ορεινή περιοχή της βορείου
Πελοποννήσου, in: *Acts of the
Second Local Congress of Achaean
Studies,* Kalavryta June 1983
(Athens 1986), 65-74.

Syriopoulos, K. 1983a
*Εισαγωγή εις την Αρχαίαν Ελληνικήν
Ιστορίαν. Οι Μεταβατικοί χρόνοι. Από
της Μυκηναϊκής εις την Αρχαϊκήν
Περίοδον, 1200 – 700 π.Χ.,* vols. A-
B. Athens.

Syriopoulos, K. 1987
Το τέλος του μυκηναϊκού
πολιτισμού εις την Ηλείαν και οι
ιστορικοί κάτοικοι αυτής, in: *Acts of
the Second Local Congress of Elian
Studies,* Amalias November 1987
(Athens 1989), 227-240.

Tartaron, T.F. & Zachos, K. 1994
The Mycenaeans and Epirus, The
Regions of the Mycenaean World,
in: *First International Interdisciplinary
Symposium,* Lamia 25-29/9/1994
(1999), 57-76.

Tegou, E. 1999
Θολωτός τάφος της Πρώιμης
Εποχής του Σιδήρου στην
Παντάνασσα Αμαρίου, in: *Crema-
tions in Late Bronze and Early Iron
Age,* Rhodes 29.4 – 02.5.1999,
forthcoming.

Themelis, P. 1965
Δοκιμαστική ανασκαφή εις την
Ηλειακήν Πύλον, *ADelt* 20, B2
Chron., 215-219.

Themelis, P. 1968
Υστεροελλαδικός τύμβος
Μακρυσίων, *AAA* I 2, 126-127.

Themelis, P. 1968a
Σκιλλούς, *ADelt* 23, A, 284-292.

Themelis, P. 1974
Μαραθών: Πρόσφατα ευρήματα
και η μάχη, *ADelt* 29, A, 226-244.

Theocharis, D. 1964
Θολωτός μυκηναϊκός τάφος Αγίου
Αντωνίου (Φαρσάλων), *ADelt* 19,
B2 Chron., 261.

Theocharis, D. 1966
Άγιος Αντώνιος Φαρσάλων, *ADelt*
21, B2 Chron., 253-254.

Theocharis, D. 1969
Θολωτοί μυκηναϊκοί τάφοι επί της
Όσσης, *AAA* II 2, 165-167.

Theocharis, D. 1969a
Ανασκαφή μυκηναϊκών θολωτών
τάφων Σπηλιάς Όσσης, *ADelt* 24,
B2 Chron., 223.

Theocharis D.-M. 1970
Εκ του νεκροταφείου της Ιωλκού,
AAA III 2, 198-203.

Thomopoulos, S.N. 1950
Ιστορία της Πόλεως Πατρών. Patrae.

Tomlinson, R.A. 1996
Achaia. Portes Achaias, *AR* 42, 15.

Touchais, G. 1996
Chronique des fouilles et
découvertes archéologiques en
Grèce 1995, *BCH* 120/III, 1170-
1171.

Toufexis, G. 1991
Φάρσαλα (κοινότητα Ερέτριας),
ADelt 46, B Chron., 222.

Travlos, J. 1988
*Bildlexikon zur Topographie des Anti-
ken Attika.* Tübingen.

Triantafyllou, K. 1995
Ιστορικόν Λεξικόν των Πατρών, vols. 1-2. Patrae.

Tsaravopoulos, A. & Zafiriou, N. 1995
Αρχαιότητες των Ψαρών, in: *Τα Ηρωικά Ψαρά, ΕΠΤΑ ΗΜΕΡΕΣ* (leaflet of Kathimerini newspaper), 27.08.1995, 2-5.

Tsountas, C. 1898
Κυκλαδικά, *AE*, 136-211.

Tsountas, C. 1899
Κυκλαδικά, *AE*, 74-134.

Tsountas, C. & Manatt, J.I. 1897
The Mycenaean Age. A Study of the Monuments and Culture of Pre-Homeric Greece. London.

Ünal, A., A. Ertekin & Ediz, I. 1990-91
The Hittite sword from Boğazköy – Hattuša, found 1991, and its Akkadian inscription, *Müze* 4, 46-52.

Vagiakakos, D.B. 1986
Παρατηρήσεις επί του συγχρόνου τοπωνυμικού της Αργολίδος, in: *Acts of the Second Local Congress of Argolian Studies,* Argos 30/5-1/6 1986 (Athens 1989), 339-360.

Valmin, N.S. 1927-28
Continued explorations in Eastern Triphylia, *BullLund,* 171-224.

Vanschoonwinkel, J. 1991
L' Egée et la Méditerranée Orientale à la Fin du IIe Millénaire. Louvaine-la-Neuve.

Vasilogamvrou, A. 1995
Πρωτοελλαδικό νεκροταφείο στο Καλαμάκι Ελαιοχωρίου – Λουσικών Αχαΐας, in: *Acts of the Fifth International Congress of Peloponnesian Studies,* Argos – Nauplio 1995 (Athens 1998), 366-399.

Vasilogamvrou, A. 1995a
Υστεροελλαδικές επεμβάσεις σε πρωτοελλαδικό νεκροταφείο, στο Καλαμάκι Ελαιοχωρίου – Λουσικών Αχαΐας, in: *Acts of International Congress,* Dymaia – Vouprasio, Kato Achaia June 1995, in print.

Vasilogamvrou, A. 1998
ΥΕ οικισμός στο Λάππα Αχαΐας, in: *Forschungen in der Peloponnes. 1898-1998: 100 Jahre des Österreichisches Instituts Athen,* Athens 5-7 March 1998, in print.

Vatin, C. 1969
Médéon de Phocide. Rapport provisoire. Paris.

Verdelis, N. 1951
Ανασκαφικαί έρευναι εν Θεσσαλία, *Prakt,* 129-163.

Verdelis, N. 1952
Ανασκαφικαί έρευναι εν Θεσσαλία. Β. Ανασκαφή Φαρσάλων, *Prakt,* 185-204.

Verdelis, N. 1953
Ανασκαφικαί έρευναι εν Θεσσαλία. Β. Ανασκαφή Φαρσάλων, *Prakt,* 127-132.

Vermeule, E.T. 1960
The Mycenaeans in Achaia, *AJA* 64, 1-20.

Vermeule, E.T. 1964
Greece in the Bronze Age. Chicago - London.

Vikatou, O. 1996-97
Θαλαμοειδής τάφος στη Βροχίτσα Ηλείας, *Peloponnesiaka* 22, 304-313.

Vlachopoulos, A.G. 1995
Η Υστεροελλαδική III Γ Περίοδος στη Νάξο. Τα Ταφικά Σύνολα και οι Συσχετισμοί τους με το Αιγαίο (unpublished PhD Thesis, University of Athens).

Vokotopoulou, I. 1969
Νέοι κιβωτιόσχημοι τάφοι της ΥΕΙΙΙΒ-Γ περιόδου εξ Ηπείρου, *AE,* 179-207.

Vordhos, A. 1995
Αραβωνίτσα, *ADelt* 50, Β Chron., in print.

Voutsaki, S. 1985
Middle and Late Bronze Age Burials in Messenia, Greece: Spatial Aspects, MPhil. Dissertation, University of Cambridge.

Voutsaki, S. 1992
Society and Culture in the Mycenaean World: An Analysis of Mortuary Practices in the Argolid, Thessaly and the Dodecanese (Unpublished PhD Thesis, University of Cambridge).

Voutsaki, S. 1998
Mortuary evidence, symbolic meanings and social change: a comparison between Messenia and the Argolid in the Mycenaean period, in: *Cemetery and Society in the Aegean Bronze Age,* K. Branigan, ed., Sheffield, 41-58.

Wace, A.J.B. 1946
The prehistoric exploration of the Greek mainland, *BCH* 70, 628-638.

Wace, A.J.B. & M.S. Thompson 1912
Prehistoric Thessaly. Cambridge.

Wardle, K.A. 1972
The Greek Bronze Age West of the Pindus: a study of the period ca. 3000-1000 B.C. in Epirus, Aetoloakarnania, the Ionian Islands and Albania, with reference to the Aegean, Adriatic and Balkan Regions (Unpublished PhD Thesis, University of London).

Wardle, K.A. 1977
Cultural groups of the Late Bronze and Early Iron Age in north west Greece, *Codišnjak centar za Balkanološka Ispitivanja* XV, 153-199.

Waterhouse, H. & Hope Simpson, R. 1960
Prehistoric Laconia, Part I, *BSA* 55, 67-107.

Waterhouse, H. & Hope Simpson, R. 1961
Prehistoric Laconia, Part II, *BSA* 56, 114-173.

Wide, S. 1896
Aphidna in Nordattika, *AM* 21, 385-409.

Wolters, P. 1889
Mykenische Vasen aus dem nordlichen Griechenland, *AM* 14, 262-270.

Xanthoudidis, S. 1904
Εκ Κρήτης, *AE*, 1-56.

Xydis, Th. 1971
Ερύμανθος, *Peloponnesiaka* 8, 147-175.

Yialouris, N. 1965
Μυκηναϊκός τύμβος Σαμικού, *ADelt* 20, A, 6-40.

Yialouris, N. 1966
Σωστικαί ανασκαφαί και τυχαία ευρήματα, *ADelt* 21, B1 Chron., 170-173.

Zapheiropoulos, N.S. 1952
Ανασκαφικαί έρευναι εις περιφέρεια Φαρών Αχαΐας, *Prakt*, 396-412.

Zapheiropoulos, N.S. 1956
Ανασκαφικαί έρευναι εις περιφέρεια Φαρών Αχαΐας, *Prakt,* 197ff.

Zapheiropoulos, N.S. 1957
Ανασκαφή Φαρών, *Prakt*, 114-117.

Zapheiropoulos, N.S. 1957a
Αχαΐα. Φαραί, *Ergon*, 69-70.

Zapheiropoulos, N.S. 1958
Ανασκαφή εν Φαραίς, *Prakt*, 167-176.

Zapheiropoulos, N.S. 1965
Νάξος. Λυγαρίδια, *ADelt* 20, B3 Chron., 505-506.

Zavadil, M. 1995
Bronzezeitliche Tumuli der Westpeloponnes, Magister Arbeit, Wien.

The "Mystery" of Psathi
Some Early Minoan Clay Strips and a Sealing

Dimitra Mytilineou & Erik Hallager

Abstract

During a rescue excavation at the site of Psathi in Crete in 1980, a large amount of unstratified Pre-palatial material was unearthed. The material consisted mainly of pottery, while it contained also 3,124 small, flat, narrow fragments of clay strips, mostly with string impressions on the surface and often with extra clay applied upon the strings. Such artefacts have to the knowledge of the authors not previously been published from prehistoric sites in the Aegean, and the study of the clay strips, together with practical experiments, leads us to suggest that they may have been used as "buffers" and "stabilizers" when the local poor-quality pottery was fired. In addition to these finds the site produced one of the very rarely found true sealings from the Pre-palatial period in Crete.

Psathi is a low hill by the sea, 6 km west of Khania and belonging to the municipality of Nea Kydonia. In 1980 the site was excavated by the 25th Ephoreia of Khania.[1] The excavators, Y. Tzedakis and V. Niniou, investigated the area by opening trial trenches, which yielded a great quantity of sherds, but no architectural remains. All the pottery was unstratified due to agricultural activity in the area and the natural bed-rock was very close to the surface.

The pottery is handmade and has been dated to the EM IIB period and to the transitional EM III/MM IA period: these are the only periods represented among the Psathi material. The quality, the type and the forms show that the vessels had a mainly practical and strictly secular character and were locally made. A small number of high quality sherds imported from Khania implies close contacts with that

settlement and probably also with Kastri on Kythera. To judge from the pottery, the site of Psathi was a small Pre-palatial settlement with an agricultural economy, which was abandoned peacefully, at least as far as it can be judged by the absence of burning on the sherds.[2]

The finds from Psathi consisted almost entirely of pottery, but one seal impression was unearthed and scattered among the sherds from all the trenches was 3,124[3] pieces of what we have called *teniakia* (ταινιάκια), the Greek word for small strips (ταινία). A *tenia* may be defined as a flat, narrow, curved strip of clay which has been attached to a smooth object by the help of strings, the impressions of which are seen on the surface of the clay and which are often covered with a second piece of clay.

With the exception of a single fragment found at the Daskalogianni excavations at Khania in 1997 in an EM III/MM IA context,[4] we know of no other prehistoric site in Greece which has produced similar finds. To our knowledge none has so far been found *in situ* and thus only the objects themselves can provide clues as to their function. With eight doubtful exceptions[5] none of the teniakia are complete. The preserved length of the fragments varies from 0.6 to 7.8 cm,[6] while the width is usually completely preserved; this varies from 0.6 to 3.5 cm.[7] The thickness of the teniakia is typically 0.5-0.6 cm.[8]

After an initial examination we realized that the fragments – although probably coming from the same activity – were of different types, shapes and profiles. Accordingly we defined different criteria, which we thought useful for further investigation; we examined every fragment and entered all the information on a database.

Description

The clay of the teniakia is probably only one local fabric similar to that of the pottery. In general terms the clay used is fine, in most cases firm and pure, although it sometimes contains relatively large grits. The teniakia were baked in a badly controlled temperature, which resulted in different appearances of the individual pieces. To the eye these fell into six categories: 1. very hard well fired black pieces found on 150 teniakia; 2. a little less hard, but still well fired black to grey pieces found on 708 teniakia; 3. soft grey pieces found on 694 teniakia; 4. hard well fired buff to red in colour found on 518 teniakia; 5. softish, less well fired red/pink to grey colour found on 754 teniakia; 6. well, but unevenly fired pieces which often in the same piece show both black and red colour from the firing found on 281 teniakia. 19 pieces did not fall into the above categories. The pottery from Psathi did not show any signs of secondary burning, while the teniakia often had the appearance of being over-fired.

The teniakia were divided into eight different types or elements according to physical appearance:

Type 1: the pieces where extra clay had been added on top of the string (Fig. 1). 727 (23%) teniakia had extra clay added.
Type 2: the pieces where string marks were visible on the surface of the clay (Fig. 2). String marks on surface were found on 2,149 pieces (69%).
Type 3: flat end pieces, i.e. the end of a teniaki had just been smoothed flat (Fig. 3, bottom row). 218 such end pieces (7%) have been identified with reasonable certainty.
Type 4: raised end pieces, i.e. the end of a teniaki had been pressed against something which gave the end a small upwards bent (Fig. 3 top row and Fig. 11). 249 raised end pieces (8%) were identified

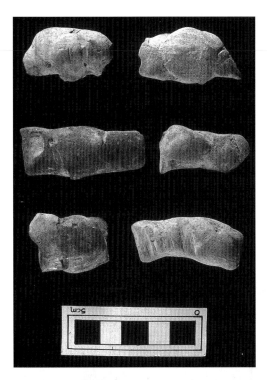

Fig. 1. Six examples of Type 1 with extra clay applied.

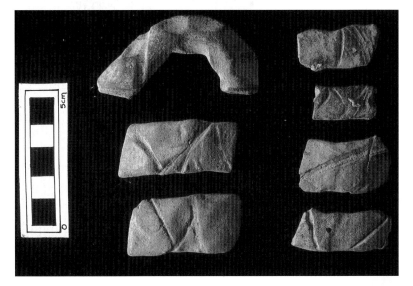

with reasonable certainty.
Type 5: consists of a small group of narrow pieces with triangular section and without string marks (Fig. 4, second row, right). Only 30 such pieces (1%) were identified and may be a sub-type of Type 7 cf. below.
Type 6: are flat pieces without string impressions. 391 fragments of this type (13%) were noted.
Type 7: pieces with small depressions probably from fingers (Fig. 4, second row,

Fig. 2. Seven teniakia of Type 2. Upper left is a combination of type 2 and type 7.

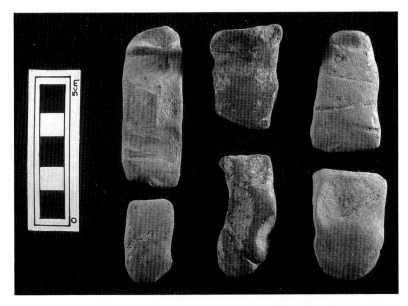

Fig. 3. Upper row: Type 4, end pieces with raised end: bottom row: Type 3, end pieces with flat

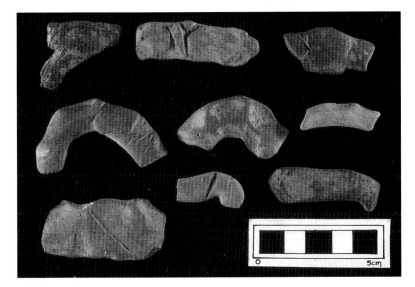

Fig. 4. Different shapes of teniakia.

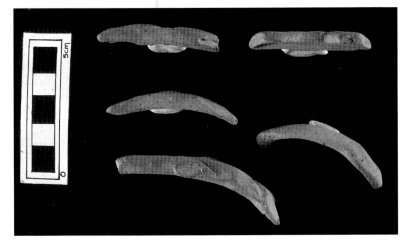

Fig. 5. Different profiles of teniakia.

middle). Such depressions were noted on 293 pieces (9%).

Type 8: miscellaneous pieces, with diverging shapes from the ordinary strip type. Quite often they had been pressed against something giving the teniakia curves in different directions, as if they had been pressed against a spout. 135 pieces (4%) of these anomalies were found.

These eight types or elements more often than not appear in combinations. For example are 249 pieces combinations of Type 1 and Type 2 (Fig. 12), while these combination pieces may be combined with further elements as for example depressions from fingers (Type 7) (Fig. 2 left column, top) or they may be end pieces (Types 3 and 4). With the possible exception of Type 5 (as we have defined it[9]) all sorts of combinations appear, which show that they are all elements that might be found in a complete/ordinary tenia.

The shape of a teniaki varies a great deal, from being straight to almost circular or S-curved. The straight pieces we called strips while the curved ones were subdivided into slightly curved, curved or much curved. Only the Type 8 pieces had a somewhat irregular appearance. The categories are as follows (Fig. 4):

unclear shape	10
circular	50
oval	20
much curved	144
curved	717
slightly curved	369
S-curved	1
irregular	1
strip	1811

Also the profile of a teniaki varies somewhat from almost flat to much curved, while a very few Type 8 were described as being uneven. The categories are as follows (Fig. 5):

unclear profile	1
almost flat	216
slightly curved	481
curved	2148
much curved	275
uneven	3

All teniakia were examined for finger-prints, i.e. pieces where papillary lines could be distinguished. This investigation only took into consideration whether papillary lines could be seen or not. With a few exceptions only a relatively small part of a teniaki had papillary lines (Fig. 4, bottom, right). The result was as follows:

uncertain	33
faint	375
yes	737
clear	36
no	1943

Considering that all tenias were hand-made, very often with extra clay applied, and considering that the tenias were probably a waste-product, which did not require special surface treatment, it may seem surprising that only *c.* 25% carried reasonably clear finger prints. On pieces with depressions from fingers we never found papillary lines – probably because the fingers were squeezed in the clay?

The string marks deserved special attention. In this connection there was one thing we noted from the beginning and which proved to be consistent on all pieces with string marks: in no instance did the string mark reach the bottom of the teniaki. This means that the tenias were applied to objects larger than them-selves (Fig. 6b).[10] The string marks run in all directions, i.e. straight across a teniaki, in oblique directions and lengthwise. When more than one string impression is preserved, the strings often crossed each other (Figs. 2 and 9, top). Most of the string marks ran obliquely over the pieces as noted on 1,578 examples, while string marks going across was noted on 696 pieces. What may, at a first thought, seem surprising: as many as 442 pieces had the string marks running along the length of the teniaki. The number of string marks found on a single teniaki varied from 0 (type 6) to 9.[11] We also made notes as to whether the string had cut deep into the clay, whether only light traces were seen or whether it was somewhere in between. When more than one string impression

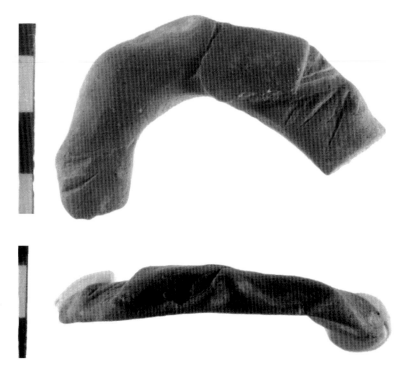

occurred, we often noted differences in depth; for example one string cutting lightly, the other deep (Fig. 7). The three main categories were noted in almost equal amounts (deep: 813; light: 672; medium: 757). In several cases we noted that a finger had been pressed over the string after it was in place (Fig. 7). The strings themselves were apparently of two types: the one a rather simple and fine organic string perhaps strips from palm leaves or "kalami" (Fig. 8a-b) while the other type, for which we have no sugges-tions, often showed traces of windings.[12] In general the string marks were fine leav-ing impressions in width from *c.* 0.5 to less than 0.01cm (Fig. 2).

Fig. 6a-b. 15/0346, a Type 1/2 teniaki where the string-hole in the profile is clearly seen not to go down to the edge of the teniaki.

Fig. 7. 16/2229, a Type 2 where the clay has been pressed over one string and where a different depth of string marks is clearly noted.

with an unusually broad
and clear string mark shown
in plasticine impression
to the right.

When examining terracotta objects with string impressions, one is inclined first of all to study the reverse (or bottom) of the object in order to find out what the object had been attached to. In one way

against which the tenia was pressed must have been relatively smooth. In cross-section the bottom was slightly bent, while the profile varies from almost flat till much curved, cf. above (Fig. 5). Many of the teniakia were worn

In the preceding discussion the teniakia have been presented as if they were plain or oddly shaped strips, but there are a few exceptions to this rule in that a piece may display three or even four broken ends. Some pieces are broken in a T shape[13] or a Y[14] (three broken ends), an X[15] or a double T[16] (Figs. 4, upper row, left and 10). These pieces show that in a few cases a tenia is not a single band, but composite bands applied to the object.

All together the 3,124 teniakia have a length of 88.762 m, which means that the

Fig. 9. Obverse, profile and reverse of four teniakia.

the teniakia were absolutely uniform in that the surface of all pieces were smooth and without impressions (Fig. 9, bottom). This shows that the surface of the object

Fig. 10. A double T- teniaki. Could be compared to what is seen on Fig. 16.

average length of a fragment is 2.84 cm in length and the average width is 1.63 cm. We have noted 468 end pieces or possible end pieces. If a tenia always has two ends and if the collected pieces are representative of what once existed we might argue that the material represents 234 pieces (468 ends/2). Thus the average length of a tenia would be 37.9 cm (8876.2 cm/234) and a tenia piece was broken up into 13 teniakia. As will become apparent below, we believe that this playing with numbers is of little relevance, partly because we shall argue that the tenias were of different length and partly because we do not believe that all tenias necessarily had an end, i.e. they might have been a continuous band around the object.

Fig. 11. An uprised end piece (type 4) fitting to a rim/body/handle fragment from Psathi.

The object

We believe that what has up till now been described as 'the object' is pottery. Pots are curved in all kinds of directions and are bigger than the tenias, which explains why the strings never went down to the edge or bottom of the teniakia. Moreover Pre-palatial pottery often has a fine smooth surface. Pottery would thus fulfil the conditions described above. In addition, we have tried to fit teniakia to Pre-palatial (and later) pottery and it was not difficult to find areas on the vases where the teniakia fitted. This was especially clearly seen with raised end pieces (Type 4) and certain types of handles as well as with "pressed against" pieces and out-curving rims and spouts. In short we believe that the teniakia sat either on handles (both vertical (Fig. 11) and horizontal) or as wavy bands around the upper part of (smaller?) vessels. These reconstructions would be consistent with the string impressions. Thus for example are all 199 surely identified end pieces of Type 4, with the odd exception of 16/1852, with string marks going either across and/or obliquely as shown in the reconstruction. Of the same end-type 56 are more than 4 cm long and they are with one exception all curved in profile as one would expect. Out of the 1230 pieces with a curved

shape, most of which would have belonged to the wavy-band-type, only 227 had string marks going across. These 227 pieces could not, of course, have belonged to the wavy-band type, but might have been sitting on horizontal handles – or perhaps on the side of vertical handles.

The teniakia

If we are right in our assumption that the teniakia were attached to handles and upper parts of vessels, we can be fairly certain that they were not attached while the vase was being made. Firstly, if the clay of both vase and tenia was wet the strings would hardly have been needed, and secondly, traces of tenia impressions would have been found on at least some of the recovered sherds, and this was not the case. It therefore seems reasonable to conclude that the teniakia were added on the vases after they had a hard dry surface.

An early practical experiment with plasticine showed us that strings would be needed while the teniakia were applied to the vases and it seems likely that many of the extra pieces of clay added (and covering strings, Type 1) were added for two purposes. The first would clearly be to keep the string in place during the "binding-up process"; the second to cover string ends, as is shown on some of the pieces where there was only one or three string holes below the added clay. The need to keep several strings in place is, for example, also seen on Fig. 12. The added

Fig. 12. 16/2285 which
shows that several strings had
been kept in place by the
extra applied clay.

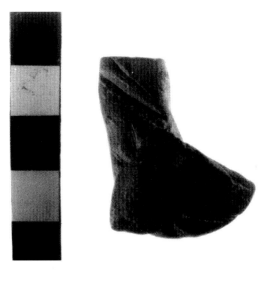

clay is thus of a purely practical nature. This feature was found on roughly 1/4 of the pieces. This would seem a large quantity, and would indicate that the "binding-up process" was not always simple.

A few more observations must also be stressed:

- As no care has been taken for their appearance, teniakia give the impression of secular, clearly practical purpose.

- It is obvious that they were intended to accomplish a specific result and not as complete objects in themselves.

- It seems that they were needed for a certain time and not for permanent use, as they were attached with perishable material, namely strings.

- Each tenia could be used only once.

A practical experiment

All the above observations forced us to abandon two ideas we had about the possible function of the teniakia. One was that they might have been applied to the pottery during the firing process to reduce the amount of oxygen in order to give some kind of decoration to the vases – but not a single sherd from the entire Psathi material could confirm this theory. Our second idea was that the teniakia had somehow been part of a sealing procedure: for example, if a piece of gut had covered the rim of the vase and was kept in place by teniakia. But this idea also had

to be abandoned, because not a single fragment of a tenia preserved impressions of folding which a piece of gut (or thin leather) would have inevitably given, when pulled over the sides of a vase. We had other ideas, which also had to be rejected.

At this point, when the hard evidence of the teniakia themselves had reduced all our ideas to nothing, DM contacted a local potter, Aspasia Vasilikaki, to discuss our problems further with her. And this proved most fruitful. Study of the pottery and the teniakia lead to the idea that the teniakia could have been applied to the vases in order to avoid them breaking during the process of firing in the kiln. Such an explanation would not violate any observation we had made, and Mrs. Vasilikaki kindly agreed to make a practical experiment together with DM to test if such a procedure would produce items similar to those found at Psathi.[17]

During the entire experiment attempts were made to stay as close as possible to the prehistoric techniques, constructing handmade vessels and using tools and materials which the prehistoric man could find and use. The experiment was carried out in four stages.

Stage 1. Preparation of the clay
On 3 December 1998, AV and DM collected earth from four different places near Psathi (west and south-west of the excavation site). After the earth was sieved, water was added to prepare the clay for the experiment. When the experiment started on 9 August 1999 the clay from Psathi proved to be useless, since it was not homogeneous or plastic at all. Therefore, DM returned to Psathi searching for better earth quality and found a fine earth-like powder from a location south of the site; this material was near the surface, due to the construction of a new road. The earth is yellow with small grey grits. The clay prepared from the new soil was again problematic, but better than the previous ones, so it was used with the addition of red Cretan clay (from Moires in the Messara plain) in a proportion of 1:1. For

some of the vessels a coarse English clay named "rakou" was also used; this is more resistant in high temperatures.

Stage 2. The construction of the vessels
Fifteen vases similar to Early Minoan shapes were produced in one week (Fig. 13):
2 teapots (1 wheel made from *rakou* and one from mixed clay)
1 jug (from mixed clay)
2 small "jars" (1 wheel made from Cretan clay and one from mixed clay)
4 goblets with foot (two from *rakou* and two from mixed clay)
6 cups (two from pure Psathi clay, and four from mixed clay)

The forms were not exactly identical to the Psathi ones, but they had the characteristics needed for the teniakia: handles, rims, wavy rims, bases and spouts). Teniakia were applied to two of the vases (one cup and one "jar") when the clay was still wet, while the remaining vases were left to dry slowly for two or three days. Then the exterior, and interior of the open vessels, was slightly polished with a sea-pebble and olive oil, and in some cases with a light solution of red clay.

Stage 3. The teniakia
The clay used for the teniakia was the same as that used for most of the vases, i.e.

Fig. 14. A tea pot with teniakia applied in different directions.

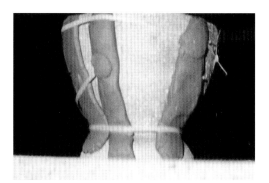

Fig. 15. A cup with vertical teniakia applied.

Fig. 16. A pot with horizontal and crossing teniakia applied.

Fig. 17. The fifteen vases with teniakia placed in the oven before they were covered with sherds and wood.

of most of the vases after they had dried. We tried to imitate all the possible types; shape, directions, back-side anomalies and string marks found on the originals (Figs. 14-16). After the teniakia dried on the vessels they were seen to be very loose and fragile – some fell off on the first touch. Therefore, on four vases, the teniakia were attached immediately before they were put into the fire in order to see what would happen when wet teniakia were baked.

Stage 4. Baking the vases
On 3 September 1999 the vases were fired in an open hearth. We opened a shallow hole in the ground (10 to 20 cm deep) where we put a layer of thin branches from olive trees. The vases were placed on the branches, very close to one another, making a small conical construction (Fig. 17). The vases were then covered by sherds[19] in order to protect them from direct fire. Then branches were put around and upon the construction and we fired the vases, adding wood when necessary.

The firing process lasted for about two hours and a temperature of at least 700 degrees C was reached.[20] During the first

Fig. 18. A collection of the teniakia from the experiment. In all cases counterparts could be found among the original material. Only the ones from the experiment tends to be larger than those found at Psathi – but then they have not been rejected on a dump yet.

the mixed clay. The string used came from the plant *athanatos*, which is a type of cactus with large leaves with thorns. Many fibres were joined, which resulted in a very strong string, similar in appearance to the second type observed on the teniakia.[18] Attempts were also made to produce strings from "kalami"– but with no success, probably due to ignorance of the correct processing.

Teniakia were attached around the body

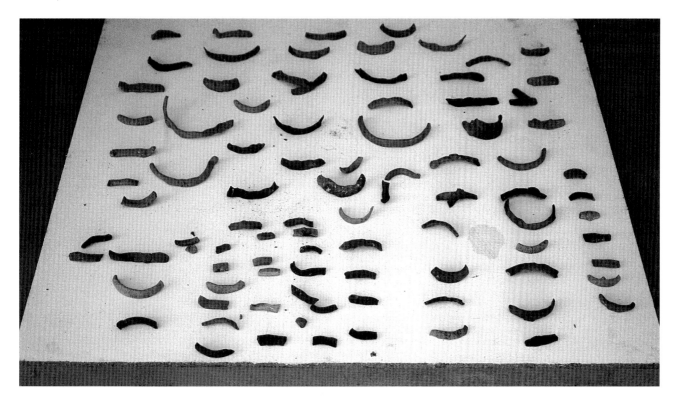

half hour (between 150 and 300 degrees) we heard the sound of breaking vases.

The result was checked the next morning. Fortunately only the wheel made jar was completely broken (it was still a little wet), whereas most of the other vases were almost complete. Of relevance to our problem: the teniakia fell from the vases without leaving any sign on the surface of the vessels, and we did not observe any difference between those which were put into the fire wet and those which were dry. Only the teniakia which were attached to the two wet vases did not fall off (one seen in Fig. 13, lower, right). They were difficult to detach and they left signs (scars?) on the vases.

The teniakia themselves looked identical to the original ones – except for the colour of the clay. They had similar forms, shapes, profiles, string marks and "anomalies" (Fig. 18). And most importantly, the reverse of the teniakia had the same smooth surface as the original ones. Furthermore, it should also be noted that impressions from papillary lines – like on the original material – were quite limited.

Conclusion

The practical experiment has thus more than strongly suggested that the teniakia were attached to vases and that they were fired with them. The small size and thinness of the teniakia caused most of them to be over-fired. The experiment seemed to show that the teniakia were attached to the vases when they were completely dry and that they were attached immediately before the vases were baked.

As to why the teniakia were attached to the pottery in this fashion we are not certain, but the potters with whom DM has discussed the problem have suggested a very plausible solution.[21] The quality of the Psathi clay is rather poor and the fire in which the vases were baked was not well controlled. Under this condition, teniakia attached to the vases as described, may have served a two-fold purpose during the critical moment of the firing process (between 150 and 300 degrees):[22]

they offer a very effective protection against fire and could thus protect the vases from breaking by the suddenly increased temperature, while the string tightens the surface and thus keeps the shape intact.

Naturally the practical experiment does not prove that the above explanation for the teniakia is the correct one, but it seems the best we can offer for the "mystery" of Psathi. Should it prove correct, it seems that at least part of the deposits excavated at Psathi are waste products from pottery production. And in this connection one asks whether this is a local phenomenon or whether excavations from other prehistoric settlements (presumably with low-quality pottery) had not struck upon waste from pottery production.

Fig. 19. The seal impression Π 9600. Scale 2:1.

Fig. 20. Reverse of the seal impression Π 9600, probably revealing impressions from rough basketry. Scale 2:1.

Fig. 21. Drawing of the seal
impression Π 9600. Scale
2:1.

The sealing

Among the material from Psathi was found a single fragment of a sealing[23] – a welcome find, since so little is know about seal *use* in Pre-palatial Crete.

Catalogue (Figs. 19-21)
Mus.no. Π 9600. Clay sealing, fragment fractured all way round. Clay: soft, light brown, finely gritted, slightly porous. Probably non-local clay. Worn on all sides. No string holes. Pres. Ø 2.66 x 1.84, Th. 0.93. On the reverse are seen three small grooves, indicating that the sealing may perhaps have been pressed against some kind of rough basketry. The worn state of the reverse makes it impossible to decide with certainty. Seal: along the longitudinal axis of the sealing the surface is very straight while on the short side it is slightly curved indicating that a large cylinder or a slightly incurved large stamp may have been used to impress the design, which consists of a complicated, geometric linear design around a cross or swastika. Parallels for the motif may be found at CMS II.1, nos. 66 and 351 and perhaps CMS V.1, no. 80.

As mentioned our knowledge of Pre-palatial seal use is – in contrast to the situation on the contemporary mainland – rather limited. Only 21 possible pieces have been published and of these, 10 were found on pottery, loom weights and a spindle whorl.[24] Of the eleven "true" Pre-palatial sealings, the Psathi example recalls the one found below the palace at Malia[25] and a sealing found at the recent excavations at Mochlos.[26] They remind one of the Psathi sealing in that they are flat, fractured all round, with an indistinct impression on the reverse, no string hole, and with a simple linear geometric design for motif. In all three cases it is impossible to decide whether these sealing fragments are part of larger decorated terracotta object or pottery decoration as is found several times on the mainland during the EH II period[27] or whether they may have been fragments from canonical sealings. If our observations are correct, that the Psathi sealing was sitting on basketry and that it was produced from non-local clay we may argue for a genuine sealing procedure with administrative implications, as several of the other Pre-palatial sealings clearly indicate.[28]

Notes

We are most grateful to Mrs. Maria Andreadaki-Vlasaki who encouraged us to undertake this study and to the Ministry of Culture for the permission to publish the terracotta objects from the excavation at Psathi. We wish to thank Olga Krzyszkowska, who has corrected the English text.

Figs. 13-18 are by D.M. while the remaining are by E.H.

NOTE 1
Tzedakis 1980, 507-518.

NOTE 2
Mytilineou 1997-98, 195-236.

NOTE 3
Actually 3,186 pieces were inventoried from which a few joins were made and of which 48 on a second investigation seemed more likely to be pot sherds than teniakia.

NOTE 4
We are grateful to Mrs. Maria Andreadaki-Vlasaki for permission to mention this find here.

NOTE 5
16/2065, 16/2186, 16/0397, 16/1725, 16/0970, 16/1072, 16/1083, 16/1188.

NOTE 6
Only 474 were preserved at a length of 4.0 cm or more.

NOTE 7
98% of the measurable pieces, however, had a width between 1.0 and 2.5 cm.

NOTE 8
We did not measure the thickness of all teniakia, since they appeared rather uniform. From the random sample measured 72% were 0.5-0.6 cm while 14% were thinner and 14% thicker.

NOTE 9
It should be noted that the typical triangular shape of Type 5 was noted in 9 instances with string impressions for which reason

Type 5 should not be excluded, but just be considered to have an exceptional cross-section.

NOTE 10
A good example of objects also bound with clay and strings is the Minoan flat-based nodule where however the object was more narrow than the clay packed around it, for which reason the string marks were seen at the bottom or the very edge of the bottom, cf. Hallager 1996 I, 135-145, figs. 47-56.

NOTE 11
On the Type 2 pieces we found the following distribution:
1 725
2 688
3 398
4 181
5 72
6 23
7 10
9 1

NOTE 12
We wish to thank Dr. Anaya Sarpaki for discussions and suggestions concerning the nature of the strings.

NOTE 13
16/0904, 16/2458, 16/0118, and 16/2193.

NOTE 14
16/1147.

NOTE 15
16/1140.

NOTE 16
16/1776.

NOTE 17
We wish to thank warmly Aspasia, without whose help we could not have carried out the practical experiment, and also a special thanks to Anastasia Tzigounaki, who first proposed that the teniakia might have played a role in connection with producing of pot-

tery. We also thank the potter Polytimi Biliona for her help in making of the vessels.

NOTE 18
Athanatos was not the plant used to make the Minoan strings, since it was only introduced in Crete *c*. 500 years ago; from then on it was used for strings until the beginning of the 20th Century.

NOTE 19
These sherds were from modern pottery.

NOTE 20
By 700 degrees the clay becomes red-hot, and one vase which we extracted from the fire had reached this state.

NOTE 21
We are grateful to Mr. Mathios Liodakis, who helped in the firing of the vases and offered a lot of his knowledge on the conclusions of the experiment.

NOTE 22
After 300 degrees the vases are stable, and do not need teniakia.

NOTE 23
In trench 8, level 1.

NOTE 24
Vlasaki & Hallager 1995, 254 and Table 1.

NOTE 25
Hue & Pelon 1992, 31ff., figs. 33-34.

NOTE 26
Soles & Davaras 1992, 436. We are grateful to J. Soles for showing us the piece and for his permission to mention our observations here.

NOTE 27
For example, Tiryns, cf. CMS V.2 nos 526-572 and Lerna, cf. CMS V.1, 120-149.

NOTE 28
Vlasaki & Hallager 1995, 268-270.

Bibliography

Hallager, E. 1996
The Minoan Roundel and other Sealed Documents in the Neopalatial Linear A Administration, I-II (Aegaeum 14). Liège.

Hue, M. & O. Pelon 1992
La salle à piliers du palais de Malia et ses antécédents, *BCH* 116, 1-36.

Mytilineou, D. 1997-98
Προανακτορική κεραμική από τη θέση Ψαθί Κυδωνίας, *Kritiki Estia* 6, 195-236.

Soles, J. & C. Davaras 1992
Excavations at Mochlos 1989, *Hesperia* 61, 414-445.

Tzedakis, Y. 1980
Αρχαιότητες και μνημεία Δυτικής Κρήτης, *ADelt* 35 Chron, 507-518.

Vlasaki, M. & E. Hallager 1995
Evidence for seal use in Pre-palatial Western Crete, in: *Sceaux minoens et mycéniens,* ed. W. Müller (CMS Beiheft 5). Berlin, 251-270.

A Fragment of an Early Etruscan Bronze Throne in Olympia?

Ingrid Strøm

Among the early Etruscan bronze objects in Olympia is a fragmentary relief plate with fine, green patina and Orientalizing ornamentation, Ol. IV. 1007 (Fig. 1).[1] It is made up of three small, joining fragments and measures in all 19.6 cm in width, its height varying between 5.7 and 7.12 cm. It is decorated in two curving friezes, one of overlapping double arcs and one of connected palmettes, the exact type of which cannot be deduced because of the break – they may represent a series of linked Phoenician palmettes.[2] The two friezes are separated by a relief line, measuring ca. 42 cm in diameter, with small raised points on either side. Below the arcs is a plain, undecorated part.

Since the back of the plate is now covered in wax, its thickness cannot be determined nor details of its original form, although – even in its present state – it seems to show a curvature in horizontal as well as in vertical direction, the former a little more pronounced at the palmette frieze than

below. A small hole in the right-hand, triangular fragment with arcs does not penetrate the plate and there is no reason to believe that the plate was fastened to another material.

Further technical observations are possible from the front of the plate: The double arcs vary in outer width – between 5.96 and 6.56 cm – as well as in height which, although in no case fully preserved, varies around 3.5 cm; the space between the two parallel lines of the arcs differs at their ends; the small, raised points at the relief line are irregularly placed, now on the line, now at one or the other side of it. Since the ornaments are not identical in detail, they cannot have been set with identical stamps, but must have been punched free-hand from the back. Most details are engraved: The outlines of the arcs, of each palmette petal and of each connecting link between the palmettes as well as the inner oblique lines of these links. The curved tips of the palmette pet-

Fig. 1. Ol. IV 1007. Fragment of Bronze Relief. Olympia. Deutsches Archäologisches Institut. Athen. Neg. No. 77. 299.

Fig. 2. Fragments of Etruscan shields with stamped decoration.
A. Oxford Ashmolean Mueum. Inv. No. 1982. 222. Museum Photo.
B. Br. Mus. Inv. No. 55.10 - 4.1. Museum Photo.

als are slightly more raised than the rest of the ornament. Obviously a South Etruscan Orientalizing bronze relief of the 7th Century BC,[3] neither its local workshop nor its exact chronology can be immediately given.

Interpretation

Several scholars have identified this fragmentary relief with part of a South Etruscan round bronze shield,[4] the numbers of which are steadily increasing.[5] For technical reasons alone such an interpretation is not possible, since all known South Etruscan Orientalizing bronze shields are decorated in stamped motives and not one is engraved.[6] In my opinion, these observations are conclusive in themselves; but also in its ornamentation the fragment stands apart from early Etruscan bronze shields: Connected palmettes and arcs are characteristic of Late Orientalizing Etruscan shields of Group B II only (Geiger 3 a-b) (Fig. 2A);[7] however, those of the Olympia fragment show different details. As I observed in 1971: "... the palmette decoration of its upper part differs in character from the palmettes of Etruscan shields, while the arcs below all lack the palmette or star terminals which apparently are never missing on Etruscan shields or other stamped bronze objects with this type of decoration".[8] Other palmette types of B II are fuller and may remind more of the palmettes of the Olympia fragment, but they are always unconnected, either single or antithetically placed double ones (Fig. 2B).[9] The plain part below the arcs is a sign of an undecorated zone, foreign to the Orientalizing shields, except for the few, ornamentally diverging shields of B III (Geiger Group 2d).[10]

Stylistically, the Olympia fragment corresponds with the Late Orientalizing B II stamped bronze reliefs as well as with metal reliefs in free-hand drawing found in the Bernardini and Barberini Tombs in Palestrina and the Regolini-Galassi Tomb in Cerveteri,[11] three tombs the Orientalizing shields of which all were of B I type

(Geiger 2a, b and c).[12] The production of B I started in the first quarter of the 7th Century BC[13] and the two Palestrina tombs are dated to around 675 BC and the second quarter of the 7th Century BC, respectively,[14] the Regolini-Galassi Tomb, in my opinion, to shortly after 650 BC.[15]

Although their absolute chronology is not certain, the B II stamped shields chiefly belong to the second half of the 7th Cent. BC, possibly continuing into the early 6th Cent. BC.[16] However, three objects of stamped bronze relief, apparently representing a transitional phase with a combination of B I and B II stamped ornaments: a trapezoid standard,[17] a rectangular box serving as urn (Fig. 3) and the mountings of a four-wheeled carriage, were found in Veji, Monte Michele, Tomb 5, dated to the second quarter of the 7th Century BC.[18] The typically B I ornaments of small bosses and narrow cable pattern are used together with palmettes and rosettes, characteristic of B II reliefs only. Specific ornaments, such as the Phoenician palmettes of the standard, the leaf rosettes of the urn and the carriage, and the small single palmettes of the urn plates, are either unique or rare in the normal B II repertory and indicate a local Veji production. The stamped bronze reliefs of Monte Michele, Tomb 5, point to a date not much later than around 650 BC for the fully developed B II style. From the above comparisons, an absolute chronology of the Olympia fragment to around 650 BC or perhaps slightly earlier is probably not far out of date.[19]

Never having accepted the Olympia fragment as part of an Etruscan shield, I some years ago tentatively proposed to identify it with a fragment of the high back of a South Etruscan barrel-shaped bronze throne.[20] With its large inner diameter (42 cm), on the outside of which was at least one broad, ornamental frieze, it is part of an object of considerable size and the only other possibility that comes to my mind is a two-wheeled chariot, either its high,

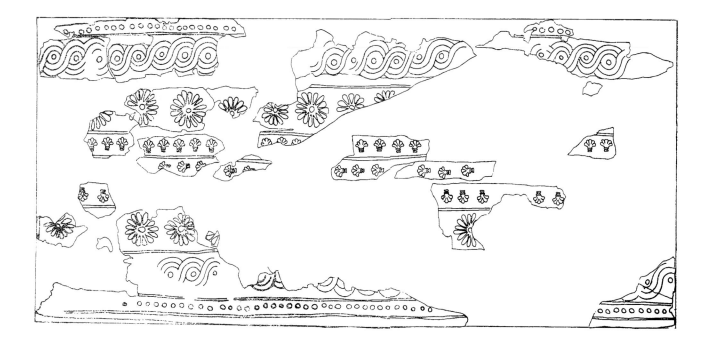

Fig. 3. Veji, Monte Michele, Tomb 5. Rectangular urn, bronze relief with stamped ornaments. StEtr LI, 552, fig. 5.

curved back or the semi-curved side of its foot-board.[21] We have examples of bronze reliefs for thrones as well as for chariots coming from the same workshops as the shields and other objects with stamped ornamentation,[22] which may account for the close stylistic correspondence between the Olympia fragment and Etruscan Late Orientalizing stamped bronze reliefs. However, there is no sign of Ol. IV 1007 having been fastened to another material as was the case for the chariot plates, and if my observations regarding the curvature of the Olympia relief are correct, they do not conform well with the straight back or the flat foot-board of a two-wheeled chariot.[23] On the other hand, the curvature of the relief would fit perfectly with the normal flaring back of Etruscan bronze thrones in free-hand relief decoration, as they are known from Chiusi (Fig. 4).[24] On this evidence alone, an identification with a two-wheeled chariot cannot be entirely rejected, but there are other reasons for ruling it out[25] and I find an identification of the Olympia fragment with part of a South Etruscan Early Orientalizing bronze throne the one most likely.

The Etruscan Thrones

The Orientalizing Chiusi thrones with free decoration form a long line of development throughout the second half of the 7th Century BC and into the early 6th Century BC.[26] In Chiusi, the local barrel-shaped throne functions as seat for the urn and forms part of grave furniture comprising also a bronze table. The context is presumably that of the dead person seated at his burial meal.[27] Throne and table alike may have the same free-hand relief decoration of animals and fabulous creatures, rosettes and linked palmettes on arcs (Fig. 4), in which last-mentioned features the Olympia fragment resembles them. Their decoration has close counterparts in South Etruscan Orientalizing art from which they must have been inspired.[28]

The few South Etruscan Orientalizing bronze thrones known today do not have free-hand decoration, but the same stamped motives as the B I shields[29] and, in my opinion, in one case, also as B II.[30]

The centres of production of the stamped Orientalizing South Etruscan bronze reliefs are still a matter of dispute. Definitely, Tarquinia had an important workshop of shields, Veji and Vulci at least of

Fig. 4. Chiusi bronze throne. The British Museum. Cat. Bronzes, No. 600. Museum Photo.

other stamped metal reliefs and most likely Caere too, while there is evidence of workshops in other Etruscanized regions such as Latium and the Faliscan area.[31] Presumably the stamped bronze reliefs, Geometric as well as Orientalizing, were produced locally in most major towns[32] and an attempt at establishing different workshops will require detailed studies not only of shields, but of other stamped bronze reliefs (urns, flasks, tripods etc.) as well.[33]

As regards the known South Etruscan Orientalizing bronze thrones with stamped motives, Jurgeit appears to waver between a Tarquinia and a Vulci workshop.[34] Other scholars point to Caere, mostly because of stone thrones having been carved out in several chamber tombs at Cerveteri – although neither in Tarquinia nor in Vulci.[35] On the other hand, the only secure provenance is that of the Barberini Tomb in Palestrina in Latium.[36]

However, since the local Chiusi thrones are the only identified Etruscan bronze thrones with free-hand Orientalizing relief decoration, they should, in my opinion, be drawn into the discussion. Their style strongly suggests South Etruscan models (Fig. 4) and although I formerly saw the barrel-shaped stamped bronze thrones as their immediate predecessors,[37] they may just as well have been inspired by South Etruscan bronze thrones with large-scale, free-hand relief decoration in which arcs and palmettes played a corresponding role. We still do not have any examples from South Etruria, but our knowledge of Orientalizing metal workshops in Etruria and Etruscanized Italy is steadily increasing.[38]

Looking at the funerary sphere of Chiusi upper classes in the 7th Century BC with their imports of South Etruscan objects of stamped bronze plates,[39] their local grave furniture of tables and thrones in bronze reliefs imitating South Etruscan style,[40] their types of chamber tombs and – not least – their tomb-paintings under obviously South Etruscan influence, I concluded in 1989 that "Tarquinia and Veji could just as easily as Cerveteri be the chief source of influence on Chiusi" and observed that: "The tomb-paintings point more specifically towards influence from Veji".[41] I also mentioned the fact that the Tiber formed an important inland route between Veji and Chiusi not open to Tarquinia.[42] In general, our knowledge of the inland contacts of Veji to the Faliscan area and further north on the one hand[43] and, on the other, to Latium and further south, reaching Pithecusa and the Western Greek colonies, is well-established.[44]

In contrast to the rather small Chiusi thrones, functioning as seat for the canopic urn, the South Etruscan bronze thrones are large[45] and the stone thrones were either empty or part of statues as apparent e.g. from the two tufa statues of the first half of the 7th Century BC in Caere, Tomba delle Statue, each representing a male person seated on a throne.[46] From

the placing of the empty thrones in the "-atrium" of the tomb, Prayon and Colonna interpret them as seats for the heads of the family, while Colonna sees the Caere statues placed at the entrance of the tomb, as re-presentations of the forefathers.[47] Although originally just household furniture, in 7th Century BC Etruria, the thrones were held in veneration.

Some years ago, a fragment of a similar tufa statue was found in the Piccazzano necropolis at Veji, the lower part of a person seated on a barrel-shaped throne.[48] Since Veji also had an important production of Orientalizing bronze reliefs (Fig. 3), this town should have the same claim to a possible production of bronze thrones as Caere.

In both the Veji and the Caere statues, the person's feet rest on a footstool, each side of which is formed as a volute. Whereas the thrones are of local origin, Colonna and v. Hase regard the footstools as Near Eastern imitations and one of many signs of North Syrian sculptors having worked in Caere.[49] Although the Veji statue is badly preserved, it seems reasonable to transfer these conclusions to Veji. A similar footstool is worked in relief in a chamber tomb in Vignanello in the Faliscan area and others are represented on the assembly frieze of the 6th Century BC Upper Building of Poggio Civitate (Murlo). Several volute footstools were found in tombs in Etruria and Latium, in both male and female burials: there are wooden examples in four Verucchio tombs, while foot-stools in bronze relief with Geometric stamped ornamentation are known from tombs in Trevignano Romano at Lago di Bracciano and in Castel di Decima and Laurentina in Latium[50] as well as – the earliest of all – in Veji, Casale del Fosso, Tomb 871,[51] which is dated to around 720 BC.[52] The other tombs are of the 7th Century BC. Apart from the two Caere statues, the known examples of this kind of footstool chiefly come from the inland areas of Etruria and Etruscanized Italy, in regions under influence from Veji.[53]

Although the volute footstools might be used together with folding chairs,[54] such wooden footstools were found with wooden barrel-shaped thrones in three Verucchio tombs of the 7th Century BC[55] and presumably the two pieces of furniture should be viewed as an entity, even though the wooden seat has perished in tombs with bronze footstools.[56] The grave furniture accompanying the footstools always give evidence of both wealth – with e.g. gold or silver fibulae and other kinds of jewellery – and a high social status for the deceased person.[57] The tombs, whether with male or female burials, contained two-wheeled chariots; originally the chariots for men served for transporting the warrior to and from the battle field, but already before the end of the 8th Century BC the chariots were used for ceremonial purposes;[58] in the male tombs there are generally horse bits or harnesses;[59] there are banqueting implements such as drinking cups, amphorae, firedogs, meat spits and sometimes carving knives[60] as well as a two-wheeled bronze tray;[61] in one of the tombs there is a fan, obviously a sign of rank and ceremonially connected with the throne;[62] and in several others, a trapezoid or rounded standard. The former, specific to Etruria, the latter to Latium, apparently had a significance equal to that of the fan and a distribution almost identical with that of the volute footstool.[63] Again the earliest examples come from Veji, which Guldager regards as the mediator of social rituals between the elites of southern Etruria and northern Latium;[64] in some tombs there were cistai[65] and in the male burials, warriors' equipment.[66] Some of these objects, with the customs they represent, are normal to upper class Central Italic tombs of the 8th – 7th Centuries BC, while others as e.g. both the volute footstool, closely connected with the barrel-shaped throne, and the trapezoid or rounded standard seem concentrated to a specific area, covering the influential sphere of Veji. In both cases, Veji provides the earliest examples.

A lituus or scepter in Veji, Casale del Fosso, Tomb 871, signifies a high official position,[67] presumably also of religious character. E.g. the Tarquinia, Pian di Civita cult deposit at the entrance to cult house Beta contained three bronzes: an axe and a shield were placed together with a trumpet-lituus, one immediately above the other and the two last-mentioned objects ceremonially buckled. The whole area is sacral and the cult deposit was placed in two hollows, both containing fragments of the same impasto vases, the forms of which suggested a banqueting function. The three bronzes were in Deposit A. The excavators, taking into account also the sacral character of the whole area, interpret the find as a votive deposit made by a person of rank.[68] It is also worth noting that the two Cerveteri tufa statues of male persons seated on thrones were holding in their hands, one a sceptre, the other a lituus.[69] and that the woman seated on a bronze throne in the Murlo frieze, who obviously took part in an important ceremony, had in front of her another seated person, holding a lituus.[70] Undoubtedly, the barrel-shaped thrones signify a high and powerful official position in Etruscan society, partly of religious character.[71]

Early Etruscan bronzes in Greek Sanctuaries

On the other hand, one should not forget that the bronze fragment, Ol. IV 1007, was found in the Hera/Zeus Sanctuary of Olympia and must be viewed in relation also to other early Etruscan bronzes in Greek sanctuaries.[72]

The early Italic/Etruscan bronze votives in Greek sanctuaries present a varied picture. Most widely distributed are the fibulae, known all over the Greek Mainland as well as on several islands. With one early exception, they are dated to the second half of the 8th Century and the 7th Century BC and to a great extent they are of South Italian or Sicilian origin. They comprise fibulae for the male as well as the female dress and are presumably mostly private donations, whether by Greeks or Italic/Etruscans will be difficult to decide in most cases.[73] All fibulae except one come from sanctuaries.[74]

Among the dress articles are Sicilian hooks[75] and a Villanovan bronze belt which was acquired on Euboea in the early 19th century by the Danish archaeologist, P. O. Brøndsted; whether coming from a tomb or a sanctuary is not known. Such bronze belts were in Italy found in women's tombs of the 8th Century BC, mostly in the Bologna region, Latium and the Faliscan area as well as in Southern Etruria: Tarquinia, Vulci and, in particular, Veji.[76]

The early Italic/Etruscan bronze vases in Greece are dated from the 7th Century BC onwards and are known in particular from the sanctuaries of Olympia, Perachora and Samos as well as from the Argive Heraion and a tomb in Korkyra, and they include fragments of larger vessels, as e.g. North Etruscan lebetes with plastic decoration.[77] Of the utmost importance is the Italic wheeled tripod censer from Olympia, published by M. Söldner and dated to the second quarter of the 7th Century BC; its nearest parallel comes from Luceria in Apulia. M. Söldner concludes her investigations in stating that it must be an Italic dedication, definitely of religious and possibly of official character.[78] Söldner's publication opens for a renewed discussion of the identity of the dedicators of the more spectacular Italic/Etruscan early bronze finds in Greek sanctuaries, not only bronze vessels, but also armour and weapons.

The warriors' equipment of Italic/Etruscan origin found in Greek sanctuaries comprises horse bits and parts of horses' harnesses of North Etruscan types (Olympia);[79] lance heads of types probably originating in Sicily or South Italy, but with a large distribution area in Italy (Delphi and Olympia);[80] axe heads, presumably South Italic (Olympia and Dodone);[81] a South Etruscan antenna sword of the so-

called Tarquinia type, probably dated to the second half of the 8th Century BC (Samos);[82] a fragment of a greave (Olympia), for which there are parallels in Veji of the second half of the 8th Century BC;[83] helmets of types which began in the first half of the 8th Century BC and continued into the second half of the century; their counterparts are almost exclusively found in South Etruria, especially in Tarquinia and Veji (Olympia and Delphi).[84] Although some of the above pieces of warriors' equipment are of types beginning earlier than 750 BC, they may all be dated to the second half of the 8th Century BC or the early 7th Century BC, and the South Etruscan types are for the greater part connected with either Tarquinia or Veji.[85]

However, by far the largest group of warriors' equipment found in Greek sanctuaries consists of fragments of Etruscan round bronze shields with stamped Geometric ornamentation (Delphi, Dodone, Olympia and Samos). The identifiable shields of normal size[86] all belong to the same two classes of Geometric shields, A II and A IV (Geiger 1 a and 1 c).[87] The former group, with alternating stamps of concentric circles and animals, predominantly horses (Fig. 5), covers the second half of the 8th Century BC, lasting into the early 7th Century BC.[88] The A IV bronze reliefs, with Subgeometric ornamentation, begin in the last quarter of the 8th Century BC[89] and their production period covers the two quarter centuries on either side of 700 BC[90] and perhaps even the entire first half of the 7th Century BC.[91] However, since not one example of the Early Orientalizing B I shields, the production of which started in the early 7th Century BC,[92] was found in Greece, there seems no reason to date any Italic/Etruscan round bronze shield from the Greek sanctuaries later than the early 7th Century BC, their absolute chronology thus corresponding well with the rest of the warriors' equipment of the same provenances. Like the Etruscan Orientalizing shields, the Geometric ones seem to

have been produced in several localities, probably with an important centre in Tarquinia;[93] but there was definitely a major production of A II reliefs in Veji – as well as presumably in Vulci – while A IV reliefs seem to have a wider production area.[94]

In general, the Etruscan warriors' equipment found in Greek sanctuaries presents a picture which closely resembles that of the upper class warriors' burials in Central Italy in the latter half of the 8th Century BC and the 7th Century BC, with weapons and defensive armour, horse bits and harnesses, and possibly an axe. The axe may be South Italic, while the other objects seem to be genuinely Etruscan. Not all can be securely located, but the horse's gear is North Etruscan, while several more spectacular finds such as the antenna sword, the greave, the helmets and shields are South Etruscan prestige objects, apparently predominantly of Tarquinian or Vejian origin.

Several scholars have interpreted the greater part of the early Italic/Etruscan bronzes in the Greek sanctuaries – and definitely those of warriors' equipment – as spoils of war dedicated by Greeks, probably Greeks of the Western Greek colonies.[95] Some scholars regard the bronze vases as signs of trade or piracy.[96] On the other hand, the above-mentioned Olympia tripod censer can be taken as a sign of an official Italic dedication of religious character already in the second quarter of the 7th Century BC[97] and we have written evidence of official Etruscan dedications in the Archaic Period to both Delphi and Olympia.[98] Nevertheless, until recently, the two Etruscan archaeologists, M. Cristofani and G. Bartoloni, apparently were alone in seeing the early Etruscan prestigious bronzes, including the warriors' equipment, as dedications to the Greek sanctuaries by upper class Etruscans.[99]

The Function of the Geometric Round Bronze Shields

Undoubtedly of significance for this discussion is the question of the possible military function of the Etruscan round bronze shields with stamped Geometric ornamentation, as known from Greek sanctuaries.[100] Several scholars – and lately also Geiger[101] – advocate their functional purpose. Also according to Geiger, the thin metal plate requires a backing of leather or wood to provide satisfactory protection.[102] However, of such a backing there is no trace in any of these shields, neither, as often maintained, in the shield of the Tarquinia Warrior's Tomb,[103] nor in the more recent shield finds.[104] Although Geiger refers also to other circumstances speaking against their functional purpose,[105] she concludes that the Geometric bronze shields were made with a view to military use, partly because of their size and partly because of their faithful rendering of details in the handle and the attachment plates,[106] details which, in my opinion, may just as well indicate a close imitation of the battle shields, which presumably were of leather;[107] later on such details gradually become neglected.[108] At any rate, without an inner covering of leather or wood, the shields could not offer satisfactory protection in a military situation, and of such a reinforcement, we still have no evidence.[109]

Other aspects may be of relevance for the discussion. In Etruria itself, such shields have now appeared in sacrificial contexts, the Geometric shields in Verucchio and the shield at cult building Beta in the sacrificial area of Tarquinia; although Early Orientalizing, this shield is contemporary with the latest Geometric shield finds in Greek sanctuaries and apparently was produced specifically for its cult purpose.[110]

In many 8th-7th Century BC tombs, there were two or three round bronze shields, although only one helmet and one greave (for either the left or the right leg), a plurality which weakens the conception of the shields as effectively used armour; they were placed in a position covering the whole body or in an essentially decorative fashion, along the walls of the tomb. There are even shields in women's tombs. As noted by Bartoloni and De Santis, the shields are not so much a sign of a warrior as a symbol of rank and membership of the élite class.[111]

Another type of Italic/Etruscan Geometric bronze shields with corresponding stamped ornamentation was recently studied by Colonna, the double shield or ancile shield. It is made up of two smaller round shields, ca. 30-40 cm in diameter, either fastened together in a fixed position or connected with an intermediate oval plate. One of the two certain finds of ancile shields had definitely been used, since it was heavily repaired. However, in the other find, the only one in its original context, Veji. Casale del Fosso, Tomb 1036 – a male burial of the third quarter of the 8th Century BC of a person of very high rank – two such shields covered the whole body, showing the same plurality as the round shields, possibly indicating a specific burial ritual.[112]

In Olympia, there may be one fragment of an ancile shield and possibly one small shield with counterparts in Etruria; their significance is still uncertain.[113] They have Geometric ornamentation, but are often found in 7th Century BC tombs, in some cases together with shields of normal size, and they may have a ceremonial function.[114] Perhaps they should be viewed in the light of the earlier tradition, of the 10th to 9th Centuries BC, of placing bronze miniature shields and miniature warriors' equipment in general in the more wealthy tombs, especially characteristic of Latium, but also seen in Bisenzio and Veji. The miniature shields are of both above-mentioned types, round shields as well as ancile or double shields.[115] The miniature weapons thus give definite evidence that both shield types were used in military actions in Central Italy as far back as the 10th Century BC. Since no shields of normal size are known in Central Italy until the earliest bronze shields around the middle of the 8th Century BC were placed in tombs, the battle shields must have been made of perishable material. A strange disparity concerns the ancile shields. Although they continued in use until Classical times and in connection with certain ceremonies far into the Roman period,[116] the ancile shields of bronze apparently were only placed in Italic/Etruscan tombs during a very short period, already around 725 BC being superseded by the round bronze shields, and one of their few tomb contexts indicates ceremonial use.[117] The military use of the metallic ancile or double shield, for which one of its shield finds appears to give evidence,[118] apparently was abandoned almost immediately. The real battle shields continued to be made of a different material, presumably of leather on a wooden frame.[119] And we have no evidence that they were placed in the tombs.

Not only miniature shields, but also miniature bronzes of other parts of the warriors' outfit, such as lances and swords, were found in the 10th – 9th Century BC Central Italic tombs, to be gradually replaced by the same metal objects in normal size only in the course of the 8th Century BC.[120] For the 8th-7th Century BC aristocratic tombs, Etruscan archaeologists more and more stress the symbolic value of the military equipment in bronze, not only shields, but also helmets of impressive size, unfit for military use, and lances, meant for parades only.[121] The bronze arms and armour in Early Etruscan tombs seem to represent the last stage of a long tradition of placing not the actual arms and armour in the warriors' tombs, but symbolic objects which more and more acquire a prestigious character and become signs of the high rank of the deceased person, of his social status as a member of the ruling élite class.[122] Thus, the prestigious parts of these Etruscan bronze arms and armour apparently were not intended for actual military use, but were designed for votive offerings, for burials of upper class Etruscans and perhaps for parades.[123]

On this background, it is hardly possible to imagine that their counterparts in the Greek sanctuaries reached Greece as spoils of war, nor can one easily imagine that Etruscan objects of such venerated character were subject to mercantile transactions.[124] As suggested by Bartoloni and Cristofani,[125] the early Etruscan bronze arms and armour of prestigious character in the Greek sanctuaries should most likely be considered dedications by upperclass Etruscans in the second half of the 8th Century and the early 7th Century BC.

Early Thrones in Greece

In Etruria and Etruscan Italy, chariots as well as thrones continue to form part of the burial contexts throughout the 7th Century BC,[126] still comprising the same kind of warriors' outfit. However, as noted above, in the Greek sanctuaries such donations were not continued after the early 7th Century BC and the South Etruscan bronze relief, Ol. IV 1007, dated to around 650 BC, cannot, therefore, be interpreted in this light, but must be viewed from a different angle, as representing a new tradition. In my opinion, this chronological discrepancy rules out its identification with part of a two-wheeled chariot, a vehicle which only at a much later date received a new role in Etruria and Latium, in being used for chariot races.[127]

As regards thrones, on the other hand, we have evidence for a new tradition in the Greek sanctuaries, apparently starting shortly before 700 BC with the much valued offering of a throne to Apollo in Delphi by the Near Eastern ruler, King Midas of Phrygia. Presumably his throne was wooden and with inlaid decoration like the wooden furniture in contemporary Gordion tombs.[128]

The tradition was taken up by the Etruscan King Arimnestos dedicating a throne to Zeus in Olympia, which later was seen by Pausanias in the pronaos of the Zeus Temple and by him described as the first foreign dedication in Olympia – by which one presumably must imply the earliest foreign official dedication preserved to Pausanias' time.[129] Definitely Archaic, it is probably of 7th Century BC date.[130] Arimnestos' throne is unlikely to have been made of bronze, considering the fate of most Archaic Olympia bronzes.[131] As suggested by Völling, the Arimnestos throne was presumably a wooden throne with intaglio decoration like the impressive Verucchio thrones, especially the one in Fondo Lippi, Tomb 89, dated to around 650 BC.[132] One more piece of information favours this idea. From the root of Arimnestos' graecized name, mna/mne, his realm was by Colonna located to an inland Italian axis, reaching from Veji and Rome southwards to the Etruscanized regions of Campania and northwards to Perugia and Spina. Colonna observes that the name points more specifically to the Verucchio – Rimini area.[133]

Conclusions

Definitely not a fragment of a shield and probably not of a chariot, the South Etruscan Orientalizing bronze relief, Ol. IV 1007, part of a very large object, is, in my opinion, most likely to be interpreted as part of the back of a barrel-shaped bronze throne which just like the Arimnestos throne was donated to Zeus in Olympia by an Etruscan king. The dedication most likely took place around or shortly before 650 BC, the period for at least one other official Italic bronze donation in Olympia.[134] Possibly wanting to continue the custom of his aristocratic forefathers who had donated to Greek sanctuaries examples of their prestige arms and armour, symbolizing their high rank, and acquainted with the new tradition established by the Near Eastern ruler, King Midas of Phrygia, he dedicated to a Greek sanctuary a token of his high official position of secular as well as religious character.

There can be no doubt that his realm should be sought in South Etruria. Judging from the origin of the prestigious bronzes of the warriors' equipment found in Greek sanctuaries, Tarquinia or Veji seems the most likely home town of the ruler in question, and for both cities we have information of their close ties during the 8th-7th Centuries BC with the Greeks[135] as well as with the Near Eastern countries.[136] However, from the above comparisons with material in Etruria, Veji appears to be the most probable locality, since Tarquinia – unlike Veji – has not given evidence of the use of thrones,[137] nor did its geographical position to the same degree as Veji favour specific ties with Chiusi, with its local barrel-shaped, Orientalizing bronze thrones under strong South Etruscan influences.[138]

There are several indications of Near Eastern ties influencing the life of upper class Vejians during the period in question. Not only the probable presence here of North Syrian sculptors in the early 7th Century BC[139] but also, in particular, evinced by the banquet custom where drinking vessels of Near Eastern types were used from the second half of the 8th Century BC onwards,[140] even comprising an Assyrian lion head rhyton of bronze, dated to shortly before 700 BC, the only one of its kind known from Italy.[141] This rhyton may have reached Veji from Assyria by many routes, but it may be worth noting that among its few close counterparts outside Assyria are rhyta in Gordion at the time of King Midas as well as in the Heraeum of Samos,[142] the island situated opposite the terminal of one of the land routes which leads westwards from Gordion.[143] One cannot exclude the possibility of aristocratic Vejians having some links with the city of Gordion during the reign of King Midas.

New excavations, publications and studies may confirm or disprove my theory, but on the material available today, I see it as the most probable explanation for the presence of the bronze relief, Ol. IV 1007, in Olympia: that it is a fragmentary back of an Etruscan barrel-shaped bronze throne dedicated in Olympia around or shortly before 650 BC by a South Etruscan king of the locality where it was produced, presumably the King of Veji.

Notes

I want to thank the following scholars and institutions for permission to publish the illustrations of my paper: Dr. H.R. Goette, Deutsches Archäologisches Institut, Athen, for Fig. 1; Dr. Judith Swaddling and the Trustees of the British Museum, London, for Figs. 2 b and 4; and Dr. Michael Vickers and the Ashmolean Museum, Oxford, for Fig. 2 a. I also want to thank the Director of the Ephoria of Prehistoric and Classical Antiquities of Joannina, Konstantinos L. Zachos, for the photograph of Fig. 5 and the permission to publish it, and the Director of the Museo di Villa Giulia, Dr. Francesca Boitani for permission to publish the drawing, Fig. 3, from her excavations at Monte Michele, Veji, Finally, my sincere thanks are due to Lisbeth Havrehed for revising my English manuscript.

NOTE 1

Ol.IV 1007. Geiger, 107-108, No. 111, (with earlier references) and pl. 91 and v. Hase 1997. 298, figs. 14, 12 and 321, note 48.

I thank Dr. Thomas Völling for his help during my studies of the fragment in Olympia in 1996.

NOTE 2

Linked Phoenician palmettes, cf. e.g. Boitani 1983, pl. XCV,c (Veji, Monte Michele Tomb 5, cf. below p. 69 and notes 17-18); De Santis 1997, 122-132, figs. 13, 15; 14, 17 and 22, 1, found together with pottery with ornamentation of overlapping arcs, such as fig. 14, 22 and fig. 22, 9 – all impasto pottery from Veji, Pantano di Grano, Tombs 1-3, dated to the second quarter of the 7th Cent. BC, op. cit. p. 113. Cf. also Delpino 1997, 21, fig. 2, below right.(Veji. Casalaccio, Tomb 3).

NOTE 3

There is general agreement as to its South Etruscan stylistic character, cf. v. Hase 1979, 68 and in general, Geiger's references, above note 1. For stylistic comparisons, cf. references notes 2 and 11.

NOTE 4

Cf. above note 1, almost all Geiger's references and, most recently, both Geiger and v. Hase.

For my own views, cf. below and references notes 8 and 20.

NOTE 5

With her catalogue of 135 shields, Geiger has considerably enlarged the numbers of early Etruscan bronze shields (Strøm 1971, 20-41 (84); Stary 1981, 430-433, W 16 (92); and Bedini 1990, 64 (112)). Geiger includes the small shields which I left out, since they are too small for any possiblity of independent military use (Strøm 1971, 219-220, note 19). E.g. Geiger, 45, Nos. 8A-8C (Type 1a), and 75-77, Nos. 49-50 (Type 1g) (cf. below p. 76 and notes 112 and 114).

Even so, Geiger overlooked several shields known at the time of her publication. Of Geometric shields, e.g. Verucchio, Tomb 89 (Montanari 1987, 252, No. 128 and fig. 168 (A I = Geiger, Type 1b, cf. below note 7) and for the small shield, cf. below note 114); Laurentina – Acqua Acetosa, Tomb 70 (c. 650 BC, three shields) and Tomb 93 (late 8th Cent. BC, two shields), (Bedini 1990, 52-54, 64 and fig. 27 and Bedini 1992, 85 and fig. 6). Apparently all Geometric, stamped bronze reliefs from Laurentina are A 1 (= Geiger 1b), and the shields are always in numbers of two or three (cf. Bedini 1995, 301. For Tomb 121, cf. below note 12).

Since Geiger's publication at least two Geometric shields have been published, Osteria dell' Osa, Tomb 600 (late 8th Cent. BC, De Santis 1995, 367-368, 371 and 374, No. 7 and fig. 3); and one from Casale Marittimo, Tomb A (Emiliozzi 1997, 319 and Esposito 1999, 41 fig. 30).

For Orientalizing shields, cf. below notes 9 and 12.

There may still be more shields; I have not looked for them systematically.

NOTE 6

The most detailed technical analysis of the shields and their decoration is given by Geiger, 8-27.

NOTE 7

Strøm 1971, 52-55 and 173-174 (BII) and Geiger, 101-108 (3a-b).

Here I use my own classification, giving Geiger's in parenthesis. In general, the two classifications do not differ very much, apart from Geiger 1c and 1d (Geiger 52-60) both combining shields of my groups A I and A IV (especially Geiger 1d appears very heterogeneous), and apart from Geiger 1g (cf. above note 5 and below and note 114). However, in particular as regards the Orientalizing shields, I find my own classification more useful, since it stresses the continuity of the Early Orientalizing B I shields, with narrow cable pattern and rows of small bosses as frieze separation (references below note 12), into the Late Orientalizing B II shields, with broad cable pattern and rows of stars as frieze separation (cf. Strøm 1971, 49, 54 and 56) – in contrast with Geiger's types, 2a-b-c (Geiger, 83-97) for the former group, and Geiger 3a-b, for the latter, inserting the quite different B III as Type 2d (references below note 10).

NOTE 8

Strøm 1971, 218, note 10.

For the star terminal of the arcs, not noted on shields, cf. the bronze fragments from Chiusi. Tomba della Pania, Mon. Ined. X, 1876, pl. XXXVIIIIa, No. 2 and Strøm 1989, 22, fig. 27. For the identification of these fragments, cf. below note 30.

NOTE 9

B II, references above note 7.

Geiger overlooks several B II shields as e.g.: In the Faliscan area, Vignanello, Tomba dei Velminei: Museo del Forte di Civitacastellana, Inv. No. 26058. As stated, Baglione 1986, 141, its decoration is especially close to a group of B II shields in Karlsruhe, London and Oxford (Geiger 102-106, Nos. 102-106, pls. 96-106), and it has the same rather rare leaf rosettes as the Karlsruhe shield (Geiger 103, No. 103, cf. fig. 51a). Only, around the boss are rows of small bosses as in B I – shields. Unfortunately, the Vignanello shield was found in a 4th/3rd Cent. BC. context. I thank Paola Baglione for providing me with information and photographs of the shield.

In the Siena region, Castelnuovo Berardenga, Tomba A del Poggione (dated to c. 600 BC, Mangani 1988-89, 49, No. 108 and fig. 42 (chronology, p. 81); for No. 107, cf. below note 114).

In Picenum, Pitino di San Severino, Tomb 14, Schichilone 1973, 516: Two shields with cable pattern along the rim. Because of the chronology of the tomb, c. 600 BC, and the find of a large disk with B II decoration, I regard them as presumably B II shields.(For bibliography of the tomb, cf. Emiliozzi 1997, 318, No. 74).

NOTE 10
B III, Strøm 1971, 55-57 and 173-174; Geiger, 97-100 (2d).

NOTE 11
Cf. e.g. Canciani & v. Hase 1979, 43, No. 35, pls. 23-24 (Tomba Bernardini (silver)); Curtis 1925, 36-37, No. 72 and pl. 18 (Tomba Barberini wheeled tray, bronze); and Pareti 1947, 290-291, No. 240 (RG, the handle of a wheeled tray of bronze); (for both trays, cf. Woywowitch 1978, pl. 21). Emiliozzi 1992, 106, fig. 23 (RG, footboard of a two-wheeled chariot of bronze).

NOTE 12
B I: Strøm 1971, 48-52, Nos. B 1-9, in particular, and 173-174 and Geiger, 83-97 (2a-2c).
To Geiger's list add: Laurentina Acqua Acetosa, Tomb 121 (c. 650-625 BC, two shields) (Bedini 1990, 61 and 63-64, Cat. No. 28, (ill.)); Cerveteri, Il Tumulo di Montetosto, camera centrale (c. 675 BC, more than one shield) (Rizzo 1989, 155 and 157); and – extremely important – Tarquinia, Pian di Civita, a shield found as part of a cult deposit, at the entrance to cult building Beta, situated in a large sacrificial area; from its context, Deposit A, the shield is dated to the first quarter of the 7th Cent. BC (cf. Bonghi Jovino 1987, 63 and Chiaramonte Treré 1988, 584). Deposit A also contained two other bronzes, an axe and a trumpet-lituus. (Cf. Bonghi Jovino. 1986, 98-105; Bonghi Jovino 1987, 66-77, with the shield, pls. XXIV-XXVI; StEtr 58, 1992, 555-557; AR 1995-96, p. 52, Fig. 7; and Bonghi Jovino & Chiaramonte Treré 1997, 172-173 and pls. 125-126 and p. 165, and cf. below p. 73 and note 68). As noted by Bonghi

Jovino 1987, 69, the repertory of the shield decoration is close to the RG shield, Geiger No. 78 (cf. below), only its horses and small quadrupeds are more naturalistic. The shield is exceptional in not having a metal ring at the rim and it is de-finitely a local work (Bonghi Jovino 1987, 71 and 77).

Pitino di San Severino. Tomb 17, contained two shields (Geiger, 90, No. 75 and pls. 64-65, published one; cf. Schichilone 1973, 515 and Emiliozzi 1997, 318, No. 75).

Also to be classified as B I are five shields, unclassified by Geiger, the two identical Satricum shields (Geiger 109, Nos. 124-125, cf. Waarsenburg 1995, 261-262, Cat. No. 2.160, pl. 53) and the three shields from Colle del Forno, Tomb XI, now in the Ny Carlsberg Glyptothek, Copenhagen, Inv. Nos. H.I.N. 670-672 (Geiger, 109, Nos. 132-134). They are still unpublished, but according to information by the keeper, Jette Christiansen, they have been on exhibition since May 1983. H.I.N. 670 shows the same stamps as the Populonia, Tomba dei Flabelli shield (Geiger 86, No. 72, pl. 69 and fig. 43 A) as well as a single row of the stamps which make up the scale pattern of two RG shields (Geiger, 87 and 91, Nos. 74 and 78, pls. 62-63 and 68-69, respectively). H.I.N. 671 is very close to the last-mentioned shield, with the same stamps as Geiger, fig. 46a left (except for the middle figure); H.I.N. 672 is very similar to the earliest B II shield, from Narce Tomb 62 (Geiger 102, No. 101), except for its use of small bosses as frieze separation (cf. Strøm 1971, 28-29 and 52-54, Cat. No. 36 = B II 3, fig. 24 (not illustrated by Geiger)). For Colle del Forno XI, cf. also below note 38. I thank Jette Christiansen and the librarian, Claus Grønne, for detailed photographs of the three shields.

NOTE 13
My absolute chronology for the earliest Orientalizing B I shields, "shortly after 700 B.C." and "not later than ca. 675 B.C." (Strøm 1971, 173-174) seems to be confirmed by the absolute chronology of the Tarquinia Pian di Civita shield, cf. above note 12. Cf. also the corresponding chronology of the Vulci chariot with B I decoration (Colonna 1972, 567 and Emiliozzi 1997, 329, No. 195 and below note 22).

NOTE 14
Strøm 1971, 150-154, 157-160, and 171, and Geiger 93-97. For the Bernardini Tomb, cf. also Canciani & v. Hase 1979, 10: The beginning of the second quarter of the century, i.e. slightly later than the date proposed by me.

NOTE 15
The suggested absolute chronology of RG, to the third quarter of the 7th Cent. BC (Strøm 1971, 160-168 and 171) is generally regarded as too late, cf. e.g. Colonna 1972, 569, who stresses the suspicious provenance of the LPC/Transitional pottery fragments, and Geiger, 57 and 59. However, also the East Greek bird skyphos with rays (Pareti 1947, 342-343, No. 381 and pl. XLIX) is definitely later than 650 BC (cf. Strøm 1971, 112 and 168 with note 149 and – for the type – most recently Cook & Dupont 1998, 26).

Apart from in RG, B I shields were found in other tombs of the third quarter of the 7th Cent. BC or later, as e.g. Laurentina Acqua Acetosa, Tomb 121 and Colle del Forno, XI (cf. above note 12).

Colonna and di Paolo 1997, 154-168, have convincingly shown that the finds in the cella and the antecamera – separated only by a half-wall – belong to the same burial, the differences in their contexts relating to different ritual functions. My discussion in 1971 of the distribution of the material on three burials is therefore now out of date.

NOTE 16
Strøm 1971, 173-174, based, in particular, on the chronology of Narce Tomb 62 with three early B II shields (cf. Geiger 102, Nos. 99-101) and several finds in Chiusi tombs, (Strøm 1971, 195-196).

Neither Colonna 1972, 569, nor Geiger, 102 and 106, accept the suggested continuation of the type into the 6th Cent. BC. As regards the date of the beginning of the style, I now agree with Colonna, loc. cit. (Cf. below).

NOTE 17
Guldager 1994, 23, No. 15.
The best illustration of the trapezoid standard in Veji, Monte Michele Tomb 5, is EAA, Sec.Sup. V, 1997, opposite p. 969. The Phoenician palmettes are normally found on stamped gold and silver reliefs only (cf. Strøm 1971, 85 and Strøm 1990, 93).

The bronze plates of trapezoid or rounded form (the former type in Etruria, the latter in the Faliscan area and Latium) are generally interpreted as fans (cf. Moretti 1970, 23-26 and Guldager 1994). However, I fail to see how such a solid plate could be used as a fan, which as far as I know is made either of feathers or of some other kind of light perishable material, folded or put together in a way to provide flows of air. (Cf. also Magi 1969, 124-125: The Pre-Hellenistic fans were chiefly made of palm laves). Nor do I in the trapezoid form observe any attempt at imitating a fan such as is the case e.g. with the bronze "fans" from Populonia. Tomba dei Flabelli (cf. below note 62). However, judging from their tomb contexts in general, such bronze standards definitely were equivalent with the fan as a sign of a high social status of the deceased person (Guldager 1994, 14 and 20). For the tomb context of Veji, Monte Michele, Tomb 5, cf. below note 18.

NOTE 18
Boitani 1982, Boitani 1983 and Boitani 1997 and Emiliozzi 1997, 325, No. 152.

Veji, Monte Michele, Tomb 5, is a family tomb with four, almost contemporary burials, the most important of which is the urn burial of a male person in the main chamber; the urn (Fig. 3) was placed on a four-wheeled carriage; there were weapons of iron, banqueting implements which included drinking vessels, fire-dogs and spits, as well as several prestigious objects (cf. above note 17, and below notes 58, 61, 62 and 67). For the grave furniture as found, cf. Boitani 1982, fig. 5, and for absolute chronology, most recently Boitani 1997, 33.

Concerning the ornaments of the bronze plates, the single palmettes are smaller than normal on B II reliefs, while leaf rosettes are comparatively rare (cf. above note 9, the Vignanello shield).

NOTE 19
Cf. also above note 2 for references to stylistically close ornamentation of Veji impasto pottery in contexts of the second quarter of the 7th Cent. BC.

NOTE 20
Strøm 1989, 26, note 41, cf. Strøm 1971, 218, note 10. Cf. Steingräber 1979, 23-24, Type I a.

Jurgeit, 1990, 23, note 87, suggests the same identification for another Olympia rim fragment, Br 1321, (Geiger, 81, No. 61, pl. 59 and v. Hase 1997, 298 and fig. 14, 13). Jurgeit's suggestion will be difficult to prove. This fragment as well as the rim fragment, Geiger, 81-82, No. 69 and pl. 59, are also listed among the Greek shield fragments from Olympia (Bol 1989, 1-2 and 105, Cat. Nos. A 5 and A 7 and pl. 1). The former is definitely Etruscan, the latter, without an inner ring of bronze or iron, probably not.

Jurgeit 1990 refers to Strøm 1989, 25, note 41, for the suggestion that the Arimnestos throne is a bronze throne, a theory which I no longer uphold, cf. below pp. 77-78 and note 131.

NOTE 21
Cf. e.g. the Monteleone, Castro and San Mariano chariots, Emiliozzi 1997, 179-190 and 203-225 and pls. XII-XIII and XX-XXII for the chariot back and Emiliozzi 1992, 106, fig. 23 for the footboard of the RG chariot.

NOTE 22
For thrones, cf. references below notes 29-30; for two-wheeled chariots, cf. the Vulci chariot (B I) (Emiliozzi 1997, 139-153 and pls. III-IV) and for four-wheeled carriages, the Veji, Monte Michele, Tomb 5 chariot (cf. above note 18) and the Castellina in Chianti carriage (B II) (Woywowitch 1978, 144-145, No. 62, pl. 11 and Emiliozzi 1997, 320, No. 98).

NOTE 23
The metal plates of the chariots were fastened onto another material, wood or leather (Emiliozzi 1997, 96 and 148, the Vulci chariot). However, there need not be traces of fastening in such a small inner fragment as Ol. IV. 1007. For the straight metal plates for back and footboard of the two-wheeled chariots, cf. references above, notes 21-22.

NOTE 24
For technical details of the best known Chiusi bronze thrones, cf. Vlad Borelli 1973, 211-220; Strøm 1986; Hockey 1987 and Strøm 1989.

For Chiusi thrones with flaring back, here Fig. 4 and Strøm 1989, 7 and notes 2-3.

Of the South Etruscan bronze thrones, at least the Louvre throne has a flaring back (references below note 29).

NOTE 25
Cf. below p. 77.

NOTE 26
Strøm 1986 and 1989.

Taking into account my acceptance of the earlier chronology of the B II reliefs, cf. above p. 69, with which the Chiusi thrones are stylistically related (cf. Strøm 1989, 20), I am now inclined to date the Orientalizing Chiusi thrones from shortly after 650 BC onwards, having earlier found close stylistic correspondence with the metal reliefs of the Barberini Tomb and RG (cf. Strøm 1986, 56, note 8, and for the chronology of these tombs, above p. 69 and notes 14-15).

NOTE 27
Cf. Strøm 1989, 16.

NOTE 28
Strøm 1986, 56, note 8 and Strøm 1989, 10 and 20-21; cf. also the detail of raised points at the ends of the palmette petals of the Olympia fragment which is a characteristic feature of the Chiusi bronzes in question (cf. e.g. Strøm 1989, figs. 9 and 11).

NOTE 29
Cf. Strøm 1986, 55, note 5, thrones No. 1 (the Barberini throne) and No. 2 (the throne in the Louvre Museum, Inv. No. Br. 4408, cf. Etrusques, 128, No. 95) and most comprehensively, Jurgeit 1990, with the publication of fragments of a third throne of the Barberini type in Badisches Landesmuseum, Karlsruhe (Jurgeit 1990, fig. 1 and pls. 3-5). After having later had the opportunity to study the Louvre throne on exhibition, I withdraw my former scepticism about its genuineness (Strøm 1986, cf. Jurgeit 1990, 4, note 15).

NOTE 30
Jurgeit 1990, 4-5, disputes my interpretation of the published B II fragments from Tomba della Pania, Chiusi, as fragments of the throne described by Helbig, 1874, 206 (cf. Strøm 1986, 55, note 5, Throne No. 3, and Strøm 1989, 20 and fig. 27) and follows Bianchi Bandinelli and other scholars in identifying the seat mentioned by Helbig as a support for a local canopic urn and the stamped bronze fragments as coming from the so-called "pavimento" (Helbig 1874, 205). However, Helbig mentions human skeletal remains found close to the bed in the plundered tomb and thus also an inhumation burial. I do not find Helbig's words "Incrustazione del pavimento" in his draft for the text to the illustration, Mon. Ined. X, pl. XXXVIIIa, conclusive (Jurgeit 1990), since he apparently changed his mind and in the published text (Helbig 1877, 405) just wrote "posto sul suolo". At any rate, as stated, Strøm 1971, 222, note 48, the ornamentation of one or two of the fragments illustrated by Helbig is placed in curved friezes and cannot possibly come from the rectangularly divided bronze plates which Helbig describes as the "pavimento"; the same applies, if Steingräber is correct in his interpretation of the fragments as parts of a kline or a table, which are also rectangular (Steingräber 1979, 194, No. 8 and Steingräber, 1993, 172).

NOTE 31
Although I still regard Tarquinia as an important centre of production, my former views of this site as the centre for all

Orientalizing B I-B II shields – as well as some of the Geometric groups – (Strøm 1971, 56) have changed (cf. Strøm 1989, 20 and Strøm 1990, 94). Here I refer also to Caere, Veji and Vulci as well as (for B III = Geiger 2 d) to the Faliscan area, which last-mentioned attribution is accepted by Geiger (cf. Strøm 1971, 57, and Geiger, 118). For Veji, cf. above p. 69 and notes 17-18, for Vulci, above note 22, and for Caere, the shield above note 12 and cf. also below note 35. Bedini 1990, 64, convincingly argues for Geometric workshops in Latium, and since the Orientalizing shields from Laurentina, Tomb 121 (cf. above note 12), differ in details from other known B I shields, such a conclusion is extremely likely also for the Orientalizing period.

In her discussion of the problem, Geiger, 115-118, does not consider the Orientalizing stamped metal reliefs from Veji, nor at all mentions the Tarquinia, Pian di Civita shield, presumably made specifically for the occasion and definitely a local work (cf. above p. 69 and notes 17-18 and 12, respectively). I do not find her conclusions about a major centre at Marsigliana exporting Orientalizing shields to other Etruscan towns, sufficiently studied or well founded.

NOTE 32
For the Geometric stamped bronze reliefs, cf. below pp. 74-75 and note 93.

NOTE 33
Colonna 1972, 567, quite correctly criticised my book, Strøm 1971, on this point, in which Geiger, 115-118, follows the same lines as I did. On the other hand, today the material for such comparative studies is overwhelmingly large and should be examined by more than one scholar, each collecting various kinds of stamped bronze plates from a specific town or region.

NOTE 34
Cf. Jurgeit 1990, 28-30.

NOTE 35
Cf. Helbig 1969, 753-754 (Dohrn) and Steingräber 1979, 199, Cat. No. 28.
I adopt Jurgeit's term of Type Ia/Ib for the stone thrones (Jurgeit 1990, 22, note 85), because of the very slight difference between the two types (cf. Steingräber 1979, 24-25 and 149-151). For the stone thrones in general, cf. Steingräber 1979, 313-352. For the Caere thrones, chiefly of Type Ia/ Ib, cf. in particular, Colonna & v. Hase 1984, 55-56, Nos. 1-15 and for other localities (not comprising Tarquinia or Vulci), Nos. 16-23.

NOTE 36
Cf. above note 29 and for the Barberini Tomb in general, references above note 14.

NOTE 37
Strøm 1989, 19-20. For their South Etruscan stylistic elements in general, cf. references above note 28.

NOTE 38
Cf. e.g. the comparatively recent acknowledgement of a specific Sabine bronze relief production of Orientalizing style as exemplified by the bronze reliefs in the Ny Carlsberg Glyptothek, Copenhagen, Johansen 1971 and 1979, including the reliefs of the two chariots from Colle del Forno, Tomb XI. Cf. for the chariots, Emiliozzi 1997, 291-300, with absolute chronology (c. 600 BC) 293-294 (Emiliozzi and Santoro) and p. 319, No. 88. For the excavations of the tomb, cf. in particular Santoro 1977, 259-270, and Santoro 1986, 114-118.

NOTE 39
Cf. Strøm 1971, 35-37, Nos. 62-65, and 222, note 48.

NOTE 40
Strøm 1989, 19-20.

NOTE 41
Cf. Strøm 1989, 21-23.

NOTE 42
Cf. Strøm 1989, 22-23 and fig. 28.

NOTE 43
Cf. Baglione 1986, 131-134 and 142, Baglione & De Lucia Brolli 1990, 89-96 and 102 and Baglione & De Lucia Brolli 1997, for the Faliscan area and e.g. Colonna 1986, 95, for influences reaching further north. Cf. also Bartoloni 1986a, 52, in particular regarding Vejian influences on Verucchio and the Bologna area. According to Bartoloni and Colonna, the Tiber route was fading out in the second half of the 8th Cent. BC, but from the above references, one gets the impression of a revival in the late 8th and the 7th Centuries BC.

NOTE 44
Cf. e.g. Bartoloni 1986 a, 52-53; Bartoloni 1986b, 105-107; Bartoloni 1989a, 186; Bartoloni 1989b; Ridgway 1992, 129-137; De Santis 1995, 365-366 (in general), and 372-373 (Osteria dell'Osa, Tomb 600); Hoffmann 1996; Martelli 1997 and Toms 1997.

NOTE 45
The Barberini and Louvre thrones measure

92-93 cm in height, while the estimated height of the Karlsruhe throne is c. 90 cm (Jurgeit 1990, 10).

NOTE 46
For stone thrones, cf. above note 35. The Caere tufa statues (actually in high relief and the thrones of Steingräber type Ia/I b), Colonna & v. Hase, 1984. For absolute chronology, either the first or the second quarter of the 7th Cent. BC. cf. op. cit. pp. 29 and 47; Damgaard Andersen 1993, 45-46, No. 43, with other references.

NOTE 47
Colonna in Colonna & v. Hase 1984, 35-41, with reference to Prayon 1975, 109-112 for the former conclusion. Cf. also Steingräber 1997, 108-109.

NOTE 48
Strøm 1989, 21 and Strøm 1997, 246-247, fig. 1.
The throne is of Steingräber, Type Ia/I b (barrel-shaped, but with a straight front, cf. above note 35).
For a small votive terracotta from the Portonaccio sanctuary at Veji with the same motive of a person seated on a throne, cf. Colonna – v. Hase 1984, 48, note 96 and pl. XVIc.

NOTE 49
The volute footstool, Steingräber 1979, 46 and 187, pl. 14, Type S.
Colonna & v. Hase 1984, 46 and 57 for North Syrian models of the footstool (cf. also Gubel 1987, 235-236, Type VIIa) and pp. 47-48 and 52-53 for North Syrian sculptors working in Caere.

NOTE 50
Colonna & v. Hase 1984, 45-46, fig. 17 (Vignanello Chamber Tomb XI) and 57-59, the list, Appendice II.
No. 2, Castel di Decima. Tomb 153, is still unpublished.
For No. 3, Laurentina Acqua Acetosa, Tomb 70, see now also Bedini 1990, 54-55, Cat. No. 19 ill., and Bedini 1992, 85 and 92-93, Cat. No. 114 ill. and p. 85, fig. 6, and for such footstools also in Tombs 73-74 and 93, cf. Bedini 1990, 154 and Bedini 1992, 83. For the Verucchio footstools (of which Colonna lists only one), see the Moroni Necropolis, Tomb 24 (Gentili 1985, 76 and 80, No. 35 and pl. XXXVII) and below note 55.
For the footstools on the Murlo frieze, cf. below note 54.

NOTE 51

According to Colonna, Colonna & v. Hase 1984, 57, No. 1, the footstool in Veji, Casale del Fosso 871, is almost identical with the two in Trevignano Romano, Tomba dei Flabelli, Nos. 4-5, pl. XX c. (A IV stamped bronze reliefs).

For Veji, Casale del Fosso Tomb 871, cf. Bartoloni et. al. 1994, 25 and fig. 8 and for its tomb context in general, cf. Strøm 1971, 140-141; Müller-Karpe 1974, with pls. 22-25; Buranelli 1981, 39 (which I have not seen); Geiger, 49; and Buranelli, Drago & Paolini 1997, 69-73 with notes 30-31 and 42 and figs. 8-14.

There are drinking cups and amphorae, and several objects of stamped bronze relief: An A I shield (Strøm 1971, 27 and 42-44, Cat. No. 28 and Geiger, 49 (1b), No. 9 and Buranelli, Drago & Paolini 1997, 69 and fig. 8); a flask (Marzoli 1989, 35-36, Cat. No. 13, pl. 16); and in A IV relief (Geiger 1c) apart from the footstool, also a wheeled tray (Müller-Karpe 1974, pl. 23, 1) and a trapezoid standard (Guldager, 1994, 8-9 and 21, Cat. No. 7, fig. 3 and Buranelli, Drago & Paolini 1997, 71, fig. 11). Apart from the shield, its warriors' equipment comprises a crested helmet of such exaggerated height that it is not considered functional (cf. v. Hase 1988, 203 and Buranelli, Drago & Paolini 1997, 69 and fig. 14), a sword, lances, horse bits and remains of a two-wheeled chariot (Emiliozzi 1997, 324, No. 148); and among its more precious objects is a belt-clasp of two stamped gold plaques (Strøm 1971, 65-66 and 77-80, Cat. No. S 28 = S I 2), a wooden lituus in gold foil, Müller-Karpe 1974, pl. 25, 2, and a deep silver foil cup of Near Eastern type (Buranelli, Drago & Paolini, 71, fig. 12, cf. below note 139).

NOTE 52

From its local pottery, Veji, Casale del Fosso, 871 can be placed in the transition period, Veji II/Veji III A, around or shortly after 720 (cf. below note 88).

Important for its absolute chronology is the local imitation of a Corinthian Geometric skyphos, the original of which is dated to the third quarter of the 8th Cent. BC (cf. Strøm 1971, 141, and Buranelli, Drago & Paolini 1997, 73, note 42 and fig. 12). Colonna 1972, 568, excludes the Assyrian lion rhyton of bronze from the tomb context, which I – following Brown – used as a chronological fixed point (Strøm 1971, 129 and 140-141; it is still listed by Geiger, 49, No. 9 and, p. 51, used for her chronology). Colonna's absolute chronology for Veji, Casale del Fosso 871 to ca. 720 B.C. (Colonna 1984, 57) seems now the most reasonable. However, since the lion rhyton was exhibited in Museo di Villa Giulia together with material from Veji 871 (Brown 1960, 12-13, pl. VI and a better illustration in Rathje 1979, fig. I), it presumably was found in Veji.

The grave furniture of Veji, Tomb 871, is closely related with and only slightly earlier than that of the Tarquinia Warrior's Tomb in Berlin, which Geiger, 50-52, dates to shortly before 700 BC. Following Kilian 1977, 40-52, Geiger bases her chronology of the Tarquinia tomb on the alleged local pottery finds. However, apart from the Italo-Geometric bird askos, the pottery cannot with certainty be attributed to this tomb, cf. Strøm 1971, 142-143, where I stressed the considerable increase in pottery from Helbig's first publication in 1869 to his second in 1874. Today I agree with Kilian 1977, 52, that the Marzi brothers are not to blame in this case. (For other revelations of Helbig's transactions with unreliable results, cf. e.g. Guarducci 1980 and Moltesen 1981 and 1987). As I stated in 1971 – e.g. loc. cit. as regards this tomb – if such an old excavation is to be of any chronological value, "the evaluation of its furniture must .... be confined solely to the absolutely reliable objects." The alleged pottery finds of the Tarquinia Warrior's Tomb does not allow of a lowering of the date of Veji, Casaledel Fosso, 871.

NOTE 53
Cf. above notes 43-44.

NOTE 54
E.g. the assembly scene of the 6th Cent. B.C. terracotta frieze of the Upper Building, second building phase, in Poggio Civitate (Murlo), shows two seated persons using different kinds of volute footstools, a man seated on a folding chair and behind him a woman on a barrel-shaped throne, obviously made of bronze (illustrated in almost all works on this building, cf. e.g. Poggio Civitate, pl. XXXVII and Phillips 1993, 44, figs. 52-53).

For a summary of the discussion regarding the interpretation of the scene, whether gods, officials, members of the local aristocratic family etc., cf. Phillips 1993, 42-43. The subjects of the Murlo friezes are now being studied by Annette Rathje (cf. Rathje 1993 and Rathje 1994, 95), who believes that all four frieze-subjects together represent an ideological programme. The assembly scene covered 50 frieze plates (cf. v. Mehren 1993).

NOTE 55
Verucchio. Necropoli Fondo Lippi, Tombs 85 and 89, Montanari 1987, 239-241 (Gentili), No. 77 and fig. 160 (throne) and No. 78 and fig. 161 (footstool) (Tomb 85) and pp. 243-247, Nos. 93a-b and fig. 162 (throne) and No. 94, fig. 163 (footstool) (Tomb 89). (Cf. for Tomb 89 also Elles 1995, figs. 51-53 and Kossack 1992). Necropoli Moroni, Tomb 26, Gentili 1985, 25-26 and 88-89, Nos. 53 and 61, pl. 43-44. Tomb B /1971, Montanari 1987, 218 (Gentili), cf. Martelli 1995, 19, note 20. All four wooden thrones have intaglio decoration.

NOTE 56
Cf. e.g. Bedini 1992, 85 referring to Laurentina Acqua Acetosa, Tomb 70, for a perished wooden throne.

NOTE 57
Bedini 1992, 83-84, and Bedini 1995, 301, lists the groups of grave furniture specific to the aristocratic tombs of Laurentina Acqua Acetosa, but also to other upper class tombs in Etruria and Etruscanized Italy. Cf. also e.g. Bartoloni et.al. 1982 and the tombs above notes 14-15 and 18.

NOTE 58
For the significance of the two-wheeled chariot in Central Italy, cf. most recently Emiliozzi 1997, 1-2 (Emiliozzi) and 15-23 (Colonna) and for the list of two-wheeled chariots, op. cit. pp. 311-335: No. 148, Veji, Casale del Fosso, 871 (cf. above note 51); Nos. 142-143, Trevignano Romano, Tomba dei Flabelli; Nos. 227-228, Verucchio, Fondo Lippi, Tomb 89 (two chariots); No. 233, Verucchio, Necropoli Moroni, Tomb 26; and Nos. 29-32, Laurentina Acqua Acetosa, Tombs 70, 73-74 and 93.

The two-wheeled chariots are generally found in aristocratic tombs of the 7th Cent. BC, e.g. also in Palestrina, the Bernardini and Barberini Tombs (cf. above note 14); Cerveteri, RG (cf. above note 15); and Veji, Monte Michele Tomb 5 (cf. above note 18 and cf. Emiliozzi 1997, 311-335, Nos. 24-25, 103 and 153, respectively). The two last-mentioned tombs also had a four-wheeled carriage, used for the *ekphora* of the body which in Veji, Monte Michele Tomb 5, was then cremated (Emiliozzi 1997, 311-335, Nos. 102 and 152, respectively, and p. 15 and cf. for Veji. Monte Michele 5, also here Fig. 3).

Galeotti 1986-88, 82, observed a constructional difference in the two-wheeled chariots for men and women, indicating different forms of chariots, and since horse bits are lacking in most female tombs (cf.

note 59) their chariots presumably were drawn not by horses, but by mules (Bedini 1992, 85 and Emiliozzi 1997, 15). However, Casale Marittimo. Tomb A, had remains of two two-wheeled chariots, one of each type (Esposito 1999, 44 - 47).

NOTE 59
Horse bits or harnesses, cf. Veji, Casale del Fosso, Tomb 871 (above note 51); Laurentina Acqua Acetosa, Tombs 73 and 93 (Emiliozzi 1997, 314, Nos. 30 and 32); Trevignano Romano, Tomba dei Flabelli (Emiliozzi 1997, 324, Nos. 142-143) and Verucchio, Fondo Lippi, Tombs 85 and 89 (Montanari 1987, 235, Nos. 61-62 and fig. 157 and p. 256, Nos. 154-155 and fig. 169). The Verucchio tombs do not appear to follow the burial customs as strictly as the Latium tombs, having horse bits in the above woman's grave, Tomb 85, and a cista with the male burial, Tomb 89 (cf. above note 58 and below note 65).

NOTE 60
Veji, Casale del Fosso, Tomb 871 (above note 51); Laurentina Acqua Acetosa, in general (Bedini 1992, 83 and Bedini 1995, 301), and for Tomb 70 (Bedini 1990, 58-59, Nos. 23-24; Bedini 1992, 87-93, Cat. Nos. 76-109 and 111-112, Nos. 124-125, ill.); Verucchio, Fondo Lippi, Tomb 89 (Montanari 1988, 254, No. 135, (knife)); Verucchio, Necropoli Moroni, Tombs 24 and 26 (Gentili 1985, 76-78 (Nos. 2-15) 85-86 (Nos. 3-27); Trevignano Romano, Tomba dei Flabelli (Moretti 1970, 26-31, Nos. 11-18, pls. VI and VIII); and Castel di Decima, Tomb 153 (Zevi 1977, 272-273 and Naissance, Cat. Nos. 427-496).

Also the above-mentioned tombs, notes 14-15 and 18 had banqueting equipment.

NOTE 61
Veji, Tomb 871 (above note 51) (and for Veji, the Garucci Tomb (with A I decoration), cf. Woywowitsch 1978, 54, No. 121 and pl. 25); Laurentina Acqua Acetosa, Tomb 93 (Bedini 1990, 54), Tomb 70 (Bedini 1990, 57-58, Cat. No. 22, ill. and Bedini 1992, 92-93, Cat. No. 114, cf. p. 885, fig. 6 (the whole tomb context)) and Tomb 121 (Bedini 1990, 62, No. 26); and for Latium tombs in general (cf. Bedini 1990, 58).

Cf. also Woywowitch 1978, 121, pl. 21, for Tomba Bernardini, Tomba Barberini (also with a bronze throne, cf. above note 29) and RG (cf. above notes 11 and 14-15). Possibly also Veji, Monte Michele, Tomb 5 (above note 18), cf. Boitani 1983, 547, pl. CI.

NOTE 62
Verucchio, Fondo Lippi, Tomba 89 (Montanari 1987, 248-249, No. 109, fig. 164 and Elles 1995, 69 and fig. 56, a wooden handle for a fan, cf. Guldager 1994, 23, No. 15). The appearance of the fan can best be deduced from the bronze imitations of fans in Populonia. Tomba dei Flabelli, Guldager 1994, 23-24, Nos. 19-21.

For the significance of the fan, cf. Guldager 1994, 13-18. Behind the woman seated on the bronze throne on the assembly scene of the Murlo frieze is a standing female attendant fanning her. For other real fans in early Etruscan tombs, cf. Guldager 1994, 21-24, Nos. 10 and 12-13, Castel di Decima, Tomb 50 and Marsigliana d'Albegna, Banditella, Circolo degi Avori, respectively.

I wonder whether the ivory finial in Veji, Monte Michele, Tomb 5 (Boitani 1983, pl. CI and Boitani 1997, 34-35, fig. 6) may come from a fan; it appears rather close to the Marsigliana fan finials, of which two are mentioned above, while four others are listed in Etrusker, 156-157, Cat. Nos. 209-212, as possibly parts of fans.

NOTE 63
Veji, Casale del Fosso, Tomb 871 (Guldager 1994, 21, No. 7, cf. above note 52); Laurentina Acqua Acetosa, Tombs 70, 73-74 and 93 (Guldager 1994, 21-23, Nos. 3, 11 and 17-18). Trevignano Romano, Tomba dei Flabelli (Guldager 1994, 24, No. 22 (two examples)). Martelli 1995, 19-20, note 20, adds several examples to Guldager's list. referring also to Osteria dell'Osa, Tomb 600, with the only published trapezoid standard from Latium; in its decoration it is close to the earliest trapezoid standard, Veji, QF, Tomb Z 15 A, Guldager 1994, 21, Cat. No. 1, (cf. De Santis 1995, 369 and fig. 2. 13).

For the type, cf. in general, Guldager 1994, and cf. above note 17 for discussion of the interpretation of this object.

NOTE 64
Guldager 1994, Cat. Nos. 1 and 2 are the earliest examples, both from Veji II B tombs. For the social role of Veji, cf. Guldager 1994, 20.

NOTE 65
Cf. Montanari 1987, 249 and fig. 163 (Verucchio Tomb 89, cf. above note 59) and Gentili 1985, 79 (No. 16) and 89, No. 58 (Verucchio, Necropoli Moroni, Tombs 24 and 26) and cf. Bedini 1992, 84, for the general occurrence of cistai in women's tombs in Latium, and cf. Bedini 1990, 56-

57, Cat. No. 21, ill. (Laurentina. Acqua Acetosa Tomb 70) and Zevi 1977, 277 (Castel di Decima 153).

NOTE 66
Veji, Casale del Fosso, Tomb 871 (above note 51): Verucchio, Fondo Lippi, Tomb 89 (Montanari 1987, 252-253, Nos. 126-127 (helmets) and No. 128 (shield), figs. 167-168; for the small shield, No. 129, cf. below note 114) and Verucchio, Necropoli Moroni, Tomb 26 (cf. Emiliozzi 1997, 332-333); Laurentina Acqua Acetosa, Tombs 73 and 93 (cf. Emiliozzi 1997, 314, No. 30 and 32); Trevignano Romano. Tomba dei Flabelli (cf. Emiliozzi 1997, 324, Nos. 142-143).

Again the above-mentioned tombs, notes 14-15 and 18, have the same equipment.

NOTE 67
For the lituus or scepter in Veji, Tomb 871, cf above note 51. (Cf. also Monte Michele. Tomb 5, a wooden scepter with silver foil and, as finial, a bronze knob with intarsia decoration in iron. Boitani 1983, 545 and 553-554 and pl. XCVIII a-b, and Boitani 1997, 34-35, fig. 5).

Boitani 1983, note 48, refers to other sceptres in early tombs. For a possible lituus as well as a sceptre in Veji, Casale del Fosso, Tomb 1036, cf. Colonna 1991, 70, note 22, and 69, respectively, and De Santis 1995, 372. For this tomb, cf. below pp. 74 and 76 and notes 83 and 112.

Also the fragmentary ivory object in Casale Marittimo. Tomb A, is presumably a lituus (Esposito 1999, 54).

NOTE 68
Tarquinia, Pian di Civita, for the cult deposit in general and the shield, cf. above note 12. (According to Carancini 1984, 240-245, in Central Italy this type of axe was never found in tombs and axes did not form part of the military equipment. The fine decoration of the Tarquinia axe signifies its representative character, symbolic of the rank of its dedicator); for the pottery, cf. in particular Chiaramonte Treré 1988; and for the interpretation, see the conclusions, Bonghi Jovino 1987, 75-76; Chiaramonti Treré 1988, 585 and Bonghi Jovino, 1991, 700; and Chiaramonte Treré 1997, 175. For the sacrificial area in general, cf. also Chiaramonte Treré 1987.

In Casale Marittimo. Tomb A, a ceremonial axe was found together with two other axes (Esposito 1999, 53 - 54, fig. 46).

NOTE 69
Colonna – v. Hase 1984, 30-34, fig. 11 and pl. VI b.

NOTE 70
Cf. above note 54.

NOTE 71
Cf. also above p. 72 and note 47 for the interpretation of the thrones and statues in the Cerveteri tombs and cf. e.g. Rasenna, 38-39, where M. Torelli points to throne, scepter, double axe, and chariot as signs of power.

NOTE 72
Since Furtwängler's publication of the bronzes in Ol. IV, the early Etruscan bronzes in Greek sanctuaries have been studied by many scholars, cf. in particular, Karo 1937; Kilian 1973 and 1977 a, b and c; Herrmann 1983; Gras 1985, 651-675; Kyrieleis 1986 and v. Hase 1979, 1981, 1995 and – most recently – 1997, where most earlier references are given.

NOTE 73
Cf. in particular, Kilian 1973, 4 (with notes 21-26), 27-28 and maps 1-2; v. Hase 1979, 69-72; Gras 1985, 655-662 and v. Hase 1997, 297, here also for absolute chronology; the early Olympia fibula, fig. 4, 1. Cf. also Strøm 1998, 38-39, for the Argive Heraion fibulae, and 92, notes 10-11 and note 14, for my views on the problem of the dedicators.

NOTE 74
The Exochi fibula was found in Tomb Z, Friis Johansen 1957, 73-74 (Z 27), 184 and fig. 16.

NOTE 75
Kilian 1977 a, 436, note 42 and fig. 3 a-d, cf. v. Hase 1997, 297, fig. 6, 1-4.

NOTE 76
The Euboea belt, now in the Bibliothèque Nationale de Paris, Babelon – Blanchet 1895, 662-663, No. 2029. Brøndsted 1837, 19, note 19, pl. VII; Close-Brooks 1967b; Gras 1985, 671-672 and fig. 91 a. According to v. Hase 1997, 294, Brøndsted acquired it in Greece with the provenance of Euboea, but actually Brøndsted bought it himself on Euboea, cf. Brøndsted, loc. cit. and Close-Brooks 1976b, 22.
According to Close-Brooks 1967b, 23, such belts were most numerous in Veji II A (for chronology, cf. below note 88). For their distribution, cf. Kossack 1949/50, 132 (fig. 1) and 145- 147; Lazio pl. IX and pl. XXXVI and note, p. 197 (both with references to Tarquinia), and cf. also for Veji, loc. cit. as well as Close-Brooks 1967b; Not. 1976, 181 and fig. 27 (QF. Tomb I 17, 17);

Tomb 973 and 1032 in Casale del Fosso (Buranelli, Drago & Paolino 1997, 69-70 and figs. 19 and 20) and Tombs 732 and 780 in Grotta di Camicia (Berardetti – Drago 1997, 52 and figs. 19 and 22). For Vulci, cf. Hall Dohan 1942, 95, No. 25 and pl. L and Falconi Amorelli 1966, 10-11, No. 24, fig. 4.

NOTE 77
Cf. Herrmann 1983; Gras 1985, 672-675, Kyrieleis 1986; and v. Hase 1997, 309-317 and figs. 21-22 (The North Etruscan bronze vases). For the basin with raised points on the rim in the Argive Heraion, cf. also Strøm 1998, 39.

NOTE 78
Söldner, 1994, with conclusions, 225-226.

NOTE 79
v. Hase 1997, 299 and 313-314, figs 18-19, with reference to Kilian 1977 c, 121-122, fig. 1.
Horse bits do not presuppose the presence of chariots; separate horse bits have a symbolic value as "pars pro toto", cf. v. Hase 1969 and Bartoloni et al. 1982, 264 and Stary 1981, 94.

NOTE 80
Kilian 1977a, 437-438 and fig. 4; Herrmann 1983, 281-283, figs. 15-17 and v. Hase 1997, 298 and fig. 13. One of the lance heads, of exceptional size, has incised ornamentation, cf. Herrmann 1983, 282, fig. 15.

NOTE 81
Ol. Forsch. I, pl. 73k, cf. Kilian 1977a, 438 and Carapanos 1878, pl. 54, 6, cf. Gras 1985, 671.

NOTE 82
Kilian-Dirlmeier 1993, 127-128, 161 and 168, No. 445, pl. 58 and v. Hase 1997, 298 and fig. 11.

NOTE 83
Herrmann 1983, 279-282 and fig. 14, with reference to Veji, Casale del Fosso, Tomb 1036. Cf. v. Merhart 1956-57, 92-93, figs. 4.4 and 8.5. For the tomb, cf. also below note 112 and for its chronology, cf. Colonna 1991, 69, note 14.

NOTE 84
Kilian 1977a, ill. figs. 1-2; Gras 1985, 667-668; v. Hase 1988, 197-199, Nos. 17-18, and 202 and fig. 2 and v. Hase 1997, 298 and figs. 8-10. The Delphi fragment is definitely of "Variante III", chiefly dated to the second half of the 8th Cent. BC, the Olympia fragment possibly so.

NOTE 85
Apart from one early Sicilian/South Italic fibula (cf. above note 73) and the Villanoan II belt (cf. above note 76), v. Hase dates most Italic/Etruscan bronzes in Greek sanctuaries later than 750 BC (cf. v. Hase, 1979, 64-66 and 72-77, revising Kilian's chronology, and v. Hase 1997, 297-299).

NOTE 86
As regards the Olympia fragments, Geiger Nos 61 and 69 (cf. above note 20) the latter should probably be excluded from the list as well as of course, Geiger No. 111 = Ol. 1007. Some of the fragments are so small that an idenfication with a shield cannot be certain e.g. Geiger, 81, Nos. 60 and 65, pl. 69, and most other fragments on pl. 69 cannot be classified with certainty, nor can the attachment plates from Olympia and Delphi, Geiger, 74, Nos. 47-48.
Geiger 109, No. 127, pl. 91, may belong to Geiger Type 1g, since its decoration is very close to that of Geiger No. 50, cf. above note 5 and below p. 76 and note 112, while Geiger, 81, No. 62, pl. 59 seems to be a rim fragment (although the actual rim is not preserved) with a diameter of only 26 cm, cf. Herrmann 1983, 293, No. 13; if so, it possibly belongs with the small shields, below p. 76 and note 114.

NOTE 87
Geiger, 44-45, Nos. 6-8 (Olympia) and p. 81, No. 59 (Dodone), all A II (= Geiger 1a) and Geiger, 56-59, Nos. 28-31 (Olympia) and p. 57, No. 21 (Samos), all A IV (= Geiger 1c). (For photos, see Herrmann 1983 and v. Hase 1997, 298-299 and figs. 14-15).
Geiger, 81, No. 59 lists the Dodone fragment among her not securely classified Geometric shields. It is definitely a rim fragment of an A II (Geiger 1a) shield (here Fig. 5).

NOTE 88
The Veji tomb, QF 1-66-AA 1, has the earliest example of an A II shield (Geiger 43-46, Type 1 a, No. 1). Since its grave furniture combines elements of the phases Veji II A and II B, it should be dated within the third quarter of the 8th Cent. BC. Geiger, however, dates the tomb to around 760 or 750 BC, following the absolute Veji chronology of Close-Brooks 1967a. Close-Brooks' relative chronology has since been verified, although divided into more phases (Toms 1986), but her absolute Veji chronology was revised by Descoeudres – Kearsley 1983, 52: Veji II A, ca. 780-730, and Veji II B, ca. 750-720. (Cf. also Gierow 1977, 24-30). The revised chronology, to which Gei-

ger does not refer in her diagram, Geiger, 6, seems in the main accepted (cf. e.g. Ridgway et. al. 1985, 140-141; Bartoloni 1989a, 98-102 and Bartoloni 1989b, 125 (Veji II, 780/770-730/720); Ridgway 1991, 159-160) although not by Guidi 1993, 99-100, who bases his chronology not on imported Greek pottery, but on correlations with Latium, Pontecagnano and the Bologna area. However, also Guidi dates Veji QF 1-66-AA 1 to the third quarter of the 8th Cent. BC, Guidi 1993, 116-120.

(In general one cannot help wondering that Geiger's bibliography, in a book published in 1994, does not list a single publication later than 1983).

The latest datable A II shield comes from Palestrina. The Castellani Tomb, Strøm 1971, 23 and 44-45, Cat. No. 10 and A II 1; for the chronology of the tomb, cf. pp. 155-156 and 170, first quarter of the 7th Cent. BC. Geiger, 43-44, No. 2, accepts this chronology.

NOTE 89
A shield, transitional AI/AIV was found in Tomba Artiaco. Cumae (Strøm 1971, 21 and 46-47, Cat. Nr. 5 = A I 2, fig. 5). Because of the few scattered concentric circle ornaments I placed it in my group A I, while Geiger, 57-58, No. 22, classifies it as 1 c. Tomba Artiaco is dated to ca. 700 BC, (- Strøm 1971, 146-148, cf. Strøm 1990, 90-91, and Geiger, 58-60). However, Veji, Casale del Fosso, Tomb 871, dated to ca. 720 BC, contains several stamped bronze reliefs with A IV ornamentation, cf. above note 51 and for chronology of the tomb, note 52.

NOTE 90
Cf. Strøm 1971, 23-24 (Cat. No. 12 = A IV 4), 46-47 and 154-156 (the Castellani Tomb, cf. above note 88). Geiger, 46, places the shield in her group 1 d (cf. above note 7).

NOTE 91
The latest A IV shields were found in RG, Geiger, 56-57, Nos. 15-19, pls. 22-29; for the absolute chronology of the tomb, cf. above note 15.

NOTE 92
Cf. above notes 12-13.

NOTE 93
Both Kilian 1977, 73, and Bartoloni 1989a, 197, suggested the existence of several local workshops, which now seems to be accepted by most scholars, cf. Montanari 1987, 259 (Gentili) and references above note 31 to Bedini for Geometric Latium

workshops, and cf. v. Hase 1979, 66, for a possible Geometric workshop in Cerveteri. For Veji and Vulci, cf. note 94.

In general, I am sceptical about the importance which Geiger, 115-118, ascribes to Marsigliana (cf. above note 31). She bases her views almost exclusively on the types of pendants, even attributing to Marsigliana a specific pendant type found only in Tarquinia, Verucchio and Vetulonia, Geiger 116-117. Although sharing the now almost general view of many local workshops, I still see Tarquinia as an important centre (cf. above note 31, and cf. Bartoloni 1989a, 197).

NOTE 94
For a possible A II production in both Veji and Vulci, cf. Strøm 1971, 57 and Marzoli 1989, 44-45, while Geiger, 116 and 118, refers the whole production to Veji.

A IV reliefs were also found in Veji, e.g. in Casale del Fosso, Tomb 871 (cf. above note 51), as well as in Tarquinia, cf. e.g. Hencken 1968 I, fig. 179.

NOTE 95
Cf. e.g. Kilian 1977c, 124 and Kilian 1983; v. Hase 1979, 74; Herrmann 1983, 288 and 358; Kilian-Dirlmeier 1993, 161 and v. Hase 1997, 307-309; (v. Hase 1997, 322, note 57, refers to Strøm 1971, 56, for my then views of Etruscan shields possibly having reached Greece via the Western Greek colonies; however, I did not consider them spoils of war).

NOTE 96
E.g. Kyrieleis 1986, 134, cf. the discussion Gras 1985, 699-700, and v. Hase 1997, 317.

NOTE 97
Cf. above p. 74 and note 78.

NOTE 98
The Arimnestos throne, cf. below pp. 77 - 78 and note 128-132, and the two Etruscan treasuries in Delphi, dedicated by Spina and Agylla (Caere), cf. Bommelaer & Laroche 1991, 231-232, No. 342 and cf. the general discussion, Gras 1985, 681-689.

NOTE 99
Cristofani 1978, 41 and in the discussion, Herrmann 1983, 357; Bartoloni 1989a, 197.

As regards the antenna sword from Samos, Kilian-Dirlmeier 1993, 160-161, mentions the same possiblility, but concludes spoils of war to be the most plausible explanation for its presence in the Greek sanctuary. Cf. v. Hase 1997, 307.

NOTE 100
For the ancile or double shields, not with certainty known from Greek sanctuaries, cf. below p. 76 and note 112.

NOTE 101
Cf. references above note 95, regarding war spoils. According to Geiger, 110-114, the Geometric shields, in contrast to the Orientalizing ones, were real battle shields.

NOTE 102
Geiger, 110-113, with reference to the tests by J. Coles.

Only one of the small shields, Geiger, 76, No. 50, may have had a wooden backing, cf. above note 5 and below note 112.

NOTE 103
E.g. Kilian 1977, 26, Cat. No. 1, and Kilian 1983, in both cases he refers to Helbig, 1869, 259, for a leather backing of the shield. However, apparently Helbig did not actually observe such remains. There is a notable difference to his statement about the shoulder plate in the same tomb: "il cui fodero di tela è ancora benissimo conservato", and that regarding the shield, where in more general words, he says: "Lo scudo anche esso di bronzo stampato e foderato di cuojo era appoggiato sul petto". Helbig 1869, 258-259. For the Tarquinia Warrior's Tomb, cf. also above note 53.

NOTE 104
Geiger, 113, refutes the apparent evidence of the Verucchio shields (cf. Gentili 1969, 307) and when in the 1970's I was allowed by Professor Gentili to study the Verucchio shield fragments, I observed remnants of organic material on both the inside and the outside of the fragments, in which case they cannot derive from an inner leather coating.

NOTE 105
As e.g. that they do not show traces of battle or wear and that the fastenings of the handle and the attachment plates do not leave room for a leather covering, which according to Coles' tests should have a thickness of at least half a centimetre (Geiger, 110-113, cf. Strøm 1971, 19). Geiger's reference to Kilian's suggestion that the fastening of the handle and attachment plates pressed the leather so thin as not to leave any space in between appears to me an academic construction, Geiger, 113 with note 10.

NOTE 106
Esp. Geiger, 112-113.

NOTE 107
Cf. Colonna 1991, 101-102, regarding the ancile or double shields, cf. below p. 76 and note 112.

NOTE 108
I. e. the same explanation as is given by Geiger, 113, for the absence or decline of such details on the Orientalizing shields.

NOTE 109
Cf. Rieth 1964, for a later Etruscan shield with inner leather and wooden backing.

NOTE 110
The Verucchio shields, Geiger, 49 (No. 10) and 57-58 (Nos. 20 and 25). Although the shields were not found in a secure cult context, Gentili 1969, 298-299, considers them a votive or ritual offering, because they were found outside the actual habitation area and placed one inside the other in a normal votive deposit fashion. For the cult deposit of the Tarquinia shield, cf. above p. 73 and notes 12 and 68.

NOTE 111
For Geometric shields in numbers of two or three in single tombs, cf. e.g. above note 5, Laurentina Acqua Acetosa and Osteria dell'Osa, Tomb 600, and references, above note 88, to Palestrina. Tomba Castellani; cf. Veji, the Garrucci Tomb (Strøm 1971, 26-27, Nos. 26-27 (A II) and Geiger, 44, Nos. 4-5 (1a)) and Castel di Decima. Tomb 21 (cf. Bartoloni et al. 1982, 263. Cf. in general, Colonna 1991 79-81 and Bartoloni & De Santis 1995, 279 (here the observation about the changing significance of the shields) and cf. below and note 114 for the possibility of a specific burial ritus).

For shields placed along the wall of the tomb, cf. Laurentina Acqua Acetosa, Tombs 70, 93 and 121 (cf. above notes 5 and 12) and cf. Bedini 1992, 83 and 85, and Bedini 1995, 301) in the same ways they were said to be found in RG (Pareti 1947, 292) and in several tombs with Orientalizing shields.

Bedini 1990, 64, refers to shields in women's tombs in Laurentina Acqua Acetosa, Tomb 70 and in Pitino S. Severino, Tomb 17 (Early Orientalizing = Geiger, 90, No. 75 and cf. above note 12) and to Albore Livadhi 1975, 53-54, note 5, Cumae, Tombs 11 and 56, with Etruscan Geometric shields used as cover for urns in women's burials (A IV shields, cf. Strøm, 20-21).

NOTE 112
Colonna 1991. For the repaired Norchia shield, cf. in particular, pp. 55-63, and for Veji, Casale del Fosso, Tomb 1036, pp. 69-81 with earlier references as well as absolute chronology, note 14; for the shields as found, cf. figs. 12 and 14-16 and for their fastening, fig. 17. For the tomb context, cf. also above notes 67 and 83.

Possibly the small shields, Geiger, Nos. 49-50, Type 1g, cf. above note 5, are parts of ancile shields, one of which, No. 50, from Tuscania, may have had a wooden backing; the tomb of No. 49, Bisenzio, Olmo Bello, Tomb 8, is dated to the third quarter of the 8th Cent. BC like Veji, Casale del Fosso, Tomb 1036. The Bisenzio shield has holes for fastening along the rim and the inside of the buckle of the Tuscania shield shows a construction identical with that of the Veji ancile shields.

For suggestion of a specific burial ritual connected with the plurality of shields, cf. Bartoloni – De Santis 1995, 280-281.

NOTE 113
Cf. above note 86, Geiger, Nos. 127 and 62, and cf. notes 112 and 114, respectively.

NOTE 114
Colonna 1991, 81-82, interprets the two extra, small shields of Veji, Tomb 1036, as cuirass-disks, but such an interpretation is not possible for the small shields in Tombs 70 and 340 of the Villanovan necropolis of Benacci (Bologna), Morigi Govi & Tovoli 1993, 1-5, who suggest a ceremonial role and refer also to the extra, small shield in Verucchio. Fondo Lippi, Tomb 89 (Montanari 1987, 252, Cat. 129 and fig. 168). Another was found in Castelnuovo Berardenga (Mangani 1988-89, No. 107, figs. 40-41): For the shields of normal size in the same two tombs, cf. above notes 5 and 9. Morigi Govi & Tovoli 1993, 9, notes 16-17 also refer to small shields in Bisenzio and Narce tombs.

NOTE 115
Colonna 1991, 63-68 and Bartoloni & De Santis 1995, 278-279.

NOTE 116
Cf. Colonna 1991, 84-97 and for the time when the Etruscans abandoned the ancile shield, in particular pp. 89-90.

NOTE 117
Veji Tomb 1036, cf. references above notes 67 and 112. Its context signifies a person of extremely high rank, probably also of religious character and the plurality of its

shields indicates their function in a burial ritual. For the chronology of Bisenzio, Olmo Bello, Tomb 8, cf. also note 112.

NOTE 118
The Norchia shield, above note 112.

NOTE 119
Cf. above p. 76 and note 107.

NOTE 120
Cf. Colonna 1991, figs. 9 and 40, and Bartoloni & De Santis 1995, 279 with references.

NOTE 121
For an extra lance of bronze meant for parades, besides the iron lances of the Latium tombs, cf. e.g. Bartoloni et al. 1982, 263-264, and Bedini 1992, 83-84, and for the same interpretation of the very large iron lance heads in Veji, Monte Michele, Tomb 5 (above note 18), cf. Boitani 1983, 551-553. And cf. above note 51 for the same significance of the extremely high helmet in Veji Tomb 871. This interpretation should apply also e.g. to the correspondingly high helmet in Veruchio, Fondo Lippi Tomb 89 (cf. Montanari 1987, 252, No. 126 (Gentili).

NOTE 122
Bartoloni & De Santis 1995, 279-281.

Although there seems a contradiction in the summary, p. 281, where the functionality of the same objects is stressed as regards a short period in the 8th Cent. BC. As stated above, the only certain example is the Norchia ancile shield, whereas the two ancile shields in Veji, Tomb 1036, complied with the custom of non-functional plurality of the round bronze shields, cf. above p. 76 and notes 111 and 112.

NOTE 123
Cf. Strøm 1971, 19, for the shields.

NOTE 124
This conclusion concerns at least the shields, the antenna sword (above note 82), and the decorated, disproportionately large lance head in Olympia (above note 80), but presumably also the helmets (above notes 84 and 121) and probably also other parts of the warriors' equipment in Greek sanctuaries.

NOTE 125
Cf. above note 99.

NOTE 126
Cf. above pp. 70 and 72-73 and notes 26, 29-30, 50-51 and 55 (for thrones and volute footstools) and note 58 (for two-wheeled chariots, which were found in several more tombs than here listed, cf. Emiliozzi 1997, 310-335, Catalogue).

NOTE 127
Cf. Emiliozzi 1997, 18 (Colonna). Apart from the fact that the Etruscans as barbarians did not have access to the Olympic Games and therefore had no reason for dedicating racing chariots.

NOTE 128
Cf. Herodotus 1.14 and most thoroughly Muscarella 1989, 334-335.

NOTE 129
The Arimnestos throne, Pausanias 5.12.5, cf. in particular, Karo 1937, 316; Eckstein 1969, 67-69; Steingräber 1979, 148-149; Jurgeit 1990, 22; Kossack 1992, 234; Colonna 1993, 44-56; and Völling 1998, 243.

NOTE 130
Colonna 1993, 50-53, definitely before 490 BC. Colonna suggests a Late Archaic date; however, in my opinion, not with convincing arguments. I agree with Steingräber, Jurgeit and Völling (cf. preceding note) that a 7th Cent. BC date is more likely. Colonna's chronology for Arimnestos' throne seems connected with the identification that (following Eckstein 1969, 67-69, cf. Colonna 1993, 46-48) he gives of the very large stone foundation in the pronaos of the Zeus Temple as the basis for Arimnestos'throne. Colonna compares it with Etruscan stone thrones. In my opinion, a throne of a light material which had no need for such a weighty basis is much more likely, see below. Nor do I find it possible from Pausanias' words to determine the exact position of Arimnestos' throne in the pronaos of the temple.

NOTE 131
This in contrast to my former views, cf. above note 20.

NOTE 132
The Verucchio thrones, cf. above note 55. Although both Jurgeit 1990, 22, and Kossack, 1992, 234, refer to the Verucchio throne from Tomb 89 for comparisons with Arimnestos' throne, Völling 1998, 243, seems the first to actually suggest that it is a throne of this type.

NOTE 133
Colonna 1993, 53-56.
Colonna's conclusions that the throne was a donation by a king in Etruscan Campania, from either Nola or Capua, is closely connected with his late chronology of the Arimnestos throne (cf. above note 130), since the Campanian towns were prosperous in the late 6th Cent. BC, Verucchio on the other hand on the decline. Against the location to a Campanian town speaks, in my opinion, also the lack of such throne finds in Campania, whereas the suggested 7th Cent. BC date for the Arimnestos throne above (cf. above note 130) fits in well with the chronology of the aristocratic Verucchio tombs, Tomb 89 being dated c. 650 BC (Montanari 1987, 243 (Gentili).

NOTE 134
Cf. Söldner 1994, 225-226.

NOTE 135
Cf. Bartoloni 1989a, 183-186. Delpino 1989, and Ridgway 1992, 128.
For Veji, cf. also Bartoloni 1986; Ridgway 1992, 129-136; Hoffmann 1996; Martelli 1997 and Toms 1997.

NOTE 136
Apart from Near Eastern imports and close imitations, especially in pottery, both towns give evidence of Near Eastern links of a different kind. For Tarquinia, cf. e.g. indications of immigrant North Syrian gold- and silver smiths having worked in South Etruria around 700 BC, Tarquinia apparently being one important centre for this work (Strøm 1971, 212, and Strøm 1990, 93-94) and cf. the Near Eastern technical details (pilaster construction) in the architecture of cult house Beta on the Acropolis of Tarquinia, suggesting co-operation of a Near Eastern architect (Bonghi Jovino 1991,

178-181, Bonghi Jovino 1992 and Bonghi Jovino & Chiaramonte Treré 1997, 170-171 and Prayon 1998, 38-39).
The first to suggest that Near Eastern craftsmen settled in Etruscan Italy around 700 BC, was Brown 1960, 1-3, who observed signs of a co-operation of North Syrian ivory workers and local craftsmen in Etruria and Latium, seeing this immigration as a result of Sargon II's conquests in the late 8th Cent. BC. Such immigrations must have comprised also other persons than craftsmen (cf. Strøm 1984, 356) and had also non-material influence on the Etruscan society.
For Veji, cf. notes 139-141.

NOTE 137
Cf. above p. 71 and note 35 for stone thrones not having been found in Tarquinia tombs and notes 48 and 51 for thrones and volute footstools in Veji.

NOTE 138
Cf. above p. 72.

NOTE 139
Cf. the Veji statue above p. 72 and note 48.

NOTE 140
Cf. Rathje 1997, esp. p. 204.

NOTE 141
The lion head rhyton, formerly attributed to Casale del Fosso, Tomb 871, was at any rate found in Veji, cf. above note 51. For the function of these rhyta as drinking vessels, cf. Reade 1995, 44-47, figs. 9 and 11-13.

NOTE 142
For Gordion, cf. Young 1981, 121-123, MM 45-46, pls. 62-63, and for Samos, Jantzen 1972, 71 and 74, Nos. B 275 and pl. 73 and Kyrieleis 1986b, 189 and Colour Plate II c.

NOTE 143
Cf. references Strøm 1998, 101, note 130.

Abbreviations

ANATHEMA
Atti del Convegno Internazionale
ANATHEMA: Regime delle
offerte e vita dei santuari nel Mediterraneo antico. Roma, 15-18 giugno 1989. *Scienze dell'Antichità* 3-4
(1989-1990).
Roma 1991.

Annali
*Annali dell' Istituto di Corrispondenza
Archeologica.*
Roma. 1829-1885.

Atti
*Atti del Secondo congresso Internazionale Etrusco. Firenze 26 maggio-2
giugno 1985. I-III.* Roma 1989.

Bull.
Bullettino dell' Istituto di Corrispondenza Archeologica.
Roma 1829-1885.

Deliciae Fictiles
Rystedt, E., Wikander, C. &
Wikander, Ö. (Eds.)
*Deliciae Fictiles. Proceedings of the First
International Conference on Central
Italic Architectural Terracottas at the
Swedish Institute in Rome, 10-12
December 1990.* Stockholm 1993.

EAA Sec.Sup.
*Enciclopedia dell'Arte Antica, Classica
et Orientale.* Secondo Supplemento
1971-1994. Vols. I-V. 1994-1997
Roma.

Etrusker
*Etrusker in der Toskana. Etruskische
Gräber der Frühzeit.*
Museum für Kunst und Gewerbe.
Hamburg. Ab 18. Juni 1987.
Firenze 1987.

Etrusques
Les Etrusques et l'Europe. Galeries
Nationales du Grand Palais. Paris.
15 septembre-14 décembre 1992.
Milan 1992.

Geiger
Geiger, A., *Treibverzierte Bronzerundschilde der italischen Eisenzeit aus
Italien und Griechenland.* PBF III 1.
1994.

Lazio
Civiltà del Lazio primitivo. Palazzo
delle Esposizioni. Roma 1976.

Mon. Ined.
*Monumenti Inediti pubblicati dell'
Instituto di Corrispondenza Archeologica per gli Anni 1829-1885.* I-XII.
Roma.

Naissance
Naissance de Rome. Petit Palais.
Mars-mai 1977.
Paris 1977.

Necropoli Praeneste
La Necropoli di Praeneste. "Periodi
orientalizzante e medio repubblicana". *Atti del 20 Convegno di Studi
Archeologici.* Palestrina 21/22. Aprile
1990. Palestrina 1992.

Nuovi Tesori
Nuovi tesori dell'antica Tuscia. Catalogo della Mostra.
Viterbo 1970.

Ol. IV.
Furtwängler, A., *Die Bronzen und
die übrigen kleineren Funde,* in: Curtius, E. & Adler, F., *Olympia. Die
Ergebnisse der von dem Deutschen
Reich veranstalteten Ausgrabung. IV.*
Berlin 1890.

PBF.
Prähistorische Bronzefunde I-.
München/Stuttgart 1969-.

Poggio Civitate.
Poggio Civitate (Murlo. Siena). Il Santuario Arcaico. Catalogo della Mostra
Firenze-Siena. Firenze 1970.

QF.
Necropoli Quattro Fontanili. (Veji).

Rassenna
M. Pallottino et al., *Storia e Civiltà
degli Etruschi.* Milano 1986.

RG.
Tomba Regolini-Galassi (Cerveteri).

Bibliography

Albore Livadie, C. 1975
Remarques sur un groupe de tombes de Cumes. Contribution à l'Etude de la Société et de la Colonisation Eubéennes, 53-58. *Cahiers du Centre Jean Bérard*, II. Naples.

Babelon, E. & Blanchet, J.-A. 1895
Catalogue des Bronzes Anciens de la Bibliothèque Nationale. Paris.

Baglione, M.P. 1986
Il Tevere e i Falisci. *Archeologia Laziale* VII.2, *QuadAEI* 12, 124-142.

Baglione, M.P. & De Lucia Brolli, M.A. 1990
Nuovi dati sulla necropoli de "I Tufi" di Narce, in: *La Civiltà dei Falisci. Atti XV Convegno di Studi Etruschi ed Italici* (Cività Castellani 1987), Firenze, 61-102.

Baglione, M.P. & De Lucia Brolli, M.A. 1997
Veio e i Falisci, in: *Bartoloni 1997*, 145-171.

Bartoloni, G. et al. 1982
Aspetti dell'ideologia funeraria nella necropoli di Castel di Decima, in: *Gnoli & Vernant 1982*, 257-273.

Bartoloni, G. & Grottanelli, C. 1984
I carri a due ruote nelle tombe femminili del Lazio e dell' Etruria, *OPUS* III, 383-396.

Bartoloni, G. 1986a
Relazioni interregionali nell'VIII

secolo a.C.: Bologna-Etruria mineraria-Valle Tiberina, *StDocA* II, 45-56.

Bartoloni, G. 1986b
I Latini e il Tevere, *Archeologia Laziale* VII, 2, 98-110.

Bartoloni, G. 1989a
La cultura villanoviana. All' inizio della storia etrusca. Urbino.

Bartoloni, G. 1989b
Veio nell'VIII secolo a.C. e le prime relazioni con l'ambiente greco, in: *Atti I*, 117-128, Roma.

Bartoloni, G. 1991
Veio e il Tevere. Considerazioni sul ruolo della communità Tiberina negli scambi tra Nord e Sud Italia durante la prima età del ferro, *Dial.* 9, 35-48.

Bartoloni, G. et al. 1994
Veio tra IX e VI. sec. a. C.: primi risultati sull'analisi comparata delle necropoli Veiente, *ArchCl* XLVI, 1-46.

Bartoloni, G. & De Santis, A. 1995
La deposizione di scudi nelle tombe di VIII e VII secolo a.C. nell'Italia Centrale Tirrenica, in: *Preistoria e Protostoria in Etruria. Atti del Secondo Incontro di Studi*, Milano.

Bartoloni, G. (ed.) 1997
Le necropoli arcaiche di Veio. Giornata di studio in memoria di Massimo Pallottino. Roma.

Bedini, A. & Cordano, F. 1977
L'ottavo secolo nel Lazio e l'inizio dell'orientalizzante antico. Alla luce di recenti scoperti nella necropoli di Castel di Decima, *PP* CLXXV, 274-311.

Bedini, A. 1990
Abitato protostorico in località Acqua Acetosa Laurentina, in: *Archeologia a Roma. La materia e la tecnica nell'arte antica*, eds. Di Mino, M.R. & Bertinetti, M. Terme di Diocleziano, aprile-dicembre 1990, Roma, 48-64.

Bedini, A. 1992
Le site de Laurentina Acqua Acetosa, in: *Rome 1000 Ans de Civilisation*, eds. La Regina & A. Verona, 83-96.

Bedini, A. 1995
Laurentina – Acqua Acetosa, *EAA, Sec. Sup.* III, 300-302.

Berardinetti, A. & Drago, L. 1997
La necropoli di Grotta Gramiccia, in: *Bartoloni 1997*, 39-61.

Boitani F. 1982
Veio: nuovi rinvenimenti nella necropoli di Monte Michele, in: *Archeologia nella Tuscia*, Roma, 95-103.

Boitani, F. 1983
Veio: la tomba "principesca" della necropoli di Monte Michele, *StEtr* LI (1985), 535-556.

Boitani, F. 1997
Recenti scoperti a Veio, in: *Bartoloni 1997*, 33-37.

Bol, P.C. 1989
Argivische Schilde. *Ol. Forsch* XVII. Berlin.

Bommelaer, J.-F. & Laroche, D. 1991
Guide de Delphes. Le Site. Paris.

Bonghi Jovino, M. 1986
Gli Etruschi di Tarquinia. Modena.

Bonghi Jovino, M. 1987
Gli scavi nell'abitato di Tarquinia e la scoperta dei "bronzi" in un preliminare inquadramento, in: *Bonghi Jovino & Chiaramonte Treré 1987*, 59-77.

Bonghi Jovino, M. & Chiaramonte Treré, C. (eds.) 1987
Tarquinia: Ricerche, Scavi e Prospettive, in: *La Lombardia per gli Etruschi. Atti del Convegno Internazionale di Studi*. Milano 24-25 Giugno 1986, Modena.

Bonghi Jovino, M. 1991
Osservazioni sui sistemi di costruzione a Tarquinia: techniche locali ed impiego del "muro a pilastri" fenicio, *ArchCl* XLIII, 171-191.

Bonghi Jovino, M. 1992
Aggiornamenti sull'"area sacra" di Tarquinia e nuove considerazioni sulla tromba-lituo, in: *ANATHEMA*, 679-694.

Bonghi Jovino, M. & Chiaramonte Treré, C. 1997
Tarquinia. Testimonianze archeologiche e ricostruzione storica. Scavi sistematici nell'abitato, campagne 1982-1988. Tarchna I. Roma.

Bonghi Jovino, M. (ed.) 1998
Archeologia della città. Quindici anni di scavo a Tarquinia. Dal documento alla ricostruzione – appunti per un dibattito. Milano.

Brown, W.L. 1960
The Etruscan Lion. Oxford.

Brøndsted, P.J. 1837
Die Bronzen von Siris. Kopenhagen.

Buranelli, F. 1981.
Proposta di interpretazione dello sviluppo topografico nella necropoli di Casale del Fosso a Veio, in: Peroni, R., *Necropoli e usi funerari dell'età del ferro*, Bari, 19-45.

Buranelli, F., Drago, L. & Paolini, L. 1997
La necropoli di Casale del Fosso, in: *Bartoloni 1997*, 63-83.

Canciani, F. & Hase, Fr.-W. v.
La Tomba Bernardini di Palestrina. Roma.

Carancini, G.L. 1984
Früheisenzeitliche Äxte und Beile in Italien, in: *PBF* IX, 12.

Carapanos, C. 1878
Dodone et Ses Ruines. Paris.

Chiaramonte Treré, C. 1987
Altri dati dagli scavi alla Civita sugli aspetti cultuali e rituali, in: *Bonghi Jovino & Chiaramonte Treré 1987*, 79-105.

Chiaramonte Treré, C. 1988
I depositi all'ingresso dell' edificio tarquiniese: nuovi dati sui costumi rituali etruschi, *MEFRA* 100, 565-600.

Chiaramonte Treré, C. 1992
Alcuni dati sulla prassi rituale etrusca, in: *ANATHEMA*, 695-704.

Close-Brooks, J. 1967a
Considerazioni sulla cronologia delle facies arcaiche dell'Etruria, *StEtr.* XXXV, 323-329.

Close-Brooks, J. 1967b
A Villanovan Belt from Euboea, *BICS* 14, 22-24.

Colonna, G. 1972
Review of Strøm 1971, *StEtr.* XL, 565-569.

Colonna, G. & Hase, Fr.-W. v. 1984
Alle origine della statuaria etrusca: La Tomba delle Statue presso Ceri, *StEtr.* LII (1986), 13-59.

Colonna, G. 1986
Il Tevere e gli Etruschi. *Archeologia Laziale* VII, 2. *QuadAEI* 12, 90-97.

Colonna, G. 1991
Gli scudi bilobati dell'Italia centrale e l'ancile dei Salii, *ArchCl* XLIII, 55-122.

Colonna, G. 1993
Doni di Etruschi e di altri Barbari occidentali nei santuari panellenici, in: *I grandi santuari della Grecia e l'Occidente*, ed. A. Mastrocinque, Trento, 43-67.

Colonna, G. & Di Paolo, E. 1997
Il letto vuoto, la distribuzione del corredo e la "finestra" della Tomba Regolini-Galassi, in: *Etrusca et Italica. Scritti in ricordo di Massimo Pallottino I*, eds. Nardi, G. & Pandolfini, M., Pisa/Roma, 131-172.

Cook, R.M. & Dupont, P. 1998
East Greek Pottery. London/New York.

Cristofani, M. 1978
L'Arte degli Etruschi. Produzione e consumo. Torino.

Cristofani, M. 1983
In: *Herrmann 1983*, Discussion, 357.

Cristofani, M.(ed.) 1985
Civiltà degli Etruschi. Firenze. Museo Archeologico. 16 maggio-20 ottobre 1985. Milano.

Curtis, C.D. 1925
The Barberini Tomb, *MemAcAd* V, 9-52.

Damgaard Andersen, H. 1993
The Etruscan Ancestral Cult – Its Origin and Development and the Importance of Anthropomorphization, *ARID* XXI, 1993, 7-79.

Delpino, F. 1989
L'ellenizazione dell'Etruria villanoviana: sui rapporti tra Grecia ed Etruria fra IX e VIII secolo a. C., in: *Atti I*, 105-116.

Delpino, F. 1997
Massimo Pallottino a Veio, in: *Bartoloni 1997*, 19-26.

De Santis, A. 1995
Contatti fra Etruria e Lazio antico alla fine dell'VIII secolo a.C.: La tomba di guerriero di Osteria dell'Osa, in: *Settlement and Economy in Italy 1500 BC-AD 1500. Papers of the Fifth Conference of Italian Archaeology*, ed. Christie N., Oxbow Monographs, 365-375.

De Santis, A. 1997
Alcuni considerazioni sul territorio Veiente in età orientalizzante e arcaica, in: *Bartoloni 1997a*, 101-143.

Descoeudres, J.-P. & Kearsley, R. 1983
Greek Pottery at Veii: Another Look, *BSA* LXXVIII, 9-53.

Eckstein, F. 1969
ANAΘHMATA. Studien zu den Weihgeschenken strengen Stils im Heiligtum von Olympia. Berlin.

Elles, P. von 1995
Museo Civico Archeologico. Guida Catalogo. Verucchio.

Emiliozzi, A. 1992
I resti del carro Bernardini nel quadro dell'attestazione coeve dell' area medio-italiana, in: *Necropoli Praeneste*, 85-108.

Emiliozzi, A. 1997
Carri da guerra e principi Etruschi. Catalogo della Mostra. Viterbo, Palazzo dei Papi, 24 maggio 1997-31 gennaio 1998. Roma.

Esposito, A.M. 1999
Principi e guerrieri. La necropoli etrusca di Casale Marittimo. Milano.

Falconi Amorelli, M.T. 1966
Tomba villanoviana con bronzetto nuragico, *ArchCl* 18, 1-15.

Friis Johansen, K. 1957
Exochi, ein frührhodisches Gräberfeld, in: *ActaArch* XXVIII, 1-192.

Galeotti, L. 1986-88
Considerazione sul carro a due ruote nell'Etruria e nel Latium Vetus, *ArchCl* XXXVIII-XL, 94-104.

Gaultier, F & Briquel, D. (eds.) 1997
Les Etrusques, les plus religieux des hommes. Etat de la recherche sur la religion Etrusque. Actes du colloque international. Galeries nationales du Grand Palais 17-18-19 novembre 1992. Paris.

Gentili, G.V. 1969
Gli scudi bronzei dello stanziamento protostorico di Verucchio e il problema della loro funzione nell'armamento villanoviano, *Studi Romagnoli* XX, 295-331.

Gentili, G.V. 1985
Il villanoviano verucchiese nella Romagna Orientale ed il sepolcreto Moroni, *StDocA* I.

Gierow, P.G. 1977.
Absolute Chronology of the Iron Age Culture of Latium in the Light of Recent Excavations. Lund.

Gnoli, G. & Vernant, J.P. (eds.) 1982
La mort, les morts dans les sociétes anciennes. Cambridge.

Gras, M. 1985
Trafics Tyrrhéniens archaïques, *BEFRA* 258. Roma.

Guarducci, M. 1980
La cosidetta fibula prenestina. Antiquari eruditi e falsari nella Roma dell'Ottocento, *MemAccLinc* 24, 411-574.

Gubel, E. 1987
Phoenician furniture. Studia Phoenicia 7. Leuven.

Guidi, A. 1993
La necropoli veiente dei Quattro Fontanili nel quadro della fase recente della prima Età del Ferro Italiana. Firenze.

Guldager, P. Bilde 1994
Ritual and Power: The Fan as a Sign of Rank in Central Italian Society, *ARID* XXII, 7-34.

Hall Dohan, E. 1942
Italic Tomb-Groups in the University Museum. Philadelphia. Philadelphia/London/Oxford.

Hase, Fr.-W. v. 1969
Die Trensen der Früheisenzeit in Italien, in: *PBF* XVI, 1.

Hase, Fr.-W. v. 1979
Zur Interpretation villanovazeit-
licher und frühetruskischer Funde
in Griechenland und der Ägäis,
Kleine Schriften aus dem vorgeschichtli-
chen Seminar, Marburg, Hft. 5, 62-99.

Hase, Fr.-W. v. 1981
Zum Beginn des Fernhandels von
und nach Etrurien unter besonder-
er Berücksichtigung der frühesten
mittelitalischen Funde in Griechenland, in: *Die Aufnahme fremder*
Kultureinflüsse in Etrurien und das
Problem des Retardierens in der etrus-
kischen Kunst, Mannheim 8.-10. 2.
1980, Mannheim, 9-24.

Hase, Fr.-W. v. 1988
Früheisenzeitliche Kammhelme aus
Italien. Antike Helme. Sammlung
Lipperheide und andere Bestände
des Antikenmuseums Berlin.
RGZM Monographien, Band 14,
Mainz, 195-211 and 447-449.

Hase, Fr.-W. v. 1995
Ägäische, griechische und vorder-
asiatische Einflüsse auf das tyrrhe-
nische Mittelitalien. Beiträge zur
Urnenfelderzeit nördlich und süd-
lich der Alpen. *RGZM Monogra-*
phien, Band 35, 239-286.

Hase, Fr.-W. v. 1997
Présences étrusques et italiques
dans les sanctuaires grecs (VIIIe-
VIIe siècle av.J.-C.), in: *Gaultier-*
Brique 1997, 293- 323.

Helbig, W. 1874
Scavi di Chiusi, *Bull.* 1874, 203-210.

Helbig, W. 1877
Oggetti trovati in una tomba chiusina, *Annali* 1877, 397-410.

Helbig, W. 1969
Führer durch die öffentlichen Samm-
lungen klassischer Altertümer in Rom
(IV. Auflage, Hrsg. v. H. Speier).
Band III. Tübingen.

Hencken, H. 1968
Tarquinia, Villanovans and Early
Etruscans I-II. Cambridge Mass.

Herrmann, H.-V. 1983
Altitalisches und Etruskisches in
Olympia, *ASAtene* LXI (1984),
271-294 and 357-358 (discussion).

Hockey, M. 1987
Reconstruction of an Etruscan
Bronze Tomb Throne, *The Conser-*
vator, 11, 38-41.

Hoffmann, L. 1996
Civilization on Barbarian soil? An
evaluation of Geometric pottery at
the Quattro Fontanili necropolis, in:
Die Akten des Internationalen Kollo-
quiums "Interaction in the Iron Age:
Phoenicians, Greeks and the Indige-
neous Peoples of the Western Mediterra-
nean". Amsterdam 26 und 27 März
1992. *HambBeitr* 19-20 (1992-
1993), 115-138.

Jantzen, U. 1972
Ägyptische und Orientaische Bronzen
aus dem Heraion von Samos. Samos
VIII. Bonn.

Johansen, F. 1971
Reliefs en bronze d'Etrurie. Copen-
hague.

Johansen, F. 1979
Etruskiske broncerelieffer i Glypto-
teket, *MeddelGlypt.* 36, 67-87.

Jurgeit, F. 1990
Fragmente eines etruskischen
Rundthrones in Karlsruhe, *RM* 97,
1-32.

Karo, G. 1937
Etruskisches in Griechenland,
AEphem 100, 316-320.

Kilian, K. 1973
Zum italischen und griechischen
Fibelhandwerk des 8. und 7. Jahr-
hunderts, *HambBeitr.* III, 1, 1-39.

Kilian, K. 1975.
Trachtzubehör der Eisenzeit zwis-
chen Ägäis und Adria, *PZ* 50, 9-
140.

Kilian, K. 1977a
Zwei italische Kammhelme aus
Griechenland, *BCH Suppl.* IV, 429-
442.

Kilian, K. 1977b
Das Kriegergrab von Tarquinia.
Beigaben aus Metall und Holz, *JdI*
92, 24-98.

Kilian, K. 1977c
Zwei italienische Neufunde der
Früheisenzeit aus Olympia, *AKorrBl*
7, 121-126.

Kilian, K. 1983.
In: *Herrmann 1983,* Discussion, pp.
357-358.

Kilian-Dirlmeier, I. 1993
Die Schwerter in Griechenland
(ausserhalb der Peloponnes), Bul-
garien und Albanien, *PBF* IV, 12.

Kossack, G. 1949/50
Über italische Cinturoni, *PZ*
XXXIV, 132-147.

Kossack, G. 1992
Lebensbilder, mythische
Bilderzählung und Kultfestbilder.
Bemerkungen zu Bildszenen auf
einer Thronlehne von Verrucchio,
in: *Festschrift zum 50jährigen Beste-*
hen des Institutes für Ur- und
Frühgeschichte der Leopold-Franzens-
Universität Innsbruck, eds. Lippert, A.
& Spindler, K. Bonn, 231-246.

Kyrieleis, H. 1986a
Etruskische Bronzen aus dem Heraion von Samos, *AM* 101, 127-
136.

Kyrieleis, H. 1986b
Chios and Samos in the Archaic
Period, in: *Chios. A conference at the*

Homereion in Chios, eds. Boardman, J. & Vaphopoulou-Richardson, C.E., Oxford, 187-204.

Magi, F. 1969
L'ossuario di Montescudaio, in: *Atti del primo simposio internazionale di protostoria italiana, Fondazione per il Museo "Claudio Faina"* Orvieto. Roma, 121-133.

Mangani, A. 1988-1989
Castelnuovi Berardenga (Siena). L'orientalizzante recente in Etruria settentrionale: Tomba A della necropoli principesca del Poggione (1980). *NSc.* XLII-XLIII, 5-82.

Martelli, M. 1995
Circolazioni dei beni, santuari e stile del potere nell' Orientalizzante, in: *Atti VII Giornata Archeologica. Viaggi e commerci nell'antichità*,- Università di Genova. Facoltà di Lettere, 9-26.

Marzoli, D. 1989
Bronzefeldflaschen in Italien, in: *PBF* II, 4.

Mehren, M. v. 1993
The Murlo Frieze Plaques, in: *Deliciae Fictiles*, 139-145.

Merhart, G.V. 1956-1957
Geschnürte Schienen, *BerRGK*, 37-38, 91-147.

Moltesen, M. 1981
En forfalskningshistorie, *Meddel-Glypt* 37, 51-69.

Moltesen, M. 1987
Wolfgang Helbig. Brygger Jacobsens Agent i Rom 1887-1914. København.

Montanari, G.B. 1987
La Formazione della città in Emilia Romagna. II. Bologna. Museo Civico Archeologico. 26 settembre 1987-24 gennaio 1988. Bologna.

Moretti, M. 1970
Trevignano Romano. Tomba dei Flabelli. *In Nuovi Tesori*, Viterbo, 23-31.

Morigi Govi, C. - Tovoli, S. 1993
Due piccoli scudi di bronzo e il problema dell'armamento nella societa villanoviana Bolognese, *ArchCl* XLV, 1-54.

Müller-Karpe, H. 1974
Beiträge zu italienischen und griechischen Bronzefunden, in: *PBF* XX, 1.

Muscarella, O.W. 1989
King Midas of Phrygia and the Greeks, in: *Anatolia and the Ancient Near East. Studies in Honor of Tahsin Özgüc*, eds. Emre, K. et al., Ankara, 333-344.

Pareti, L. 1947
La Tomba Regolini-Galassi del Museo Gregoriano Etrusco e la civiltà della Italia centrale nel sec. VII a. c. Città del Vaticano.

Phillips, K.M. 1993
In the Hills of Tuscany. Recent Excavations at the Etruscan Site of Poggio Civitate (Murlo, Siena). Philadelphia.

Prayon, F. 1975
Frühetruskische Grab-und Hausarchitektur. RM Erg.H. 22. Heidelberg.

Prayon, F. 1998
Una disamina, in: *Bonghi Jovino 1998*, 35-39.

Rathje, A. 1979
Oriental Imports in Etruria in the Eight and Seventh Centuries B.C.: Their Origins and Implications, in: *Italy Before the Romans*, eds. Ridgway, D. and F.R., London/New York/San Francisco, 145-183.

Rathje, A. 1993
Il fregio di Murlo: Status sulle considerazioni, in: *Deliciae Fictiles*, 135-138.

Rathje, A. 1994
Banquet and Ideology. Some New Considerations about Banquetting at Poggio Civitate, in: *Murlo and the Etruscans. Art and Society in Ancient Etruria*, eds. De Puma, R.D. & Small, J.P., Wisconsin, 95-99.

Rathje, A. 1997
Gli Etruschi e gli altri: il caso di Veio, in: *Bartoloni 1997*, 201-205.

Reade, J.E. 1995
The Symposium in Ancient Mesopotamia: Archaeological Evidence, in: *In vino veritas*, eds. Murray, O. & Tecusan, M., Oxford, 35-56.

Ridgway, D., Deriu, A. & Boitani, F. 1985
Provenance and Firing Techniques of Geometric Pottery from Veii: A Mössbauer Investigation, *BSA* 80, 139-150.

Ridgway, D. 1991
In margine al Villanoviano evoluto di Veio, *ArchCl* XLIII, 157-167.

Ridgway, D. 1992
The First Western Greeks. Cambridge.

Rieth, A. 1964
Ein etruskischer Rundschild, in: *AA* 79, 101-110.

Rizzo, M.A. 1989
Cerveteri – Il Tumulo di Montetosto, in: *Atti I*, 153–161.

Santoro, P. 1977
Colle del Forno. Loc. Montelibretti (Roma). Relazione di scavo sulle campagne 1971-1974 nella necropoli, *NSc* 1977, 211-298.

Santoro, P. 1986
I Sabini e il Tevere. *Archeologia Laziale* VII, 2, *QuadAEI* 12, 111-123.

Schichilone, G. 1973
San Severino Marche, *StEtr* XLI, 515-517.

Söldner, M. 1994
Ein italischer Dreifusswagen in Olympia, *OlBer.* IX, 209-226.

Stary, P.F. 1981.
Zur früheisenzeitlichen Bewaffnung und Kampfesweise in Mittelitalien. Marburger Studien zur Vor- und Frühgeschichte. Band 3.

Steingräber, S. 1979
Etruskische Möbel. Rom.

Steingräber S. 1993
L'Architettura funeraria chiusina, in: *La Civiltà di Chiusi e del suo territorio, Chianciano Terme 28. maggio-1. giugno 1989.*
Atti del XVII Convegno di Studi Etruschi ed Italici, firenze 171-182.

Steingräber, S. 1997
Le culte des morts et les monuments de pierre des nécropoles étrusques, in: *Gaultier-Briquel 1997,* 97-116.

Strøm, I. 1971
Problems Concerning the Origin and Development of the Etruscan Orientalizing Style. Odense.

Strøm, I. 1984
Aspetti delle aristocrazie fra VIII e VII sec. a. C. Problemi riguardanti l'influsso dei paesi mediterranei sulla formazione delle città etrusche e il ruolo delle aristocrazie, *OPUS* III, 355-365.

Strøm, I. 1986
Decorated bronze sheet from a chair, in: *Italian Iron Age Artefacts in the British Museum. Papers of the Sixth British Museum Classical Colloquium,* ed. Swaddling, J., London, 53-57.

Strøm, I. 1989
Orientalising Bronze Reliefs from Chiusi, *ARID* XVII-XVIII, 7-27.

Strøm, I. 1990
Relations between Etruria and Campania around 700 BC, in: *Greek Colonists and Native Populations. Proceedings of the First Australian Congress of Classical Archaeology held in honour of Emeritus Professor A.D. Trendall. Sydney 9-14 July 1985,* ed. Descoeudres, J.-P., Oxford, 87-97.

Strøm, I. 1997.
Conclusioni, in: *Bartoloni 1997,* 245-247.

Strøm, I. 1998.
The Early Sanctuary of the Argive Heraion and its External Relations (8th - Early 6th Cent. B.C.) Bronze Imports and Archaic Greek Bronzes, *ProcDIA* II, 37-125.

Toms, J. 1986
The relative chronology of the Villanovan cemetery of Quattro Fontanili at Veii, *AION* VIII, 41-97.

Toms, J. 1997
La prima ceramica geometrica a Veio, in: *Bartoloni 1997,* 85-88.

Vlad Borelli, L. 1973
Il canopo di Dolciano: evidenze e perplessità dopo un restauro, *StEtr* XLI, 203-236.

Völling, T. 1998
Ein phrygischer Gürtel aus Olympia, *AA* 1998, 243-252.

Waarsenburg, D.J. 1995
Satricum III. The Northwest Necropolis of Satricum. An Iron Age Cemetery in Latium Vetus. Amsterdam.

Woytowitsch, E. 1978
Die Wagen der Bronze- und frühen Eisenzeit in Italien, in: *PBF* XVII, 1.

Zevi, F. 1977
Alcuni aspetti della necropoli di Castel di Decima, *PP* CLXXV, 241-273.

Young, R.S. 1981
Three Great Early Tumuli. The Gordion Excavations. Final Reports. Volume I. Philadelphia.

The Utopia of Xenophon

Bodil Due

I have given my article the title Xenophon's Utopia to announce in advance the angle from which I intend to present the *Cyropaedia*. Utopia is – as so much of our literary, political or philosophical terminology – derived from Greek, although not a term actually used in Antiquity. We owe it to Thomas More who coined it in 1516 for his book describing an imaginary island with a perfect social and political system. It means a no-where land, from *οὐ* and *τόπος*, and is used to designate an idealized place or model-state, or the description of, or dream of, or plan to create such a place.

In my opinion it makes sense to use the term to describe Xenophon's work on the education of the founder of the Achaemenid dynasty in the same way as it makes sense to describe Plato's *Republic* as a Utopia. They both discuss many different subjects in these works, e.g. justice, marriage, slavery, the division of labour; but their main concern is how to establish a sound and stable human society. The two works are admittedly very different in form, in style, and in content, but I suggest regarding them as contributions to the lively debate in the 4th century BC on the ideal form of government, the ideal leader and the good society. There were other participants – Isocrates and Aristotle – in that debate, but I shall restrict myself here to Xenophon and Plato.

What I intend to do is first to justify such an interpretation of Xenophon's work; secondly to make a short comparison between Xenophon and Plato as regards their attempts to solve the problems they were facing, and thirdly, to comment briefly on the present state of Xenophontic scholarship, especially as regards the *Cyropaedia*.

I. To make my first point, I shall begin by giving a short summary of the content of the book. The title means the upbringing and education of Cyrus; its subject is the life from cradle to grave so to speak, of Cyrus the Great. Thus the setting is Asia in the 6th century BC. The division into 8 books is not Xenophon's and cuts across the natural structure of contents, which is: A formal introduction where Xenophon speaks directly in the first person as the author to his reader (1.1), and as a complement to this an epilogue, again in the first person (8.8). These two chapters form a frame around the main story, which falls in three parts of very uneven length. The first part (1.2-1.6.46) deals with Cyrus' birth, his upbringing and education until his first military command. The second and by far the longest part (2.1-7.5.36) describes his adventures and conquests, among which Sardis and Babylon are the most important. The third part (7.5.37-8.7) gives an account of Cyrus' ideology and administration of his empire, ending with his death.

It has been argued that only the first book answers to the title,[1] but the description in that book of Persian education makes it clear that education is to be taken in a wider sense, meaning education as something which goes on all through life, something which only death brings to an end. Understood in this way, the title applies to the whole work and gives in itself a clue to Xenophon's intentions.[2]

But the most informative passage on the aim of Xenophon is the first chapter, which formed the first part of the frame. James Tatum very appropriately named it the Poetics of the work.[3] There, Xenophon tells his readers about the circumstances and speculations that made him compose the work. He defines his subject as that of ruling and informs us that ruling over human beings seemed impossible, until he found it illustrated in a positive and even excellent way by Cyrus the Great. Therefore he wants to examine Cyrus' family, character and education. His point of departure is the sad reality of political instability in his own time as the very first sentence shows:

The reflection once came to us how many democracies have been overthrown by people who preferred to live under any form of government other than a democracy; and again, how many monarchies and how many oligarchies in times past have been abolished by the people; and how many of those individuals who have aspired to tyranny have either been deposed of once and for all and then very quickly, or if they have continued in power, no matter how short a time, they are objects of wonder as having proved to be wise and happy men.[4]

Xenophon proceeds to comment, not on tyrants or kings but on ordinary men and their relations to their household-slaves, thereby demonstrating that the problem of leadership exists on all levels of human life, in the family as in the state, in the *oikos* as in the *polis*. And he brings in analogies from husbandry, showing shepherds as having an easier task than politicians.

The subject is thus widened to encompass social relations in general; and the aim becomes to demonstrate what values and virtues are important to create a harmonious and stable society and how these can be acquired.

Xenophon gives his answer not in abstract instructions, but through the example of one well-known historical person. And he does not do so through an objective, his-

torically correct narrative. He selects and changes the historical facts to make them fit his purpose. Cyrus was a popular figure in Greek literature, and the Greek audience was presumably familiar with his life and career, for instance through the *Histories* of Herodotus and maybe also through the Persian history of Ctesias, the Greek physician and writer who lived at the court of Artaxerxes, the brother of Cyrus the Younger, and who wrote a *Persica*, which, as we can see from the preserved fragments, was full of gossip and scandals. Xenophon, on the contrary, erases all that might be obnoxious to the harmonious picture he wants to create. To give only one example; he changes the death of Cyrus from the violent one Herodotus gives us, to a peaceful one. In Herodotus 1.201ff. Cyrus dies on the battlefield and is even mocked in death by his conqueror, the queen of the Massagetae, who cuts off his head and drowns it in blood. In Xenophon's version he dies in old age, surrounded by his family and friends, telling them his last will as befits a monarch.[5]

It is therefore better to understand Xenophon's work as fiction, not history. Cicero understood this. In a famous letter to his brother, describing the perfect provincial governor, he writes that Xenophon described Cyrus not to provide a historically true picture, but a representation of a just empire.[6]

Throughout the books, Xenophon depicts Cyrus' actions and behaviour in different situations and towards different characters in order to show the qualities, which in his view were necessary to improve or redeem the sad, confusing conditions of human life. And these qualities are kindness, clemency and concern for other people combined with strength, discipline, especially self-discipline, and the capacity for moral as well as physical endurance. Xenophon describes his hero vis-à-vis his family, friends, enemies, allies, subordinates and slaves, men and women, thus covering the whole social spectre. He pictures him in war and peace, in serious and relaxed surroundings, as a child, a young man, a grown-up and as an old man, thus covering all stages of human life. And he does so always in a paradigmatic and didactic way and always with the conditions of his own times in perspective. To give an example:

In book 2 Cyrus introduces a principle of reward according to merit to his army. The subject is brought up by one of his friends among the Persian aristocrats, but is advocated also by members of the rank and file. Cyrus' motives are reported in the following way:

Now Cyrus wished for the sake of the peers themselves that this measure should be passed, for he thought that they also would be better if they knew that they would be judged by their works and would receive rewards according to merits.[7]

He thus sees the principle as a stimulating and provocative tool and puts the matter to the vote in spite of the warnings of his aristocratic friend who asks:

And do you really believe that the common soldiers will adopt a resolution that each one shall not have an equal share, but that the best shall have preference both in honours and in gifts?[8]

His suspicion is proved ill advised; the rank and file support the proposal, confident of themselves and of their leader's justice and generosity. Later, at his court in Babylon, Cyrus sticks to this principle: recognizing special efforts with special privileges, but also withdrawing them again if people stop making an effort.[9]

Behind this principle it is easy to spot a reaction to the democratic principle of ἰσομοιρία or arithmetical equality to which democratic Athens was committed. Xenophon champions the opinion that people are not equal and therefore should not be treated as if they were. Total arithmetical equality meant to him that persons who were not equal from a moral point of view were given the same opportunities.

Accordingly, if morally inferior persons had the same rights as their betters, the outcome would be that injustice ruled.

Another point where the critique of his own times is evident is in the all-important theme of education. As stated earlier, Xenophon gives in book 1 a description of Persian education, contrasting it explicitly with education in most city-states. In our societies, he says,[10] parents are left free to educate their children as they choose, and adults are left free to live as they please. Prohibitions are laid down only afterwards against certain forms of behaviour and certain punishments are prescribed for certain crimes. The Persian system, on the other hand, is directed towards prevention rather than cure. Education is a public matter, common to all, and goes on all through life with different programmes and functions according to age. In the programme for the boys – girls and, later in the programme for the adults, women being left out – he stresses the moral components. Justice is, he says, considered the most important basic element much as reading and writing in the Greek or Athenian system.

Self-control and obedience, too, are elements of central importance, best learned through the example of the elders. Another item is ascetic or abstemious living. Besides these moral accomplishments the boys are taught practical skills such as shooting or throwing a spear, to which hunting is added at a later stage, as a preparation for war.

The education thus covers both body and soul. This holistic attitude is also preserved for the grown-ups. Hard physical training is a must, even when Cyrus is later installed in Babylon, because the physical efforts are supposed to have a psychological aspect as well, preventing their newly won power from having a corruptive influence on him and on his friends. The purpose of life is ἀρετή, understood as the ability to resist temptations and upholding virtues such as justice, piety, respect for others, loyalty, generosity and tolerance. The possession of these virtues justifies the possession of power. Only those who actually are the best, οἱ ἄριστοι, deserve to reign.

The truth of this is brought home in the last section of the work where Xenophon relates what happened after Cyrus' death. The passage in question, i. e. the last chapter, has been much discussed and some take it to be an interpolation. I hold the opinion that it is genuine, and interpret its meaning and function to be to stress once more the necessity of moral integrity in the leader. Cyrus possessed it, his sons did not, and therefore he was able to stay in power and was obeyed willingly by his subjects. His sons lost it all.

Apart from this ideal picture or dream of the perfect leader, who in a way is greater than life, as are the heroes in Greek tragedy, Xenophon is eager to stress the moral component in ordinary life, even in purely practical pursuits, because they, too, have a social implication. One example among many:

In describing the situation before the first battle (5.3.46ff.) he underlines as important Cyrus' ability to remember the names of his officers and soldiers, using analogies from the world of artisans, physicians and fathers of families, thereby making the point instructive for everyone who has to make decisions of social importance. And his conclusion with regard to the detrimental consequences of collective responsibility carries conviction on more than one level. Again it is easy to spot a connection to certain elements and episodes in Athenian society and history.[11] And again I find it reasonable to interpret Xenophon's aim as that of pointing to another and better human society than the one he and his contemporaries knew.

Against the background of the various and unsuccessful attempts to create a stable empire in the 5th and 4th century BC, – attempts made by Athens, Sparta and Thessaly – Xenophon advocates a system built on tolerance and self-restraint instead of oppression and brutality. He recommends that the leader wins the loyalty of his subjects by affection and generosity, and that the vanquished nations be treated with kindness and clemency. The empire he envisages is a multi-ethnical one where the ruling class consists of people from many different nationalities, composed of individuals who each have attained their position by their personal merits and achievements, not by nationality, birth or riches. Thus Cyrus' friends are Persians, Medes, Armenians, Bactrians and others. Xenophon's Utopia has a strong affinity to the attempt later made by Alexander – or maybe it is more correct to interpret Alexander's dream of a fusion between Greeks and Persians as inspired by the ideology of Xenophon's Cyrus.[12] Alexander, however, did not succeed, whereas in Cyrus' world the fusion between the Persians and Medes is said to have occurred without any conflict at all.

II. Passing now to a short comparison with Plato: I said earlier that Cicero read the *Cyropaedia* as a representation of a just empire. To create such a state was also the ambition of Plato in the *Republic* and later in the *Laws*. In this article I shall restrict myself to the *Republic*. In this work Plato constructs a system divided in classes, which each has a specific function to fulfil. The kings and rulers are philosophers who have earned their right to rule by being the best. Different rights, duties and rewards are bestowed upon the different classes according to their function in society. There is therefore equality within the different classes, but not between them. As in Xenophon, this is a reaction against the arithmetical equality, which was advocated by Athenian democracy. And as in Xenophon's Utopia, education plays a dominant role in Plato's. In the *Republic* the upbringing and education of the guardians are described in great detail. Apart from justice, most importance is attached to obedience, training and abstemious living, as was the case in the *Cyropaedia*.

Luxury is likewise viewed as the road to decadence. Training is also seen as having a psychological effect and there is the same linking together of the health of body and mind. The idea that the leader has a moral obligation to be better than everyone else, and totally without flaws, is valid for the guardians and especially for the philosophers, as it was for Cyrus and his friends. And the ultimate and declared goal for both writers is stability.

Nevertheless the differences between them are obvious. Xenophon chose a hierarchic system based on the personal qualities of one individual. His ideal state is built on an analogy between οἶκος and πόλις. His leader feels responsible for all members of the community just as a father does for all the members of his οἶκος, and he is in return regarded as a father by his subjects. Stability is secured by personal bonds and emotions. The reign envisaged is not a Greek city-state, but an empire of huge proportions.

Plato stays within the framework of the city-state and within the Greek world. But in his Utopia private households are abolished and the traditional οἶκος is eliminated. Contrary to Xenophon, he does include women in education, at least in the class of the guardians; but marriage and children are not a private or personal matter, but a public affair arranged and controlled by the rulers. The purpose of this is to prevent the development of specific bonds or inclinations for specific persons. If parents do not know their children or children their parents, there will not be any paternal or filial love. The members of the different classes are supposed to identify themselves with the polis because they do not have any individuality, except as a member of their class and state. Individuality, personal bonds and especially personal property are seen as the root of conflict. Thus where Xenophon stressed the importance of the individual, Plato tried to minimize the individualistic element as much as possible.

To conclude: Xenophon gave a pseudo-historical reconstruction of the life and career of a character well established in Greek literature, using practical illustration and exemplification; Plato described an abstract ideal state analysing the problem systematically and in the abstract. Xenophon, apparently in nostalgia, looked to the past, although a fictitious past; Plato looked to the future, but actually they both had their own times in mind, trying to remedy what they agreed was far from perfect.

III. To pass now to my third and last item: Xenophontic scholarship especially as regards the *Cyropaedia*. Xenophon and his Utopia were much admired in earlier times from the Romans to the 18th century.[13] But in this century he, and especially the *Cyropaedia*, fell out of fashion. Xenophon was considered a dull, second-rate author, and as late as in 1968 G. L. Cawkwell called the *Cyropaedia* one of the most tedious works from Antiquity.[14] Since then Xenophontic scholarship has undergone not a renaissance, but a metamorphosis. These are the words used in the invitation to a forthcoming international conference with the title: *The world of Xenophon*. In the invitation, the organizers Christopher Tuplin and Graham Oliver speculate on the reason for this change of heart; and I shall end my article by doing so for the *Cyropaedia* in particular. During the last nine years, no less than four monographs have been dedicated to that particular work. In 1989 James Tatum published his *Xenophon's Imperial Fiction*, and in the same year came my own *The Cyropaedia, Xenophon's Aims and Methods*; in 1993 came Deborah Levine Gera's *Xenophon's Cyropaedia. Style, Genre and Literary Technique,* and in 1995 C. Müeller-Goldingen published *Untersuchungen zu Xenophon's Kyrupaedie.*[15] In 1992 a new German-Greek edition was published by Rainer Nickel; in the same year came a Spanish-Greek edition by Alvarez Rosa de Santiago, and in 1996 Franco Ferrari published an edition with an Italian translation and notes. This new interest is based on several trends in scholarship: 1. A literary interest in genre studies and in the Ancient Novel, 2. A new trend of socio-economic history, the so-called civic humanism or conceptual history, 3. The history of mentality, and 4. The remarkable development in Achaemenid Persian Studies. Xenophon knew more about Persia than most of his contemporaries and is not easily accused of having quite the simplified prejudices about East and West or Europeans and Orientals that Saïd's famous Book from 1975 succeeded in showing as inherent in the minds of so many Greek and European authors. St. Hirsch' book *The Friendship of the Barbarians* opened this line in 1985, and since then a number of contributions have been published in the *Achaemenid History*: the Proceedings of a number of conferences held in Groningen and London since 1981.

The current discussion of multi-ethnic societies may, too, have tipped the scales in favour of the *Cyropaedia*. It has, undoubtedly, increased interest in the Hellenistic period in general; and Xenophon was in many ways a forerunner of Hellenistic values and conceptions. And last, but not least, the world-wide interest in moral questions, in ethical behaviour, in political correctness and in leadership or – to use a modern term, very appropriate for Xenophon – management may serve as an explanation. In 1985 Helene Sancisi-Weerdenburg stated: "In short, The Cyropaedia contains too much virtue for our age".[16] That appears no longer to be the case.

Notes

NOTE 1
Breitenbach 1967, 1707a.

NOTE 2
See Higgins 1977, 54; Nickel 1989, 57;
Tatum 1989, 90f. and Due 1989, 15.

NOTE 3
Tatum 1989, 37 ff.

NOTE 4
Cyr. 1.1. The translations are all W. Miller's
from the Loeb-editions 1914 (London).

NOTE 5
In Ctesias he dies after having been
wounded in battle, but surrounded by his
sons.

NOTE 6
Cic. *Q. fr.* 1.1.23.

NOTE 7
Cyr. 2.2.21.

NOTE 8
Cyr. 2.2.20.

NOTE 9
Cyr. 8.4.3ff.

NOTE 10
Cyr. 1.2.2.

NOTE 11
Xenophon gave an example in his historical work, the *Hellenica*, with the description
in 1.7 of the trial of the generals after the
battle of Arginousai.

NOTE 12
See Due 1993, 53ff.

NOTE 13
See for this the excellent chapter, "The rise
of a novel" in James Tatum 1989, 36 ff.

NOTE 14
G. L. Cawkwell, 1968, 50ff.

NOTE 15
In Princeton N.Y, Aarhus, Oxford and
Stuttgart, respectively.

NOTE 16
H. Sancisi-Weerdenburg, 1985, 459ff.

Bibliography

Breitenbach, H.R. 1967
Xenophon, in: RE IXA,2 cols
1567ff. Stuttgart.

Cawkwell, G-L. 1966-68
A Diet of Xenophon, *Didaskalos* II,
2, 50 ff.

Due, B. 1989
*The Cyropaedia, Xenophon's Aims and
Methods.* Aarhus

Due, B. 1993
Alexander's Inspiration and Ideas,
in: *Alexander the Great, Reality and
Myth* (Analecta Romana Instituti
Danici, suppl. XX), Rome 53ff.

Ferrari, F. 1995
Senofonte, Ciropedia. 2 vols. Milano

Levine Gera, D. 1993
*Xenophon's Cyropaedia, Style, Genre
and Literary Technique.* Oxford

Higgins, W.E. 1977
Xenophon the Athenian. Albany N.Y.

Hirsch, St. W. 1985
The Friendship of the Barbarians.
Hanover and London

Nickel, R. 1979
Xenophon (Erträge der Forschung,
Bd 111). Darmstadt

Nickel, R. 1992
*Xenophon, Kyrupaedie. Die Erziehung
des Kyros.* Greek & German. Tusculum

Sancisi-Weerdenburg, H. 1985
The death of Cyrus: Xenophon's
Cyropaedia as a source for Iranian
History, A*cta Iranica* 25, 459-472.

Sancisi-Weerdenburg, H. 1987
The fifth oriental Monarchy, and
Hellenocentrism. Cyropaedia VIII
and its influence, in: *Achaemenid
History II: The Greek sources,* Leiden,117- 131

Schmeling, G. (ed.) 1996
The Novel in the Ancient World. Leiden, New york, Köln

Tatum, J. 1989
Xenophon's Imperial Fiction. Princeton N.Y.

Tuplin, Ch. 1990
Persian Decor in Cyropaedia, in:
*Achaemenid History V: The roots of the
Europaean Tradition,* Leiden, 17-29

Cultic Theatres and Ritual Drama in Ancient Greece[1]

Inge Nielsen

Introduction:

The subject of this article is to illuminate an obscure aspect of Greek religion, namely the ritual drama, by studying an installation, which is often present in Greek sanctuaries, namely the cultic theatre. I shall argue that this structure primarily constituted the setting for ritual dramas, rather than only for well-known rituals such as sacrifices or, sometimes, for literary drama, that is, basically, tragedy, comedy, and satyr play. The ritual drama may be defined as a dramatic ritual based on the myth of the god and thus furnished with a plot, performed at the great seasonal feasts. In contrast to the literary drama, the ritual drama *must* treat the myth of the god at whose feast it was performed. The reason why the ritual drama was so important in ancient religions is that it constituted a good way to learn and to understand the contents of the cults in a basically non-literary society.

Ritual dramas were first performed at the great agrarian feasts of the fertility gods in the Near East and in Egypt. It is thus no coincidence that it was exactly in connection with this type of gods that we have the first signs of the ritual drama in Greece, and neither that it was in connection with one of them, Dionysos, that the literary drama was developed. That such ritual dramas continued to be performed also in the poleis may not surprise us, since most of the inhabitants were still occupied on the land. Besides, these gods might change and enlarge their repertoire when the society to which they belonged, changed. For example was this the case in the orientalizing period, that is, the Late

8th – 7th century BC, when contacts with the Orient were re-established after the Dark Ages. Another such time of change was the Hellenistic period (330-30 BC), when the basically agrarian society developed into a cosmopolitan one, with travelling merchants and slaves dispersing all over the known world.

As far as Greek drama is concerned, it is almost exclusively the literary drama that comes to mind, and for very good reasons, since Greece was the place where this unique drama form originated. Of course scholars have also focused on the origin/s of tragedy, comedy and satyr plays, the most common opinion being that they originated from Greek chorus performances at the great feasts.[2] Only a few scholars, and then mostly historians of religion and anthropologists, have compared the early stages of Greek drama with drama forms existing in other cultures in antiquity.[3] I shall argue that it is very important to include the Oriental, that is, Egyptian, Near Eastern and Anatolian, drama forms in this connection, too. For although the ultimate result of the development of drama in Greece was the unique literary drama, the early stages were by no means unique, indeed, they seem to constitute a loan during the prolific orientalizing period from the Oriental ritual drama, which was known in these areas from early on.

In Egypt, such dramas are documented as early as the Old Kingdom, in the form of texts constituting librettos as well as of depictions showing such performances.[4] They were especially connected to the myth of Osiris. From the Ptolemaic peri-

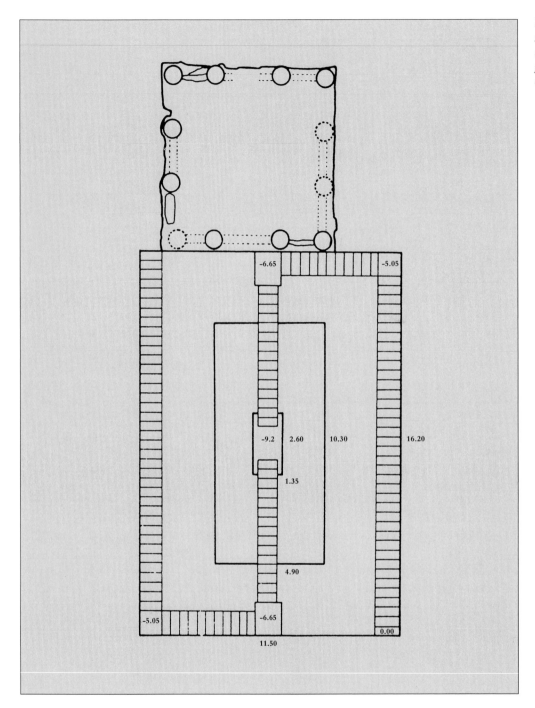

Fig. 1. The sacred lake in the sanctuary in Tod in the Nile delta. To this lake, a well-preserved pavilion was attached (from Gessler-Löhr 1983, Abb. 68).

od we even have an entire ritual drama preserved with illustrations in relief from the temple of Edfou, taking as its theme the fight between Horus, the owner of the sanctuary, and Seth, disguised as a hippopotamus.[5] This drama, the Triumph of Horus, constituted at the same time a symbol of the first beginning of Egyptian kingship and Egypt´s perpetual triumph over her enemies. These Egyptian dramas were normally enacted around the sacred lakes in the great temenoi. Related to these lakes were pavilions and platforms, on which the acting priests and priestesses, many of whom were carrying masks, stood, and where the images of the gods were placed during the performances[6] (Fig. 1). The chorus stood around the lake, as did the worshippers, who participated with outcries etc. in the drama as well.

In the Near East, the documents recording such dramas are primarily written on clay tablets, and may be in the form of literary adaptations of such drama texts and of librettos, as well as constitute a kind of book of words for the rituals.[7] But also the presence of masks of various types indicates dramatic performances here from as early as the early 2nd Millennium BC.[8] There is evidence for the performance of ritual dramas already in Sumeria, and they were well-known also by the Assyrians, the Canaanites, the Israelites, and the Phoenicians. The subjects were normally myths related to the great fertility goddess, Inanna/Isthar/Asherah/Astarte, and her paredroi, young gods of crises, whether called Dumuzi, Tammuz, Baal or Adonis. They were mostly performed at the great feasts in the spring, that is, the New Year feasts. Finally the Hittites in Anatolia apparently also included such dramas in the rituals of their gods, primarily, to judge from the texts preserved on clay-tablets, in connection with the Purulli feast.[9] Here, the fertility god Telipinu playing the main role, as a god who in anger disappeared with the corn, a theme also known from the myth of Demeter. Other subjects typical of ritual dramas are fights between gods and daemons or monsters, and the disappearance

and return of the young gods signifying the renewal of life in plants as well as animals and humans. Finally the sacred marriage rite, *hieros gamos*, between goddess and young god, often impersonated by the king, signified the beginning of a new fruitful year. Thus kings played a central role in these dramas all over the Orient.

In the Greek area, the direct sources for the existence of ritual dramas are fewer. In return, much information may be gleaned from liturgical hymns, from epic poems, and from the literary drama texts.[10] Also, masks of a special type have been found in the Greek sanctuaries, and vase paintings often show masked mythical figures[11] (Fig. 2). Last, but not least, a permanent setting for these dramas, the cultic theatre was developed in these sanctuaries. While this setting, as we shall see, differed considerably from the Oriental ones, the subjects for the ritual dramas in Greece were rather similar. Thus the ritual drama was always based on the myth of the god and dependent on the feast at which it was performed. In Athens, for example, one may mention the myth of the hieros gamos between Dionysos and Ariadne played by the archon basileus and his wife, the basilinna, at the Anthesteria feast. This was originally a vine grower´s festival, and probably also a kind of transitional feast for the youth.[12] The feasts of the Thesmophoria, for Demeter, apparently included the disappearance of the corn due to the anger of the goddess, as recounted in the Homeric hymn, as well as the abduction and return of Persephone.[13] In the sanctuary of Artemis Ortheia in Sparta, the drama was, like the goddess, apparently of Oriental origin. It included a fight between monster and young paredros, according to the masks found there, and also, to judge from the hymns of Alkman, the hieros gamos.[14] Also in Samothrace, there are indications for a ritual drama including a hieros gamos, this time with Kadmos and Harmoneia as protagonists, as well as, probably, a fight with the dragon.[15] A similar fight is recorded in Delphi, this time between Apollo and Python at the

feast called Septarion. We hear from Plutarch that Apollo was played by a youth followed by young men with torches. A table was set up in front of the hut of Python. The table was then turned over and the hut set on fire, and when Python was killed, they ran away to all sides.[16] Finally, of the many myths related to Dionysos we have evidence that at least some were used for ritual dramas as well, including his childhood on Mount Nysa and the Pentheus story (v.i.).

The performers of these dramas were, in the beginning, primarily the priests and officials of the sanctuaries, as was the case in the Orient. From the Hellenistic period, however, it became increasingly the members of the cultic groups, *koina*, related to the god and/or the sanctuary, who performed. Especially well known are the Dionysian Technitai, groups of professional actors who first appear in the 4th century BC, and who primarily performed in the literary dramas; but there were many oth-

Fig. 3. Grave stele from Magnesia in Asia Minor showing a member of a Dionysian boukoloi koina. He is clad in bukskin and carries a mask (from Merkelbach 1988, Zeichnung 3).

Fig. 4. The "theatre" in the west court of the palace of Phaistos, dating from the first palatial period (1900-1700 BC (photo IN).

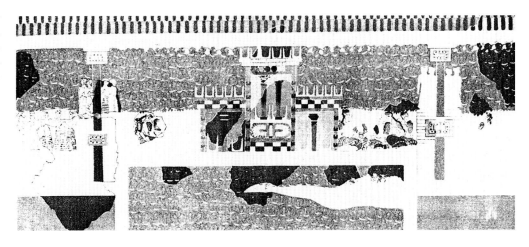

Fig. 5. Drawing of the Grand Stand Fresco from the palace of Knossos, where at lest some of the audience surveying ceremonies in the courtyard is represented as seated (from Marinatos 1993, fig. 5).

ers. These koina are among the most interesting and characteristic institutions in the Hellenistic and Roman world.[17] For example, the members of the famous Iobacchoi koinon in Athens apparently participated in dramatic performances, since various roles as gods played by them are mentioned in the inscription recording the rules of this association. Also, we have an inscription of such a *thiasos* from Magnesia in Asia Minor, which refers to a performance of the childhood of Dionysos. Thus the parts of *pappas*, that is, foster-father, undoubtedly Silenus, and of *hypotrophos*, that is nurse, which might be Ino or one of the Nymphs of Nysa are mentioned. And Lucian, who wrote in the 2nd century AD, recounts that the Ionians witnessed performances with corybants, satyrs, and *bukoloi* (that is, initiates into the mysteries of Dionysos), at a public Dionysos feast (Fig. 3). He states that the performers were men of a high esteem in the city, and not professionals; one may imagine that they were members of Dionysian thiasoi.[18]

The Setting

A very important source for the existence of ritual dramas in Greece is the presence of a setting for them, the cultic theatre.[19] While in the Orient these settings were rather ephemeral or multi-functional, a specific building was apparently regarded as necessary in Greece, and was to become a very visible element in the Greek sanc-

tuaries. I shall in this connection only briefly mention the interesting theatrical structures found in some Minoan palaces, since they may well be a result of an early contact with the Near East and with Egypt, if, which seems possible, ritual dramas were indeed performed in them[20] (Fig. 4). What is interesting as far as these structures and the depictions of them in the wall paintings are concerned, is that they reveal a tradition for the spectators to be seated on such occasions, documented here for the first time; in the Near East and in Egypt worshippers stood during the rituals (Fig. 5). This difference persists during the entire antiquity.

In the Greek mainland, there are no signs of theatrical installations neither in the Mycaenean palaces, nor in the sanctuaries of the Dark Ages. Thus it was apparently in the orientalizing period, when contacts with the Near East and Egypt were re-established, that the first signs of ritual dramas and settings for them, turn up in the Greek sanctuaries, although there may well already have existed some kind of dramatic performances in the local cults. The Phoenician traders who roamed the Mediterranean did not only deal in merchandise, but also settled in trading colonies in the Greek area, and introduced their own gods, such as Asherah, Astarte, Adonis and Melchart, to this new environment. These gods then underwent a Greek interpretation, to Artemis Ortheia and Aphrodite, to a Greek Adonis, and to

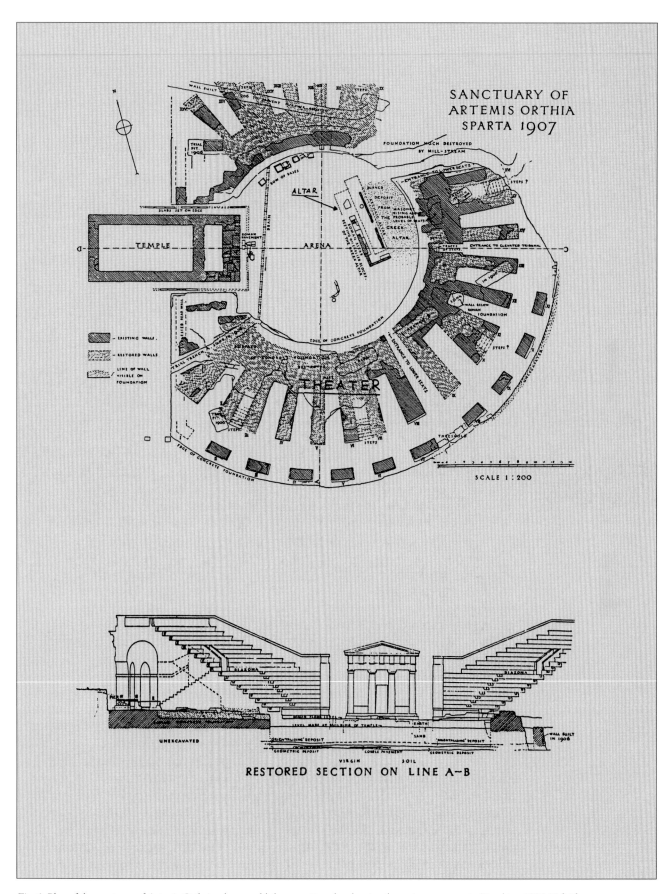

Fig. 6. Plan of the sanctuary of Artemis Ortheia, above, and below, a section also showing the various pavements (Dawkins 1929, Taf. 3f).

Fig. 7. Sparta. The round structure with steps and orthostates, situated on the southern slope of the Acropolis (photo IN).

Heracles. It was precisely in the sanctuary of one of these gods, (Artemis) Ortheia, that we have the first indication that ritual dramas were performed. Thus it has recently been shown that the hymns, which Alkman wrote to this goddess already in the late 7th century BC, have a great similarity to hymns reflecting ritual dramas in Sumeria.[21] Also, masks of the two types common also in the Near East, namely a demonic mask and one of a young man, have been found in this sanctuary, on and below a round area with a pavement dating to around 600 BC[22] (Fig. 2). That this area flanked by the altar was, in fact, an orchestra from the beginning is indicated by its having been transformed into a proper cultic theatre in the late Hellenistic period, although it is only monumentally preserved from the Roman period (Fig. 6). Another indication that there was, indeed, an early theatre there is the presence of a similar, round, structure

in Sparta itself, on the southern slope of the Acropolis, dating back to the 5th century BC and probably i.a. used for ritual purposes, perhaps in connection with the feast of Apollo Karneios[23] (Fig. 7).

Many cultic theatres were like the one in the sanctuary of Ortheia transformed in later times, so that their original form remains uncertain, although we are positive that they existed. This is the case with two cultic theatres in Athens. The oldest one existed already in the middle of the 6th century BC on the Agora. This *hieros kyklos*, a designation proving that this structure, or orchestra, was round, was situated near the altar of the Twelve gods west of the Panathenaic Way.[24] It was used both for political purposes and for rituals in connection, undoubtedly, with the sanctuary of Dionysos Lenaios, to which cult ritual dramas were often related, as were, later, literary ones. Although there

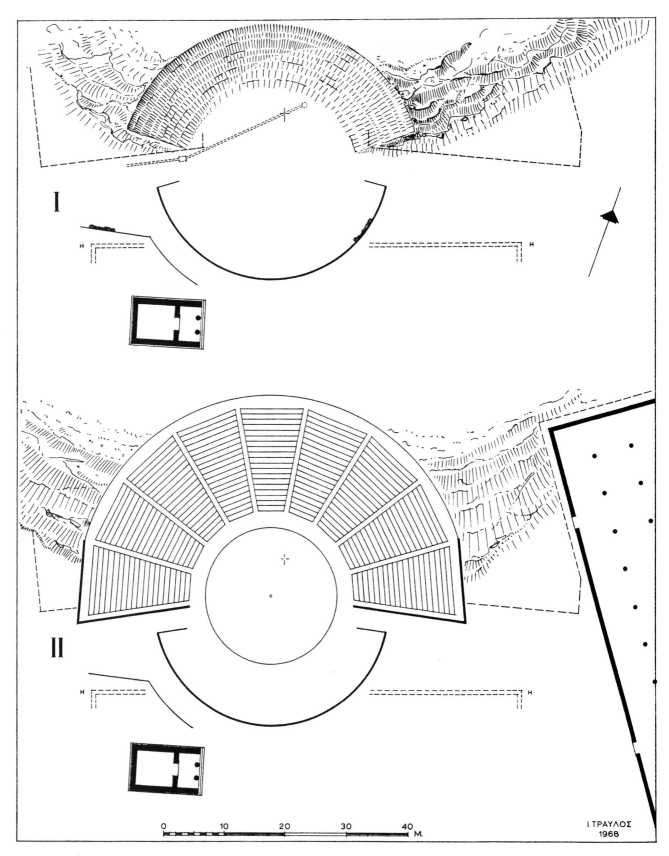

I

II

I.ΤΡΑΥΛΟΣ
1968

0   10   20   30   40
M.

Fig. 8. Athens. Plan of the sanctuary of Dionysos before the restoration by Lycurgus. In fact, the orchestra may well have been rectangular in these early phases. (from Travlos 1971, fig. 677).

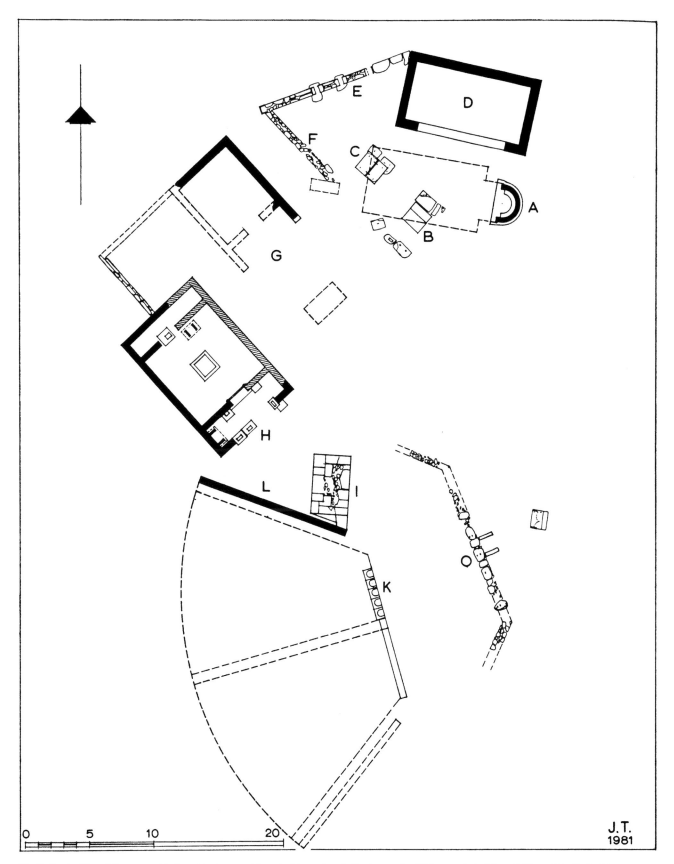

Fig. 9. Ikaria. Plan of the agora with the cultic theatre, with prohedria, and probably the temple of Dionysos in building G. That of Apollo Pythios is building H (from Travlos 1988, fig. 98).

were no permanent seats in this theatre, we hear of scaffoldings with seats in wood, *ikria*, from the written sources, and traces of such seats have, in fact, been found even earlier in the Achaean colony of Metapontum in Southern Italy.[25] It was on an occasion of the collapse of these Athenian ikria that the dramatic performances were finally moved to the sanctuary of Dionysos Eleuthereus on the southern slope of the Acropolis. In its first phases this famous theatre consisted only of an orchestra of uncertain form, but probably rectangular in shape, and a slope and later wooden seats for the spectators, and there was no barrier between the theatre and the old temple of Dionysos, whose statue we know surveyed the performances[26] (Fig. 8). But when this theatre was finally monumentalized with stone seats and a permanent stage building in the 4th century BC, it became at the same time isolated from the sanctuary of Dionysos and placed outside the temenos wall. It was now used exclusively for literary dramas in connection with the panhellenic festival of the Great Dionysia and for popular assemblies. One may imagine that the ritual dramas, which were undoubtedly still performed in connection with this cult, now took place in front of the new temple in the temenos itself.

At the same time as the first cultic theatres were built in Athens, similar structures were raised in the Attic demes. They were related to the same cult, that of Dionysos Lenaios, whose main feast, the rural Dionysia, a very old agrarian festival, was the scene of ritual dramas from far back. The earliest cultic theatres have been found in the demes which were traditionally closely related to the myth of Dionysos, namely his arrival in Attica, taking place in Thorikos, and his first introduction of vine there, which happened in Ikaria. The latter deme was also said to be the home of the first "literary" tragedian, Thespis, as well as of Susarion, connected with the early stages of the comedy, both

Fig. 10. The cultic theatre of Thoricos. In front, the altar, and in the distance, the temple. The temple court, in the middle, was flanked by the seats on one side, and supported by a terrace wall on the other (photo IN).

belonging to the middle of the 6th century BC. The cultic theatre of Ikaria goes back at least to the 5th century BC and is situated in the agora, where Dionysos Lenaios was traditionally worshipped.[27] It is a very primitive structure, consisting only of a slope and a supporting wall for the orchestra. Later, prohedria seats were added, but there is no trace of a stage (Fig. 9). One may compare with the cultic theatre in Rhamnous, from the same period.[28] The same is also the case in Thorikos, where, however, the theatre developed further than that of Ikaria, for although the first theatre consisted only of a slope facing a terrace with the temple at one end, stone seats were added in the 5th and 4th century BC[29] (Fig. 10). In all instances, the seats always remained basically linear, something which is typical of many cultic theatres, undoubtedly a reflection of the early ikria of wood placed at one side of the orchestra, as in the agora of Athens. Also dedicated to Dionysos and closely related to those of Thoricos and Athens,

was the theatre of Eretria, in Euboea, which dates back to the 5th century BC and is placed perpendicular to the temple, which in its present form dates from the 4th century BC[30] (Fig. 11).

It is, however, worth noting that although Dionysos was the god of literary drama par excellence, this was not the case with ritual drama, in fact only rather few theatres have been found in his sanctuaries outside Attica. Even in Attica, the sanctuaries of other gods were furnished with cultic theatres from an early period, too. This was for example the case with Amphiaraos, a healing god, in whose sanctuary a primitive cultic theatre with stone seats was built in its first phase in the centre of the sanctuary facing the altars (Fig. 12). It was later almost entirely pulled down and replaced by another, more canonical festival theatre at the edge of the sanctuary.[31] Also Apollo was furnished with such rites from early on. This was as mentioned the case in Delphi, where an archaic ritual drama, mentioned by Plutarch, took as its theme the god´s fight over the sanctuary with its original owner, the snake-god Python, son of Gaia. This took place on an orchestra placed just below the temple, in the area in front of the Stoa of the Athenians, whose steps could thus be used by the spectators. Later, others seats, in form of exedrae, were put up around this area.[32] Another example is the cultic theatre from the 5th century BC in the sanctuary of Apollo Temitis in Syracuse[33] (Fig. 13).

From the 4th century BC onwards, quite a lot of cultic theatres have been preserved in Greek sanctuaries all over the Greek world, belonging to many different gods and with a great variety of shapes. These cultic theatres differed both in architecture and in function from the canonic theatres, which at this time were being built in many Greek cities, partly for the literary drama festivals, and partly to accommodate popular assemblies. Thus the cultic theatres always remained rather primitive

Fig. 12. Oropos. The old cultic theatre facing the altars of the sanctuary of Amphieraros (photo IN).

Fig. 13. Syracuse. The cultic theatre placed on the slope of the Acropolis, just beside the great theatre. It belonged to the sanctuary of Apollo Temitis. The orchestra has disappeared, only the rock-cut seats are left (photo IN).

Fig. 14. Lycosura. The sanctuary of Despoina, with a theatron which at the same time functioned as a terrace wall. The temple was placed very close to the theatron (photo IN).

in form, and are sometimes even difficult to distinguish from terrace walls and staircases, since it is the *theatron*, that is, literally, the place from where one sees, which is normally preserved. But it was not these seats which were the main thing in the cultic theatre, but the area on which the chorus and the priests and officials performed, namely the orchestra. This indicates the great importance of the chorus,

which had ultimately developed from the worshippers themselves performing in the ritual drama. In most sanctuaries, the central area with the altar in front of the temple and with the seats (theatron) facing it constituted the orchestra. Stages were seldom present, instead, the temple facade could sometimes be used as a backdrop, and its steps and pronaos, as well as the altar could constitute a multiple stage. The relationship between temple and theatron never became systematically organized in the Greek sanctuaries, although cultic theatres continued to exist until late Antiquity, this was only to happen in Italy.

A good example of such a theatron, well preserved since it is cut into the rock, is the small one recently found in Corinth, in the sanctuary of the old agrarian goddesses Demeter and Core, to whose cult ritual dramas had belonged from an early period. The theatron was placed on the uppermost terrace and could only house c. 85 spectators. The performance was probably set on the terrace below, constituting the main terrace of the sanctuary, where the temple and their altar was situated.[34] Another theatron has been found in Lykousura, for related goddesses, Despoina, Demeter, and Artemis, in the form of a terrace-like structure along the side of the temple and further along the narrow temenos[35] (Fig. 14). A similar placement is also seen in Demeter's sanctuary in Pergamon, and from the same period, i.e. late 4th to early 3rd century BC. This large structure, which was 30 m long and had 11 rows of seats, functioned at the same time as a terrace wall[36] (Fig. 15). Whether the interesting structure with seats in Eleusis, facing the Southern Court, belonged to this period or only to the 2nd century AD, is uncertain. In any case it is clearly a theatron for watching what went on in this court. The rites may have had connections to the mysteries, where we know that dramas were per-

Fig. 15. Pergamon. A similar situation as in Lycusura applies in this monumental sanctuary of Demeter; here, however, the theatron faced a great altar and continued along the entire length of the sanctuary (photo IN).

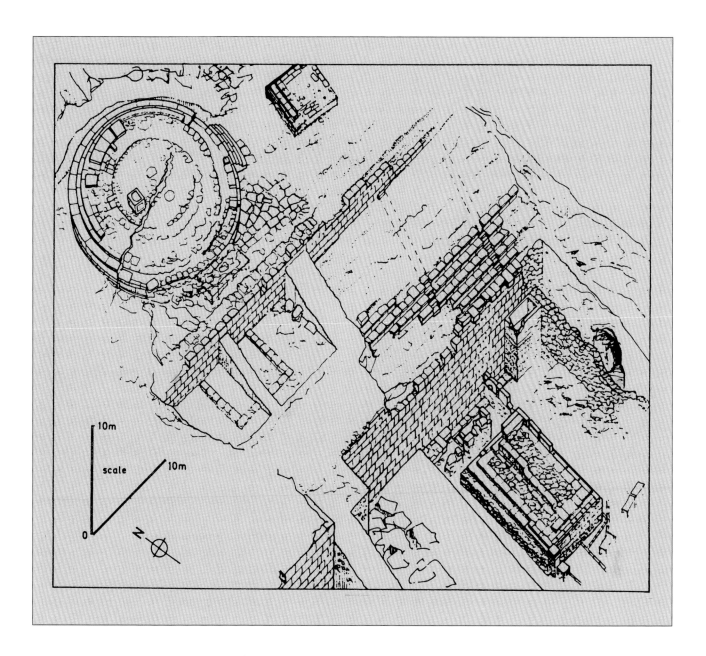

Fig. 16. Knidos. Reconstruction of the theatron, which is here situated on a terrace wall spanning the level between the upper sanctuary of Aphrodite and the lower one of Apollo Karneios. It faced the latter's altar (from Bankel 1997, Abb. 1).

formed in the temenos, but it is also a possibility that the ritual dramas performed here were connected to the Thesmophoria festival.[37] For related chthonic gods, a cultic theatre was also built in Morgantina in Sicily at that time, while on Rhodes, Dionysos Smintheus probably had a sanctuary in Lindos with a fine theatre resting on the slope of the acropolis. At least the Danish expedition related this theatre to a building, which may well have belonged to this god. In nearby Asia Minor ritual dramas connected to Dionysos are well documented.[38] And in the Sanctuary of Apollo Karneios in Knidos, a

cultic theatre was built on the terrace wall dividing it from the sanctuary of Aphrodite with the round temple housing Praxiteles' famous statue of the goddess[39] (Fig. 16). Apollo Karneios was a pan-Doric god who was famous for his feasts, which seem to have included performances of various kinds, to judge from the sources on them especially from Sparta.

In the later Hellenistic period, a cultic theatre was built in the 2nd century BC in the famous sanctuary on Samothrace, which was dedicated to Electra, a relative of Cybele, together with other Megaloi

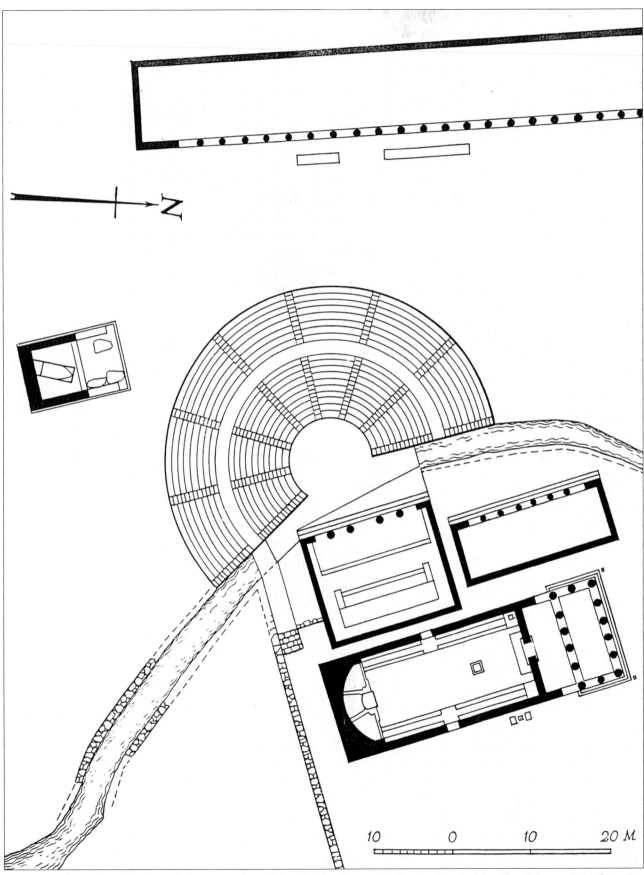

Fig. 17. Samothrace. Plan of the theatron built just across the wadi from the Altar Court, which functioned as a backdrop (from Lehmann 1964, fig. 117).

Theoi. The theatron faced the so-called Altar Court, functioning as a backdrop, on the other side of a brook, which ran dry in the summer[40] (Fig. 17). Closely attached to this cult were Kadmos, the Tyrian prince and later king of Thebes, and Harmoneia, the daughter of Electra and wife of Kadmos. In fact their myth seemingly constituted the subject of a ritual drama which was performed here, during the summer festival (see n. 15). Whether the same or a related subject was also used in the cultic theatre found in the sanctuary of the related gods Kabeiros and Pais near Thebes is unknown. This cultic theatre was coeval with the one on Samothrace, but locally made vases from the 5th to 4th century BC found in the sanctuary showed grotesque figures in dramatic scenes, indicating that the tradition to perform ritual dramas went further back in time in this sanctuary.[41] As in the sanctuary of Ortheia of Sparta, it was the temple itself that functioned as a backdrop for the theatron in Thebes.

The Oriental Cults in the West

In the Hellenistic period a new wave of Oriental cults invaded the Greek area. Although not the main topic of this article, it is, all the same, worth mentioning how these new cults, that is, from Egypt Isis, Osiris, Harpocrates, Anubis and Sarapis, from the Near East Atargatis and Hadad, and from Anatolia Cybele and Attis, adapted to their new homelands in this regard.[42] If ritual dramas were important for the indigenous cults, this was, as already the Phoenicians had experienced, even more the case with the foreign gods, trying to find new worshippers. These cults had to be presented in the most favourable light to prospective new adepts. Since the liturgy was often in a foreign language, at least in the beginning, and since the contents would seem exotic for a Greek, which was indeed one of the reasons why he would be attracted to them, it was very important to be able to explain the cult and its contents, and this could for example be done through the performance of ritual dramas. The parts of the liturgies that were kept and the parts that were left out show to what extent the cult had to adapt to the new society.

Again, this development may be gleaned from the literary religious texts, including hymns and aretalogies, connected to these cults. At the same time, new subjects were added, including myths on how the cult was introduced into the Greek area. The question here is whether the Oriental cults took over the setting for ritual dramas developed in the previous centuries in the Greek sanctuaries, i.e. the cultic theatres, or whether they kept the settings normally used in their sanctuaries in the homelands. This has also to do with the status of the worshippers. The Greek tradition to be seated on these occasions in a certain way made an audience out of the worshippers to a greater extent than when these remained standing in the temenos. At the same time, such a standing audience necessitated that the actors/priests were raised to be seen, often by means of platforms and the like. This was less necessary if the audience was seated on a slope, and in fact stages are seldom present in the early cultic theatres, although there may have been single platforms there.

When studying the sanctuaries of the Oriental cults in the west it is interesting to note that only three of them with certainty included a theatron. The earliest known theatron in a sanctuary for a foreign deity was also the most primitive, namely the one in the sanctuary of Cybele in Rome, where it formed an integral part from the beginning, that is, around 200 BC, when this goddess was invited to Rome to help against Hannibal.[43] Here, the temple was placed behind the theatron, a model, which was later developed to perfection in the great sanctuaries in central Italy, among others that of Praeneste (Fig. 18). The next example is found on Delos. Here, a cultic theatre was built into the sanctuary of the Syrian gods Atargatis and Hadad in the late 2nd centu-

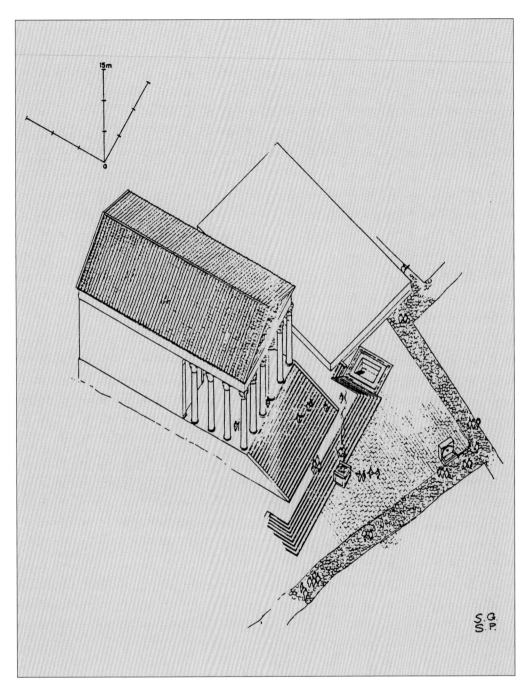

Fig. 18. Rome. Reconstruction of the sanctuary of Cybele on the Palatine. Its first phase included a theatron placed in front of the temple, as was the rule in Italy, with this one constituting the first example (from Pensabene 1982).

ry BC[44] (Fig. 19). It is interesting that this happened in connection with the Athenian conquest of the island, when the sanctuary became official and received annual Greek priests. The third example is to be found in connection with yet another deity, namely Isis, in what is probably her sanctuary in the centre of Syracuse (Fig. 20). Although this sanctuary may go back to the 2nd century BC, the cultic theatre, here uncharacteristically placed behind the temple, was first added in the 1st or 2nd century AD, when the sanctuary apparently changed its status.[45] In all three cases it thus seems that these western style drama installations were first added when the sanctuary in question became official, and thus heavily hellenized or romanized.

This could indicate that in most cases, the Oriental cults chose not to include settings from the host countries for the per-

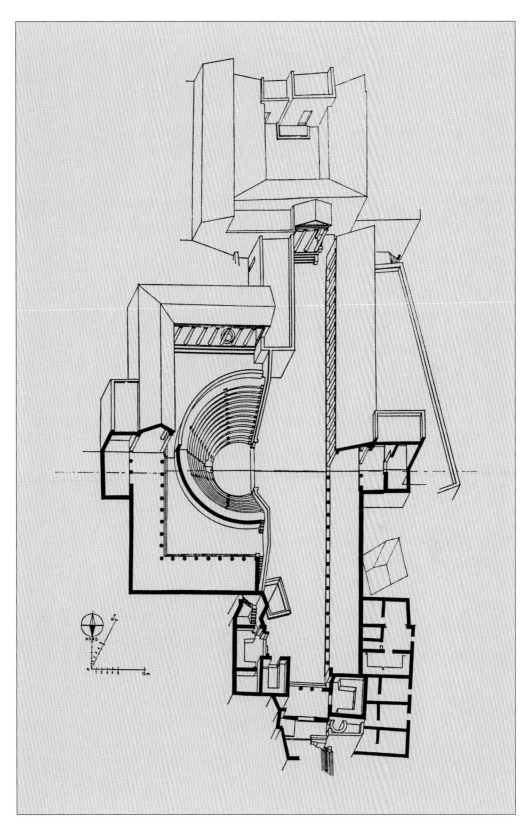

Fig. 19. Delos. Reconstruction of the sanctuary of the Syrian gods. Here, the fine theatron faced the large oblong courtyard, and the throne of the goddess (from Will 1985, fig. 47).

formance of their old ritual dramas in their new sanctuaries. Rather, it seems that they kept their traditional way of per-forming these dramas, whether in the dromos, on a sacred lake, or on platforms, often in front of the temple, in the sanctuaries of the Egyptian gods, or around the altars in the temenoi of the Phoenicio-Syrian gods. On the other hand there are, in fact, examples of an introduction of such theatra in the sanctuaries of these gods even in their homelands. Although this did not happen often, and not until the late Hellenistic period, it is all the same interesting that these structures were used in sanctuaries where the rituals performed were undoubtedly of an only little hellenizied type. Such theatra have been found in Anatolia in the main city of Cybele, Pessinus, dating from Tiberian times (Fig. 21), and in Syria in the Hellenistic colony of Dura Europos, from 1st-3rd century AD (Fig. 22), and in the Hauran, a Nabataean area, from the late 1st century BC. Lately such a cultic theatre has also been found inside a temple in Petra.[46]

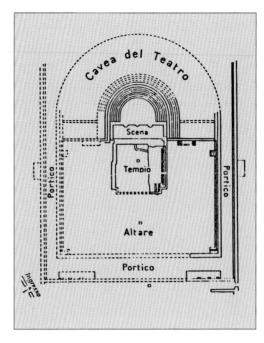

Fig. 20. Syracuse. Plan of the sanctuary, which was probably dedicated to Isis. Here, the theatron is uncharacteristically placed behind the temple (from Coarelli & Torelli 1984).

Conclusion

In general, one may say that the cultic theatres, which were built in the sanctuaries in Greece, whether they belonged to the Greek or the Oriental gods, never became truly monumental. Thus they were normally not of the canonical kind with horseshoe or semicircular formed auditorium, round orchestra, and elaborate stage building. It is clear that what was needed was a place from where the worshippers, when seated, could see what went on in the central area of the sanctu-

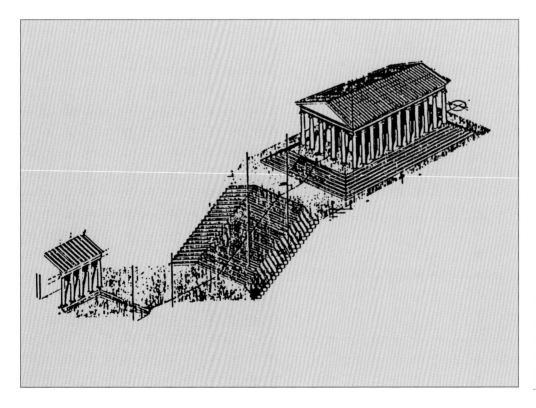

Fig. 21. Pessinus. Reconstruction of the temple and theatron of, probably, Cybele, the main goddess here. Note that the situation is the same as in Italy (from Polacco 1987, fig. 2).

Fig. 22. Dura Europos. One
of the pecular cultic theatres
placed in the pronaoi of many
of the temples of goddesses in
this town (photo IN).

ary, around the altar and in front of the temple. Whether this theatron was constructed in wood, cut into the rock, or built in stone, was a matter of economy; its function did not change. Also, these theatra always remained rather small, generally housing a maximum of 500-1000 adepts, and often even fewer. Stage buildings were only rarely present. The props needed for the performance of a ritual drama were already present in the sanctuary in the form of the temple and the altar, which could also be used as platform as could, sometimes, the frontal staircase of the temple. In fact this was still the kind of theatre in which the first and most famous tragedies, comedies and satyr plays were performed in Athens during the 5th century BC in the sanctuary of Dionysos Eleuthereus. At this time, the same theatron could undoubtedly also still be used for ritual dramas, since it had not yet been isolated from the sanctuary by a supporting wall. This happened in the late 4th century BC, in a period when the city theatres reached their canonical form. But in parallel with the construction of these great theatres, so characteristic of ancient Greece, the primitive cultic theatres continued to function in many Greek sanctuaries until late antiquity.

Notes

NOTE 1
This Article is a summary of part of my book on Cultic theatres and Ritual Drama, (Nielsen forthcoming). A short version was held as a lecture at the annual meeting of the Danish Institute at Athens in March, 1999, and at the international seminar on *Celebrations. Sanctuaries and the Vestiges of Cult Activity*, held by the Norwegian Institute at Athens, May 1999.

NOTE 2
See for a good survey of the enormous scholarship in this field, e.g. Pickard-Cambridge 1962, 60ff; Adrados 1975; Kolb 1981, 26ff; Friedrich 1983; Polacco 1990, 23ff.

NOTE 3
This was i.a. done by the so-called Cambridge Ritualists, ultimately based on Frazer's Golden Bough, J. Harrison (1912), G Murray, (1912) and F.M. Cornford (1914), and later, in a moderated form, by Polacco 1987, 1990, and Adrados, 1975, and in the seminar entitled *L'Anthropologie et Théatre Antique*, published 1987. For the tendency in later years to reconcile these theories, see the good summary by Friedrich 1983.

NOTE 4
See Sethe 1928; Drioton 1942; Gaster 1966.

NOTE 5
See Fairman 1974, who has made a reconstruction of this drama and even arranged for it to be performed in several cities in Britain. Cf. Podemann Sørensen 1986.

NOTE 6
See for these lakes, Gessler-Löhr 1983; she does not, however, combine them specifically with dramatic performances.

NOTE 7
See for these texts, Gaster 1966, de Moor 1971.

NOTE 8
See Carter 1987.

NOTE 9
See for these texts, Gaster 1966.

NOTE 10
Thus according to Polacco 1987, the Greek *hymnologoi*, especially those of the Homeric hymns, did nothing but "translate" liturgical dramatic forms, which were older, as was the case in the Orient.

NOTE 11
See for the masks, which have i.a. been found in the sanctuary of Artemis Ortheia in Sparta, and in the Heraia of Tiryns, Argos and Samos, Carter 1987; for the vase-paintings, see Bieber 1961 and Pickard-Cambridge 1962.

NOTE 12
See for this feast, Pickard-Cambridge 1968, 1ff; Burkert 1985, 237ff. This enactment is depicted on the choes vases, which belonged to this feast; i.a. a procession to the sanctuary with wedding cart is seen, in which the *archon basileus*, clad as Dionysos, is sitting while the *basilinna* is about to enter it (see Bieber 1961, fig. 218).

NOTE 13
This was undoubtedly a liturgical hymn song at the seasonal feasts of Demeter, cf. Gaster 1966, 452ff.

NOTE 14
See Carter 1987, 1988.

NOTE 15
See Scholia to Euripides, *Phoenissae*, 7; Nonnus, *Dion*. 3.61-78, One may mention also two decrees with names of the poets Dymas of Iasos (early 2nd century BC) and Herodes of Priene (2nd century BC), who both (according to Salviat in Charpouthier, Salac and Salviat 1956), or at least the former (according to Lehmann 1964) had written plays to be performed at the great summer feast. The former is honoured for having written a drama on Dardanos' myth, the latter for having written two new works for this occasion, one on the myth of the brothers Dardanos and Iasion (sons of the main goddess Electra and brothers of Harmoneia), and the other on Kadmos and Harmoneia.

NOTE 16
See for this drama, Plut. *De def. or.* 418 A-B, cf. Laurens 1987.

NOTE 17
Such koina were also of a very great importance in a society that moved from the locally based polis society towards the cosmopolitan milieu of the Hellenistic and Roman world. In this period, the many merchants, officials and slaves that travelled all over the known world needed a place where they could feel at home and find friends and assistants in a foreign city. These associations could have more or less specific functions, and be both basically secular and basically religious. But most often they were both. Such associations were especially typical of the foreign, mostly Oriental gods, whose worshippers more than others needed a basis since they were often, at least in the beginning, foreign to the society in which they lived (v.i.). See for these koina, Poland 1909.

NOTE 18
See for the Iobacchoi, *IG* II-III,1,2, 1368 = *SEG* 3, 1109, dated to c. 178 AD. The inscription from Magnesia, *I Magn*. 117; Lucian, *de Salt*. 79.1

NOTE 19
See for these structures, which have not always been identified as cultic theatres, in general Anti 1947; Anti and Polacco 1969; Ginouvès 1972; Kolb 1981.

NOTE 20
See for these Minoan structures in general, Anti 1947; Ginouvès 1972, 53f; Kolb 1981, 103f; Stoessel 1987, 4ff; Marinatos 1993, 46ff, with references.

NOTE 21
See Carter 1988.

NOTE 22
See for the masks, Dickens in Dawkins 1929 and Carter 1987; for the excavations in the sanctuary, where more than 3000 fragments of masks have been found, see Dawkins 1929.

NOTE 23
See for this structure, Waldstein & Meader 1893; Christou in *BCH* 89, 1965, 717-723, v. G Daux. For the feast, Kolb 1981, 79ff.

NOTE 24
See Kolb 1981, with references.

NOTE 25
See Mertens 1982.

NOTE 26
See Dörpfeld and Reich 1896, who regarded the orchestra as being round, an opinion challenged first by Anti 1947, 55ff; and later i.a. by Gebhardt 1974; Wurster 1979.

NOTE 27
See for this theatre, preliminary reports in *AJA* 4, 1888, 421; 5, 1889, 154ff, 354ff; Ginouvès 1972, 64; Kolb 1981, 72ff; Biers and Boyd 1982; Rossetto & Sartorio II, 199.

NOTE 28
See for Rhamnous, Pouilloux 1954, chpt. VI; B. Petrakos in *Praktika* 1975ff; Kolb 1981, 66ff; Rossetto & Sartorio II, 221.

NOTE 29
See Mussche 1967 and 1968; Ginouvès 1972, 59; Kolb 1981, 63ff.; Rossetto & Sartorio II, 308.

NOTE 30
See Fiechter 1937; Auberson & Schefold 1982, 46-52; Rossetto & Sartorio II, 215.

NOTE 31
See Petrakos 1968, 98-99; Ginouvès 1972, 66ff. The old theatron, which goes back at least to the late 5th century BC, is recorded in an inscription mentioning: *ek tou theatrou tou kata ton bomon* (*IG* VII 4255, 29).

NOTE 32
See for this area, which is now difficult to imagine because of the late paved street crossing it, *FD* III, 3, 87f, 207-13; Amandry in *BCH* 63, 1939, 89-119; Bomelaer & Laroche 1991, 146f.

NOTE 33
See for this sanctuary, Gentili 1952; Kolb 1981, 91ff.

NOTE 34
See the recent publication by Bookidis & Stroud 1997, 254ff.

NOTE 35
See Orlandini 1969-70; Leonardos 1986.

NOTE 36
See Bohtz 1981; Radt 1988, 206ff.

NOTE 37
See Mylonas 1961, 137ff; Travlos 1988, 97.

NOTE 38
See for Morgantina, Ginouvès 1972, 71ff; Stillwell 1967; Kolb 1975, 226ff.; Rossetto & Sartorio III 26. For Lindos, see Dyggve 1960; Rossetto & Sartorio III, 26.

NOTE 39
See Love 1972 and 1973; latest Bankel 1997.

NOTE 40
Chapouthier, Salac & Salviat 1956; Lehmann 1964.

NOTE 41
See Heyder & Mallwitz 1978.

NOTE 42
See for a detailed treatment of this phenomenon, Turcan 1989; Nielsen forthcoming.

NOTE 43
See for this sanctuary, Pensabene 1982, 1988, and 1996. These seats were removed in the rebuilding of 111 BC, instead the frontal staircase was probably used.

NOTE 44
See Will 1985, 150ff.

NOTE 45
See Coarelli & Torelli 1984, 242f; Wilson 1988.

NOTE 46
See for Pessinus, Waelkens 1986; Polacco 1987 Devreker & Vermeulen 1998; for Dura Europos, Downey 1988; for Hauran, Butler 1916; for Petra, M. Sharp Joukowsky in *JDAI* 1995ff.

Bibliography

Adrados, F.R. 1975
Festival, Comedy and Tragedy. The Greek Origins of Theatre. London.

Anti, C. 1947
Teatri greci arcaici da Minosse à Pericle. Padova.

Anti, C. & Polacco, L. 1969
Nuove ricerche sui teatri greci archaici. Padova.

Auberson, P. & Schefold, K. 1982
Führer durch Eretria. Bern.

L'Anthropologie et Théatre antique 1987
L'Anthropologie et Théatre antique. Actes de colloque international de Montpellier 6-8 mars 1986, ed. P. Chiron-Bistaque, Montpellier.

Bankel, H. 1997
Der hellenistische Rundtempel und sein Altar. Vorbericht, *AA,* 51-71.

Bieber, M. 1961
The History of the Greek and Roman Theater. Princeton N.J.

Biers, W.R. & Boyd, T.D. 1982
Ikarion in Attica: 1888-1981, *Hesperia* 51, 1-18.

Bohtz, C.H. 1981
Das Demeter-Heiligtum. Altertümer von Pergamon XIII. Berlin.

Bomelaer, J.-F. & Laroche, D. 1991
Guide de Delphes. Le Site. Paris.

Bookidis, N. & Stroud, R.S. 1997
The Sanctuary of Demeter and Kore. Topography and Architecture. Corinth XVIII, III. Princeton N.J.

Burkert, W. 1985
Greek Religion. Cambridge Mass.

Butler, H.C. 1916
Architecture and other Arts. Publications of the Princeton University Archaeological Expedition to Syria II A. Princeton.

Carter, J. Burr 1987
The Masks of Ortheia, *AJA* 91, 355-383.

Carter J. Burr 1988
Masks and Poetry in Early Sparta, in: *Early Greek Cult Practice,* eds. Robin Hägg et al., Stockholm, 89-98.

Chapouthier, F., Salac, A. & Salviat, F. 1956
Le Théatre de Samothrace, *BCH* 80, 118-146.

Coarelli, F. & Torelli, M. 1984
Sicilia. Guide Archeologiche Laterza. Roma/Bari.

Cornford, F. Macdonald 1961
The Origin of Attic Comedy, ed. with foreword and additional notes by T.H. Gaster. New York (1st edn. 1914).

Dawkins, R.M. 1929
The Sanctuary of Artemis Orthia at Sparta. London.

Devreker, J. & Vermeulen, F. 1998
Fouilles et prospections à Pessinonte: campagne de 1996, *Anatolia Antiqua* VI, 249-258 (esp. 249-253).

Dörpfeld, W. & Reich, E. 1896
Das Griechische Theater. Athen.

Downey, S. 1988
Mesopotamian Religious Architecture. Alexander through the Parthians. Princeton N.J.

Drioton, E. 1942
Le Théatre Égyptien. Cairo.

Dyggve, E. 1960
Le Sanctuaire d'Athena Lindia et l'architecture Lindienne. Lindos III,II, Berlin and Copenhagen (spec. p. 399ff).

Fairman, H.W. 1974
The Triumph of Horus. An Ancient Egyptian Sacred Drama. London.

Fiechter, E.R. 1930
Das Theater in Oropos. Stuttgart.

Fiechter, E. 1937
Das Theater in Eretria. Stuttgart.

Friedrich, R. 1983
Drama and ritual, in: *Drama and Religion. Themes in Drama* 5, ed. James Redmond, Cambridge, 159-223.

Gaster, T.H. 1966
Thespis. Ritual, myth and Drama in the Ancient Near East. New York.

Gebhard, E. 1974
The form of the orchestra in the early Greek theater, *Hesperia* 43, 428-440.

Gentili, G.V. 1952. Nuovo esempio di "theatron" con gradinata rettilinea a Siracusa, *Dioniso* 15, 122-130.

Gessler-Löhr, B. 1983
Die heiligen Seen ägyptischer Tempel. Ein Beitrag zur Deutung sakraler Baukunst im alten Ägypten (Hildesheimer ägyptologische Beiträge 21). Hildesheim.

Ginouvès, R. 1972
Le Théâtron à gradins droits et l'odéon d'Argos (École Française d'Athenes, Etudes Peloponesiennes VI). Paris.

Harrison, J.E. 1912
Themis. A Study of the Social Origins of Greek Religion. Cambridge.

Heyder, W, & Mallwitz, A. 1978
Die Bauten im Kabirenheiligtum bei Theben. Das Kabirenheiligtum bei Theben, II. Berlin.

Kolb, F. 1975
Agora und Theater in Morgantina, *Kokalos* 21, 226-230.

Kolb, F. 1981
Agora und Theater, Volks-und Festversammlung (Archäologische Forschungen 9). Berlin.

Laurens, A-F. 1987
Les masques chypriotes, in: *L'Anthropologie et Théatre antique 1987*, 23-36.

Lehmann, K. 1964
The Altar Court. Samothrace 4,2. New York (spec. pp. 136-146).

Leonardos, B. 1986
Naos Despoines, *Praktika* 1986, 101-126.

Love, I.C. 1972
A Preliminary Report of the Excavations at Knidos 1971, *AJA* 76, 393ff.

Love, I.C. 1973
A Preliminary Report of the Excavations at Knidos 1972, *AJA* 77, 419-424.

Marinatos, N. 1993
Minoan Religion. Ritual, Image, and Symbol. Columbia J.C.

Mertens, D. 1982
Metaponto: il teatro-ekklesiasterion, *BdA* 16, 1-60.

de Moor, J.C. 1971
The seasonal pattern in the Ugaritic Myth of Ba'lu (Alten Orient und Altes Testament, Bd. 16). Kevelaer.

Murray 1912
Excursus on the ritual form preserved in Greek tragedy, in: *Harrison 1912*, 340-363.

Mussche, H.F. et al. 1968
Thorikos I. Rapport Preliminaire sur la premiere campagne de fouilles (with a contribution on the theatre by T. Hackens pp. 39-46). Bruxelles.

Mussche, H.F. et al. 1967
Thorikos III. Rapport Preliminaire sur la troisieme campagne de fouilles (with a contribution on the theatre by T. Hackens pp. 75-96). Bruxelles.

Mylonas, E. 1961
Eleusis and the Eleusinian Mysteries. Princeton.

Nielsen, I forthcoming.
Cultic Theatres and Ritual Drama. A study of Regional Development and Religious Interchange between East and West in Antiquity. Aarhus.

Orlandini, G.A. 1969-70
Considerazioni sul Megaron di Despoina à Licosura, *ASAtene* N.S. 31-32, 343-357.

Pensabene, P. 1982
Nuove indagini nell'area del tempio di Cibele, in: *La soteriologia dei culti orientali nell'Impero Romano*, eds. U. Bianchi & M.J.Vermaseren (EPRO 92), Leiden, 68-98.

Pensabene, P. 1988
Scavi nell'area del tempio della Vittoria e del santuario della Magna Mater sul Palatino, *ArchLaz*, 54-67.

Pensabene, P. 1996
Magna Mater, aedes. In: *LTUR* III, 206-208.

Petrakos, B. 1968.
O Oropos kai to hieron tou Amphiaraou. Athens.

Pickard-Cambridge, A. 1962
Dithyramb, Tragedy and Comedy, 2nd ed. revised by T.B.L. Webster. Oxford.

Pickard-Cambridge, A. 1968. *The Dramatic Festivals of Athens*, 2nd rev. ed. by J. Gould and D.M. Lewis. Oxford.

Podeman Sørensen, J. 1986
Three varieties of ritual drama, *Temenos* 22, 79-92.

Polacco, L. 1987
Rites des saisons et drames sacrés chez les Grecs, in: *L'Anthropologie et Théatre antique 1987*, 9-22.

Polacco, L. 1990
Il teatro di Dioniso Eleutero ad Atene. Roma.

Poland, F. 1909
Geschichte des griechischen Vereinswesen. Leipzig.

Pouilloux, J. 1954
La Fortresse de Rhamnonte. Paris.

Radt, W. 1988
Pergamon. Geschichte und Bauten, Funde und Erforschung einer antiken Metropole. Köln.

Rossetto, P & Sartorio, G. Pisani, et al. 1994-1996
Teatri greci e romani. Alle origini del linguaggio rappresentato. Censimento analitico. vols. I-III. Torino.

Sethe, K. 1928
Dramatische Texte zu Altägyptischen Mysterienspielen I-II, in: *Untersuchungen zur Geschichte und Altertumskunde Ägyptens* X,1-2. Leipzig.

Stillwell, R. 1967
The theatre of Morgantina, *AJA* 71, 245-46.

Stoessl, F. 1987
Die Vorgeschichte des griechischen Theaters. Darmstadt.

Travlos, J. 1971
A Pictorial Dictionary of Ancient Athens. London.

Travlos, J. 1988
Bildlexikon zur Topographie des Antiken Attika. Tübingen.

Turcan, R. 1989
Les cultes orientaux dans le monde romain. Paris, 2nd edn. 1992. English edition 1996.

Waelkens, M. 1986
The imperial sanctuary at Pessinus. Archaeological, Epigraphical and Numismatic Evidence for its date and identification, *Epigraphica Anatolia* 7, 37-73.

Waldstein, C. & Meader, C.L. 1893
Reports on excavations at Sparta in 1893, *AJA* 8, 410-428.

Will, E. 1985
Le Sanctuaire de la Déesse Syrienne. Exploration Archéologique de Delos XXXV. Paris.

Wilson, R.J.A. 1988
Towns of Sicily during the Roman Empire, in: ANRW 11, 1, 90-206.

Wurster, W. 1979
Die neuen Untersuchungen am Dionysos Theater in Athen, *Architectura* 9, 58-76

Typology of the Greek Theatre Building in Late Classical and Hellenistic Times[1]

Rune Frederiksen

Introduction

When we refer to the Greek theatre in the architectural sense with terms such as *Greek Theatre* or *Greek Theatre Building* we are referring to a complex and not to a building. In Greek antiquity the theatre did not develop into a harmonious architectural building,[2] a fact which is reflected in the traditional view that the developed theatre consisted, basically, of three separate elements: the koilon, the orchestra and the scene building.[3] The koilon and the orchestra are, however, often treated to-gether,[4] which makes sense since, as suggested by E. Gebhard followed by F. Kolb, the design of the orchestra seems to be determined by that of the koilon.[5] On this view the theatre is an architectural complex composed not of three but of *two* main elements: on the one hand the *koilon/orchestra* (hereafter referred to as *theatre building*) and on the other hand the *scene building*. This is not only a formal architectural point but a point rooted in chronology as well: the theatre building reached its fully developed form in the late Classical and Early Hellenistic periods, whereas

Fig.1. The theatre at Delphoi from the W. Example of 2:1 relation between steps in stairway and rows of seats. (Photo: R. Frederiksen)

Fig.2. The theatre at Aigeira from the E. Example of 1:1 relation between steps in stairway and rows of seats. (Photo: R. Frederiksen)

the development and perfection of the stone *skene* is a Hellenistic phenomenon.[6] This study deals with the architecture of the theatre building-element of the complex: the canon of it and its different types of design.

As far as the architectural development of the theatre building is concerned, the theatres of Dionysos at Athens and of Epidauros are considered, with good reason, to constitute its culmination because of their architectural splendour and perfection.[7] They have, moreover, attracted special attention on account of their unique state of preservation. The date of the important restructuring of the theatre of Dionysos, phase III between 350-325 BC, commonly referred to as the Lykourgan phase, seems firm.[8] The date of the Epidauros theatre is more uncertain; but it was probably constructed in the early 3rd century, the *epitheatron* being added ca. 170 BC.[9] Following the general idea that the theatre of Dionysos and the theatre of Epidauros played a leading role in the creation of the canon of the monumental theatre building, they are often referred to as models for the construction of other theatres (treated below).[10] No matter how central a role these two theatres played, an architectural canon definitely developed for the theatre building from around the time of their construction: the semicircular design.

Looking beyond the canon, the two key monuments in Athens and at Epidauros represent two different ways of planning the theatre building, including elements like the *euripos* and the *proedria*.[11] The theatre of Dionysos is often referred to by scholars as U or horseshoe shaped,[12] whereas the theatre of Epidauros is described as more-than-semicircular or symmetrically-rounded.[13] The similarities in the form of the koilon (and to a lesser degree also of the scene building) between the Theatre of Dionysos and a number of other Greek theatres (e.g. Eretria phase II, Peiraieus-Zea and Segesta) were pointed out at the very dawn of research on the Greek theatre in Dörpfeld and Reisch, *Das Griechische Theater*.[14] Later more buildings of similar form have been added, and it makes sense to define this group of theatre buildings as a distinct type (Fig. 4). Apart from the U-shaped type, Dörpfeld defined two other types in his discussion of the Greek theatre according to Vitruvius (*De architectura,* 5.7).[15] The observations of Dörpfeld were repeated and the types more clearly established by Dilke in his article: *The Greek Theatre Cavea.*[16] These other two types are variations of the same basic idea, of what was called the more-than-semicircular koilon, where the koilon wings keep on bending around the orchestra at or around the point where they extend beyond 180°: the real more-than-semicircular type and the elliptical type (Figs. 3 & 5, treated in detail below).

In the general literature on Greek architecture as well as specialised works on the Greek theatre the distinction between these three types of theatre building or the descriptive terminology of them, is not always clear;[17] sometimes precise terminology is used but not explained,[18] and often distinctions are not made at all.[19] The reason why the focus on the variations of the canon and what they constitute has been a rare undertaking, is probably that the variations are in fact conceived of as simply *variations* of basically the same monumental building rather than as individual types. It is proposed here to subject the problem to a more penetrating investigation in order to arrive at a clearer understanding of the variations or types. Such an endeavour is called for because the source material has expanded dramatically since the days of Dörpfeld, Dilke and Bieber. Of great importance is the giant work *Teatri Greci e Romani* (*TGR*) which appeared in 1994, and which presented a *Corpus Theatrorum Antiquorum* for the first time in the history of research on the Greek and Roman theatre. In one of the introductory articles[20] the total number of Greek theatres is given as 167, but if we adopt the approach used in the same work, the correct number is more likely to be somewhere on the other side of 200[21] of which the majority date from the Hellenistic period. This study will consider only ruins preserved and studied well enough to enable us to draw conclusions as to their date and original design. This leaves us with some 98 theatres, which is in fact a very good sample of the ancient total. We do not have to fear too much that crucial

Fig.3. Stylized version of canon (type B, semicircular). Inspired from Megalopolis. (R. Frederiksen)

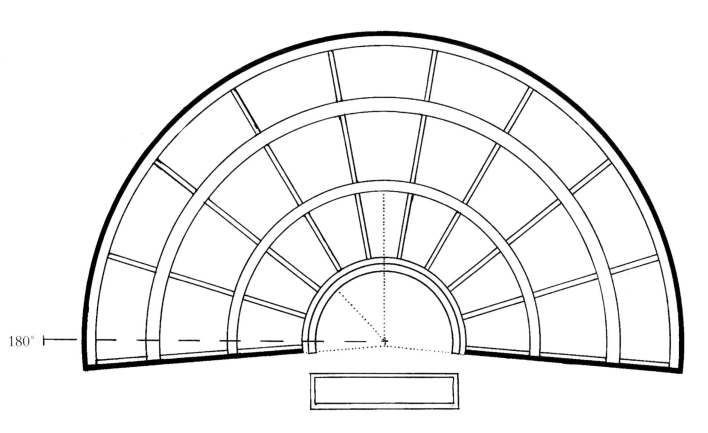

180°

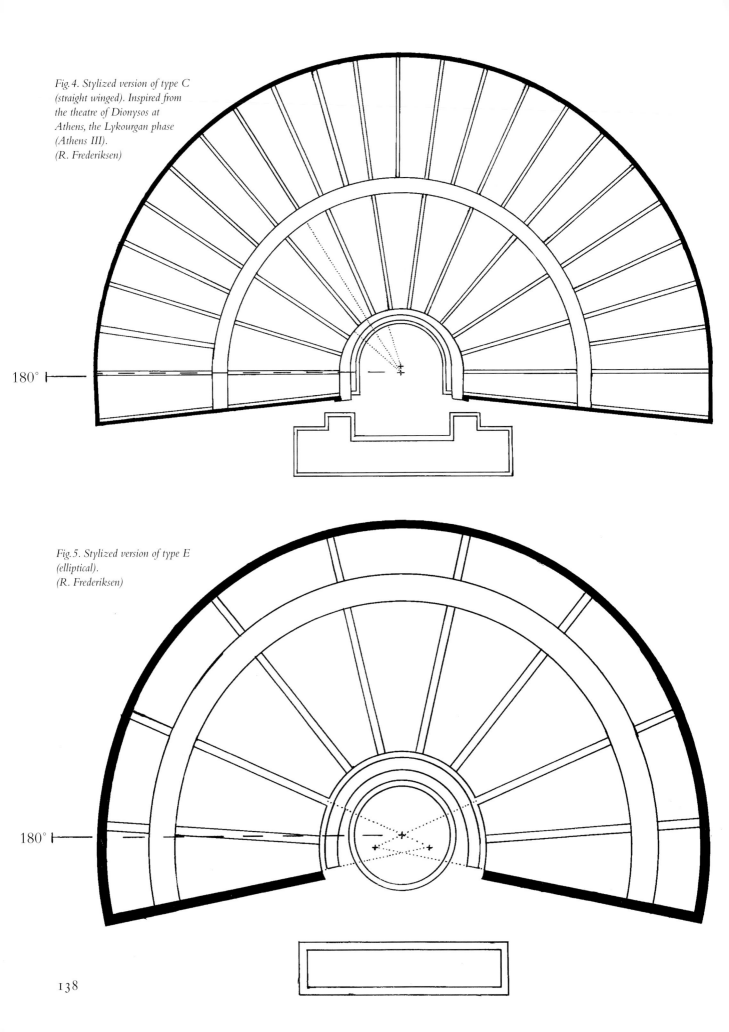

Fig.4. Stylized version of type C
(straight winged). Inspired from
the theatre of Dionysos at
Athens, the Lykourgan phase
(Athens III).
(R. Frederiksen)

180°

Fig.5. Stylized version of type E
(elliptical).
(R. Frederiksen)

180°

evidence is lost or hidden. The monuments are listed with references in an appendix (p. 167ff.).[22]

After a brief outline of theatre typology before late Classical times I shall discuss the canon in general terms. Then the groups of monuments corresponding to the different types will be summed up, along with information on the level of detail, such as stairs and rows of seats, with focus on the theatre building. Finally it will be discussed to what extent the classification comprises a real typology, and possible explanations for the existence of these different architectural types will be considered. The focus on the need for classification is not, however, maintained blindly without respect for reality, since reality, as von Gerkan pointed out, offers hundreds of unique monuments: "Jedes der verschiedenen Theater ist durchaus Individuum und in seiner ihm eigentümlichen Form entworfen und gebaut worden".[23]

Forerunners

The number of preserved Archaic buildings is low and the lack of similarities between them makes any architectural typology impossible.[24]

The Classical period yields the first type of theatre building (A),[25] the theatres with linear rows of seats hewn out of the rock at *Argos* 1, *Chaironeia* I and *Syrakousai* 1. All three examples date, in all probability, to the 5th century BC.[26] From the 5th century we know of monumentalised phases also in e.g. the *theatre of Dionysos at Athens* I-II, *Eretria* I, *Isthmia* I, *Korinthos* I, *Metapontion* III and *Thorikos* II, but the evidence from these localities is either too poor or too varied to form the basis of any typology.

In the 4th century at least four new types of theatre were introduced, defined from the shape of the theatre-building, three of which continued in the Hellenistic period. The type that was not continued (type D) is the small group of simple construction without a monumentalised koilon other than a straight proedria as the dominating element and supporting walls for the orchestra which was probably square (*Ikarion*, *Rhamnous* and *Tegea* I).[27] The other types (B, C, F and G) as well as the Hellenistic type (E) will be treated in detail below, but first their common features, the canon, must be dealt with.

The Hellenistic Theatre

At the same time as the appearance of the developed and monumentalised theatre building there was a boom in the number of new theatres built and many of the old buildings were reconstructed, generally according to the new semicircular canon and,[28] more specifically as types, principally those already mentioned. The diffusion of the canonical theatre and its different designs took place practically all over the Greek world: more than 50% of the theatres included in this study were built in Greece proper, especially in the late 4th and 3rd century. Next Magna Graecia is an area with many theatres built down to the 2nd century, when Asia Minor took over as the area where most theatres were built. This picture of regional shifts in the intensity of building activity mirrors the general changes which took place within the Greek world from late Classical to late Hellenistic times.[29]

Because of this increasing building activity, and because of the increasing preference for building in stone, we know far more about this period than about earlier periods. So we must accept the fact that a significant part of our knowledge about the architectural development through the Classical and early Hellenistic periods will remain inferior when compared to the period of the big boom.

The theatres were built primarily in or near the urban centres of cities and in major extra-urban sanctuaries, as in Classical times (exceptions to city locations are indicated individually in the appendix). The location was a slope of a hill in or close to the built-up areas.[30] Although all

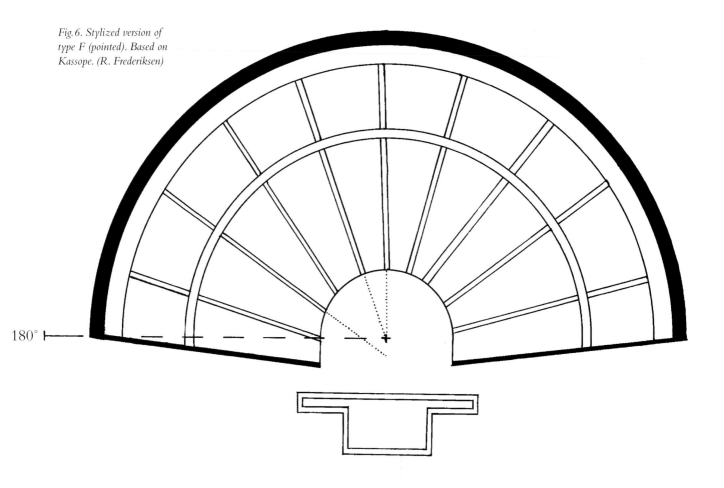

Fig.6. Stylized version of type F (pointed). Based on Kassope. (R. Frederiksen)

180°

orientations are found, the standard orientation of the buildings seems to have been east and south,[31] which is only natural, since the location of the cities themselves was often on the eastern and southern slopes of hills and mountains.[32]

Koilon

The 'invention' of the monumentalised semicircular koilon is undoubtedly to be dated back to early Classical or perhaps even Archaic times. The dating of this innovation depends on the interpretation of Metapontion II, a structure admittedly not proved to resemble the later semicircular koila in detail, but still basically consisting of two semicircular, antithetically placed and sloping koila.[33] The existence of these koila makes it very unlikely that the semicircular design was invented just like that, be it Athens or anywhere else, about 150 years later. This observation corroborates other evidence for a gradual development of the canonical semicircular

design (see below p. 150). A parallel example of such gradual architectural development is the Greek temple where it is observed too that the basic layout of the building type is also established from the very beginning of the emergence of the monument, or at least from a very early point,[34] and around the core of which the canon gradually develops (more on the establishment of the canon below p. 149f.). Even though the canon of the theatre was established in late Classical times, it is correct to state that it was primarily a Hellenistic phenomenon,[35] because of the numbers of theatres in that period.

The development towards a canonical expression of the basic idea of the semicircular koilon is clearly the result of a growing popularity of the structure, documented both by the growing size of theatres and their increasing numbers. This again was rooted in the growing popularity of the activities that took place in the theatre

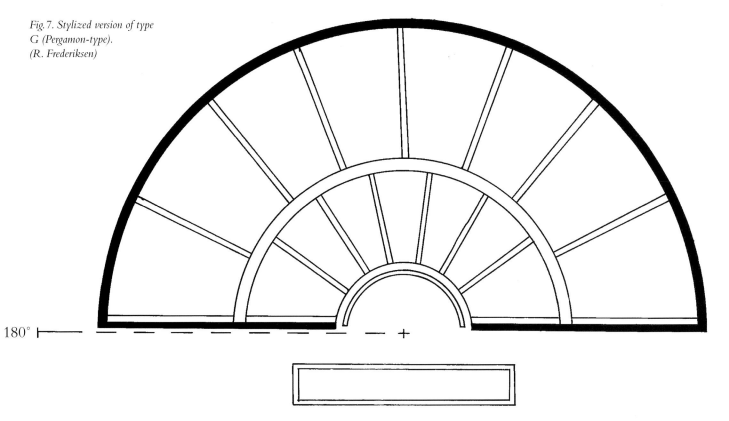

Fig. 7. Stylized version of type G (Pergamon-type). (R. Frederiksen)

180°

and the growing population figures.[36] These developments required architectural structures that allowed as many people as possible to see and hear as well as possible.[37] A good indication of this relationship between shape and size is the fact that all the theatres that can be described as having an irregular, or at least *unique* shape, are to be found in the category of small theatres (*e.g. Chaironeia* II, '*Makyneia*' in West Lokris, *Arkadian Orchomenos*, *Phleious* in the Argolid and *Trakhones* in Attika).[38] This is also the case with the Archaic and Classical theatre of *Thorikos* (I-III), the linear type A theatres of the 5th century and type D of the 4th century. The latest examples of theatres that do not follow the canon appear in the 3rd century BC. Later the canon takes over completely and thus there is both a broad chronological side to the canon, and a more firm side. So size definitely plays a role in the development towards the semicircular canon. Although no single tendency in respect of size is discernible and significant changing tendencies over time cannot, accordingly, be identified, it would pro

bably be fair to say that the majority of buildings built during Hellenistic times are to be placed between the upper end of small and in the medium size category, which means that the monuments often have a diameter of between 50 and 70 metres (see note 38 for size categories).

A canonical semicircular koilon is normally designed as a segment between 180° and 210° of a circle (cf. Fig. 3),[39] and sometimes the entire koilon of a theatre building (rows of seats, stairways, *diazomata,* etc.) follows a single layout throughout, from the innermost rows near the proedria or euripos up to the surrounding *analemma* (*e.g. Antiphellos*, *Epidauros*, *Kassope*, *Megalopolis* and *Oinoanda*). But a number of structures do not show such a consistency in the design, with the result that the typological focus has been on the orchestra and the area around the lowest tiers of the koilon in the works of e.g. Dörpfeld, Fiechter and Bieber.[40] Often such lack of consistency can be explained by the fact that a structure is built in a dense urban context, where important

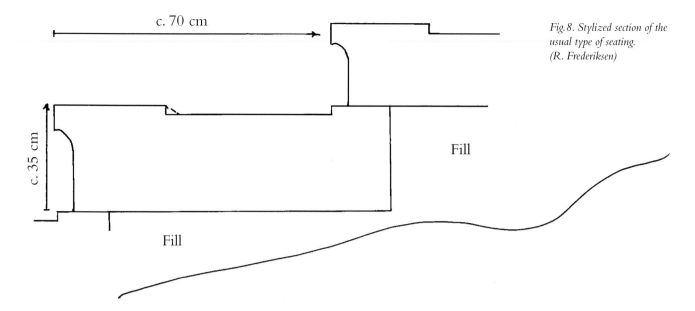

c. 70 cm

c. 35 cm

Fill

Fill

Fig. 8. Stylized section of the usual type of seating. (R. Frederiksen)

adjacent buildings or building complexes might hinder the completion of the *epitheatron*, or some of it, that had been begun in the *ima cavea* (*e.g. Athens* III, *Delphoi* and *Knidos* 1).[41] Other reasons for not completing a design could be local geomorphologic conditions as it is seen for instance at the theatre of *Pergamon* (treated below p. 155). In spite of the fact that the completion of a design from the centre to the periphery is not predominant among the known theatres, it is very likely that that design was perceived as the ideal, (*Epidauros* I-II is a good example),[42] and that it was adhered to wherever possible. This is clearly the opinion of Dilke (1948) who hints more directly at the arrangement of the wings i.e. the koilon, when he discusses the different designs (below p. 149ff.).

The division of the koilon into horizontal sections and vertical *kerkides* is determined by the number of stairways and *diazomata*. Generally speaking, the number of sections and kerkides correspond to the size of the theatres so that large buildings have many and smaller ones fewer.[43] Most small theatres naturally have no diazoma and never more than one (*i.e.* two sections). But it is perhaps surprising that many of the medium-sized and even some of the large theatres show no sign of diazomata.[44] But, nevertheless, the tendency is clear since more than 50% in both groups have

two or three sections (e.g. *Eretria* II, *Lokroi Epizephyrioi* and *Tyndaris*), the percentage being the highest in the group of large theatres. The majority of theatres have an odd number of kerkides in the ima cavea.[45] Small ones have between 3 and 11, medium-sized and large theatres between 5-15 kerkides.[46] The average numbers in the three size categories are: 7, 8 and 10 kerkides in the ima cavea, proving that the number of kerkides, as expected, tends to grow with the size of the theatre. Commenting on the Greek Theatre of Vitruvius, which has 7 kerkides, Dilke both noted that this number is not more common than others, and that the number of kerkides in the *epitheatron*, in theatre buildings with more than one section, is normally twice the number of kerkides in the ima cavea (corresponding to Vitruvius' Greek theatre).[47] The number of *kerkides* in the *epitheatron* compared to the *ima cavea* is sometimes the same, or sometimes even less. The latter instances are by and large confined to theatres where the shape of the *ima cavea* is not continued in the *epitheatron*, often because of topographical circumstances.

The number of the flights of steps that separate the kerkides is very often one more than the number of kerkides due to the fact that the koilon is flanked at the end of the wings (at the *parodos* walls) by

Fig. 8b. The theatre of Dionysos at Athens from the
S. Usual type of seating
(re-erected section).
(Photo: R. Frederiksen)

such a stairway (cf. Fig. 3). It sometimes
happens, however, that the number is one
fewer, meaning that the koilon ends in
kerkides and not stairs. This is rare in
buildings of medium or large dimensions,
and accordingly corroborates the fact that

size determines the canon as well as
prompts a higher degree of monumentality and elaboration. The stairs themselves
are very often constructed of simple
blocks. Two steps to one row of seats must
have been considered the ideal of com-
fort, as the relation is the same almost
everywhere (Fig. 1).[48] The depth and
height of the individual steps of course
varies with the sloping of the individual
koila. Rare varieties are seen in *Eretria* II,
where we find four steps per three rows of
seats, and in *Aigeira, Athens* III, *Sikyon* and
(possibly) *Peiraieus-Zea*[49] where the relation is one to one (constructed with an
individual sloping, see Fig. 2). Finally, the
separations between the kerkides in a few
theatres may be described as ramps (*Aigai*
and *Elis*), that is, with no regular steps, in
correspondence with the monumental

Fig. 8a. The theatre of Asklepios at Epidauros from the
NE. Usual type of seating. (Photo: R. Frederiksen)

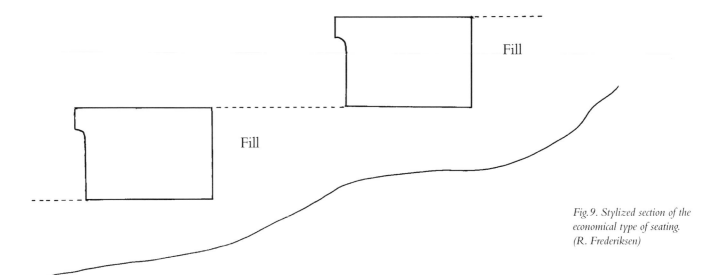

Fill

Fill

Fig. 9. Stylized section of the economical type of seating. (R. Frederiksen)

poverty of the other elements of the koila at these two localities of which the former apparently had only one row of regular stone-seats, the latter none.[50]

Another general characteristic of the Hellenistic theatre is the furnishing of stone seats. A few theatres constructed in the late Classical and Hellenistic periods probably had wooden or partially wooden seats.[51] The existence of wooden seats is often indicated negatively by the absence of blocks, but in general it is impossible to say with certainty whether this lack of

Fig. 9a. The polis theatre of Epidauros (mod. Paleia Epidauros) from the W. Economical type of seating. (Photo: R. Frederiksen)

blocks is caused by later quarrying or whether it is in fact an indication of the use of perishable materials such as wood.

On the basis of construction or style, seats may be divided into several types.[52] The average dimensions of those different types are the same: a depth around 70 cm and a height around 35 cm (cf. Fig. 8). Variations are great, especially in the Greek homeland, while dimensions, as far as the depth of the seats are concerned, are more fixed around 70 cm in Magna Graecia, with a few exceptions. That these dimensions are prevalent is very natural, as they fit the dimensions of the average sitting person; at the same time they control the sloping of the canonical theatres, which is, accordingly, always between 20 and 30 degrees (e.g. *Athens* III, 23°; *Epidauros* I, 27°; *Korinthos* II, 20°; *Megalopolis* 25°).

The *usual type* of seating (Figs. 8 & 8a,b) is used from late Classical and throughout the Hellenistic period.[53] This very common type possibly originated in *Athens* III[54] and is used down to the 1st century BC (e.g. *Kibyra*). Characteristic of this mostly monolithic seating facility is a forward projecting fillet on the front and a recess for the feet, sometimes the fillet or the recess lacks. Dilke distinguishes between this type on the one hand and all other types on the other, which he lists under 'economical seating'.[55] This may be a reasonable way of dividing the material, but if the focus were functionalistic rather than on cost more examples could be added to the usual type. Sometimes the usual type is not monolithic but constructed of for example one type of stone for the seats and another for the footrest part or the footrest part may be just a fill of earth and rubble (Figs. 9 & 9a). But the basic idea is still that of the usual type: the recess and the fillet that provide space for the feet and a comfortable angle for the legs of the seated audience. These more economical versions of the usual type are more frequent in the 4th century than lat-

Fig. 10. The large theatre at Argos (2) from S. Simple type of seating. (Photo: R. Frederiksen)

er.[56] Whatever the construction of the usual type I find that the fundamental stylistic alternative to it is the *simple type* (my expression) (Figs. 10 & 10a) which is just like a flight of steps, but with the same basic dimensions as the rows of seats of the usual type normally have. The simple type, naturally very common in rock-cut theatres, seems to be confined to Greece proper in the 4th and 3rd centuries and it is not very common among medium-sized and large theatres. Within the mixed *economical* group, Dilke count the seating of *Magnesia on the Maeander* and *Priene* which are quite alike, and to which we can compare the seating of *Boiotian Orchomenos*. It is a rare type of seating, which most probably is caused by the fact that its construction results in poor chances of preservation: stone plates resting on square blocks like benches, placed on rows of the simple type that actually work as a base for the benches. The stone plates and the blocks disappear easily, which makes it quite possible that in some theatres, where we have identified rock-cut rows of seats of the simple type, there were once seats of this economical type. To regard this small group as economical is not reasonable, since the plates used for seating in *Priene* were of marble. But of course in the majority of instances where types of the economical seating were combined with

earth, or constructed with a cheaper local stone, the term makes more sense (e.g. *Arkadian Orchomenos*, fig. 11).

The *proedria* is clearly identified in many theatres as a part of the koilon, but often at the same time as a separate section.[57] The basic type throughout the Hellenistic period consists of stone benches placed in front of every *kerkis* in the ima cavea, either replacing the first regular row of seats (*e.g. Argos* 2, *Korinthos* II, *Delos*, *Epidauros* and *Boiotian Orchomenos*) or constructed as an independent section separated from the koilon proper by a gangway (*e.g. Herakleia Minoa*, *Iaitas*, *Megalopolis* and *Sikyon*). In both cases the proedria follows the overall design of the koilon. Often the proedria section is constructed of stone of a different quality, and often ornaments and profiles are carved, presenting highly varied decorations. An additional upper proedria of this type, in front of the kerkides of the epitheatron, comes to the fore in the 3rd and 2nd centuries BC, probably as a result of the general changes in drama which moved the focal point of event from the orchestra to the roof of the proskenion. This development obviously gave the spectators sitting in the upper part of the koilon a better view, and on that consideration it is only natural that such seats of honour, at least in part, were moved to

this area.[58] Proedria could, it seems, be as simple as just blocks or plates of a different kind of stone than the rest of the koilon, as for instance in *Pleuron*.[59]

The sometimes elaborate stone thrones found in some theatres are interpreted as another type of proedria. This type may coexist with the benches just described, as for instance in *Arkadian Orchomenos*, *Priene* and *Stratos*, and it seems to consist of 3 to 5 individual stone thrones placed around the edge – but still clearly within the area – of the *orchestra* (e.g *Ephesos*, *Oropos* II, *Priene* and *Stratos*).[60]

Many theatre buildings were furnished with an euripos to lead rainwater from the koilon away from the area of the orchestra where it would otherwise have remained. It is accordingly always placed at the edge of the orchestra, but some buildings have additional euripoi along the diazomata, as Argos 2. Euripoi vary a lot in design and

construction, but from a basic point of view there existed two types.[61] One is the wide, low and open type (e.g. *Epidauros* and *Eretria* II); the other the narrower, deeper and closed type (e.g. *Athens* III and *Korinthos* II). Here, as with the proedria, it is a general rule that the euripos follows the design of the koilon/orchestra. The well-built euripoi are mostly found in larger theatre buildings, where they were also most needed because of the larger amounts of rainwater collected by koila of such buildings.

Orchestra

The orchestra is undoubtedly the earliest architectural part of the theatre. But in architectural terms the orchestra remains insignificant and as a rule it is determined in form by the koilon.[62] The first evidence for a circular orchestra is in 3rd century *Epidauros* I, and the evidence at all for circular orchestrai throughout the entire history of the Greek theatre is scarce. Apart from *Epidauros* I, it is found in: *Argos* 2, *Korinthos* II[63] and *Stratos*.[64] The idea that a circular *orchestra* was an obligatory element of the fully developed theatre originates with Dörpfeld and the impact that this idea has had on later research may reasonably be called 'the Dörpfeld orthodoxy'.[65] No matter how one interprets the actual proofs of the circular orchestra, both of the Classical and Hellenistic era, we can state without qualifications that it simply did not exist in the great majority of buildings of the Hellenistic period, and accordingly, the circular orchestra cannot be regarded as a typical part of the canonical theatre building. This may also be deduced from the fact that the proskenion in most theatres was moved so close to the koilon that it simply did not leave enough space for a circular orchestra (*e.g. Aphrodisias, Arykanda, Delos, Mantineia* II, *Tegea* II and *Tyndaris*).[66]

The orchestra's lack of architectural importance may also be deduced from the few attempts that were made to furnish the orchestra with a stone surface, as it is found for instance in Priene. There are difficulties in interpreting the 'smoothed rock' orchestrai found in not a few theatres (*e.g. Argos* 2, *Korinthos* II and *Boiotian Orchomenos*); whether they were normally covered by a layer of sand or beaten earth is naturally impossible to know. Traces of such layers have been found at for example *Morgantina* and *Solous*. Because of this lack of architectural importance and/or preservation of the early orchestra, we have no knowledge about it. It is only the appearance of the koilon that makes the orchestra visible to the archaeologist – indirectly, by the room that was made for it by the koilon. Accordingly the shape of the orchestra varies depending on the different shapes of the koilon, a fact that justifies the reasonable conclusion that the orchestra was of minor architectural importance.

Scene building

In this article the scene building will be treated according to the role it plays in building typology of the theatre building and not in particular detail, because this is a huge subject in itself.[67]

The increasing importance of the scene building in the Hellenistic period is not only demonstrated by the fact that it was given a more monumentalised and permanent form in stone, but is also indicated by the changing design of the koilon which seems to have been influenced not only, as stated above, by a growing audience but also by the growing importance of the scene building. Thus the function of the koilon was divided, so to speak, between two interests: the focus on the orchestra and on the scene building respectively.[68] Thus much was still controlled by the influence of the heritage of the Classical era; the theatre kept its semi-circular design, which means that the orchestra must still have been of importance. Otherwise we might have witnessed the introduction of such seating facilities as are characteristic of 'frontal focus theatres', like some of the present day theatres, or as we know them from cinemas.

The scene building is normally classified as one of two principal types: the *paraskenia* type or the *proskenion* type. But a combination of both is also known. The paraskenia type originated in the late Classical period, and is most frequent among the early monumentalised theatres, while the proskenion type originated in the beginning of the 3rd century BC and became an integrated part of the canonical theatre complex during the Hellenistic period.[69]

Although the theatre building is the visually more dominant feature of a Greek theatre, the scene building has been brought forth as the element determining a specific type of theatre, namely theatres built more or less in the same design as the *Theatre of Dionysos*: the *parascenium type theatre*.[70] This approach embraces both main elements of the theatre and is an example of a typology where the scene building is the focus of attention. A few theatres in the latter half of the Hellenistic period were conceived of and constructed as a single building rather than as a building complex (see note 2). But the paraskenia type of scene building does not occur consistently in connection with a specific variation/ type of theatre building. Accordingly, we cannot use 'paraskenium type theatre' as a typology to cover the entire complex of a Greek theatre. We should separate the theatre building-element from the scene building and develop independent typologies for each of them.

The *proskenion* is not a fixed or static part of the scene building. Its style and dimensions, vary considerably: the style is sometimes Ionic, but more often Doric[71]; and the dimensions, i.e. the number of columns, width of intercolumniations and the diameter of the individual columns or pillars, are dependent on the theatre: the larger the theatre building the higher the number of intercolumniations and the wider the distance between the individual columns.[72]

So we have different types of scene building and within these types we have different modes of using the architectural orders; it seems that there is no correlation between the type of scene-building and architectural style.

Types of Theatre Building in Late Classical and Hellenistic Times

TYPE B. Semicircular
(Dörpfeld & Reisch 1896, 170 Fig. 67 No. I; Dilke 1948, 141 No. I).)
The pre-eminent characteristic of type B is the regular more-than-semicircular design of the theatre building. The koilon wings bend with the same radius from the point of 180° as the central semicircular part of the koilon, giving a continuous bend and the characteristic regular semicircular shape (Fig. 3). The seats, and all the other details of the koilon, and the orchestra, are laid out as circles drawn from the same centre, which at the same

time is the centre of the orchestra (Fig. 3).[73] There are few exceptions, such as *Korinthos* II, where the orchestra has been drawn closer to the innermost central part of the koilon, and some other exceptions such as changes in the orientation of the kerkides and the stairways, towards radiating that use more than one centre (*e.g. Dodone* treated below p. 158).

The finishing of the koilon with the frontal parodos-walls can be done in more than one way in this type. Frequent is the design incorporating kerkides of equal form and size, all radiating from the same centre. This type of design naturally entails that the angle relation between the parodos walls and the centre of the orchestra is the same, or approximately the same, as that between the lines drawn from the other elements of the koilon and the centre: all the major lines would, if continued, finish in the same centre (e.g. *Antiphellos, Argos* 2, *Balbyra, Kibyra* and *Megalopolis*, see Fig. 3). More often, however, such continuations of the parodos-walls would not meet exactly at this point, but a little bit below, i.e. in direction of the scene building (e.g. *Aphrodisias, Delos, Kibyra, Kyanae* and *Rhodiapolis*, see Fig. 3). The reason for this is partly that the koilon nearly always ends in stairways of the same width all the way up, as opposed to the kerkides which widen more and more upwards, but is also caused by the width of the parodos-walls themselves. But often these details do not add up to the difference in distance between the centre of the koilon design and the point where the artificial continuations of the parodos-walls meet, which means either that the two outermost kerkides do not widen upwards as much as the rest or that they are wider in their inner part than the rest. In extreme cases the parodos-walls are built on line (e.g. *Byllis* and *Dodone*).

Type B is described as the most simple and obvious way to design a monumental Greek theatre[74] and for that reason it is considered by some to be the earliest expression of the canon; it is also the common type in the beginning of the Hellenistic period.[75] This view on the chronological priority of this type seems logical. But on closer inspection, no 4th century theatre can positively be said to antedate the second half of the 4th century BC; *Aigai*, *Lokroi Epizephyrioi*, *Mantineia* I and *Megalopolis* are some of the oldest examples. This leads to the conclusion that the introduction of type B is more or less contemporary with the 'more advanced' type C (*Athens* III). Excavations have not clarified which type is the elder.[76] It is a major problem that we know that many of the theatres rebuilt in the later fourth century had predecessors, but that these have been destroyed by the reconstructions. The few exceptions, such as the change from *Chaironeia* I to II and *Oropos* I to II, have yielded evidence only for the general change from *linear* and *unique* design to or towards the canon. Though we cannot at present *prove* that the simple semicircular type is the oldest type, we may assume with Dilke that it was so, on account of its simplicity.[77]

The question of simple *versus* advanced types brings us to the next issue raised by Dörpfeld, *i.e.* the high number of theatres of type B.[78] After having studied the many excavation plans it is my impression that we may safely say that it *was* the most common type. 50 of the 98 theatres listed in the appendix may be considered as belonging to type B, that is 50%.[79] The type is represented all over the Greek world (its absence from Africa is probably not significant) and it is built continuously throughout and down to the end of Hellenistic times (late examples are *Aphrodisias*, *Rhodiapolis* and *Stratonikeia*).

The individual buildings of type B listed in the appendix show many variations. First of all theatres like *Elis*, *Philippoi* and *Tegea* II should be discussed. They cannot be more than possible examples of this the most simple type of monumental canonised Greek theatre. *Tegea* II is considered as a type B, because the shape of the analemma, which can be followed all the way

round, points in that direction. The analemma evidence from *Philippoi* is not as strong as in *Tegea* II, but to this we may add that the later Roman alterations of the Hellenistic theatre of *Philippoi* echo a type B design, which makes it probable that the predecessor was in fact built in type B design. *Elis* is a possible B because of the contours that can be drawn from the excavation plan of the Austrian expeditions. The fact that the parodos walls meet in an obtuse angle (placing this koilon within the vast majority of koila that take up more than 180° of the circle), and that the side-analemmata at the ends of the koilon wings are not parallel, suggest a type B design together with the form of the euripos. In *Elis*, which can be dated to c. 300 BC, we see an early expression of the monumentalised Greek theatre. The koilon is laid out with radiating ramps, dividing it according to the canon, but without blocks in stone. Another type B theatre, *Aigai*, shares the primitive ramps with *Elis* and is even older, perhaps as old as the beginning of the 2nd half of the 4th century BC. But at *Aigai* the form of the orchestra-edge/euripos and first row of seats is more clearly indicative of a type B design. The excavator Andronikos observed that the koilon wings are straight.[80] From the plan it can be observed that only the extreme one or two metres of the preserved row of seats are straight, while it takes at least an entire kerkis in order to reach an effect strong enough to be indicative of type C (cf. below); but more important is that these endings of the wings are not parallel, as they are in type C buildings (cf. below), so we cannot include *Aigai* in the list of type C.

As far as size is concerned the most extreme examples, also of the Greek theatre in general, are to be found in theatres of type B. The largest of all Greek theatres is presumably *Megalopolis* (width of koilon 129.5 m, diam. of orchestra 30.2 m) and one of the smallest is *Leontion* (width of koilon ca. 25 m, diam. of orchestra 9,3 m). Between these two extremes we find all sizes: small, medium and large.

Level of detail

All the types of solution for the construction of seats, proedria, euripos etc. are found in connection with type B theatre building design. The proedria is far more often encountered in middle-sized and large theatre buildings than in small ones, and the more elaborate euripoi, not very frequent compared to the high number of theatres of this type, are almost confined to large buildings; the low and wide type is found only once (*Stratos*). Many type B theatres have seating of the usual type, some of these without fillet or recess, and a number are constructed with simple or different economical seating.

TYPE C. Straight-winged

(Dörpfeld & Reisch 1896, 170 No. II Fig. 68; Dilke 1948, 141 No. II).

A common feature is a koilon with straight wings, as the rows of seats of the two outermost kerkides are straight and not curved like the others, and the inner edges of the koilon wings as well as the upper, at least of the ima cavea, are parallel (Fig. 4). The semicircular part of the koilon and orchestra are often designed from the same centre. *Athens* III, *Oiniadai* and *Peiraieus-Zea* are, however, exceptions to that since the orchestra is moved closer towards the koilon like type B *Korinthos* II (cf. Fig. 4). Dinsmoor claims that this is a characteristic shared by the buildings designed or remodelled on inspiration from *Athens* III,[81] which is true of *Oiniadai* and *Peiraieus-Zea*, but not of *Eretria* II.

Focusing only on the design of the theatre building we can list the following buildings without much discussion: *Aigeira*, *Athens* III, *Eretria* II, *Isthmia* II,[82] *Oiniadai* and *Peiraieus-Zea*. Dilke, Dinsmoor and Gogos have listed some buildings as being of this type; but apart from the six ones mentioned above there are considerable variations between them.[83] De Bernardi Ferrero lists theatres from Asia Minor and for some reason she includes *Letoon*, which does not, however, fall easily within the definitions of the type as can be deduced from Ferrero's own plan.[84] The innermost area of the theatre has not yet been fully excavated (the orchestra has been identified through trial excavations), but if we go by the probability of consistency in the layout, especially in the innermost area of the theatre building, it should be expected that the rest of the theatre at *Letoon* falls within type B.[85] *Assos* is correctly included by Dinsmoor and Dilke, *Akrai* and *Termessos* are wrongly included by Dilke, since they do not have straight wings. Dinsmoor includes *Segesta*, which is probably correct. It can be deduced from the excavation plan that the innermost row of blocks seems to form straight lines beyond the point of 180°. *Oropos* II is preserved just as bad as *Segesta* but can equally tentatively be interpreted as type C. *Pleuron*, which is listed by Gogos, is, however, definitely not of this type, for the wings are not straight at all.[86] Furthermore, *Herakleia Minoa* and *Iaitas* of Sicily, *Boiotian Orchomenos* and the theatre on the Mounichian hill at *Peiraieus* should be added.[87] More uncertain, but pointing in the direction of type C, are the traces of the recently excavated large theatre of *Messene* in the Peloponnese. So far only the straight and parallel analemmata and parodos walls have been published, but the characteristic straight side-analemmata indicate a depth of the koilon which could correspond to a construction with straight wings (type C); but of course this must remain an assumption, for the time being. As concrete examples of design-consistency between koilon and analemma among type C theatres, we can point to *Eretria* II, *Oiniadai* and *Peiraieus-Zea*. The peripheries of the other theatres of type C are either difficult to trace or have a shape determined by adjacent topographical factors (e.g. *Aigeira* and *Athens* III). From the plan showing the poorly preserved fourth phase of the Greek theatre under the Roman amphitheatre at *Kyrene* it could be maintained that we have one more theatre of type C. But the few remains point equally in the direction of type F, where it has been listed in this study (see below p. 154), and that is as far as we can get on the basis of the evidence available at present.

So we end up with between 12-14 theatres of type C, depending on the interpretation of *Kyrene* IV and *Messene*. Thus type C is the second most common type of theatre building and not the most frequent one as was maintained by Bieber.[88] The type does not vary from the general picture of the monumentalised theatres as far as the division into sections and kerkides go. The same observation can be made on size, which means that the majority of buildings are to be found around the upper end of the small and in the middle category.

Level of detail

There is more to say about the layout of theatres of this type, which are not at all identical as far as the construction of the theatre building is concerned. They can be divided into several minor sub-groups depending on what we choose to focus on. We find an uneven number of kerkides in the ima cavea as a common characteristic of *Aigeira*, *Athens* III, *Eretria* II, *Iaitas*, *Oiniadai* and *Peiraieus-Zea*. In combination with that, we see in the same theatres that the transverse line, at the point of 180° divides the curving *kerkides* from the straight ones at or near the stairways (Fig. 4). The characteristic U-shape is followed strictly in the design of euripos and proedria in the theatres of *Aigeira*, *Athens* III and *Peiraieus-Zea* and all three are orientated in almost the same direction (between S & SSE). In *Eretria* II it is not known whether there were actually proedria benches in front of all the kerkides and in *Oiniadai* a proedria is not identified. The euripoi of these two theatres are both of the low and wide type, though *Oiniadai* is a strange combination of this type and the *narrow* one.

All common types of seat are found in type C theatre buildings and we see the use of both the narrow and the wide type of euripos as noted above. But the frequency of both usual monolithic seating, elaborate euripos and proedria is higher for type C than for type B. When we include the scene building in the comparison we see no specific type occurrence; perhaps except for some local parallels. We have at least five examples of scene buildings of the paraskenia type, the rest being of the proskenion type, and although the Doric style is predominant we find both the Doric and the Ionic in both types of scene building. The theatre buildings of *Athens* III, *Eretria* II and *Peiraieus-Zea* are almost identical, and while *Eretria* II and *Athens* III both had a scene building furnished with a proskenion in the Doric order, *Peiraieus-Zea* is suspected to have had a Ionic *proskenion* (though see note 109). That theory is not at all impossible, considering the fact that the proskenion was Ionic in *Oiniadai* and had a plan closely resembling the three mentioned above. It is clear that within this type some theatres are more alike than others, and it seems that the detailed resemblance, both in the layout and on the level of detail, between some of the theatres, is to be explained by local traditions. Accordingly it must be concluded that the choice of a type C design was not a choice which automatically limited the number of opportunities on the level of detail.

Type C was constructed from the late Classical period (*Athens* III) to at least sometime in the 2nd century BC (*Peiraieus-Zea*),[89] and we find the type in mainland Greece, Sicily and South Italy, Asia Minor, and perhaps in North Africa (*Kyrene*). The present addition to the previous attempts at listing this type does not change the fact that this type of theatre is rarer than type B which is interesting, because we find it scattered all around the Greek world and in a broad span of time.

Especially on account of the date of the theatre of Dionysos, but perhaps also because of scholarly Athenocentricity, the 'invention', not only of type C, but of the fully developed canon as such is considered by some to have been a purely Athenian project, invented and built for the first time there.[90] Others consider it the result of a gradual development, which happened to find its first monumental expression at Athens.[91] Others again follow the idea of 'invention' by specific architects, but hold that the place of invention need not necessarily to have been Athens.[92] As stated above I find that there is clear evidence for a gradual development of the canon. It is possible that the earliest expression of the C-version was *Athens* III and it may be regarded as some sort of prototype; but a direct copying of it was probably only done in one instance, in the most obvious place, namely *Peiraieus-Zea*, the harbour of Athens.

TYPE E. Elliptical
(Dörpfeld & Reisch 1896, 170 No. IV Fig. 70; Dilke 1948, 142 No. IV).
Characteristic of theatres of this type is the elliptic plan of the theatre building (Fig. 5). The elliptic shape can be obtained in different ways essentially by letting koilon and orchestra use the same centre for the innermost part of the koilon (by and large the part within the innermost 160 – 170°), while two new centres are used for the outermost two or four kerkides, normally referred to as the three-centre-method (see Fig. 5). This design results in a more or less elliptical shape, in Dilke's words "being from dominating to almost not visible at first glance".[93] The shape depends on the distance between the centres after which the rows of seats, proedria, euripos and diazomata, etc. are drawn.

There are about 10 theatres of this type which means that it is third in number after B and C.[94] Some of them, as *Epidauros, Magnesia on the Maeander* and *Priene*, are built according to the 'three-centre' method.[95] The remainder (*Demetrias, Ephesos, Kadyanda, Lindos, Maroneia, Oinoanda* and *Syrakousai* 2 V) are perhaps also constructed on that principle, but it is difficult to say with certainty, since the buildings are either poorly preserved or poorly investigated. Dinsmoor has suggested that *Korinthos* II was built according to E design,[96] thus rejecting the interpretation proposed by the excavator Stillwell who reconstructed it as a type B theatre. And Dilke suggested that *Oropos* II was of E type, but this is hardly confirmed by the excavation plans.[97]

They all clearly show the elliptic aspect in at least the lower part of the ima cavea and in the area around the edge of the orchestra. This elliptical plan is the one that resembles Vitruvius' Greek Theatre the most, and in fact most of the 10 theatres in this group are to be placed somewhere between the layout of *Epidauros* and Vitruvius' Greek Theatre. In at least five of them the change of centre occurs around the stairways that separate the kerkides of the inner ca. 180° from the two outermost kerkides, thus resembling Vitruvius, and in the rest we see a tendency towards a change of centre before the point of 180° (as can be seen in the stylized example Fig. 5).

The oldest member of this type is probably the well-preserved and fine theatre at *Priene* dated to around 300 BC,[98] followed a little later by the theatre at *Epidauros I*. The remaining buildings were built later, during the 3rd and 2nd centuries BC, and more than half is found in Asia Minor, a fact that should not be pressed unduly since that area produced the most buildings in that period.

Type E theatres exist in all sizes, half of them small, and also the section and kerkides division show the same norm as the general picture.

Level of detail
At least two types of seat is seen, both types of euripos and also as many combinations as possible between types of scene building and architectural orders used for the proskenion. Significant is the two instances of plate-on-block (*Magnesia* and *Priene*) seating, members of Dilke's economical type, but which are not necessarily economical. At least *Priene* has rather refined and elaborate marble seating. As it was observed in connection with type C we may also conclude here that the frequency of normal monolithic seating, proedria and elaborate euripos is higher than in type B.

Moreover, as was the case with type C

theatres, we find within the group of the 10 type E theatres examples of a few theatres that are very much alike, as *Priene* and *Magnesia on the Maeander*, e.g. the same unusual type of seating and again, as observed in connection with the phenomenon in type C, local inspiration may offer a logical explanation, as the two localities are situated quite close to each other. As with *Athens* III in relation to type C, it is difficult to determine whether any of the type E theatres was in fact the prototype; perhaps it is even more difficult in the case of type E, since there is no candidate that could be regarded as a prototype for clear chronological reasons.

TYPE F. *Pointed*

A small group of four to five theatres show a similarity in the layout of the theatre building that separates it from the above mentioned types. The theatre of *Hephaistia* on Lemnos, the theatre of *Kassope*, the ones at *Methymna* and *Thasos*, and possibly the theatre of *Kyrene* (cf. above 151), are all laid out with a plan of the koilon that produces a pointed shape (Fig. 6). At least in *Kassope* and *Thasos* the innermost part of the koilon near the area of the lowest tiers and the edge of the orchestra resembles type C, but upwards from the first row of seats to the last of the outermost kerkides (and this is common for all members of the type) the cone-shape of normal kerkides is not maintained. The parodos-walls are recessed to such a degree that the entire koilon becomes pointed towards the scene-building, which produces an effect the exact opposite of the wedge-shaped space between koilon and scene building that we normally find in canonical theatres.[99] The type originated in the late Classical/early Hellenistic period and examples of this type are to be dated here or later in the 3rd century, except for *Methymna* which is vaguely dated to sometime in the Hellenistic period.

Level of detail

The information on the level of detail from the small number of buildings of this type is scarce due to lack of investigation and the bad state of preservation; and thus it would not be appropriate to comment on it in this context. However, it is worth mentioning, that *Kassope* and *Hephaistia* were laid out with an even number of kerkides in the ima cavea resulting in a central stairway. This is not a significant characteristic of this type for, as noted earlier, this relatively unusual solution is to be found with a small group of type B buildings as well.

Kassope shows a peculiarity in the stairways that radiate not from one centre, but from different centres between the centre of the orchestra and the scene-building (see Fig. 6).

TYPE G. *'Pergamon type'*

The last group of theatres left to be discussed as a type has got a ground plan resembling that of *Pergamon*, or at least the ima cavea of it. A common feature is that the parodos walls are built on line instead of (if continued) meeting in an angle in the orchestra, which produces the effect of a true (180°) or sometimes reduced (less than 180°) semicircle (Fig. 7). The group of theatres that share this architectural feature is not normally referred to as an individual type except by De Bernardi Ferrero.[100] I have my doubts as to whether it should be defined as a type. The characteristics of this type are defined negatively: lack of the part of the koilon that goes beyond the real semicircular part of 180°, which with its diverging forms constitute the other types of theatre building. On the other hand, the buildings of type G still have that characteristic in common, and the reason for this koilon form, which later became the standard in the Roman theatre, may be that it was not necessary for the localities in question to build more than a semicircle. Perhaps they had enough seats in what a koilon of this type could offer.

Apart from the previously mentioned theatre at *Pergamon* we can list at least five more buildings with the above-mentioned characteristics in the layout:[101] *Ambrakia* and *Bouthrotos* in Epeiros, *Metapontion* IV and *Akrai* in Magna Graecia, and

154

'*Perperene*' (mod. Asaga-Bei-Köi) in the neighbourhood of *Pergamon*. From this we see a wide geographic diffusion, while the chronological span is more narrow, this is the late 4th and 3rd centuries BC.

It is quite obvious that local topographical conditions influenced this particular design of the koilon in *Pergamon*. The theatre here is placed on a very steep hillside, resulting in one of the steepest koila in the Greek world. If that dramatic sloping was to be maintained in possible kerkides constructed in the area extending 180°, so that the *koilon* would show a normal segment of a circle (between 180° and 210°), the parodos-walls supporting this koilon at the front would have to have been enormous, and perhaps too complicated to construct. Moreover the way the theatre is placed, attached to a narrow terrace sanctuary, would not allow the koilon to protrude more than it already does because of lack of space. That fact probably also explains why the scene building there was never built in stone (it had to be removed when not in use).[102] The other theatres with a ground plan like this are not located in topographical and geomorphological surroundings similar to those of *Pergamon*. In the case of *Akrai* the scene building is placed so close to the theatre building that an extension of the koilon beyond the 180° would have been absurd. People sitting in those areas would not have been able to see anything. At *Metapontion* the geomorphologic surroundings are in fact the opposite of those at *Pergamon*, since the theatre here is built on level ground, except for the slight artificial sloping. That results in a situation which does not create the same difficulties as in *Pergamon* for the construction of kerkides and parodos walls. So here, as in *Bouthrotos*, there seems to be no obvious explanation for this particular design. As to *Ambrakia*, the smallest of all monumental theatres found to this date, it is at present impossible to interpret the immediate ancient surroundings, as they have not been excavated because of their location in the middle of modern Arta.

The Typology of the Greek Theatre Building

In the previous section the surviving theatre buildings were discussed and grouped on the basis of their overall design. It will now be examined to what extent it makes sense to focus on the material in that way.

The appearance of the different types of design of the canon is to be explained basically as the birth of the canon itself.[103] As mentioned earlier, the growth in the number of spectators required the canon in order to facilitate an optimal view and acoustic conditions for as many people as possible. The emergence of type B was a fundamental step forward as the earliest expression of the canon. A koilon of this type could expand up to a segment of 210° or so of a circle, but not more than that, because there had to be room for the parodoi and the scene building; *Lokroi Epizephyrioi* is a rare example of a segment of a lot more than 210°. It may be observed that the scene building takes up more and more of the orchestra area, proportionally corresponding to the size of the theatre, hindering the tendency to expanding the koilon beyond 180°. The scene building simply had to be moved closer to the main body of the audience sitting, often far away, in the central part of the koilon (e.g. *Megalopolis* and *Pergamon*).[104] This phenomenon, also connected with the viewing problems, increases in importance during the Hellenistic era because of the growing size of the theatre building.[105] The rows of seats could then be expanded upwards, until the distance between the audience sitting in the uppermost seats and the actors in the orchestra and on the scene building became too long. In my opinion this is the case for the theatre of *Argos* 2 with a *koilon* of at least 81 rows of seats. The maximum distance from which an average ancient Greek could see or hear satisfactorily simply constitutes an upper limit to the size of theatre buildings, if all the seats were to be equally useful. As the scene building became more and more important as the focal point, the seats in the outermost area of the wings of the type B-koilon became less useful, or at least less desirable: the people there had to sit in an inconvenient position and turn their heads in order to be able to see the action.[106] The many examples of type B theatres, for which it can be observed that the outermost kerkides do not widen as much upwards as the rest, are clearly to be interpreted as attempts to minimize those disadvantages of the type B design.

Attempts at solving these particular problems most probably led to the introduction of type C. The outermost kerkides, which would have had the unpopular orientation in the type B design, were straightened out, so that the view from there became a compromise between the focus on orchestra and scene building. These straight rows of seats could be and were indeed in some theatres extended, not only to solve the problem of view, but also most probably to give room for more spectators in the lowermost area of the koilon where the distance between spectators and actors was shorter (e.g. Herakleia Minoa and perhaps Messene). Because of such an elongation of the koilon wings, the scene building had to be moved farther away from the central semicircular part of the koilon, in an extreme situation resulting in a bad view for the better part of the spectators who sat in that area. So there was a maximum limit to such elongation of the wings in this type, especially in large theatre buildings.

A compromise between the attempt to provide a good view from the wings while not pushing the scene building too far back is the elliptical type E. This type of theatre building design is clearly the most sophisticated, since it combines the optimal solutions to the need for space for the audience (extension of the koilon beyond 180°), a comfortable and good view from the outermost kerkides towards the scene of action (the orchestra and scene building), and finally the keeping of as short a distance as possible between the central part of the koilon and the scene building.

The pointed Type F is a kind of developed type C, where the bad view from the outer and uppermost seats was eliminated in a very concrete way: the koila of this type were simply constructed without the bad or at times even useless areas of the outermost kerkides that the other types had. The fact that the type F koilon was constructed with so much thought to the scene building is in perfect harmony with the idea of a growing popularity of the scene building during the 3rd century BC. On the other hand, the removal of the 'bad sectors' in the F-design resulted in fewer seats, and that is perhaps the reason why this type of design was used only rarely.

The last type (G) is as rare as type F. The type is the only one, apart from F, that really addresses the consequences of the growing importance of the scene building during the Hellenistic period. But this fact is not reflected chronologically; the G theatres are concentrated in the late 4th and 3rd centuries BC rather than late in the Hellenistic period, when they would otherwise have been a natural prelude to the Roman period, when this type took over completely.

That some solutions to the problems of the space and view were better than others is also proved by the way they appear chronologically as a natural result of experiment and experience. The typology does not fit strictly into a chronological line of development, but there does seem to be some chronological interrelation between the different types. They all appear for the first time more or less simultaneously during the second half of the 4th century BC, type E arriving a little later. The popularity of the individual types can be deduced from the frequency with which they appear over time. Type B design is used for construction of theatres from the time of the introduction of the canon until the end of Hellenistic times, and no particular century show a definite peak. The higher number of type B theatres built or rebuilt in the 4th and 3rd centuries compared with later periods is to be explained by the generally vast number of theatres built in that period. So Dilke's opinion that the type B gradually died out can no longer be maintained.[107] But this investigation, quite expectedly finding a relation between architectural development and chronology, supports the idea that type B was the oldest and the original expression of the canon. Later, type C becomes more frequent and in the 3rd century type E appears, the same century where we find more than half of the type G theatres and most of type F.

Details

The growing number of advanced ground plans during Hellenistic times shows a development that can also be observed on the level of detail, for example the previously mentioned lower frequency of economic versions of seats of the usual type in the 3rd century and later. The observations made on the simple type of seating points in that direction as well, but here we may also stress the fact, that this type is almost confined to small theatre buildings. This again suggests that growing size of theatre buildings leads to higher monumentality and elaboration.

An illustrative example of how design and detail concur is found in a group of large theatres of type B, *Dodone*, *Korinthos* II and *Sikyon*: they are all elaborate monumental buildings, with fine and well-built euripos, not very common for the type, and proedria, but significantly, typical of type B, with more or less economical solutions for the seats; *Sikyon* shows a combination of the usual type and the economic.

Size leads to higher monumentalisation and refinement, but it is important to note that it does not work the other way around. The types of theatre building that were considered to be more advanced are found in all sizes; they do not show a higher frequency in the large category than type B.

The examination of the details of the individual types demonstrated that none of the types of detail can add to or change the meaning of the typology in any consistent way. However, apart from the tendencies in refined details occurring proportionally to the sizes of theatres, individual tendencies of more refined plans (types C and E) can also be found coinciding with a higher frequency of refined details, which must be said to have an effect on the descriptive value of the typology. A support of this hierarchic interpretation of the types is, for instance, the identification of the only examples of 'primitive' ramps for stairways and kerkides without seat-blocks in designs of type B.

It is clear that the construction of a theatre building of a more advanced type was more complicated and expensive than a plain type B theatre building. So of course the choice of type and details was influenced by the economic resources of the communities financing the enterprise. The larger *poleis* of Hellas did choose all types of theatre building, but often preferred the more advanced ones to type B. This tendency can also be inferred from the fact that we simply do not find any 'advanced' theatres in connection with what we class as smaller and more 'provincial' poleis and none of the communities with 'primitive' theatres are huge poleis. These observations supports the idea that the types represent different degrees of refinement and monumentality of the canon.

Local traditions

An approach like the present that classifies buildings on the basis of their architectural design cannot cover all aspects of the many canonical, but still individually constructed theatres. There are many relevant approaches to a subject as substantial and complex as the Greek theatre. Apart from the factors discussed above, we should obviously consider the impact of local traditions in the designs of theatres and their details, expressed in many different ways, sometimes so strongly that they divert from the canon itself.[108] Even if they are mostly confined to details and perhaps only once found as an all pervasive feature, *Peiraieus-Zea* in relation to *Athens* III, a presentation of some examples will surely give a more nuanced picture of theatre architecture than the present rigid typology offers.

On the basic level of construction an Arkadian peculiarity is found in *Mantineia* I-II and *Tegea* II both of which are constructed on level ground; a way of construction that is used only rarely in Greece (other examples are *Eretria* and *Metapontion*). Both cities were situated in plains, but at least in the case of *Tegea* there were minor hills within the area of (or at least close to) the urban centre with natural sloping that could have been used for a theatre. It is likely that the Tegeans learned from the earlier theatre in *Mantineia* I-II and thus, for whatever reason, chose to place their theatre in answer to needs considered of higher priority than the cheaper construction at a hill had offered.

On the overall theatre building design level, it has been observed that some type C theatres in the Attika-Euboia area and some type E theatres in Asia Minor show close similarities (see above). Another example is the design of '*Perperene*' copied from the design of nearby *Pergamon*. The practical circumstances given as possible explanations for the design of *Pergamon* cannot be yielded at '*Perperene*', so here, it seems, is an example of stylistic inspiration. But even at the narrow local level, where the similarity of buildings in a few cases is almost complete, there are all the same always differences. A good example of this is the transposed orchestra in *Athens* III, an idea which is copied in the later theatre *Peiraieus-Zea*, but not in *Eretria* II, which in fact with its wide and shallow euripos is a hybrid of *Athens* III and *Epidauros* (type E). Even *Athens* III and *Peiraieus-Zea*, built by the same polis and considered to be quite alike, may have differed in regard to the scene building that was built in the Doric order in *Athens* III and (perhaps) in the Ionic in *Peiraieus-Zea*.[109]

Both in the theatre at *Megalopolis* and the theatre in the sanctuary at *Epidauros*, type B and E respectively, the epitheatra are not expanded as much as the ima caveae, so that the analemmata fronts there are not equal to the outermost seats or stairs in the individual sections. That is, on the other hand, the norm for the canon as such. This is a local way to compensate for the bad sectors in the outer and uppermost parts of the koilon, giving the same advantages in this direction as in the type F (pointed) design.

On the level of detail many examples of local tendencies can be given: in the Greek theatre building the stairways most often radiate from the centre of the orchestra, underlining the centrally oriented idea as the basic rule in the architecture of the Greek theatre. A few exceptions to that rule can, however, be observed, again with strong local roots. In *Dodone* and the large theatre of *Kassope* the stairways of the innermost part of the koilon follow the norm, while the outermost break it and bend more in the direction of the scene building (see Fig. 6). This bending of the orientation of the stairways does not have a practical function on the same level as the actual shape of the koilon wings in the way of optimalizing the visual and acoustic qualities of the theatre building. In my opinion it is an example of details on the secondary level that are influenced by the design choices made on the primary level. *Kassope* with its type F-koilon, designed for a good view of the scene building at the expense of an optimal number of spectators, is an obvious place to expect this change of radiation in the stairways. The same can be said of *Dodone*, which is admittedly type B, but at the same time designed with a straight frontal analemma, showing that here, too, the attention paid to the view of the scenebuilding took priority, so that the least attractive areas of the koilon were avoided. That the two examples of this phenomenon are to be found in Epeiros, and also quite close to each other, is undoubtedly an example of the power of local inspiration.[110]

The 'one sloping step pr. one row of seats' stairways in the theatres of *Aigeira*, *Athens* III, *Peiraieus-Zea* and *Sikyon* is also a good example of a phenomenon with some local significance. Dwelling on stairs we see an Argolid-Corinthian peculiarity in a central stairway 'cutting the theatre building in two', in *Argos* 2, *Epidauros,* and

Korinthos II. The former two are of type B, the latter of type E, and here we have a good proof of local habits, with an unknown practical significance, if any, that run counter not only to the types but also to the canon. This phenomenon is rarely seen in Greek theatres, but it is nonetheless also found as far away as *Alexandria Oxiana* and *Apollonia* in Kyrenaika. Accordingly it cannot be classified exclusively as a local north-east Peloponnesian feature. Further supporting the identification of a north-eastern Peloponnesian local tradition in theatre architecture is the fact that *Argos* 2 and *Korinthos* II, now together with *Stratos* in Epeiros, resemble each other in the circular orchestra in a quadrangular/trapezoidal enclosure.[111] The fact that they share all these peculiarities (in fact almost unique for them) is very important in the discussion of the meaning and relevance of the typology, and proves that it is not sufficient as the only tool for the architectonical description of the theatre building.

The canon and its types in new cities

Another aspect that could be studied in more detail is how the topographical context can be said to have an influence on the design of the theatre. Theatres built in connection with planned poleis and sanctuaries, as opposed to theatres built in self-grown poleis and sanctuaries, give good evidence for clear examples of the different types of theatre building, and also confirm the appearance of the types in a more or less chronological line of development. Of course, the development of the theatre took place everywhere, but one would expect to find the most articulated expression of new ideas in the architecture of the theatre, as well as in all the other types of monumental buildings of the Greeks, in planned new urban areas. Naturally, there were often local topographical or financial circumstances which limited the opportunities of the architects, both in regard to the choice of theatre building type and in regard to the choice of details.

A few examples will show that the evidence from planned poleis does in fact support the chronological side of the typology. Built in the period apparently immediately after the 'Tearless Battle' in 368 BC[112] as an integrated part of the artificially created urban centre of the polis of Megalopolis, and without a predecessor to force it to keep within the frames of an eventual local tradition, the huge theatre of *Megalopolis* became one of the earliest and finest type B theatres, the earliest expression of the canon. The element of display was perhaps important in this case, since the whole ideology of Megalopolis, as proclaimed by the name itself, was one of resource accumulation. Of course, the city served an immediate and practical purpose as a defence-bastion-city for southern Arkadia against Sparta; but to convince both insiders and outsiders of Megalopolis that the project would work, the monumental architecture such as city walls, temples, theatres, etc. had better be impressive. In the case of the theatre this assumption would be corroborated if we were able to prove that it was far larger than necessary, but this is not possible.[113] The theatre here was constructed to house a high number of people, and at that time the obvious choice of theatre building was a type B.

Another example is the urban circumstances around the theatre building in *Kassope*, perhaps the most perfect type F specimen. The plan of this large theatre seems very conscious, just as the rest of *Kassope* was, and typical of a city built from scratch in the 'Hippodamian tradition' after a synoikismos of 350 BC.[114] Unfortunately we do not know precisely when the theatre was built. The German scholars working at Kassope date most of the public buildings to the time after 230 BC when Kassope was autonomous and a member of the Epeirot League.[115] Even though there is a considerable time span between the foundation of the city and the construction of the theatre I believe that the overall planning was thought out from the start; maybe there was a more primitive structure serving as a theatre until the 'real one' was constructed. Even if there was a monumental predecessor for the theatre to determine the scope of the new building, it would not be older than the 3rd quarter of the 4th century BC. The architectural choices were based on the available architectural knowledge that existed, not just locally but also generally in late Classical Greece. Among them was the idea that the theatre building did not necessarily have to be of type B, but could be of type F, as it came to be at *Kassope*, a universal type, but also furnished with some local features as pointed out above.

As a last example of the types in new cities *Priene* will do. The city was relocated some time in the 4th century BC, and the general opinion is that the new city was built from scratch.[116] The theatre of *Priene* stands today as one of the finest examples of type E design, perhaps even the earliest expression of it, and also generally as one of the best preserved theatres. It was left almost untouched by Roman building activity and the preservation is good. But it is to be noted that the design of the ima cavea is not completed in the epitheatron, most probably because, as opposed to the theatres at *Kassope* and *Megalopolis*, the building was fitted into the orthogonal plan of the city. Even in this reduced form it was not possible to keep it within the *insulae* of Priene.[117]

Conclusion

The choice of type of theatre building is not, as pointed out above, a choice between a few all-covering concepts. Of course theatres such as *Athens* III and *Epidauros* were used as models of inspiration for architects all over the Greek world, but the lack on examples of conceptual copying, even from these two important theatres, underline to what extent we have to regard the theatre as a building composition. The choice of overall planning is of course central, but still just one out of several elements in a building composition incorporating details too. All choices are determined by change of fashion/development of new ideas, practical matters like size requirements and local topographical conditions, financial ability, and also by local tradition. The lack of typological connection between theatre building and scene building of course means that the typology B-G is not a typology of the Greek theatre – such a typology cannot be established – but a typology of the most dominating and characteristic part: the theatre building.[118] That we are dealing with different types, and not just variations of the canon, is proved by the tendencies to different degrees of monumentality that the types and the details stand for.

That the types of theatre building more or less followed the general economic capacity, number of spectators, etc. of the poleis or sanctuaries that built them is to be expected. The element of display should not be underestimated.[119] Here we only have to refer to the polis of Athens and the sanctuary of Epidauros, controlled by the polis Epidauros, both of which were visited by many people from the Greek world and the rest of the Mediterranean. At both places, the theatre played perhaps the most important role not only as the architectural and topographical *locus par excellence* generally in the architectural plan of the cities; but also as the place where the climax of events during festivals took place. Of course Athens and Epidauros had to have beautiful theatres that could impress all foreigners and thus play their part of the architectural orchestra that should confirm and legitimate the important role of these localities. But in my opinion Isler perhaps gives the representational value too much credit as opposed to the practical when he writes: " The introduction of the circular plan marked a turning point in the progression from purely utilitarian to representative architecture at a time when the theatre, which was not only used to stage performances but also to hold citizens' meetings, became the symbol of the free Greek city ".[120] I do not believe that it is possible, nor that it makes sense, to distinguish between the practical and the representational explanation for the emergence of the monumental theatre. They go hand in hand.

Notes

NOTE 1
I would like to thank my supervisor Annette Rathje for good help during the writing of this work which began as an MA thesis. Furthermore I am indebted to Tobias Fischer-Hansen, Pelle Oliver Larsen, Thomas Heine Nielsen, Pernille Flensted-Jensen & Lene Rubinstein for many corrections and suggestions. Also, thanks are due to Kjeld de Fine Licht for having read an early draft, and to the Danish Institute at Athens for its never failing help and friendly attitude, and finally to the foundation *Christian og Emma Blinkenbergs Rejselegat* and the Copenhagen Polis Centre for raising enough money for me to be able to visit more than 60 theatres between the autumn of 1995 and the summer of 1999.

NOTE 2
Bieber 1961, 73, 127; Wycherley 1962, 167, 174; Dinsmoor 1975, 318-319; Lauter 1986, 167. There are, however, a few examples of monuments where *parodos* doors unify the scene building and the *koilon* into one whole, i.e. into a theatre building as such: e.g. Epidauros, sanctuary of Asklepios (e.g. Dilke 1950, 45; Dinsmoor 1975, 318-319; see, however, Wycherley 1962, 167) and Byllis in Epeiros (Ceka 1990, 227). The theatres of Magna Graecia show a step towards this unification in the Hellenistic period, which became standard in the Roman period, cf. Mitens 1988, 11.

NOTE 3
Dörpfeld & Reisch 1896, 375-379; Bieber 1961, 73; Wycherley 1962, 174; Mitens 1988, 11-12; Isler 1994, 88; Corni 1994, 134. - I use the traditional terminology, accepting its mix of Greek, Latin and modern terms. For a recent treatment of the architectural terminology of the Greek theatre, see Corni 1994, fig. at 135-136.

NOTE 4
Lauter 1986, 166ff; Isler 1994, 94ff.

NOTE 5
Discussion p. 147f. and note 62.

NOTE 6
Bieber 1961, 73; Dinsmoor 1975, 301; Implicit in Isler 1994, 96.

NOTE 7
Bieber 1961, 71-73; Lauter 1986, 168; von Gerkan 1961, 36 (on *Epidauros*).

NOTE 8
Dörpfeld & Reisch 1896, 36-40; Pickard-Cambridge 1946, 134 ff.

NOTE 9
Von Gerkan 1961, 77-80.

NOTE 10
Theatre of Dionysos as a general 'Urbild': Isler 1994, 96, 100; Wycherley (1962, 167) calls the theatre of Dionysos "... the prototype of Greek theatres". Monuments given as examples of Athens inspiration: Dinsmoor 1975, 316 (*Peiraieus-Zea, Korinthos* II and *Oiniadae*). *Epidauros* as general 'Urbild': Dilke 1948, 135 (see however Dilke 1950, 42); von Gerkan 1961, 34. Monuments given as examples of Epidauros inspiration: von Gerkan 1961, 34 (*Magnesia* and *Priene*); Dinsmoor 1975, 250, (*Magnesia*). Dörpfeld & Reisch 1896, 155 note the similarities between the paraskenia constructed in Magnesia and The Theatre of Dionysos but also the likeness in the overall plan (elliptical) between Magnesia and Epidauros (156).

NOTE 11
General treatment, see Bieber 1961, 127.

NOTE 12
Bieber 1961, 70. U shaped: Dinsmoor 1975, 317. Horseshoe shaped: Mitens 1988, 22; Gogos 1992, 27 note 52, 109; *TGR* II, 134.

NOTE 13
TGR II, 209 and Bieber 1961, 72, respectively.

NOTE 14
Dörpfeld & Reisch 1896, 99 (*Peiraieus-Zea*), 113 (*Eretria* II), 170 (*Segesta*).

NOTE 15
Dörpfeld & Reisch 1896, 169-175. For other treatments of Vitruvius' Greek theatre, see Bieber 1961, 127-128 and Dilke 1948, 132ff.

NOTE 16
Dilke 1948.

NOTE 17
Dinsmoor 1975, 316-317 consistently recognises the three types, but uses 'horseshoe plan' explicitly about the more-than-semicircular *koila*, an expression normally used for the U-shaped ones. Horseshoes look in fact more like the elliptic *koila* than the U-shaped, but I prefer to avoid the ambiguous expression horseshoe at least in a study like the present where the differences in design of the theatre building is concerned.

NOTE 18
Mitens 1988, 22 states that the Greek theatres of Magna Graecia are normally horseshoe shaped (i.e. U-shaped) except for the theatre of *Akrai* which is semicircular. In the introductory articles of *TGR* 1994 this issue is not treated in detail, but the individual catalogue texts distinguish between horseshoe (e.g. II 204, 215) and more-than-semicircular shape (e.g. II 153, 189), but use both these terms about the third elliptical type (e.g. II 209, III 441).

NOTE 19
Bieber 1961, 70 uses 'horseshoe' and U-shape synonymously, while on page 127 she correctly recognises the types and accordingly uses the correct terms. Wycherley 1962, 166, describes the characteristics of the elliptic type as if they were general to the canon. Lauter 1986, 167ff. uses 'muschelförmig' as a broad term for the monumentalised theatre as such. In the chapter on 'Theatre Classification' in *TGR* Corni writes (1994, 134): "The *cavea - koilon -* varies in shape, but is normally a circular segment that goes beyond the semicircle."

NOTE 20
Rossetto & Sartorio 1994, 64.

NOTE 21
The Corpus includes not only actual ruins, but also theatres that are only attested in literary or epigraphic sources. An important supplement to the corpus is Isler 1997 and a special study by the author about the preservation of theatres and the different sources for reconstructing the original number of buildings (*Papers from the Copenhagen Polis Centre* 6, forthcoming).

NOTE 22
Theatres listed in the appendix and mentioned in the text are italicised and often followed by Roman numerals which stands for the major phases of construction e.g. *Athens* III = the Theatre of Dionysos at Athens, the Lykourgan phase. The Arabic numerals 1 and 2, sometimes added too, are used to distinguish between more theatres at the same locality. Because the theatres are listed according to type, an alphabetical list is given at p. 167.

NOTE 23
Von Gerkan 1961, 36.

NOTE 24
Metapontion II-III and *Thorikos* I did perhaps have a square *orchestra* in common in late Archaic times (depending on the interpretation of *Thorikos*), Frederiksen 1997. Metapontion: Mertens & De Siena 1982. Thorikos: W.L. Cushing, *The Theatre of Thoricus*, PAA IV, 1885-86, 30.

NOTE 25
In my unpublished MA thesis (Frederiksen 1997) I have suggested, without much fantasy I must admit, to name the types of Greek theatre building A, B, C etc. according more or less to the way they appear chronologically as well as on the basis of their numeral frequency. (see p. 139 and 149ff.).

NOTE 26
On this type and the dating of it, see G.V. Gentili, Nuovo esempio di "theatron" con gradinata rettilinea a Siracusa, *Dioniso* XV 1952, 127; Ginouvès 1972, 40, 61-62; Anti & Polacco 1969, 42-44. To these should perhaps be added the similar structure at Stymphalos (mentioned briefly in E.H. Williams, Stymphalos: A planned city of Ancient Arcadia, *EMC* XXVII.2 1983, 200 and G. Touchais, Chronique des Fouilles en 1983, *BCH* CVIII 1984, 756, 757 Fig. 36 [indicated on a very small scale]) but we

must wait for a detailed investigation before we determine that. The interpretation of these buildings as theatres is not without problems, as the only real unambiguous architectonic member of the Greek theatre, the scene building, is missing completely from this group of buildings. For a general treatment of the problem of identification see Ginouvès 1972, 53ff. and Frederiksen 1997, and Inge Nielsen in the volume.

NOTE 27
Bulle 1928, 5-6; Dilke 1950, 40; Ginouvès 1972, 63-65. The theatre at *Trakhones* could be regarded as a type D theatre, but as there is a monumentalized koilon (or traces of it), it rather belongs to the group of *unique* monuments, where it has in fact been listed in the appendix. But, of course, nothing can be said for certain about this monument before it has been published.

NOTE 28
Dörpfeld & Reisch 1896, 375; Wycherley 1962, 170; Dinsmoor 1975, 297-98; Isler 1994, 96; Lauter 1986, 167; Rossetto and Sartorio 1994, 66, also commenting on the geographical spread.

NOTE 29
Dinsmoor 1975, 265ff; Lauter 1986, 7ff.

NOTE 30
Cf. Rossetto and Sartorio 1994, 80; Mitens 1988, 20-21 (Magna Graecia); De Bernardi Ferrero IV 1974, 18-20 (Asia Minor).

NOTE 31
Generally: Rossetto and Sartorio 1994, 79-80; von Gerkan 1961, 5 Abb. 1; Wycherley 1962, 163. Asia Minor: De Bernardi Ferrero IV 1974, 24. Magna Graecia: Mitens 1988, 33 fig. 24.

NOTE 32
A. von Gerkan, *Griechische Stadtanlagen*, Berlin 1924, 80; Wycherley 1962, 163.

NOTE 33
In this context the interpretation of the function of the monument, by the excavators called theatre-ekklesiasterion, is of less importance. Cf. Mertens & De Siena 1982 for a discussion.

NOTE 34
Cf. Dinsmoor 1975, 49.

NOTE 35
Lauter 1986, 168.

NOTE 36
Cf. Kolb 1984, 80, 133.

NOTE 37
Cf. Isler 1994, 94.

NOTE 38
I use the size definitions introduced by Rossetto and Sartorio 1994, 80: small <60 m, medium 60-80 m and large >80 m (measured at the widest point of the koilon).

NOTE 39
Dilke 1948, 139.

NOTE 40
1896, 170ff., 1930, 24 and 1961, 127, respectively. Later followed by De Bernardi Ferrero IV 1974, 76, and (though more ambiguous) Gogos 1992, 27 note 52.

NOTE 41
Further treated by Dilke 1948, 138-139, 186 ff. Cf. Wycherley 1962, 164-165 and Kolb 1984, 134, on the problem of fitting theatres into 'Hippodamian' town plans.

NOTE 42
Cf. von Gerkan 1961, 3, 33-34.

NOTE 43
See however Mitens 1988, 23, who concludes in regard to the Greek theatres in Magna Graecia: "Le dimensioni del koilon non sembra abbiano avuto importanza nei riguardi di detta suddivisione."

NOTE 44
In a not insignificant number of buildings the knowledge about the layout of the koilon remains uncertain because of lack of preservation and/or investigation, e.g. Abdera (*TGR* II 115), Koroneia (Dilke 1948, 152), the large theatre in Larissa (*TGR* II 245), Keryneia (*TGR* II 255) and Tanagra (*TGR* II 302).

NOTE 45
Dinsmoor 1975, 317.

NOTE 46
Cf. Bieber 1961, 128, making a similar general statement on that issue.

NOTE 47
Dilke 1948, 135.

NOTE 48
Gogos 1992, 31 and note 71.

NOTE 49
Pickard-Cambridge 1946, 139 note 5. See however Fiechter 1950, 37.

NOTE 50
This could be the case also in the not excavated theatres of Boiotian Koroneia (Dilke 1948, 152) and Thespiai (valley of the Muses) (*TGR* II 307).

NOTE 51
Dilke 1948, 152-153; Dinsmoor 1975, 316.

NOTE 52
Treated by Dilke 1948, 153-161.

NOTE 53
Dilke 1948, 153. He adds that this type of seating was "by no means universal even in Hellenistic times", but that statement is far too pessimistic in my opinion. Von Gerkan 1961, 35, claims that Asia Minor showed different habits for example in the use of the 'economical type' of seating exemplified by *Ephesos*, *Magnesia on Maeander* and *Priene*. This is partly true, but according to De Bernardi Ferrero IV 1974, 45, the use of monolithic seats became the norm in Asia Minor, and she gives the same exceptions as von Gerkan and adds *Pergamon* and Tralle*s* (*TGR* III 380-81).

NOTE 54
Von Gerkan 1961, 35.

NOTE 55
Dilke 1948, 153ff.

NOTE 56
According to Dilke (1948, 161) economic seating is not attested in any theatres constructed later than 150 BC.

NOTE 57
Treated by Dilke 1948, 165-181; Dinsmoor 1975, 317-318; Gogos 1992, 109 note 269.

NOTE 58
This interpretation of the upper *proedria* is debated. See von Gerkan 1921, 99f; von Gerkan 1961, 80; Gogos 1992, 110.

NOTE 59
Dinsmoor 1975, 317; Fiechter 1931, 21, suggesting this based on a find of one plate on the first row of seats.

NOTE 60
Further examples where thrones, fragments of thrones or bases have been found are e.g. *Eretria* II, *Mytilene*, *Tegea* II and *Typaneai*.

NOTE 61
For a broad description of the different types of *euripos*, see e.g. von Gerkan 1961, 35 and Dinsmoor 1975, 312.

NOTE 62
Gebhard 1974, 428ff.; Kolb 1981, 16f. Opposed to this view we have e.g. Dörpfeld & Reisch 1896, (implicit 366-367), Dilke 1948, 127 (on the early theatre), De Bernardi Ferrero IV 1974, 76 and Lauter 1986, 311, stating that it was the other way around.

NOTE 63
See however von Gerkan 1961, 34 who is sceptic about the existence of a circular orchestra here.

NOTE 64
Gebhard 1974, 428 note 2 adds *Oiniadai* and cautiously *Ephesos*. *Oiniadai* has also earlier been included among the theatres having a circular orchestra (Bieber 1961, 119), but I must admit that I am not convinced. The excavator B. Powell (A.I.A. II Ser. VIII [1904] pl. VIII) draws it in on the plan of the theatre, and describes traces of the stone ring continuing. But already Fiechter, 1931, 13, noted that the continuation of the row of white poros-stones was not traceable when he examined the theatre. The finely profiled blocks that mark the limit of the orchestra towards the euripos do not, as far as I can see, continue to form a complete circle. The orchestra, the groove in which the profiled blocks are laid, and the euripos, are all hewn out of the rock and it is easily noticed that the groove does not continue from the point were the euripos disappears to continue underground (autopsy May 1998).

NOTE 65
Dörpfeld & Reisch 1896, 376, 379 (4th cent.), 383 (entire Hellenistic period). As late as 1975 Dinsmoor, 312, writes (having all the localities in mind where we do not find the full orchestra circle) that it was imagined; Gebhard 1974, 428-440 sums up the evidence on the existence of circular orchestra before *Epidauros* and finds that there are none. A most recent follower of the Dörpfeld orthodoxy is Isler 1997, 549, giving the examples (dating from the middle of the 4th cent. BC): *Athens* III, *Elis*, *Megalopolis* and *Aigai*, none of which, however, have circular orchestrai.

NOTE 66
Cf. Dinsmoor 1975, 312.

NOTE 67
A good treatment in Dinsmoor 1975, 298-308. Among the problems with the scene-building is the possible existence of a wooden skene as such in the early phase of the monumentalised Greek theatre and whether the purpose of the proskenion was as a background for acting or as an actual stage for it. For clarifications in the discussion on these problems see e.g. Modona 1961, 30ff and Dinsmoor 1975, 298-308, for descriptions of the development of the scene building from wooden additional element to permanent stone element. Though the sources have expanded a lot since the turn of the century a good general treatment is still to be found in O. Puchstein, *Die Griechische Bühne*, Berlin 1901, but for a more recent study comprising a few key monuments see S. Gogos, Zur Typologie vorhellenistischer Theaterarchitektur, *ÖJh* 59 1989 Beiblatt, 114-158.

NOTE 68
This increasing focus on the scene building was caused by the introduction of the New Comedy, with the accompanying decreasing importance of the *choros* and the moving of the remaining main characters to the roof of the proskenion or logheion as it was called. See e.g. Dinsmoor 1975, 298; Isler 1994, 102.

NOTE 69
Isler 1994, 98.

NOTE 70
Dinsmoor 1975, 298; Isler 1994, 100.

NOTE 71
Isler 1994, 100.

NOTE 72
For some examples see Dinsmoor 1975, 303; Gogos 1992, 75ff.

NOTE 73
Dinsmoor 1975, 316.

NOTE 74
Dörpfeld & Reisch 1896, 173.

NOTE 75
Cf. Dilke 1948, 141.

NOTE 76
Isler 1994, 96.

NOTE 77
Dilke above note 75 Gogos 1992, 27 note 52 and 30 note 68, discusses the chronological and regional aspects of types B and

C and finds that they were not linked to either chronology or place, but coexisted. Gogos also refers to Fiechter's diverging suggestions on chronology. Fiechter 1935, 84-87 (probably meaning all semicircular koila) only mentions *Epidauros* and *Priene* (both type E) explicitly as being older than type C.

NOTE 78
1896, 173. Cf. Dinsmoor 1975, 316 and Corni 1994, 134.

NOTE 79
Listings of monuments previously classified as type B: Dörpfeld & Reisch 1896, 170 (the theatres mentioned here, Side, Myra and Aezani, are apparently all Roman); Dilke 1948, 141; Dinsmoor 1975, 316 (includes *Ephesos* among theatres of this type, but it belongs to type E, see below; On Asia Minor: De Bernardi Ferrero IV 1974, 76.

NOTE 80
Andronikos 1984, 46-49.

NOTE 81
1975, 316.

NOTE 82
As reconstructed by the excavator the theatre at Isthmia, despite having the common straight wings of this type, has got a koilon whose inner part does not form a complete semicircle before the wings straighten, see Gebhard 1973, Pl. IV.

NOTE 83
1948, 141, 1975, 317 and 1992, 27 note 52, respectively.

NOTE 84
IV 1974, 76 and III 1970, Tav. XIII, respectively.

NOTE 85
Only the existence of a Roman stage building has been identified so far (Isler in *TGR* III, 475). The monument is located in the extraurban sanctuary, used as a federal sanctuary for the Lycian League, and perhaps the function of the monument was as meeting place for it and therefore constructed without scene building. Until otherwise proven *Letoon* will, however, be considered a regular theatre.

NOTE 86
Corresponding to this fact the theatre of *Pleuron* is listed by Dilke (1948, 141) and Dinsmoor (1975, 316) with theatres of type B.

NOTE 87
The beautiful and well-preserved theatre at Halikarnassos is also of this type, but since it has not been published I cannot include it in this investigation, see *TGR* III, 402.

NOTE 88
1961, 127. Dilke's statement (1948, 135) to the effect that the straight-winged type C and the circular-winged type B are equally common, will also have to be regarded as out of date.

NOTE 89
Type C theatres were built in the Roman period as well, e.g. *Tralles,* probably dating to the 1. cent. AD. De Bernardi Ferrero III 1970, 111, Tav. XX. In *TGR* III, 381, dated to 1. cent. BC.

NOTE 90
Dilke 1948, 141; Wurster 1993, 20; Lauter, 1986, 167, also considering Athens to be the spot of invention, makes a distinction between Athens and Epidauros, placing the theatre of Epidauros and also the large theatre of Syrakousai as perfect specimens developed from the theatre of Dionysos.

NOTE 91
E.g. Wycherley 1962, 170. This particular problem belongs in a study of the development of the Archaic and Classical theatre and will not be treated in detail here, see e.g. Anti 1947 (in some of the analysis partly out of date but still very useful); Bieber 1961, 54-73; Anti & Polacco 1969; Gebhard 1974; Isler 1994, 86-92.

NOTE 92
Isler 1994, 94 & 96.

NOTE 93
Dilke 1948, 135.

NOTE 94
Listings of monuments previously classified as type E: Dilke 1948, 135, 142; Bieber 1961, 72, 127 figs.176a-c; Asia Minor: De Bernardi Ferrero IV 1974, 76.

NOTE 95
See *e.g.* Dörpfeld & Reisch 1896, 122-124; Dilke 1948, 142.

NOTE 96
1975, 317.

NOTE 97
Dilke 1948, 135 (inspired by Fiechter) lists *Oropos* II among theatres like *Epidauros* and *Priene* in a context where he explains their

refinements in the elliptic aspect. For a more reasonable treatment of the theatre building at *Oropos* I-II, see Anti and Polacco 1969, 17ff.

NOTE 98
Von Gerkan 1921, 62, suggests the end of 4th century or 300 BC at the latest. Discussion in Dinsmoor 1975, 298 note 2.

NOTE 99
In the case of *Kassope* Isler describes the orchestra as a horseshoe (i.e. type C) but the koilon as being less than a semicircle. This is not exactly the case. It is true that the segment of a circle decreases upwards and thus makes the opposite angle as is normally seen in Greek theatres, but the parodos walls are not recessed as much as to be within the area of 180°, and thus the koilon is in fact larger than a semicircle.

NOTE 100
De Bernardi Ferrero IV 1974, 76, note 4. On Asia Minor she lists (IV 1974, 76), apart from the ones mentioned in the text below, *Alyndos* and *Balbyra* which to my knowledge are type B, and Aspendos which is Roman (*TGR* III, 393-95).

NOTE 101
Because of the state of knowledge on the Greek theatre in the 1940s Dilke wrote the following about the alternatives to the canon (1948, 141): "Apart from irregularly built theatres, the only exception to these rules is Pergamon, where the parodos walls form a straight line, but the cavea itself only a small segment."

NOTE 102
Dinsmoor 1975, 307.

NOTE 103
See Dörpfeld & Reisch 1896, 171-173, and Dilke 1948, 135, 141, for the following practical explanations for the development of the canon and their relations to the types B, C and E.

NOTE 104
Dinsmoor 1975, 314.

NOTE 105
Bieber 1961, 127; Cf. Fiechter 1914, 72.

NOTE 106
A fragment of Alexis' *Gynaikokratia* (T. Kock, *Comicorum Atticorum Fragmenta* [Leipzig 1834] vol. II no. 41) can possibly be interpreted as if the outer kerkides were given to foreigners (or foreign women), because

they offered the least attractive view, but it will remain an open question, because the context of the fragment could change the interpretation. Cf. A.W. Pickard-Cambridge, *The Dramatic Festivals of Athens*, Oxford 1968[2], 269.

NOTE 107
1948, 141.

NOTE 108
An extreme view is found at Wycherley 1962, 219 note 18 (on the canon generally): "But the type was not rigidly fixed and local convenience was the determining factor".

NOTE 109
Nothing to confirm the diverging attitudes on this point by Isler *TGR* II, 277 and Gogos 1992, 83, is preserved.

NOTE 110
On the local Illyrian-Epeirot characteristics of the theatre architecture, see Ceka 1990, 226-227.

NOTE 111
Anti & Polacco (1981, 192) suggest to add *Syrakousai* 2 V with its deep trapezoidal groove to the group of buildings with this particular phenomenon, which is probable, though it cannot be proved that there ever was a circular *orchestra* there. They also add *Epidauros* to this group, which is true as far as the circle goes, but strange anyway as there are no traces there at all of a quadrangular/trapezoidal enclosure for it.

NOTE 112
The synoecism of Megalopolis is recently treated by T. Heine Nielsen, ΠΟΛΛΑΝ ΕΚ ΠΟΛΙΩΝ. The *Polis* Structure of Arkadia in the Archaic and Classical Periods (unpublished PhD dissertation, Copenhagen 1996), 286ff.

NOTE 113
We have quite good population figures for Megalopolis, admittedly dating some decades later than the construction of the theatre took place, but it is unlikely that they would have changed considerably in that span of time. From the year 318 we know that the number of men fit for military duty was 15.000 (including slaves and metics), and the total population estimated from that is between 60.000 to 70.000, while the capacity of the theatre building is around 20.000. With these figures in mind we can say with a high degree of probability that the theatre building of Megalopolis was not far bigger than necessary, considering the fact that the group of men fit for military duty almost alone would fill it. The 15.000 were, moreover, only the major part of the male population. As expected spectators we should add to these, depending on the local tradition at this point, the remaining part of the male population, women, children, teenagers, elderly people (including these groups from slaves and metics too). For the population numbers of Megalopolis, see B. Forsén, Population and Political Strength in some Southeastern Arkadian *Poleis*, in P. Flensted-Jensen (ed.) Further studies in the Ancient Greek *Polis*. *Papers from the Copenhagen Polis Centre 5*. Historia *Einzelschriften* 138. Stuttgart 2000, 41.

NOTE 114
Hoepfner (*et al.*) 1999, 368.

NOTE 115
Hoepfner (*et al.*) 1999, 371.

NOTE 116
Hoepfner & Schwandner 1986, 142.

NOTE 117
Hoepfner & Schwandner 1986, 154, Abb. 148.

NOTE 118
As opposed to type A of the 5th century, the theatres of which do not consist of more than the theatre building (koilon and orchestra) and thus do not rise the same problems of classification.

NOTE 119
Cf. Isler 1994, 88.

NOTE 120
1994, 96.

Alphabetical list of theatres included in the appendix (p. 169ff.)

Locality	Type				
		Herakleia Minoa	C	Oropos I	Unique
		Iaitas	C	Oropos II	C
Aigai	B	Iasos	B	Pergamon	G
Aigeira	C	Ikarion	D	'Perperene'	G
Akrai	G	Isthmia II	C	Philippoi	B
Alexandreia Oxiana	B	Kadyanda	E	Phleious	Unique
Alyndos	B	Kassope	F	Pinara	B
Ambrakia	G	Kaunos	B	Peiraieus-Mounichia	C
Antiphellos	B	Kibyra	B	Peiraieus-Zea	C
Aphrodisias	B	Knidos 1	B	Pleuron	B
Apollonia (Kyrenaika)	B	Korinthos II	B	Priene	E
Argos 1	A	Kyanai	B	Rhamnous	D
Argos 2	B	Kyrene	F(?)	Rhegion	B
Arykanda	B	Larissa 2 (Phthiotis)	B	Rhodiapolis	B
Assos	C	Leontion	B	Samothrake	B
Athens III	C	Letoon	B	Segesta	C
Babylon	B	Lindos	E	Sikyon	B
Balbyra	B	Lokroi Epizephyrioi	B	Solous	B
Bouthrotos	G	Magnesia (on Maeander)	E	Stratonikeia	B
Byllis	B	'Makyneia'	Unique	Stratos	B
Chaironeia I	A	Mantineia II	B	Syrakousai 1	A
Chaironeia II	Unique	Maroneia	E	Syrakousai 2 V	E
Delos	B	Megalopolis	B	Tegea I	D
Delphoi	B	Melos	B	Tegea II	B
Demetrias	E	Messene	C(?)	Termessos	B
Dion (Macedon)	B	Metapontion IV	G	Thasos	F
Dodone	B	Methymna	F	Thebes (Phthiotis)	B
Elis	B	Miletos	B	Thera	B
Ephesos	E	Morgantina	B	Thorikos I-III	Unique
Epidauros I-II	E	Mytilene	B	Trakhones	Unique
Epidauros, *polis* of-	B	Oiniadai	C	Tyndaris	B
Eretria II	C	Oinoanda	E	Typaneai	B
Heloros	B	Orchomenos (Arkadia)	Unique		
Hephaistia	F	Orchomenos (Boiotia)	C		

Appendix

For conventions see note 22. The dates are as a rule the ones given in *TGR* (to which a basic reference is also given where further references will be found). Then follows a specific reference to indicate what plan I have used for the study of design. There will sometimes be references to more plans as well as to some important literature published after 1994 when *TGR* appeared.

Type A

Argos 1, 5th century BC
TGR II 123; Anti & Polacco 1969, Tav. V.
- Ginouvès 1972 Plates 1 & 5.

Chaironeia I, 5th century BC
TGR II 146; Anti & Polacco 1969, Tav. I.

Syrakousai 1, 5th century BC
TGR III 33; Polacco 1990, Tav. XXX.

Type B

Aigai, 4th century BC
TGR II 317; Andronikos 1983, Fig. B.

Alexandreia Oxiana, c. 200 BC
TGR I 211; M.P. Bernhard, Campagne de Fouilles 1976-1977 à Aï Khanoum (Afghanistan), *CRAI* 1978, 431, Fig. 6.

Alyndos, 2nd century BC
TGR III 463-4; De Bernardi Ferrero II, Tav. XXIX.

Antiphellos, Hellenistic
TGR III 465; De Bernardi Ferrero II, Tav. XXIII.

Aphrodisias, 1st century BC
TGR III 429-30; De Bernardi Ferrero IV, Tav. II-III.

Apollonia, Kyrenaika, 3rd century BC
TGR III 132-3; *ibid.*

Argos 2, 3rd century BC
TGR II 125-6; G. Roux, Chronique des Fouilles en 1955, *BCH* LXXX 1956, Fig. 41 (pp. 384-85). - J.-Ch. Moretti, Travaux de l'École Française en Grèce en 1988. Argos. 4. Le théâtre, *BCH* CXIII.2 1989, 718, Fig. 21.

Arykanda, 2nd century BC
TGR III 370; De Bernardi Ferrero IV, Tav. I.

Babylon, 4th century BC
TGR II 330-2; *ibid.*

Balbyra, 2nd century BC
TGR III 460; De Bernardi Ferrero II, Tav. XIIIB.

Byllis, 3rd century BC
TGR I 222; Ceka 1990, 225, Abb. 14.

Delos, 4th - 3rd century BC
TGR II 192-4; Y. Béquignon & J. Replat, Le Tracé du Théâtre de Délos, *BCH* LI 1927, Pl. XVI-XVIII.

Delphoi, 3rd - 2nd century BC
TGR II 188-90; E. Hansen & G. Algreen-Ussing, *Fouilles de Delphes 2 Atlas*, Paris 1975, Pl. 20.

Dion, 2nd century BC
TGR II 197; *ibid.*

Dodone. Sanctuary of Zeus at Dodone, 3rd century BC
TGR II 200-2; S.I. Dakaris, To Ieron tes Dodones, *ArchDelt* 16 1960, 25, Fig. 14.

Elis, 4th century BC
TGR II 207; V. Mitsopoulou-Leon & E. Pochmarski, Elfter vorläufiger Bericht über die Grabungen in Elis, *ÖJH* 51 (1976-77) Beiblatt, 200-3, Abb. 17.

Epidauros, the *polis* of-, 4th century BC
TGR II 213; Autopsy IX 1996 (no published plan exists).

Heloros, 4th-3rd centuries BC (?)
TGR II 444; P. Orsi, Eloro: I. Campagne di Scavo del 1899, *MonAnt* 47 1966, 233 fig. 9.

Iasos, 2nd century BC
TGR III 476; De Bernardi Ferrero III, Tav. XIA.

Kaunos, 2nd century BC
TGR III 414; De Bernardi Ferrero III, Tav. XLIVA.

Kibyra, 1st century BC
TGR III 433-4; De Bernardi Ferrero I, Tav. I.

Knidos 1 ("Lower theatre"), 2nd century BC
TGR III 511-2; I.C. Love, A preliminary Report of the Excavations at Knidos, *AJA* 74 1970 Pl. 37, Fig. 2.

Korinthos II, 3rd century BC
TGR II 152-5; Stillwell 1952, Plates II-IV.

Kyanai, 3rd century BC
TGR III 529; De Bernardi Ferrero II, Tav. XXIVB.

Larissa 2, 1st century BC
TGR II 246; A. Tziafalias, Anaskaphikes Ergasies. Larisa, *ArchDelt* 40 1985 (chronika), 199, Fig 1.

Leontion, 4th (?) century BC
TGR II 251; Autopsy VI 1998 (no published plan exists).

Letoon. Extraurban sanctuary to Xanthos, 1st century BC
TGR III 475; De Bernardi Ferrero III, Tav. XIII.

Lokroi Epizephyrioi, 4th century BC
TGR II 490-1; Mitens 1988, Fig. 44 (plan by D. Mertens).

Mantinea II, 4th century BC
TGR II 313; G. Fougères, Fouilles de Mantinée, *BCH* XIV 1890, Pl. XVII.

Megalopolis, 4th century BC
TGR II 262-3; E.A. Gardner & R.V. Schultz, Excavations at Megalopolis, *JHS* 1892 suppl. 1, Fig. I. - A. Petronotis, I Megali Polis tis Arkadias, *Ancient Greek Cities* 23, Athens 1973, 229-232, Fig. 11.

Melos, Hellenistic
TGR II 264; H. Bankel, *C. Haller von Hallerstein in Griechenland 1810-1817*, Berlin 1986, 199, fig. 4.18.

Miletos, 4th century BC
TGR III 384-7; The Hellenistic koilon is poorly preserved, but the design of it is probably reflected in the later Roman Cavea. See F. Krauss, *Das Theater von Milet*, Berlin 1973, Taf. 11.

Morgantina, 3rd century BC
TGR III 26; R. Stillwell, The Theater of Morgantina, *Kokalos* X-XI 1964-65, Tav. LI Fig. 3.

Mytilene, Hellenistic
TGR II 252; B.Ch. Petrakos, (chronika), *ArchDelt* 22 1967, 450, fig. 3.

Philippoi, 4th century BC
TGR II 243-4; G. Karadedos & Ch. Koukoule-Chrysanthaki, Skepseis gia tous analemmatikous toichous kai tis parodous tou archaiou theatrou ton Philippon, *AEMT* 7 1993, 520, Fig. 1.

Pinara, 2nd century BC
TGR III 481; De Bernardi Ferrero II, Tav.
XIXA.

Pleuron, 3rd century BC
TGR II 234; Fiechter 1931, Taf. 8.

Rhegion, 4th century BC
TGR II 578; F. Martorano, Il porto e
l'ekklesiasterion di Reggio nel 344.
Ricerche di topografia e di architettura
antica su una polis italiota, *RivStorCalabr
ns* 6, 1985, Fig. 4 (heavily restored).

Rhodiapolis, 1st century BC
TGR III 491; De Bernardi Ferrero II, Tav.
XXVIIB.

Samothrake. Sanctuary of 'the Great
Gods', 2nd century BC
TGR II 288; F. Chapouthier, A. Salac & F.
Salviat, Le Théâtre de Samothrace, *BCH*
LXXX 1956, 122 Fig. 4, 139, Fig. 28.

Sikyon, 3rd century BC
TGR II 291-2; E. Fiechter, *Das Theater von
Sikyon*, Stuttgart 1931, Taf. 6.

Solous, 4th century BC
TGR III 39; V. Tusa, Edificio sacro a Sol-
unto, *Palladio* 17 1967, Fig. 7.

Stratonikeia, 1st century BC
TGR III 424; *ibid.*

Stratos, 4th century BC
TGR II 302; Autopsy VI 1998 (no published plan exists). The theatre has been
excavated recently under the direction of
Dr. E.-L. Schwandner.

Tegea II, 2nd century BC
TGR II 270; R. Vallois, Le Théâtre de
Tégée, *BCH* L 1926, Pl. V-VII.

Termessos, 2nd century BC
TGR III 443-4; De Bernardi Ferrero II,
Tav. I.

Thebes (Phthiotis), 4th century BC
TGR II 266; A. Mpatziou-Eustathiou,
Anaskafikes Ergasies, Nomos Magnesias,

Fthiotides Thebes, *ADelt* 47.1 1992, 222-5
figs. 2-3, pl. 67a, b. Plan 225 Fig. 3.

Thera, 2nd century BC
TGR II 289-90; W. Dörpfeld, Das Theater
von Thera, *AM* XXIX 1904, Taf. V.

Tyndaris, 4th century BC
TGR III 63-4; L. Bernabò Brea, Due
secoli di studi, scavi e restauro del teatro
greco di Tindari, *RIA* 14-15, 1964-65,
Tav. 1.

Typaneai, 4th century BC-Hellenistic
TGR II 235; W.M. Leake, *Travels in the
Morea*, London 1830, vol. II, 83. - E. Mey-
er, Neue Peloponnesische Wanderungen
(Bern 1957) Pl. 1. Autopsy VI 1998.

Type C

Aigeira, 3rd century BC
TGR II 204-5; Gogos 1992, Taf. 51.

Assos, Hellenistic
TGR III 392; De Bernardi Ferrero III,
Tav. VIA.

Athens, Theatre of Dionysos III, 4th century BC
TGR II 132-5; Dörpfeld & Reisch 1896
Taf. II. - E.R. Fiechter, *Das Dionysos-Theater in Athen* I. Stuttgart 1935, Taf. 1.

Eretria II, 3rd century BC
TGR II 215-6; E. Fiechter, *Das Theater in
Eretria*, Stuttgart 1937, Taf. 1.

Herakleia Minoa, 4th – 3rd century BC
TGR II 446; E. De Miro, Il Teatro di
Heraclea Minoa, *RendLinc* 21 1966,
Tav. 2.

Iaitas, 4th century BC
TGR II 513-4; Isler 1981, Tav. II,3 - See
also H.P. Isler, *AK* 36 1993.1, 59, *AK* 39
1996. I, 52 for reports on recent investigations. Cf. R.J.A. Wilson, *AR* 42 1995-96,
107.

Isthmia II. Sanctuary of Poseidon, 4th century BC
TGR II 224-6; Gebhard 1973, 23, Pl. IV.

Messene (?), 4th century BC
TGR II 258-9; *ibid*.

Oiniadai, 3rd century BC
TGR II 236; Fiechter 1931, Taf. 1.

Orchomenos (Boiotia), 4th century BC
TGR II 268-9; Autopsy X 1995 & VII 1998 (no published plan exists).

Oropos II. Sanctuary of Amphiaraos at Oropos, 3rd century BC
TGR II 227-8; Fiechter 1930, Taf. I. - Anti & Polacco 1969, Tav. III.

Peiraieus-Mounichia, Hellenistic
TGR II 276; *ibid*.

Peiraieus-Zea, 2nd century BC
TGR II 277-8; D. Philios, Ekthesis. Peri ton en Peiraiei anaskaphon, *Praktiká* 1881 Plate (unnumbered). - Fiechter 1950 Taf. 6. - E. Curtius & J.A. Kaupert, Karten von Attika, Berlin 1881, Heft I p. 67, Plate (unnumbered).

Segesta, 3rd century BC
TGR III 21-3; Isler 1981, 155, tav. V,9.

Type D

Ikarion. Deme of Athens, 4th century BC
TGR II 199; J. Travlos, *Bildlexikon zur Topographie des antiken Attika*, Tübingen 1988, Abb. 98.

Rhamnous. Deme of Athens, 4th century BC
TGR II 221; Bulle 1928, Taf. 1.

Tegea I, 4th century BC
TGR II 270; R. Vallois, Le Théatre de Tégée, *BCH* L 1926, Pl. IX.

Type E

Demetrias, 3rd century BC
TGR II 319-20; V. Milojcic, *Demetrias* III, Bonn 1980, Taf. VII.

Ephesos, 2nd century BC
TGR III 494-6; De Bernardi Ferrero III, Tav. VIIB.

Epidauros I-II. Sanctuary of Asklepios, 3rd-2nd century BC
TGR II 208-10; Gerkan 1961, Taf. 1.

Kadyanda, 2nd century BC
TGR III 523; De Bernardi Ferrero II, Tav. XVIIIC.

Lindos, PQ 3rd century BC
TGR II 279; E. Dyggve, *Lindos* III 2, Berlin-Copenhagen 1960, Pl. X, A & C.

Magnesia on Maeander, 2nd century BC
TGR III 354; De Dernardi Ferrero III, Tav. XVIIIA.

Maroneia, Hellenistic
TGR II 257; E. Pentasos, To Archaio Theatro Ste Maroneia, in *Mneme D. Lazaride. Polis kai Chora sten Archaia Makedonia Kai Thrake*, Thessaloniki 1990, 640, Fig. 2. - G. Lavvas & G. Karadedos, Vitrouvianes Epharmoges sto Theatro kai se Ysteroklasike Katoikia tes Maroneias, *op. cit.*, 659, Fig. 3.

Oinoanda, 2nd century BC
TGR III 452; De Bernardi Ferrero II, Tav. XIVC.

Priene, 4th century BC
TGR III 441-2; Gerkan 1921, Taf. VIII & XXXII.

Syrakousai 2 V, 3rd century BC
TGR III 34-7; Polacco 1990, Tav. XXX.

Type F

Hephaistia, 4th - 3rd century BC
TGR II 249; G. Libertini, scavi di Lemno, *ASAtene* I-II (Nuova Serie) 1939/40, fig. 2.

Kassope, 3rd century BC
TGR II 231; S. Dakaris, Cassopaia and the Elean Colonies, *Ancient Greek Cities* 4, Athens 1971, Fig. 53.

Kyrene IV(?), 4th century BC
TGR III 137-138; Stucchi 1975, 136, Fig. 115.

Methymna, Hellenistic
TGR II 253; H.-G. Buchholz, *Methymna*, Mainz 1975, Abb. 1 & Plan (Z) (no published plan exists).

Thasos, 4th century BC
TGR II 303-4; G. Daux (ed.), *Guide de Thasos*, Paris 1968, 51, Fig. 17.

Type G

Ambrakia, 4th century BC
TGR II 129; E. Andreou, To mikro theatro tes Ambrakias, *Ep. Chr.* XXV 1983, Fig. A.

Akrai, 3rd century BC
TGR II 548-9; L. Bernabò-Brea, *Akrai*, Catania 1956, Tav. A.

Bouthrotos, 3rd century BC
TGR I 217-8; Ceka 1990, 228, Abb. 16.

Metapontion IV, 4th century BC
TGR II 500-3; Mertens & De Siena 1982, Tav. II.

Pergamon, 3rd century BC
TGR III 396-8; De Bernardi Ferrero III, Tav. IV.

'Perperene'. The identification of this locality (mod. Asaga-Bei-Köi) as Hellenistic Perperene is uncertain.
E. Fabricius & R. Bohn, Eine Pergamenische Landstadt, *AM* XIV 1886, 8 Plan (unnumbered). - J. Stauber, *Die Bucht von Adramytteion*. IK 50.1. Bonn 1996, 291-305.

Unique

Chaironeia II, 3rd century BC
TGR II 146; Anti & Polacco 1969, Tav. I.

'Makyneia', 4th century BC?
Isler 1997, 553; The identification of this locality (mod. Palaiokastro Mamakou) as Makyneia is uncertain. Autopsy V 1998 (no published plan exists). L. Kolonas, Makyneia Naupaktias, *ADelt* XLII 1987, Chronika, 182, Pl. 93b. - Photographs published: M. Stefossi *(et al.)*, *Ancient Theatres*, Athens 1997, 122-3.

Orchomenos (Arkadia), 4th - 3rd century BC
TGR II 229; Autopsy VI 1998 (no published plan exists). Useful photograph: G. Steinhauer, *ADeltion* 29 1973-74, 301, Pl. 193a.

Oropos I. Sanctuary of Amphiaraos at Oropos, 4th century BC
TGR II 227-8; Anti & Polacco 1969, Tav. III.

Phleious, 4th century BC-Hellenistic
TGR II 117; W.R. Biers, The Theater at Phlius: Excavations 1973, *Hesperia* XLIV 1975, 52, Fig. 1.

Thorikos I-III. Deme of Athens, 6th - 4th century BC
TGR II 308-9; H.F. Mussche, I. Bingen *(et al.)*, *Thorikos 1965 III*, Gent 1967. Pl. V.

Trakhones. Deme of Athens, 4th century BC
TGR II 311-2; Autopsy V 1998 (no published plan exists).

Bibliography

Andronikos, M. 1983
Anaskaphe Verginas, *Praktiká*, (A)
46-50, Athens.

Andronikos, M. 1984
*Vergina. The Royal Tombs and the
Ancient City*. Athens.

Anti, C. 1947
Teatri Greci Arcaici da Minosse a Pericle. Padova.

Anti, C. & Polacco, L. 1969
Nuove Ricerche sui Teatri Greci Arcaici.
Padova.

Anti, C. & Polacco, L. 1981
Il Teatro Antico di Siracusa. Rimini.

Bieber, M. 1961
*The History of the Greek and Roman
Theater*. Princeton.

Bulle, H. 1928
Untersuchungen an Griechischen
Theatern, *AbhMünch* XXXV,
München.

Ceka, N. 1990
Städtebau in der vorrömischen
Periode in Südillyrien, *Akten des
XIII. internationalen Kongresses für
Klassische Archäologie Berlin 1988*,
Mainz am Rhein, 215-229.

Corni, F. 1994
Theatre Classification, in *TGR* vol.
I, 134-135.

De Bernardi Ferrero, D. I-IV 1966-
1974
Teatri Classici in Asia Minore I-IV.
Rome.

Dilke, O.A.W. 1948
The Greek Theatre Cavea, *BSA*
XLIII 1948, 125-192.

Dilke, O.A.W. 1950
Details and Chronology of Greek
Theatre Caveas, *BSA* XLV 1950,
21-62.

Dinsmoor, W.B. 1975[3]
The Architecture of Ancient Greece.
Batsford.

Dörpfeld, W. & Reisch, E. 1896
Das Griechische Theater. Athens.

Fiechter, E.R. 1914
*Die Baugeschichtliche Entwicklung des
Antiken Theaters*. München.

Fiechter, E.R. 1930
Das Theater in Oropos. Stuttgart.

Fiechter, E.R. 1931
*Die Theater von Oiniadai und Neu
Pleuron*. Stuttgart.

Fiechter, E.R. 1950
*Das Dionysos-Theater in Athen. Das
Theater im Piraieus. Das Theater auf
Thera*. Stuttgart.

Frederiksen, R. 1997
*Det Græske Teater i tiden indtil ca.
300 - en analyse af arkitektur og funktion*. Unpublished MA-thesis from
The Institute of Archaeology and

Ethnology, University of Copenhagen.

Gebhard, E. 1973
The Theater at Isthmia. Chicago.

Gebhard, E. 1974
The Form of the Orchestra in the
Early Greek Theatre, *Hesperia* 43,
428-440.

Gerkan, A. v. 1921
Das Theater von Priene. München.

Gerkan, A. v. 1961
Das Theater von Epidauros. Stuttgart.

Ginouvès, R. 1972
Le Théâtron a Gradins Droits et
L'Odéon D'Argos, *Ètudes Péloponnésiennes* VI, Paris.

Gogos, S. 1992
Das Theater von Aigeira, Ein Beitrag zum Antiken Theaterbau, Sonderschriften des *ÖAI* band 21.
Vienna.

Hoepfner, W. & Schwandner, E.-L.
1986
Haus und Stadt im Klassischen Griechenland. München.

Hoepfner, W. (*et al.*). 1999
Die Epoche der Griechen, in W.
Hoepfner (ed.), *Geschichte des
Wohnens*. Stuttgart.

Isler, H.P. 1981
Contributi per una storia del teatro antico, Il teatro greco di Iaitas e il teatro di Segesta, *NumAntCl* 10 1981, 131-164.

Isler, H.P. 1994
Ancient Theatre Architecture, in *TGR* vol. I, 86-124.

Isler, H.P. 1997
Teatro e odeon, in *EAA* suppl. II (1971-94), Rome, 549-62.

Kolb, F. 1981
Agora und Theater, Volks- und Festversammlung. AF 9. Berlin.

Kolb, F. 1984
Die Stadt im Altertum. München.

Lauter, H. 1986
Die Architektur des Hellenismus. Darmstadt.

Mertens, D. & De Siena, A. 1982
Metaponto: Il Teatro-Ekklesiasterion. *BdA* 16, 1-60.

Mitens, C. 1988
*Teatri Greci e Teatri Ispirati All'Architettura Greca in Sicilia e Nell'Italia Meridionale ca. 350-50 a.*C., AnalRom supl. XIII, Rome.

Modona, A.N. 1961
Gli Edifici Teatrali Greci e Romani. Florence.

Pickard-Cambridge, A.W. 1946
The Theatre of Dionysus in Athens. Oxford.

Polacco, L. 1990
Il Teatro Antico di Siracusa, pars altera. Padova.

Rossetto, P.C. & Sartorio, G.P. 1994
Theatre and Theatres, in *TGR* vol. I, 64-84.

Stillwell, R. 1952
The Theatre, Corinth vol. II. Princeton.

Stucchi, S. 1975
Architettura Cirenaica, Monografie di Archeologia Libica vol. IX, Rome.

TGR I-III 1994
P.C. Rossetto & G.P. Sartorio (eds.), *Teatri Greci e Romani. Alle Origini Del Linguaggio Rappresentato,* vol. I-III. Rome.

Wurster, W.W. 1993
Die Architektur des Griechischen Theaters, *AW* 1993 1, 20-42. Mainz am Rhein.

Wycherley, R.E. 1962[2]
How The Greeks Built Cities. London.

On the Gardens and Marginal Lands of Classical Attica

Jens Krasilnikoff

Throughout the 20th century scholars have been occupied with different aspects of ancient Greek farming, the subsistence basis of the Greek *poleis*. Important aspects of ancient agriculture were from an early start the subject of thorough investigations and in this process the evidence of Attica and Athens has played a dominant role. Substantial parts of the conclusions of these early works are, however, now out-dated especially because of the intensified work which has been done throughout the last 30 years.[1] The recent discussions have mainly been conducted on the basis of the literary evidence and the hetero-gene archaeological material and have mainly focused on the farmland (*agros*)[2] thereby excluding the extensive "wilder-ness" and boarderlands (*ore*) of the *poleis*. The purpose of the examinations has been to explain the different roles played by agriculture with reference to different social and economic aspects of the *poleis*. Among the various topics the positions for and against *agropastoralism* or *mixed farming* have dominated the debate since 1981 when Halstead introduced the idea of a balanced agricultural production for the bronze age societies of the eastern Medi-terranean. In the years that followed this concept was applied to other historical periods including Classical Greece. The purpose of the discussion was to deter-mine whether the ancient Greek farmer aimed at producing for subsistence or for a market with the aim of securing a surplus in cash. The latter of these forms was by some scholars claimed to be the dominant form of production in ancient Attica, and was apparently made possible because the inadequate cereal production was counter-measured by the extensive grain supply.[3]

Ever since the 19th century scholars have been working on the settlement his-tory of Greece, and Attica has received much attention. Accordingly, historians have used the results from archaeological excavations to elucidate the history of agriculture in ancient Greece. The pin-points of these excavations did not, how-ever, produce coherent results allowing for more general conclusions, and not until the results of the survey projects started to emerge 20 years ago was it possible to say something about the relationship between agriculture and settlement in Greece and ancient Attica. Still, we have not fully exploited the possibilities which the iden-tification of a differentiated settlement structure gives for the interpretation of ancient Greek farming. However, since the majority of the literary evidence relevant for the study of ancient Greek farming originates from writers of 5th and 4th century Athens, and since survey-results are available for ancient Attica, I find it useful to examine farming in Attica itself.

The purposes of this paper are first, to comment on some of the results of recent research especially concerning marginal lands and animals. Second, it is my inten-tion to demonstrate the advantages of including all levels of ancient farming, that is, to incorporate both the domestic pro-duction and the marginal land in the examination. Parallel to this, it is also my ambition to demonstrate that the incorpo-ration of gardens and marginal lands into Attic farming rather than agropastoralism contributed to the subsistence of the growing population outside Athens and Piraeus proper.

The Basics

Attica is dominated by mountains covered with a mixture of pine wood and maquis mixed with plains suitable for cereal production. In comparison with modern Greece marches, fens and wetlands were far more dominant in the past and generally one must imagine a wetter and partly more fertile landscape than today. In this richly varied landscape the inhabitants of Attica had farmed the land ever since neoliticum. Therefore, 5th and 4th century farming was based upon centuries of accumulated knowledge of how to implement the proper agricultural strategies. This inherited knowledge of how to cultivate the land and how to breed animals in the harsh climatological and environmental conditions of Attica was the only guideline available to farmers. For Attica, as for the majority of the Greek *poleis*, evidence exists of the production of cereals, olives and vine, crops which conventionally constitute the "Mediterranean triad". Several other crops have been claimed to be dominant or at least vital to ancient agricultural production, especially various kinds of pulses and fodder crops (alfalfa), and these crops all played a vital role in the debate about the very existence and nature of the so-called farm systems in ancient Greece.[4] It seems equally important to focus on the basic elements: water and nutrients.

Ancient as well as modern farming is dominated by a number of factors including the two essential determinants: the level of technology and the conditions of growth including the amounts of water and nutrients available. Scientists have in different ways tried to establish the availability of both water and nutrition in the landscapes surrounding the modern Mediterranean.[5] For the present, it is sufficient to establish that the soils of modern Greece and Attica are generally poor on nutrients and nothing indicates that this was fundamentally different in antiquity.

The majority of the farmers relied upon precipitation for water supply, since irrigation was not commonly, if ever, used in Attica.[6] Because of this the farmer aimed at preserving the limited amounts of water in the soil and this is why ancient Greek farming is often referred to as "dry farming".[7]

Both Xenophon and Theophrastus were well aware that both climate and location dictated what migth be able to grow and how the crop was to be raised. According to Theophrastus the farmer was to cultivate the crop in a way that allowed for the plant to pursue its natural course (*telos*). If this knowledge was combined with the right procedures and with some luck and the good will of the gods, the fields and the gardens would provide a surplus. It should be pointed out that the qualities and usefulness of these nutrients were not understood by the most sofisticated writers on botanical matters - Aristotle and Theophrastus - let alone by the farmers of ancient Greece and Attica. Therefore, we cannot suppose that farming in Classical antiquity was ever based upon the knowledge of nutrients and their chemical functions. Neither the Classical Greeks nor the Romans, who in many ways practised more sophisticated forms of agriculture, were able to utilize empirical knowledge of the value of nutrients for cultivation.[8] The absence of an agricultural sophistication in Greece after the Roman annexation more than suggests that the land and climate themselves were the main obstacles for such a development. It is of the utmost importance to realize that the ancient writers and farmers did not possess a thorough empirical knowledge on the nutritional and chemical aspects of farming.[9]

The Garden

Apart from cereal cultivation in *agros* two other forms of production are documented by the literary and epigraphical evidence: the garden (*kepos*) and the orchard or plantation.[10] The garden is mentioned frequently and must be considered uniform to all levels of *agros* as well as the urban and quasi-urban centers of Attica. Greens, vegetables and several kinds of fruit were the produce of the garden.[11] The *kepos* could therefore most appropriately be described as a kitchen garden, but the *kepos* also functioned as a nursery for seedlings and perhaps as an *experimentarion* where new forms of known species were grown.[12] The *kepos* was indeed one of the most specialized parts of ancient farming and the horticultural expertise was sometimes provided by a specialist, the gardener (*kepouros*). Recently, it has been suggested that the garden was less relevant to a general synthesis on ancient Greek agriculture.[13] This might be true if size and quantity were the only guidelines, but many factors point to the fact that at a specific level a very intimate relationship could exist between gardening, agriculture and animal husbandry. The evidence suggests that most gardens were located in the vicinity of the residence of the members of the *oikos*. This makes sense, since the crops of the garden demanded intensive care including frequent waterings, and it seems probable that many gardens and residences extracted water from the same source.[14] Three levels of cultivation existed in Attic farming: cereal production in *agros*, marginal production on *phelleus* and *eschatia* and the most intensive and integrated production in the garden. Although small in area the yield of the garden was relatively high and would secure a varied diet not obtainable from the traditional crops of Mediterranean agriculture. The *oikos*-level of the production could combine plenty of water and nutrients with sufficient manpower: all members of the *oikos* could presumably contribute to the outcome of the garden, while the male members of the *oikos* were in charge of the production in the *agros*, *phelleus* and *eschatia*.[15]

The evidence suggests that in those periods of history when the peninsula experienced profound demographic pressure – from the Peloponnesian War to Alexander – all levels of agricultural potential were exploited. Agriculture aimed at subsistence primarily by cultivation of the three main crops: cereals, olives and wine but all of these might frequently be transformed into commodities with the purpose of cash-generating,[16] as was most certainly the case with animal husbandry.

Domestic Breeding

Even though focus has primarily been placed on the cereal production of the *agros*, several scholars have been working with different aspects of animal husbandry. There seems to be no greater controversies concerning the species involved in ancient animal husbandry.[17] This is not, however, the case when discussions are directed towards the question of the form(s) of animal husbandry and the role of animals in agriculture and society.[18]

Although the evidence does not allow for exact estimations of the various species involved, there is no doubt that sheep and goats were the most numerous and important animals in ancient Attic farming. The good relationship that exists between nutritional requirements and reproductive qualities makes *probata* the preferred animals in an agricultural production conditioned by limited fodder and water resources. The documentation for animal flocks is, however, very limited. The Athenian forensic speeches give a few examples probably referring to wealthy farmers: Panaitius kept 84 sheep and 67 goats,[19] Demosthenes[20] relates of 50 sheep, and Isaius[21] of one stock consisting of 60 sheep and 100 goats and another[22] of goats with shephard valued at 1.300 drachmas.[23] Cattle demands considerable amounts of fodder and water and so do pigs. This is probably the reason why the evidence gives the impression that pigs were kept in small numbers and mostly found in the vicinities of farmsteads. Given the climatological and vegetational conditions of ancient Attica, *probata* were the obvious choice for animal husbandry in Classical Attica. More difficult, however, it seems to decide the nature of animal husbandry in Classical Attica. Although few scholars have been interested in or even observant of the small domestic animal breeding, this less spectacular form was commonly used. In fact, one can hardly imagine a farmstead without a fair number of different animals attached to it.[24] The limited focus on the domestic breeding is closely connected to the nature of the evidence: the archaeological material cannot contribute with decisive information - it is often difficult to decide whether evidence originates from domestic or more extensive forms of breeding. Therefore, we have to rely heavily upon the relatively few references in the literature. Several facts are nevertheless clear: domestic breeding relied potentially upon a mixture of kitchen waste, choppice and grazing off the nearest fields and maquis. Furthermore, the animals could benefit from the water available at or nearby most farmsteads. Therefore, close to the residence of the *oikos* one might expect to find the most intensive forms of production: domestic breeding and the growth of vegetables and greens in the *kepos*. If any parts of Classical farming are to be described as "intensive" the interplay between domestic breeding and cultivation of the *kepos* is one obvious candidate. Other forms of integration involve less elements such as pasturage on fallow, manuring and the nibbling of the premature barley and wheat to increase the yield.

An examination of animal husbandry in ancient Attica or Greece could originate from an examination of the domestic level of production. First, the *oikos*-level provides evidence for all animals involved in ancient farming including a number almost entirely testified at this level (poultry and pigs). Second, domestic breeding acted as outset for more extensive forms of breeding and third,[25] the domestic production expectedly provided the majority of the people of Attica with meat, wool, leather, bone, manure, etc.[26] The production of even a limited amount of animal produce seems to be important especially for the less well-off *oikoi* since the economic surplus necessary for external purchase was very limited.

In 5th and 4th century Attica there seems to have been a distinctive contrast between the *oikoi* able to invest in a number of enterprises such as cereal and fruit production, animals, wood, charcoal, mining, etc. and the ones dependant upon a few productive units (a few *pelthra* of arable land, garden and a few animals).

The Marginal Lands

The evidence suggests that the production of the basic crops of ancient Attic farming was concentrated on the four major plains of ancient Attica but that significant contributions were also supplied from the hills and mountainous regions. The cereals were either produced in smaller fields as mono crops or with olives and other tree crops. Both vine and olive are able to grow in rather poor and stony soils, and vine and olives normally produce long roots better suited for extracting the limited amounts of moisture from the land. The formation of deep roots could according to Theophrastus be accelerated by frequently digging around the crops in order to remove surface roots.[27] Furthermore, some species of modern vines during night time make good use of the warmth accumulated during daytime in soils consisting of great amounts of fist sized stones and rubble.[28] These are the reasons why vine and olive are often found on what is often called "marginal lands".[29] In this way the farmer was able to produce crops from land otherwise suited only for pasturage.

The field structure on plain and valley was designed as a "patchwork" of more or less rectangular pieces of land.[30] With a single exception no Attic estate known to us exceeds 200 *plethra* (1 plethron = 10.000 square feet). The land of Hagnias valued at two talents was big enough to sustain a thousand olive trees.[31] The estate of Timesius extended over 180 *plethra*[32] and Plutarch mentions an estate of 100 *plethra*.[33] The cultivation of marginal lands tends towards the creation of irregular fields of varying sizes. Demosthenes gives the odd example of Phainippus the inheritor of two estates (both *eschatiai*) with a common boundary of 5 or 6 miles (40 *stadies*).[34] If both lands were rectangular the accumulated area would constitute between 3.000 og 4.000 *plethra* or ten times more than the other examples known from Attica.[35] As far as possible both fields in the plains and the marginal lands would be circumscribed by fences and dikes.[36]

The normal agricultural activities involved very labour intensive processes. This was indeed true in the case of the hilly and stony regions of Attica - the *eschatiai* and *phelleis*. Agricultural production in these areas preconditioned extensive labour with rocks and soils including the construction of dikes, ditches and trenches for the regulation of the massive amounts of precipitation falling in winter and the maintenance of these constructions.[37] Modern literature on ancient Greek agriculture often points to the importance of terraces and that the Greeks constructed these to be able to extend the area of cultivable land so desperately needed in (both modern and) ancient Greece. The terraces constitute arable *lacunae* by holding back soil from erosion, moisture and thereby the important nutrients. A significant side effect of the construction of terraces, dikes and trenches is the improvement of the land itself by the collection of stones which are transported elsewere.[38] One advantage that terraces have to offer has not yet been acknowledged: the heat absorbing effect of both terraces wall and the soil behind it. The terraces, especially those facing south, are able to preserve the solar heat received during daytime. This provides the crops with a higher and more constant temperature throughout day and night, an advantage recognized by e.g. modern wine producers. The majority of the terraces identified by Lohmann in southern Attica were facing south or in southern directions. However, these orientations were not associated with cultivation by Lohmann.[39]

The ancient documentation for the construction and use of terraces is circumstantial. Ancient literature and inscriptions never mention terraces explicitly in connection with the two most commonly known types of marginal lands in ancient

Attica, *phelleis* and *eschatiai*.[40] Theophrastus does not mention it and it seems as if the Greeks did not use a terminology consistent with our modern understanding of a 'terrace.' Bradford and Lohmann among others have found and interpreted structures as ancient terraces and all of these have been dated back to the Classical period.[41] Recently, Foxhall has argued that serious doubt could be raised about the old age of the terraces identified in Attica and that the absence of terraces in ancient literature actually reflects the limited use in Classical Greek antiquity.[42] The degree of decay of the rocks and the growth rate of lichen or moss were used as the strongest arguments against a 5th and 4th century dating of the terraces identified by Lohmann in Atene. These criteria are difficult to administrate and generally hard to accept: first, the criteria used by Foxhall are without the necessary objectivity which enables them to be used on terraces in general. One can, however, apply very general criteria, e.g. does the terrace wall look as if it is "new" or "old", but this general distinction does not offer much help. We know for example very little of how a specific rock deteriorates in a specific environment and climate. Second, the application of growth rates for lichen or moss would demand a very special kind of knowledge not available for the primitive botanical fauna of Attica.

The farm structures identified by Lohmann must be interpreted in connection with the surrounding structures including terraces. No other settlement structures were erected in the interregnum between antiquity and modern times (post war 20th century),[43] and so the terraces of south western Attica must be interpreted in an ancient context. On the other hand, it is not clear why Lohmann ignores the possibility of a late Roman dating, suggesting that southern Attica was involved in the so-called "late Roman renaissance" which flourished in the 4th - 6th century A.D.

The results from the southern Argolid and the publications of Zangger and Brückner point towards another dating strategy for the terraces of Attica.[44] With the improved methods which now exist for the analysis of earth slide profiles it is possible to determine whether a specific erosion originates from the decay of specific terraces and as a consequence decrease the errors of dating.

However, the importance of Foxhall's arguments against a too optimistic interpretation of terraces should not be underestimated and the attention towards digging as an alternative to terracing is very useful. Digging is well testified by Theophrastus and the Roman authors and the purpose of this activity was to restrain the limited precipitation (moist) and to remove surface roots, thereby forcing the crop to grow deep roots, better suited for extracting the moisture of deeper soils. Thereby the same advantages are obtained by digging and one avoids the labour intensive process of constructing and maintaining terraces. Nevertheless, Foxhall maintains that terraces did exist but only in rather limited numbers and only instigated by wealthy farmers with adequate labour force at their disposal. It is not clear why Foxhall after rejecting all evidence used by previous research to indicate the existence and use of terraces in antiquity still maintains that they were actually used.

It seems plausible that the very limited documentation for terraces also reflects the rather limited extention of terraces. Some reservations primarily concerning the very landscape involved are, however, unavoidable. First, I do not agree that digging generally ought to be seen as a more cost effective alternative to terracing because the two methods appeal to two very different types of landscape. Digging around crops growing in rather steep locations would almost certainly promote erosion. That is why terracing is the only possibility available if the farmer chooses to cultivate topographical progressive landscapes. Digging only makes sense on locations not so exposed to erosion and terracing is only attractive on locations too steep for digging. Furthermore, the two methods are intertwined, since the cultivaton of tree crops and vine in terraces normally involved digging around the roots as well.

Finally, using the example of southern Attica, I find it possible to combine the positions of both Linn Foxhall and Hans Lohmann. The structures identified by Lohmann as terraces and affiliated structures in the vicinities of Charaka, Agia Photini, Legrana and Anavyssos do form significant markers in the landscape, perhaps because they are dominant among the few remaining man made structures in those particular areas. Nevertheless, if the attention is directed towards the surrounding landscape, it is obvious that even in these marginal areas of Attica the so-called terraces occupy only a minor part of the total arable landscape at the present.[45] The poor documentation for terraces simply reflects the choises made by farmers and that even in those very marginal landscapes farmers was able to choose between different strategies.

Extensive and External Breeding

Whereas most scholars ignore domestic breeding the external and extensive forms of animal husbandry have received much attention. Some scholars have focussed on the form of animal husbandry often called *transhumance* which is dictated by the climatological constraints and changes that the vegetation undergoes during the year.[46] Because of the seasonal changes in vegetation the flocks have to migrate between suitable pasturages. Other scholars have played down or even rejected the "free" pasture under the guidance of shepherds, partly with reference to the poor evidence of this, partly with reference to the possibility of incorporating animals into agropastoralism.[47] The two parties interpret the purpose of animal husbandry very differently: The "trancehumanists" put emphasis on what one might call "the necessity of the landscape" while the champions of *mixed farming* have focussed on the narrow (and potential) intimacy between agriculture and animal production. Although none of these positions are supported by substantial evidence the trancehumanists can present examples of annual migrations of flocks. Mixed farming, on the other hand, is not documented in an Athenian context and as stated above there seems to be great difficulties in accepting a widespread cultivation of fodder crops and thereby mixed farming in Attica. Intensive farming of Attica beyond the boundaries of domestic production was indeed hampered by inadequate technology including lack of knowledge and ability to distribute water and nutrients in adequate amounts and qualities.

There exists no Greek terminology which can elaborate on the subject of transhumance, and only a few of the modern versions of transhumance can be associated with an Athenian context. In 1988 Skydsgaard, nonetheless, emphasized three strong arguments for the existence of transhumance in Classical Greece. None of these exclude Attica and Athenians as actors and entrepeneurs in trancehumantic production: Skydsgaard maintained that 1) animal husbandry was a mobile enterprise - flocks migrated between pasturage. 2) Existence of agreements between *poleis* concerning common pasturage (*epinomia*) and 3) agreements between *poleis* regulating traffic over boundaries and between pasturage.[48]

Several factors do indicate, however, that transhumance proper was not a widespread activity in Classical Attica - with regard to both number of animals and people involved - and that other forms of animal breeding presumably constituted a more realistic alternative for the majority of Athenian farmers. No external flocks of animals are recorded in the Athenian evidence and no examples of Athenian flocks taken outside Attica are recorded.[49] Furthermore, only the citizens of some wealth could expectedly honorate the investment demanded in transhumance since the animals themselves represented some value and must have been of some size to be able to support a shepherd. The number of animals involved in transhumance cannot be established with any certainty at least the previous research has failed to do so,

but I expect that a cost effective flock consisted of several hundred animals. First of all, flocks of this size are not documented from Attica. If they did exist it is difficult to imagine large seasonal migrations through Attica without these causing serious problems with the land owners e.g. on the route between Parnes and the plain of Marathon. Even though Demosthenes (55) and Plutarch (*Kimon*) both refer to fences constructed with the purpose of keeping *probata* out of the fields this does not necessarily indicate widespread transhumance in Attica but could just as well be a precaution against local *probata* or even the farmer's own animals.

The vegetation and the fact that animals raised inside Attica for a large part had to rely on the maquis for grazing, scarce water supplies, population density and close to full use of the available farm potential. All these factors must have limited or even deterred potential transhumanists. Transhumance demands space and that is something Attica was very short of in the Classical period. Athenians interested in transhumance had to travel abroad or fight the Boiotians over the limited pasturage in the Parnes region. Other options were, however, available.

Although it seems evident that a full understanding of the nature of animal breeding in Classical Attica cannot yet be achieved, the last 5 years have brought about new knowledge and new ideas of how animal breeding was managed in antiquity. The key to a better understanding lies in a thorough investigation of the "nature" of the landscape, in a proper evaluation of the pasturage available, and in the roles played by animal breeding in the economy.[50] Therefore, I will advocate a third model that seems to suit Attica well (and other parts of Greece with similar vegetational and precipitorial conditions). This is perhaps "the missing link" between the small domestic flock attractive to all economies and the large transhumane breeding forms only attractive to the most wealthy farmers.

In 1983 Oliver Rackham observed that the maquis contained a considerable potential for pasturage (as it does for the gathering of firewood), and in 1995 Forbes combined this information with the data form several survey projects to form the theory of estate based animal breeding that existed on pasturage in *ore*, shoppice, shepherds and consisted of flocks of some size but notably smaller than the ones involved in transhumance.[51] Forbes claimed that this form of animal breeding had been concealed by the very way in which the previous discussions had proceeded and his aim was to unite the strong positions of the transhumanists and the agropastoralists. His general position that animal breeding has generally been underestimated, both with regard to size and economical importance, seems to be plausible.[52] There are, however, some reservations to be made. The reasoning is based upon indications rather than firm literary evidence and/or archaeological remains – no ancient writer mentions farms that fit in all together and no farm or settlement structure has been revealed which was undoubtedly intended for the kind of animal breeding suggested by Forbes. Furthermore, the idea of estate based animal breeding was not applied to a specific context or region by Forbes. This could inspire one to make an attempt.

There are good reasons to accept the general idea in the case of Attica. It seems reasonable to suggest that most flocks and animals were concentrated in those regions most densely populated, that is, the four plains and adjacent lowlands of Attica. These landscapes would supposedly constitute the types of land called *agroi* and *phelleis* in the ancient literature and epigraphic texts. In the most fertile northern regions of Attica the majority of farmers, who had their engagement concentrated in one region, would keep small flocks on local pasturage and maquis and the flocks of wealthy farmers would not exceed 150 to 200 animals. Both categories of farmers would generate a cash income from animal breeding as a mere supplement to the more important cereal production. A few wealthy farmers might choose to concentrate on the breeding of

either *probata* or horses, as one example shows.[53] In the southern part of Attica where the low precipitation produces a different kind of vegetation as compared to the north, the production was generally more extensive in nature, with regard to the raising of both crops and animals. This observation is to some extent confirmed by the latest publication on the socio-economic history of Southern Attica, including the survey conducted by Hans Lohmann. The physiological conditions that dominate Southern Attica also apply to the southern Argolid recently surveyed by American scholars.[54] None of the results yet published challenge the idea that estate based animal breeding was practised or even dominated animal production in the southern Argolid. A clarification of this question will hopefully emerge from the publications to follow.

The epigraphical evidence from Attica shows that the most attractive pasturage was either owned by privates, (religious) institutions or by the demes. The rather few examples of lease contracts that have survived until today certainly concerns some of the best or at least expensive pasturage in Attica.[55] Nothing indicates that these leases included parts of the maquis and I cannot find any reason why the vast areas of maquis in Attica were not free to utilize for any animal breeder in ancient Attica. This means, first, that most farmers were able to shift between different pasturages throughout the year, second, that hypothetically farmers were able to breed animals without having to buy or lease expensive pasturage, a luxury probably only reserved for the more wealthy farmers. Animal breeding based on the maquis and fallow fields was probably the economically most attractive form available to the majority of Athenian farmers and therefore also the most common. The forms of animal breeding, which demanded investments exceeding the expenditure on the animals themselves, were most probably exclusively reserved for the wealthy citizens, who were also potentially involved in the mining activities in southern Attica and the timber and wood enterprises of Northern Attica and central Greece. As for most other parts of ancient Greece animal breeding was a natural and logic part of farming.

On Farming and Demography

The increase in the number of people living in Athens and Attica in the Classical period was not made possible only by the development of all potential farmland available. Although I do agree with Hanson,[56] demonstrating the limited effects of warfare upon farming, naturally some effect must be attributed to warfare with regard to the demographic development. However, most scholars agree that despite temporary setbacks, for example during the Persian and Peloponnesian Wars, Attica experienced a significant growth in the number of people both living in and living off Athens and Attica during the 5th and 4th centuries B.C., until the reign of Alexander the Great.[57] The grain supply was certainly responsible for a substantial part of this development, but only in the Classical period itself, as Garnsey pointed out.[58] The majority of the documentation for the food supply of ancient Athens indicates that most was meant for the city of Athens itself and for Piraeus.[59] According to Plutarch the household of Pericles relied upon purchases from the market financed by selling off all produce after the harvest. Surely, this one example was of interest simply because Pericles apparently acted out of the ordinary, and I find it plausible that the majority of those Athenians able to do so consumed their own agricultural produce.[60] In fact, no evidence relates of any (imported) grain travelling outside the *astu*. Finally, the few examples and quantifications mentioned in the evidence might suggest that the grain imported to Piraeus and sold at Piraeus and Athens was primarily consumed by the populations of Athens and Piraeus themselves.[61] If this is correct, it implies, first, that Athenians living outside Athens were supposed to support themselves by their own produce. Second, that

a growth in the population of the countryside, i.e. the population normally self-sufficient, could only happen if the production of stablefoods could be raised accordingly, as well. This presupposes either an improvement in technology - which was certainly not the case - or an extension of the farmland available. The survey of Atene conducted by Hans Lohmann provides the best example of the latter.

The dating of the structures identified by Lohmann in southern Attica to the early Classical period at the same time suggests an early revision of the reforms of Cleisthenes. Indeed, this expansion involving one of the most marginal lands of Attica suggests many possible changes, one of them surely being the intention of creating space and subsistence for a number of *oikoi*. Another supplementary or even single explanation would be to consider the importance of the finding of the great silver motherload in Laurion in 483/2 B.C. for the specific development of Atene. Undoubtedly, a number of citizens of the southern demes were involved in mining activities. One must, however, be cautious in suggesting that citizens of the so-called "mining demes" in general were engaged in a balanced production involving both mining enterprises and farming. Whether or not silver played a role in the development of Atene there seems to be no doubt, that agriculture was an essential economic element in the region. The agricultural basis of this deme consisted to a very large degree of marginal cultivation and animal breeding. As mentioned above, terraces dominated the countryside and this more than suggests that the necessary expansion in the countryside in the Classical period was indeed a matter of transforming potential *oros* into either *agros*, *felleus* or *eschatia*.

The forms of cereal production and animal breeding practised in ancient Attica cannot be characterized as fully integrated parts of a developed agropastoralism. The know-how was either not available or on an experimental basis in 5th and 4th century Athens. The most important argument against these forms of production is simply the landscape itself, the climatological conditions prevailing and inadequate technology, making the farmer unable to sustain the delicate balance between producing fodder crops and raising cattle. Although more research has to be carried out in the farming of Hellenistic and Roman Greece, this position is most clearly illustrated by the fact that agropastoralism was not, as far as I am able to tell, practised in Roman Greece, at a time when the know-how of integrated farming was effectuated in other more fertile parts of the Roman world.

These considerations do not mean that cereal-, fruit- and animal production were separate worlds. Integrations were achieved but at a rather low level, which was indeed hampered by lack of manure, water and knowledge of how to utilize these two essentials in a more sophisticated integrated agricultural production. Cereal and animal production were supplementary elements in a rather primitive but yet effective exploitation of the limited resources of ancient Attica. In this form the products of *agros*, *phelleus*, *eschatia* and *oros* were all valuable to the Athenian farmer who by the multiple engagements was able to produce for subsistence and, if volume allowed, for the market as well. Finally, the exploitation of all the types of landscapes in Attica was also the condition for the extension of settlement. The laborious job of transforming *oros* into *agros* was indeed responsible for the transformation of early Attica into one of the most heavily exploited and populated farmlands in Classical Greece.

Notes

Warm thanks to the director of the Danish Institute at Athens Signe Isager for long and patient support and to both director Signe Isager and dr. Inge Nielsen for constructive suggestions and critical remarks for this paper. Also, I owe great debt to professor Jens Erik Skydsgaard, senior lecturer Jesper Carlsen and director Søren Dietz, all of whom have helped to extend my perceptions of landscape, settlement and agriculture. I would also like to express my gratitude towards The Danish Institute at Athens for their support and special thanks to Hanna Lassen who made it possible to study Athens and Attica from above. Finally, a warm thank to Camilla Ginge for the hard job of transforming a draft of this paper into understandable English.

NOTE 1
Cf. Sallares 1991, 1-2; Isager & Skydsgaard 1992, 3-6 for the historiography of ancient Greek farming.

NOTE 2
Cf. e.g. the publications of Amouretti 1986; Halsted 1981; Foxhall & Forbes 1982; Jameson 1982; 1994, and lately Isager & Skydsgaard 1992; Burford 1993 and Hanson 1995.

NOTE 3
Recently Lohmann 1993 used this logic to explain the economy of southern Attica in the Classical period.

NOTE 4
Halsted 1981; Gallant 1982; Hodkinson 1988; Garnsey 1988a; cf. Isager & Skydsgaard 1992, 108-14 for critical comments on agropastoralism.

NOTE 5
The amount of literature is massive. Cf. for instance the contributions in di Castrietal 1981. Vita-Finzi 1969 is outdated.

NOTE 6
The literary evidence is circumstantial and the archaeological evidence does not exist. Cf. Isager & Skydsgaard 1992, 40 and esp. 112 for further discussion.

NOTE 7
Cf. Burford 1993, 132.

NOTE 8
White 1970 is still fundamental for the study of Roman agriculture.

NOTE 9
Cf. for example Burford 1993, 100-9.

NOTE 10
Isager & Skydsgaard 1992, 41-2, on fruit. Also Burford 1993, 135-37.

NOTE 11
Cf. IG II² 10.7; Tod no. 100.15, for a metic working as a gardener; lease of garden cf. IG II² 2494. Cf. also Burford 1993, 136, note 105 and 192 for examination of metic specialists, who according to Burford were freed slaves, who continued to live by the skills which they aquired when they were slaves. *Ampelourgos* ("winedresser") in IG II² 2492. The literary documentation is massive, cf. for example Ar., *Fr.*, 679 on watering of gardens; Arist., *PA*, 668 a 14-18 for analogy between the irrigation system of the garden and the human circulatory system; *D.L.*, 7.168-9, Cleanthes of Assus, who spend his youth "drawing water in the garden". Thphr., *HP*, 7.1.2; 7 for vegetables grown in gardens; 7.5.1. on manure for gardens; 7.7.2. on wild plants previously cultivated in gardens.

NOTE 12
Cf. D. 53.15-6.

NOTE 13
Isager & Skydsgaard 1992.

NOTE 14
Cf. Plu. *Sol.*23; D. 50.4-6,61; D. 55; Ar., *fr.* 679. X. *oec.* 2.15. for water management,

farming and problems with neighbours concerning water. Also Koerner 1973 for epigraphical evidence and Crouch 1993 for water management in cities including Athens.

NOTE 15
Exceptions do occur cf. Scheidel 1990 and Burford 1993, 135, 149, 191.

NOTE 16
By "cash-generating" is meant an extensive form of production whereby the farmer aims at producing a negotiable surplus in cash and/or to replace the crops normally applied in subsistence farming. The most commonly produced *cashcrops* were olives and animal breeding - to a lesser degree vine in Attica. Cf. Forbes 1993 and 1995.

NOTE 17
Cf. Isager & Skydsgaard 1992, 85-96 for catalogue. For Horses, cf. Vigneron 1968 and Spence 1993. Cf. Arist., *HA*, 553a; Plato used the bee in *Critias* as an indicator of the environmental status. Semonides, 7 gives a description of the attractive woman in the shape of a bee. Xenophon also compares the good women with bees in his *Oikonomikos*, 7. Cf. also Forbes 1996, 92-93. Snodgrass 1983 on cattle, and Isager & Skydsgaard 1992, 89-91, 102 og 104-7 for transport.

NOTE 18
Isager & Skydsgaard 1992, 83-5, 108-14 for evidence and recent research. Cf. Forbes 1995, 325-38 for different interpretations of animal breeding in ancient Greece.

NOTE 19
Meiggs & Lewis no. 79 64-73.

NOTE 20
D. 47.52.

NOTE 21
Is. 11.41.

NOTE 22
Is. 6.33.

NOTE 23
For speculations concerning number of
goats involved, cf. Hodkinson 1988, 63 and
Burford 1993, 151 with note 143.

NOTE 24
Cf. for example Thphr., *CP*, 4.12.4 and
Aristotle, *HA*, 595a 15-19 on pigs. Isager &
Skydsgaard 1992, 85, 107 on domesticated
animals. Isager & Skydsgaard 1992, 93, state
that the pig was nicknamed *synanthropeuo-
menos* - "one, who lives together with
man", which more than indicates a domestic affiliation. Burford 1993, 110-18, 146-7,
152 makes no further delimitation between
the domestic form and other forms of animal breeding.

NOTE 25
A possible and probably also widely used
practice by farmers was to hire or purchase
expertise to administrate a combined flock
at a larger level, cf. Chaniotis 1995. Burford
apparently downgrades the importance of
flocks kept near by the farms, which does
not totally agree with Burfords accept of
the potential of both the fallow fields and
the maquis as pasturage, Burford 1993, 145-
6,149 with note 136.

NOTE 26
Including an important supplement from
participation in the common meal at religious festivals and cults. Cf. Burkert 1985
and Bruit Zaidman & Schmitt Pantel 1994.

NOTE 27
Thphr., *CP*, 5.9.8. Most important for olive
and wine cultivation, since both produce
large amounts of surface roots, cf. Thphr.,
HP, 1.6.4. For the extent of digging, cf.
Thphr., *HP*, 2.7.5; *CP*, 3.10.1; 3.12.1;
3.20.7. Cf. Foxhall 1996, 55.

NOTE 28
Cf. Renfrew 1973 for ethnobotanical
information on olives and the history of
olive growth in Isager & Skydsgaard 1992,
33-40. Cf. also Sarpaki 1992, 70 and references.

NOTE 29
Gavrielides 1976 and Forbes 1993.

NOTE 30
Cf. for example Is., 9.17-18.

NOTE 31
D., 43.69. Estimated by Burford 1993, 69
not to exceed 200 *plethra*.

NOTE 32
Langdon & Watrous 1977.

NOTE 33
Aristides, 27.1.

NOTE 34
D. 42.

NOTE 35
Cf. Burford 1993, 69, 112, contends, without giving further explanations that a more
realistic estimation would be between 500
and 600 *plethra*.

NOTE 36
For example D. 55.11. Lohmann 1993,
219-24, refers to several boundaries in
Charaka og Agrileza. It is, however, obvious
that those boundaries discovered in Agrileza do not circumscribe rich land but
instead marginal poor soils with no clear
agricultural potential. For Charaka it is evident that these boundaries describe a structure dominated by terraces. Cf. Stanton
1994 and 1996 who believes that the inter-
nal demarcation of Attica was without
importance for the majority of farmers
who lived in *komai*. The deme demarcations
according to Stanton only had relevance
for the few shepherds who existed on the
periphery of the demes.

NOTE 37
Rackham & Moody 1992, 123-30.

NOTE 38
This observation was made by professor
Skydsgaard.

NOTE 39
Cf. Lohmann
1993,171(TH42);199(CH4);202(CH26);20
3(CH33); 205(CH53);207(PH36);
222(PH48).

NOTE 40
Cf. for example IG II² 2492 where the
lease conditions of a piece of land designat-
ed *felleus* in the deme Axione is described.
The leaseholders were allowed to dig and
remove soil - but only within the boundaries of lease. Nothing indicates that this soil
was intended for terraces. Cf. Rackham &
Moody 1992 for consultation on different
types of terraces.

NOTE 41
Bradford 1956 and 1957 on Hymettus.
Lohmann 1992 and 1993 on Southern
Attica and cautious commentaries by Isager
& Skydsgaard 1992, 81-2.

NOTE 42
Foxhall 1996, 44-67.

NOTE 43
Cf. Bradford 1956 and 1957. Also Geographical Handbook Series 1944.

NOTE 44
Brückner 1990 and Zangger 1992.

NOTE 45
There is no reason to believe that this state
of affairs should have been fundamentally
different in antiquity. Cf. Rackham 1990.

NOTE 46
Cf. Georgoudi 1974, who presents the
majority of the evidence, including later
Greek examples. Also Skydsgaard 1988, 75
on Chithairon and Euboia, and Chaniotis
1995 on Crete.

NOTE 47
Hodkinson 1988; Garnsey 1988a; 1988b.
Cf. Isager & Skydsgaard 1992, 108-14, for
criticism of agropastoralism. Burford 1993,
76 uses "mixed farming" to describe both
integrated and non-integrated forms of
agriculture.

NOTE 48
Skydsgaard 1988, 80.

NOTE 49
Th., 5.42 on Panakton is the only example
of foreigners being allowed to use pasturage
considered to be Athenian by the Athenians.

NOTE 50
Forbes 1995. Also Forbes 1992 and 1993
for criticism of comparative methodology
when used to explain ancient economy.

NOTE 51
Cf. also Foxhall 1992 for the relationship
betweeen property class and landholding in
Athens.

NOTE 52
Forbes 1995, 338.

NOTE 53
X., *Mem.* 4.3.10.

NOTE 54
Cf. van Andel & Runnels 1987 and Jameson, Runnels & van Andel 1994 for the Southern Argolid. The Boiotian results can to some extent be used to say something about northern Attica cf. Rackham 1983 and especially Bintliff & Snodgrass 1985.

NOTE 55
Cf. Jameson 1982.

NOTE 56
Hanson 1983, 1995.

NOTE 57
The amount of literature is massive, e.g. Hansen 1985.

NOTE 58
Garnsey 1988a.

NOTE 59
Osborne 1987, 98-100. A few quantities are related in the evidence: Demosthens mention 400.000 *medimnoi* imported from Bosporus (it is not certain whether this quantity was imported in a single year or throughout several years). If one year basis is assumed and 1 *choeniks* (aprox. 3700 kcal/*choeniks*) were allocated the total amount would feed between 50.000 and 60.000 adults. Cf. Osborne 1987, 99, who finds that this figure would feed between 80.000 and 90.000 persons (not specified). E.g also D. 34.39 (10.000 *medimnoi*); IG II² 360.8-10, 28-30 (*3.000 medimnoi*).

NOTE 60
Plu. *Per.* 16.

NOTE 61
We are still not able to tell how the slaves in Laurion were maintained. In a forthcoming paper on the economic relations of Attica and Euboea in the Classical period I will try to shed some light on this subject.

Bibliography

Amouretti, M-C. 1986
Le Pain et L'huile dans la Gréce antique. Paris.

Amouretti, M.-C. & Brun, J.-P. (eds.) 1993
La production de vin et du L'huile en Mediterranée. BCH. Suppl. 26. Paris.

Bintliff, J. L. & Snodgrass, A. M. 1985
The Cambridge/Bradford Boeotian Expedition, *JFA* 12, 123-63.

Bottema, S. Entjes-Nieborg G. & van Zeist, W. (eds.) 1990
Man's Role in the Shaping of the Eastern Mediterranean Landscape. (1990). Proceedings og the INQUA-BAI Symposium on the Impact of Ancient Man on the Landscape of the Eastern Mediterranean Region and the Near East. Groningen, Netherlands, 6-9 March 1989. Rotterdam.

Bradford, J. 1956
"Fieldwork on aerial discoveries in Attica and Rhodes", *Antiquity* 36, 172-80.

Bradford, J. 1957
Ancient Landscapes, London.

Bruit Zaidman, L. & Schmitt Pantel, P. 1994
Religion in the ancient Greek city. Cambridge.

Brückner, H. 1990.
Changes in the Mediterranean eco-system during antiquity - a geo-morphological approach as seen in two examples, in: *Bottema et al. 1990*, 127-137.

Burford, A. 1993
Land and Labor in the Greek World. Baltimore and London.

Burkert, W. 1985
Greek Religion. Cambridge, Massachusetts.

Chaniotis, A. 1995
"Pastoralism" and "Trancehumance" in Classical and Hellenistic Crete," *Orbis Terrarum* 1, 39-89.

Coulson, W.D.E, Palagia, O., Shear jr., T.L., Shapiro, H.A. & Frost, F.J. (eds.) 1994
The Archaeology of Athens and Attica under the Democracy. Proceedings of an International Conference celebrating 2500 years since the birth of democracy in Greece, held at the American School of Classical Studies at Athens, december 4-6, 1992. Oxbow Monograph 37. Oxford.

Crouch, D. 1993
Water Management in Ancient Greek Cities. Oxford.

di Castri, F., Goodall, D.W. & Specht, R. L. (eds.) 1981
Mediterranean-Type Shrublands. Ecosystems of the World vol. 11. Amsterdam.

Dimen, M., & Friedl, E. (eds.) 1976
Regional Variation in Modern Greece and Cyprus: Towards a Perspective on the Ethnography of Greece. Annales of the New York Academy of Sciences, 268. New York.

Doukellis, P. N. & Mendoni, L. G. (eds.) 1994
Structures Rurales et Sociétés Antiques. Paris.

Forbes, H. 1992
The Ethnoarchaeological Approach to Ancient Greek Agriculture. Olive Cultivation as a Case Study, in: *Wells 1992*, 105-16.

Forbes, H. 1993
Ethnoarchaeology and the Place of the Olive in the Economy of the Southern Argolid, Greece, in: *Amouretti & Brun 1993*, 213-226.

Forbes, H. 1995
The Identification of Pastoralist Sites within the Context of Estate-based Agriculture in Ancient Greece: beyond the "Trancehumance versus Agro-pastoralism" Debate, *ABSA* 90, 325-38.

Forbes, H. 1996
The uses of the uncultivated landscape in modern Greece: a pointer to the value of the wilderness in antiquity?, in: *Shipley & Salmon 1996*, 68-97.

Foxhall, L. 1992
The control of the Attic landscape, in: *Wells 1992*, 155-59.

Foxhall, L. 1996
Feeling the earth move: cultivation techniques on steep slopes in classical antiquity, in: *Shipley & Salmon 1996*, 44-67.

Foxhall, L., & Forbes, H. A.. 1982
"SITOMETREIA: The Role of Grain as a Staple Food in Classical Antiquity", *CHIRON* Band 12, 41-90.

Gallant, T. H. 1982
Agricultural systems, land tenure, and the reforms of Solon, *ABSA* 77, 111-24.

Garnsey, P. 1988a
Famine and food supply in the Graeco-Roman World. Cambridge.

Garnsey, P. 1988b
Mountain economies in southern Europe. Thoughts on the early history, continuity and individuality of Mediterranean upland pastoralism, in: *Whittaker 1988*, 196-209.

Garnsey, P., Hopkins, M. K. & Whittaker, C. R. (eds.) 1983
Trade in the Ancient Economy. London.

Gavrielides, N. 1976
The impact of olive growing on the landscape in Fourni valley, in: *Dimen & Friedl 1976*, 143-57.

Geographical Handbook Series 1944
The British Admiralty, Naval Intelligence Division edn. 3 vols.

Georgoudi, S. 1974
"Quelques problèmes de la transhumance dans la Grèce ancienne", *REG* 87, 155-85.

Halsted, P. 1981
Counting sheep in neolithic and bronze age Greece, in: *Hodder et al. 1981*, 307-339.

Hansen, M. H. 1985
Demography and Democracy. The Number of Athenian Citizens in the Fourth Century B.C. Vojens.

Hanson, V. D. 1983
Warfare and Agriculture in Classical Greece. Pisa.

Hanson, V. D. 1995
The Other Greeks. The Family Farm and the Agrarian Roots of Western Civilization. New York.

Hodder, I. Isaac, G. & Hammond, N. (eds.) 1981
Pattern of the Past. Studies in Honour of David Clarke. Cambridge.

Hodkinson, S. 1988
Animal Husbandry in the Greek polis, in: *Whittaker 1988*, 35-74.

Isager S. & J. E. Skydsgaard. 1992
Ancient Greek Agriculture. London.

Jameson, M. H. 1982
"The leasing of land at Rhamnous", *Hesperia* suppl.19, 60-74.

Jameson, M. H. 1994
Class in the ancient Greek countryside, in: *Doukellis & Mendoni 1994*, 55-63.

Jameson, M. H., Runnels, C. N., & van Andel, T. 1994
A Greek Countryside: The Southern Argolid from Prehistory to the Present Day. Stanford.

Koerner, R., 1973
Zu Recht und Verwaltung der griechischen Wasserversorgung nach den Inschriften, *AfP* 22, 155-202.

Langdon, M. K. & Watrous, L. V. 1977
The Farm of Timesios: rock-cut inscriptions in South Attica, *Hesperia* 46, 162-77.

Lohmann, H. 1992
Agriculture and Country Life in Classical Attica, in: *Wells 1992*, 29-57.

Lohmann. H. 1993
Atene. Forschungen zu Siedlungs und Wirtschaftsstruktur des klassischen Attika. 2 vols. Köln.

Murray, O. & Price, S. (eds.) 1990
The Greek City - From Homer to Alexander. Oxford.

Osborne, R. 1987
Classical Landscape with Figures. The Ancient Greek City and its Countryside. London

Rackham, O. 1983
"Observations on the Historical Ecology of Boeotia", *ABSA* 78, 291-351.

Rackham, O. 1990
Ancient Landscapes, in: *Murray & Price 1990*, 85-111.

Rackham, O. & J. Moody, 1992
Terraces, in: *Wells 1992*, 123-30.

Renfrew, J. M. 1973
Palaeoethnobotany: The Prehistoric Food Plants of the Near East and Europe. London.

Sallares, R. 1991
The Ecology of the Ancient Greek World. London.

Sarpaki, A. 1992
The Palaeoethnobotanical Approach. The Mediterranean Triad or Is It a Quartet?, in: *Wells 1992*, 61-75.

Scheidel, W. 1990
Feldarbeit von Frauen in der antiken Landwirtschaft, *Gymnasium* 97, 405-31.

Shipley, G. & Salmon, J. (eds.) 1996
Human Landscapes in classical Antiqu-

ity. *Environment and Culture.* Leister–Nottingham Studies in Ancient Society. Volume 6. London.

Skydsgaard, J. E. 1988
Transhumance in ancient Greece, in: *Whittaker 1988*, 75-86.

Snodgrass, A. 1983
Heavy Freight in Archaic Greece, in: *Garnsey et al. 1983*.

Spence, I. G. 1993
The Cavalry of Classical Greece. A Social and Military History with Particular Reference to Athens. Oxford.

Stanton, G. R. 1994
The rural demes and Athenian politics, in: *Coulson et al. 1994*, 217-24.

Stanton, G. R. 1996
Some Inscriptions in Attic Demes, *ABSA* 91, 341-64.

van Andel, Tj., & Runnels, C. N. 1987
Beyond the Acropolis. A Rural Greek Past. Stanford.

Vigneron, P. 1968
Le Cheval dans l'antiquité Gréco-Romaine I-II. Nancy.

Vita-Finzi, C. 1969
The Mediterranean Valleys. Geological Changes in Historical Times. Cambridge.

Wells, B. (ed.) 1992
*Agriculture in Ancient Greece. Proceedings of the seventh International Sym-*posium at the Swedish Institute at Athens, 16-17 May, 1990. Stockholm.

White, K.D. 1970
Roman Farming. London.

Whittaker. C. R. (ed.) 1988
Pastoral economies in classical antiquity. PCPhS, Suppl. 14. Cambridge.

Zangger, E. 1992
Prehistoric and Historic Soils in Greece: Assessing the Natural Resources for Agriculture, in: *Wells 1992.* 13-18.

The Foundation of Nea Paphos

Tønnes Bekker-Nielsen

The founder-myth is a phenomenon found in many Greek city-states. The story of how a hero had established the city was cherished by its citizens and passed on from generation to generation. No doubt many founder-myths had a historical core: the first inhabitants of the city came from a certain region of Greece, personified in the person of the founder. In the course of time, new layers were added around the historical core. The self-perception of the citizens or the ruling élite came to be projected on to the founder-hero, and the foundation story was embellished and fictionalized.

The city-states of Cyprus, too, have their founder-myths. Lapithos on the north coast is said to have been founded by Parxander, a Spartan; Kourion on the south coast was supposedly founded by the Argives.[1] Another founder-myth concerns the famous city of Salamis, near modern Famagusta in the eastern part of the island. It begins with Telamon from Aigina: he was one of the Argonauts and became king of the neighbouring island of Salamis. Telamon fought at Troy alongside his sons Teukros and the famous Aias. Because Teukros had failed to avenge the death of his brother Aias, his father would not let him return home to Salamis. Instead, Teukros travelled far and wide before coming to Cyprus, where he founded a city in the eastern part of the island and called it Salamis in remembrance of his father's kingdom.

A modern reader will dismiss this story about the foundation of Salamis in Cyprus as an etymological myth, invented to explain the similarity in name with the island-state of Salamis near Athens. Ancient readers were apparently less skeptic, and the Teukros myth in turn provided the background to other stories. For example, Ovid relates how a boy in Salamis was passionately in love with a princess of the local dynasty, Anaxarete.[2] Another variant is given by the Roman mythographer Antoninus Liberalis, who lived in the late second or third century AD; here, the girl is called Arsinoë.[3] A very short summary is given by Plutarch, who calls the girl Paracyptousa.[4] In Ovid's story, the princess is inordinately proud of her lineage, of having the hero Teukros among her ancestors − too proud to consider the suitor's offer. According to Antoninus, the suitor was attracted not only by the beauty of the princess but by the fact that she was descended from the famous Teukros. Both versions of the story have a sad ending: the boy dies, and as punishment for her insufferable pride and callous behaviour, the princess is turned into stone.

Without doubt, the most famous of all the myths set in Cyprus was the tale of how the goddess Aphrodite was born from the sea, on the coast a short distance from the city of Palaipaphos. Old Paphos, Palaipaphos, was the original capital of the Paphian kingdom. According to legend, it was founded by Agapenor, son of Ankaios, from the Arkadian city of Tegea. He, too, fought at Troy (as one of those who had courted Helena, he was obliged to do so). In the Catalogue of Ships, he is named as a leader of the Arcadians, commanding a force of sixty ships.[5] Later, he founded the kingdom of Paphos and, according to Pausanias,[6] built the sanctuary of Aphrodite in the city of Palaipaphos. It is interesting to note that there was a temple of the Paphian Aphrodite in Tegea: this could

Fig. 1. Coin of Nikokles showing, on the obverse, Aphrodite with a crown of walls and turrets

indicate a historical connection between Agapenor, Paphos and Arcadia. Another possibility is that the story of Agapenor's foundation of Old Paphos, or part of it, was invented to explain the existence of the temple at Tegea.

There is another mythical personage linked to the origins of Palaipaphos: Kinyras, the ancestor of the Kinyrad dynasty, which for centuries held the dual office as kings of Paphos and high priests of Aphrodite. As late as in the *Histories* of Tacitus,[7] i.e., in the late first century AD, it is stated that only a descendant of Kinyras can serve as priest in the sanctuary at Palaipaphos.[8]

What about the origins of Nea Paphos? According to the standard works on the history of Cyprus, the city of New Paphos was founded by a historical person, Nikokles, the last ruler of the independent kingdom of Paphos. The city was not established on virgin soil: a small settlement at the southwestern corner of the island was renamed and promoted to be the new capital of the Paphian kingdom. Nikokles' accession to the throne of the Paphian kingdom took place before 321 BC and he died in 310, which would place the foundation of Nea Paphos in the penultimate decade of the fourth century BC.

If we turn to the sources for this period, however, we find that not a single one of them makes the connection between the person of Nikokles and the founda-tion of Nea Paphos. This is surely surprising, considering the interest of the ancients in founder-myths. It makes one wonder whether Nikokles the founder of Nea Paphos is a historical reality; or whether this is a founder-myth created by a combination of local tradition and modern historical scholarship?[9]

An inscription found in the temple of Aphrodite in Palaipaphos names Nikokles and records how he has "surrounded the widespread (*eurychoros*) city with a wreath (*stefanos*) of towers".[10] We also have coins struck in the name of Nikokles showing Aphrodite with a mural crown (Fig.1). The date of these coins has been debated, but Otto Mørkholm has argued for a date around 317 BC.[11] The mural crown – a "wreath of towers", as the inscription expressed it – is generally taken to refer to the fortification of a city.

At the time when this evidence was first recorded, little was known about the fortifications of Old Paphos. On the other hand, New Paphos was known to have had walls, large parts of which were still visible; and it was natural that both inscription and coin were interpreted to mean that Nikokles was the driving force behind the fortification of New Paphos. Today, we know that those sections of the walls surrounding Nea Paphos which have been found so far are from a date much later than the reign of Nikokles – while, on the other hand, pottery dated to the period 350-325 BC has been found in the

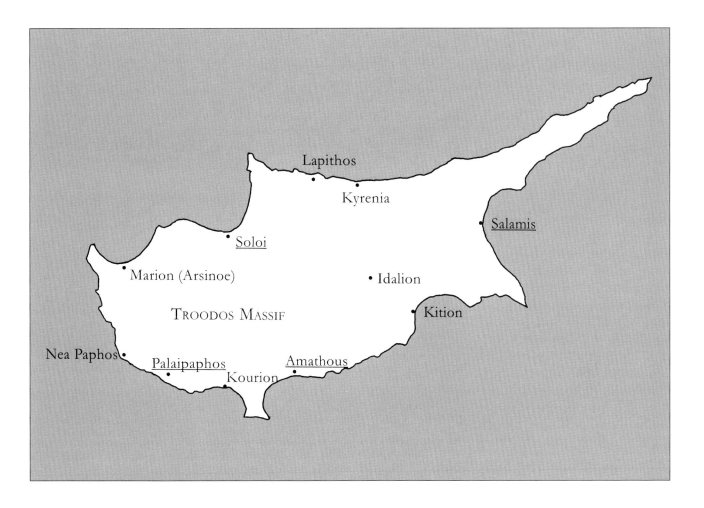

Fig. 2. Map of Cyprus c. 290 BC. Underlining indicates the cities which were allied with Ptolemy I in 321 BC.

walls of Old Paphos, consistent with a date of construction in the penultimate decade of the fourth century. Against this background, there is no longer any basis for the assumption that either the inscription, or the coins, refer to Nea Paphos. The message in both cases is quite straightforward: the words *eurychoros polis* refers to the city where the inscription was set up, i.e. Palaipaphos. And when the coins show Aphrodite with a crown of walls and towers, it alludes to the walls and towers surrounding her sanctuary – at Palaipaphos.

What does the literary evidence have to tell us about the kingdom of Paphos and the biography of Nikokles? Initially, it needs to be explained that until the first century AD, our sources do not use the epithets *palaia* or *nea*, "old" or "new", to distinguish the two cities. Both Nea Paphos and Palaipaphos are simply called "Paphos", and in addition, "Paphos" can

be used to describe the entire city-state, i.,e. the former Paphian kingdom.

Nikokles was ruler of the Paphian kingdom in 321 BC. In that year, four kings on the island concluded an alliance with Ptolemy I Soter. In a fragment of Arrian we find Nikokles, king of Paphos, listed along with Nikokreon of Salamis, Pasikrates of Soli, and Androkles of Amathous.[12]

These were troubled years in the history of the island. In 315 Seleukos, later known to us as king Seleukos I Nikator, but at this time in the service of Ptolemy I, sailed along the north coast, "took Kyrenia and Lapithos, and secured the support of Stasioikos, king of Marion", according to Diodoros.[13] Seleukos also laid siege to Kition on the south coast, forcing the king, Pygmalion, to abandon Antigonos in favour of Ptolemy. When king Ptolemy himself came to the island in 312, he had Pygmalion killed. Ptolemy also had the kings of Kyrenia, Lapithos and Marion arrested, and Marion itself was destroyed. Its inhabitants were transferred to the kingdom of Paphos and the revenues from its lands given to Nikokreon, king of Salamis, who now became *strategos* of Cyprus; in other words, Ptolemy's satrap on the island.[14]

According to the account of Diodoros, Nikokles reigned until 310.[15] Then Ptolemy, fearing that Nikokles might be negotiating with Antigonos Monophtalmos, sent two of his agents to Cyprus to have him killed. Nikokles tried to convince them of his loyalty to Ptolemy, without success. Trapped in his palace, he chose to commit suicide along with his entire household; his brothers were the last to kill themselves, having locked the doors and set fire to the building.

This was the tragic end of the independent kingdom of Paphos, as described by Diodoros. Some scholars have questioned this account, and hypothesized that Diodoros has confused Nikokles with Nikokreon of Salamis, who is known to have died in 311. On this interpretation, it is Nikokreon who is suspected of disloyalty and forced to suicide; the events take place in Salamis, not in Paphos; and Nikokles lives on as king of Paphos until c. 306. Helga Gesche, who has published a detailed survey of the sources, rejects the hypothesis that Diodoros has confused the two kings.[16]

There are, indeed, few obvious reasons why Nikokreon, who owed his position as master of the island to Ptolemy, should wish to change sides. It is more likely that Ptolemy's suspicions would be directed at Nikokles, among other things because Nikokles had fortified his capital, Palaipaphos, at the time when he was allied with Ptolemy. Perhaps Ptolemy viewed this as a provocation, perhaps as an indication that Nikokles wanted to create his own hegemony over the western part of the island. Nikokreon would surely not have wasted an opportunity to draw Ptolemy's attention to this? In his turn, Nikokles had good reason to be disaffected with Ptolemy, who had passed him over and promoted Nikokreon to master of the island.

Some have seen a connection between the forced resettlement of the population of Marion, and the foundation of Nea Paphos: in this view, the transfer of population from Marion to Paphos is a gesture of good will on the part of Ptolemy, a contribution to the success of the new city. In that case, Nikokles and Ptolemy must have been on amicable terms in 312, which makes it difficult to understand why Ptolemy should order the death of Nikokles only two years later. Does this support the theory that Diodoros has confounded Nikokles and Nikokreon? Not really. For one thing, during these years, loyalty was often short-lived; for another, Ptolemy's relations with Nikokreon must have been amicable as well, if Nikokreon received the revenues from the territory of Marion. So if there is an apparent contradiction between Ptolemy's treatment of Nikokles in 312 and 310, then there would, by the same reasoning, be an even greater contradiction between Ptolemy's treatment of Nikokreon in 312 and 311/310 (if we were to follow the hypothesis that Diodoros has got the two kings mixed up).

There is another interpretation which cannot be ignored. Ptolemy's actions in the years 312 to 310 could be elements in a larger plan to subjugate the semi-independent kinglets of Cyprus. Ptolemy deposed the kings of Kition and the north coast in 312. Had he already planned his next move against Nikokreon and Nikokles? These two kings would surely be uneasy at the fate of their royal colleagues, and dividing the spoils of Marion between them could be a ploy to reassure them.

Another question: was the population of Marion ever actually resettled, and if so, where? "To Paphos" may indicate their removal to either Old Paphos or New Paphos, or to any other community within the kingdom of Paphos. Or, for that matter, that their territory was placed under the dominion of the king of Paphos. We note that the revenues of their territory was supposedly given to Nikokreon. If the entire population had been forcibly displaced from the territory of

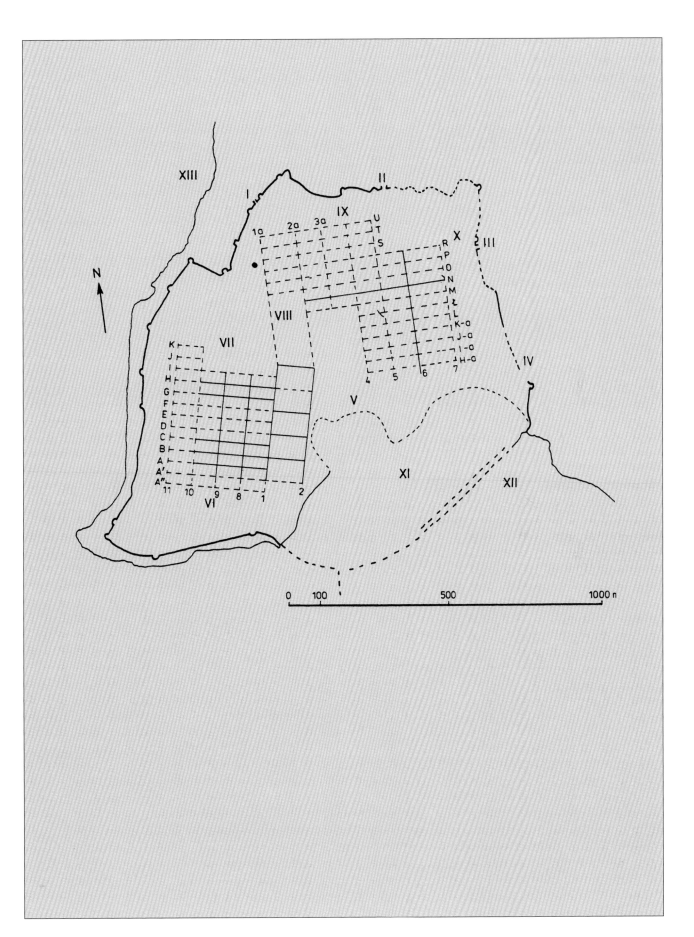

Marion, it is difficult to see where the revenues would come from.

Let us look at some of the arguments proposed in favour of Nikokles as the founder of Nea Paphos. These are summarized in the volume by Jolanta Mlynarczyk, *Nea Paphos in the Hellenistic Period*.[17] A number of points are raised, among them the account given by Diodoros of the siege of Salamis in 306. Hearing that Demetrios Poliorketes was attacking Salamis, Ptolemy sailed from Egypt with a large fleet and first mustered his naval forces at "Paphos". As mentioned earlier, this word could designate either Palaipaphos or Nea Paphos. Dr. Mlynarczyk assumes that the new harbour at Nea Paphos is meant, since the harbour at Palaipaphos was unsuitable for the purpose.[18] In that case, it would give us a *terminus ante quem* for the foundation of Nea Paphos – but this argument is inconclusive. First, we know little about the harbour conditions at Palaipaphos, but in a fragment of a poem by Sappho, she describes the city as *panormos*, that is to say, having a good harbour.[19] So we cannot *a priori* rule out the possibility that a fleet assembled at Palaipaphos, nor that the fleet anchored off the coast near the settlement that later became Nea Paphos, even if no foundation had yet taken place.

Nikokles' hypothetical rôle as founder of Nea Paphos has contemporary parallels. Seleukia and Antiochia, among many others, come to mind; but the founders of Seleukia and Antiochia gave their own names to their cities, just as Alexander gave his name to dozens of Alexandrias. So carrying this parallel through to its logical conclusion, we would expect Nikokles to found a *Nikoklia* rather than a New Paphos. There is indeed a *Nikoklia* in Cyprus; two kilometres north of Old Paphos. The foundation of this settlement is traditionally ascribed to the last of the Kinyrad kings, and it would seem natural to place a new royal residence close to the sanctuary of Old Paphos, considering the rôle of the kings as priests of Aphrodite.

The preceding arguments are some of those which have been advanced in favour of the view that Nikokles is the founder of Nea Paphos. In all fairness, we should also look at possible arguments against this view, of which there are several.

First, it is difficult to see Nikokles' motive for moving his capital more than fifteen kilometres away from the sanctuary of Aphrodite – the traditional locus of sacred authority within the Paphian kingdom. The cult was part and parcel of the legitimacy and power-base of the Kinyrads, a fact reflected in the inscriptions of Nikokles, where the titulature is "Nikokles, king of Paphos, priest of Anassa, son of Timarchos". *Anassa*, i.e. "lady" or "queen", is the local appellation for Aphrodite, and we note that the king's religious claim to legitimacy – his function as priest – is mentioned *before* the dynastic proof of legitimacy – the name of his father. As Dr. Mlynarczyk herself very precisely expresses it: "The qualification "priest of Anassa" in the inscriptions of Nikokles is not only evidence of his actual role in the cult of the goddess, but also proof of the legality of his secular power".[20]

One could theorize that Nikokles had been at cross purposes with the priests of the sanctuary and for this reason had wanted to move his residence, more or less for the same reasons that Akhnaton once moved his capital to Amarna. But there is no evidence in our sources to suggest such a development; and the fact that the Kinyrads continued to hold the office of high priests on a hereditary basis – as we know from Tacitus, quoted above – does not fit with the notion of a serious rift between dynasty and sanctuary.

Second, there is the question of fortifications. If Nikokles was establishing a new capital elsewhere, why fortify Palaipaphos? This behaviour is even more self-contradictory if we follow the traditional chronology, which would date the foundation of Nea Paphos around 320, and the coins with the mural crown – which, as we have seen, must refer to the fortification of Old Paphos – to c. 317. Why devote time and resources the old capital, right at the moment when Nikokles was preparing to vacate it? And why did he not fortify his new capital instead?

Third, an argument which is clearly weaker than the preceding two, because it is an argument *e silentio*. If Nikokles was in fact the founder of Nea Paphos, why has no tradition to this effect been preserved in any of our sources? Perhaps Nikokles was not a charismatic leader, his foreign policy may have been ineffective and his other achievements uninspiring, but his violent death makes him a tragic hero, the stuff of which myths – including founder-myths – are made. Yet apparently the citizens of Nea Paphos did not commemorate him as their founder; or if they did, then strangely enough the story has not come down to us.

Assuming that Nikokles was not the founder of Nea Paphos, the most obvious candidate is the diadoch ruler of Egypt, Ptolemy I son of Lagos, also known as the "saviour", Ptolemy Soter. At the international archaeological congress in Athens in 1983, Wiktor A. Daszewski proposed the hypothesis that Ptolemy took the initiative for the foundation of Nea Paphos around 315 BC, that is, while king Nikokles was still *de facto* and *de jure* ruler of the Paphian kingdom. In Daszewski's view, the resources of Nikokles were insufficient to fortify Palaipaphos and establish Nea Paphos at the same time. It was Ptolemy, then, not Nikokles, who founded the new city and later forcibly resettled the population of Marion at Nea Paphos. In Daszewski's interpretation, Ptolemy is the protagonist, creating "a town-base for *his* Mediterranean fleet and a foothold for *him* on Cyprus".[21]

This hypothesis has several points in its favour: for one, it explains why Nikokles and Ptolemy eventually became enemies: Nikokles must have resented this intrusion upon his sovereign territory. It also explains why there is no tradition concerning the founder of Nea Paphos: if their city had been founded by a foreign invader, the citizens may have preferred to forget the fact.

It is difficult to see why Nikokles would want to separate capital and sanctuary, weakening his own position. In the case of Ptolemy, the situation is directly reversed. Ptolemy had very good reasons to separate one from the other: to break the double power, secular and religious, of the Kinyrads. In addition, he might want to locate the capital in a place which was not marked by the memory of the last priest-king and his violent death, for which Ptolemy was to blame – assuming that Nea Paphos was founded after the death of Nikokles, that is to say after 310.

Why did Ptolemy not name the city for himself – why was *Nea Paphos* not named *Ptolemais*, a name befitting the capital of Ptolemaic Cyprus? A possible explanation is that the foundation of the new city carried unpleasant memories, which one did not want associated with the new régime; and that on the other hand, retention of the old name (and the consequent association with the Paphian Aphrodite) gave the new capital a legitimacy which the Ptolemaic rulers needed to bolster their position in the island.

The prime concern of Ptolemy was not the local political geography of western Cyprus. His was a far broader view, concerned with the need to defend Egypt against aggression from the sea. Here, Daszewski correctly emphasizes that the importance of Cyprus to Ptolemy was not primarily its function as a naval base. The decisive strategic importance of the island lay in its timber resources. Without timber, there could be no ships; and without ships, no thalassocracy – which meant leaving the shores of Egypt open to invaders. According to Diodoros, Antigonos ordered the invasion of Cyprus after a discussion concerned with the supply of shipbuilding timber.[22] And many centuries later, when the Cypriot forests were already showing signs of overexploitation, Ammianus Marcellinus could still record that Cyprus was the only island which could outfit a complete ship from its own indigenous resources.[23] There were no tall forests in the African provinces of the Ptolemaic kingdom, nor in Coele-Syria. Phoenicia, Cilicia and Rhodes had good forests, but access to these was controlled by Antigonos. So the nearest, perhaps the only, certainly the safest option available to Ptolemy were the Troodos forests of Cyprus.

Unfortunately, from an Egyptian point of view, the resources of the Troodos were difficult to exploit, since there were few good harbours on the south coast of the island. This we know, since shortly before the year 300 great expense and great effort were put into the construction of a harbour at Amathous. 5,000 stone blocks weighing several tons each were used for breakwaters and moles, yet within a few years the port silted up and was useless.[24]

It is reasonable to assume that Ptolemy wanted a bridgehead on Cyprus and access to the timber resources of the island.[25] He may well have felt uneasy about the loyalty of the Cypriot cities in general. Four cities, however, had been on his side since the treaty of 321 and were presumably more reliable than the others (Fig. 2). Of these, Soloi was on the North coast, facing away from Egypt, while Salamis was too far from the forests of the Troodos. This left Paphos and Amathous, with Amathous enjoying a more central location and in addition, being *gravida metallis*, as Ovid expresses it:[26] having metal as well as timber resources to offer.

Jean-Yves Empéreur proposes a different interpretation.[27] In his view, the harbour at Amathous was the work of Demetrios Poliorketes. The scale of the project indeed makes one think of Demetrios, the location, however, less so. Empéreur sees Amathous as an Antigonid naval base, "pour menacer les autres possessions de son ennemi". While it is true that Amathous is close to Egypt, it would be a very exposed base. And for timber exports to Greece, which seem to have been a concern of Antigonos, it would be very inconveniently located. As far as the dating evidence is concerned, a date either shortly before or shortly after 306 is possible, leaving both interpretations open.

Allow me to suggest a scenario for the events of 321 to 294. Ptolemy gained control of Cyprus through a series of alle-giances with local kings: first the four cities of Soloi, Salamis, Amathous and Paphos, then the kings of Kition and the north coast. His position grew stronger, and from 312 onwards, he systematically eliminated his allies one by one, deposing them or forcing them to suicide. We have seen how, in turn, he dealt with the kings of Lapithos and Kyrenia, Stasioikos of Marion, Pygmalion of Kition, Nikokreon of Salamis, and, the last but not the least, king Nikokles of Paphos.

Having secured his control of Cyprus, Ptolemy needed a port for timber exports and shipbuilding, perhaps also a residence for his *strategos*. His first choice was Amathous, but the building project was unsuccesful; in any case, Antigonos and Demetrios seized control of Cyprus soon after. When Ptolemy regained the island in 294, he founded a new city in the former kingdom of Paphos. Palaipaphos had been devastated by an earthquake around 300 BC, and its functions were all transferred to the new Paphos – all, that is to say, except the functions associated with the great sanctuary of Aphrodite. These remained in Palaipaphos, in the hands of the Kinyrad dynasty, at a suitable distance from the seat of political power. To retain the link between the sanctuary and the capital, a ritual procession was instituted.[28]

To summarize: the traditional dating of the foundation of Nea Paphos to 320, as well as the traditional identification of Nikokles as the founder, are in conflict with most of the evidence now available. The alternative theory of Daszewski, dating the foundation to 315 and identifying Ptolemy as the founder, solves some problems but creates others, and does not accord well with the chronology of the harbour at Amathous. But accepting a date for the foundation of Nea Paphos in or soon after 294, with Ptolemy I Soter as the founder, provides a scenario which is straightforward, both in terms of chronology and motives, and which is not contradicted by any of our sources.

Antoninus Liberalis, the mythographer, was quoted at the beginning of this article. A mythographer's vocation is writing about myths, just as the historian's vocation is writing about history. In the case of Nea Paphos it would seem that mythography and historiography have been confounded, producing not a foundation history but a foundation myth, complete with a mythical founder in the person of the tragic king Nikokles. It is a beautiful myth, but it is too good to be true.

Notes

A preliminary version of this paper, in Danish, was presented to a meeting of Scandinavian historians in Kungälv, Sweden, May 1998. I am grateful for the comments received on this and subsequent occasions, and especially to Anne Destrooper-Georgiades, Jane Fejfer, Vincent Gabrielsen, John Hayes, John Leonard and Jørgen Christian Meyer.

NOTE 1
Strabo, 14.6.3.

NOTE 2
Met. 14.698-764.

NOTE 3
Arkeophon, 39.1-6.

NOTE 4
Mor., 766 C-D.

NOTE 5
Iliad, 2.609.

NOTE 6
8.5.2; also Strabo, 14.6.3.

NOTE 7
Hist., 2.2-3

NOTE 8
Tacitus, *Hist.* (previous note) and also *Ann.* 3.62, mentions a third founder of Palaipaphos, Aërias. He is not mentioned in any other source.

NOTE 9
A necropolis along the road leading from Nea Paphos to the north is known locally as "the tombs of the kings". This identification goes back at least as far as 1878, when it is quoted by a German traveller, F. von Löher. The tombs are not royal, however, they belong to high-ranking functionaries within the Ptolemaic administration of Cyprus, and date from the third and second centuries BC.

NOTE 10
Mitford 1961, 2.

NOTE 11
Mørkholm 1978.

NOTE 12
FGrH IIB, 10.6 (p. 848).

NOTE 13
Diod. 19.62.

NOTE 14
Diod. 19.79

NOTE 15
Diod. 20.21.

NOTE 16
Gesche 1974, 122-23.

NOTE 17
Mlynarczyk 1990, 67ff.

NOTE 18
Mlynarczyk 1990, 27.

NOTE 19
Sappho et Alcaeus Fragmenta, ed. Eva-Maria Voigt, Amsterdam 1971, 35, with critical notes and additional references. The fragment is found in Strabo's description of Cyprus, *Geo.* 1.2.33. Voigt prefers to interpret *Panormos* as a place-name, not an adjective; either interpretation is possible, but the first reading – *panormos* as an adjective – is more likely in the context of Strabo's text. Wallace and Orphanides, *Sources for the History of Cyprus*, I, 124, follow H.L. Jones' translation (Loeb Classical Library): "Paphos of the spacious harbour".

NOTE 20
Mlynarczyk 1990, 70.

NOTE 21
Daszewski 1987, 174. Hohlfelder & Leonard (1993) suggest that the town was established in 315 BC, but the harbour some years later, 310/309 BC.

NOTE 22
Diod. 20.46.4-5.

NOTE 23
Ammianus, 14.8.14. Pliny, *NH* 16.203, reports that the tallest cedar tree ever recorded was felled in Cyprus, adding that it was used by Demetrios Poliorketes for the mast of a giant warship.

NOTE 24
Empéreur 1996, 164ff. The results of the harbour excavations have not yet been published in more detail.

NOTE 25
See also Hauben 1987, 217-19.

NOTE 26
Met. 10.220.

NOTE 27
Empéreur 1996, 168.

NOTE 28
Strabo, 14.6.3.

Bibliography

Daszewski, W. A. 1987
Nicocles and Ptolemy: Remarks on
the Early History of Nea Paphos,
RDAC, 171-75.

Empéreur, J.-Y. 1996
Le port externe, in: P. Aubert (ed.),
Guide d'Amathonte. Paris, 164-68.

Gesche, H. 1974
Nikokles von Paphos und Nikokreon von Salamis. *Chiron* 4, 103-
25.

Hauben, H. 1987
Cyprus and the Ptolemaic Navy,
RDAC, 213-26.

Hohlfelder, R.L. & Leonard, J.R.
1993
Underwater Explorations at
Paphos, Cyprus: The 1991 Preliminary Survey, *ASOR Annual* 51, 45-
62.

Maier, F.G. & Karageorghis, V. 1984
Paphos. History and Archaeology.
Nicosia.

Mitford, T.B. 1961
The Hellenistic Inscriptions of Old
Paphos, *BSA* 56, 1-41.

Mørkholm, O. 1978
The Alexandrian Coinage of Nikokles of Paphos, *Chiron* 8, 135-46.

Wallace, P.W. & Orphanides, A.G.
1990
Sources for the History of Cyprus, I.
Nicosia.

La colonne du Dôdékathéon à Délos[1]

Jari Pakkanen

Abstract

The temple of Twelve Gods on Delos was most probably built in the beginning of third century BC. The column shaft reconstruction presented in this paper is based on the data published by E. Will (1955). The shaft had a slight entasis with a maximum projection of 5 mm approximately in the middle of the shaft. The closest parallels for the shaft profile may be found in fourth century BC Peloponnesian architecture and the third century BC Stoa in the sanctuary of Athena at Lindos. The column height of the Dôdekatheon of 6.7 lower diameters is paralleled both in Late Classical and Early Hellenistic architecture.

Les fondations entre la Salle Hypostyle et l'Agora des Italiens à Délos ont été identifiées par R. Vallois comme les vestiges du Λωδεκάθεον, le temple des Douze Dieux, en 1929.[2] Ce temple fut probablement construit au début du IIIe siècle av. J.-C.[3] C'est un petit bâtiment dorique hexastyle, amphiprostyle, pourvu d'un pronaos mais dénué d'opistodome.[4] Les blocs conservés dans le site ont permis une reconstitution générale de ce temple ruiné; la restitution du fût de la colonne présentée ici est basée sur l'information publiée par E. Will (1955) dans sa monographie sur le bâtiment.

Bien qu'un nombre élevé de tambours et de fragments – Will a identifié 41 des 48 tambours – il n'est pas facile d'établir les données du fût: seuls 29 tambours sont utilisables pour la restitution et ceux-ci sont souvent mal conservés. Les tambours les mieux conservés sont les tambours inférieurs et une partie des deuxième du bas. Les colonnes du Dôdékathéon avaient vingt cannelures canoniques. A la base, le diamètre est de 0,69 m entre les arêtes et de 0,63 m au fond des cannelures; au sommet, les mesures correspondantes sont de 0,566 m et de 0,524 m. Le nombre des tambours dans le fût est discuté en détail plus bas. Will propose que la hauteur totale de la colonne avec le chapiteau est de 4,62 m et qu'elle n'avait ni entasis, ni inclinaison vers l'interieur.[5] R. Vallois constate seulement brièvement que l'existence d'entasis est douteuse au Dôdékathéon.[6]

Le raisonnement de Will sur l'inclination de la colonne est correct: pour construire un fût incliné, il est nécessaire que les lits de pose et d'attente du tambour inférieur ne sont pas parallèles,[7] et il est possible de vérifier le parallélisme en prenant plusieurs mesures de la hauteur du tambour sur différents côtés. Si toutes les mesures sont environ les mêmes, comme c'est le cas au Dôdékathéon,[8] les deux lits sont parallèles et le fût n'est pas incliné.[9] Toutefois, l'observation de Will sur l'entasis est erronée. De son texte, il ressort qu'il tente de vérifier l'existence d'entasis se basant sur les tambours inférieurs; il ne tient donc pas compte du fût complet.[10] Même si la courbe de l'entasis est continue, celle-ci est souvent si minime qu'il est impossible de l'observer sur un seul tambour, surtout quand les tambours sont érodés.[11]

Pour déterminer la hauteur de la colonne Will utilise la hauteur du mur et la hauteur moyenne de quatre assises des tambours. Selon lui la hauteur du mur de la cella au-dessous de l'épistyle est de 14 x 0,33 m = 4,62 m, et la hauteur totale de la colonne doit être la même.[12] Les observations de Will sur le mur sont très minu-

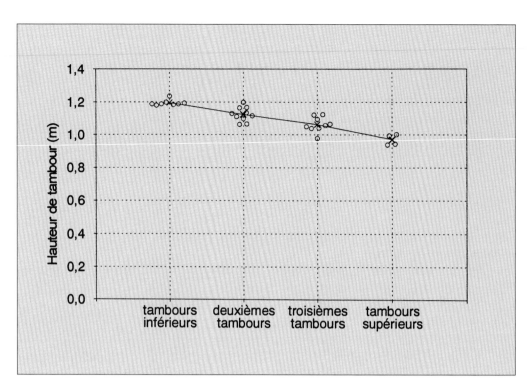

Fig. 1. Les hauteurs des tambours conservés.

tieuses, et le nombre de blocs préservés est suffisant pour établir que la hauteur d'une assise est de 0,33 m.[13] La hauteur moyenne des tambours et des chapiteaux donne 1,196 + 1,121 + 1,065 + 0,971 + 0,25 (4,60 m comme la hauteur de la colonne. Will considère la possibilité d'un fût avec cinq tambours, mais il rejette cette alternative parce que la hauteur du mur avec dix-sept assises (5,61 m) et la hauteur de la colonne (5,73 m) ne sont pas la même.[14] Je vais examiner la possibilité d'un fût avec cinq tambours en détail plus bas.

Avec quelle précision est-il possible de déterminer la hauteur du fût du Dôdékathéon en utilisant les hauteurs moyennes des tambours? Figure 1 montre un graphique des hauteurs des tambours conservés. Les petits cercles indiquent la hauteur de chaque tambour. Pour représenter toutes les observations, les cercles sont horizontalement un peu dispersés sur les deux côtés de la vraie valeur de la classe. Les croix indiquent la hauteur moyenne de chaque classe et une ligne les relie pour illustrer la tendance des hauteurs moyennes. Bien que la hauteur des

tambours varie dans chaque classe, la tendance linéaire est claire: les tambours inférieurs sont les plus longs et les tambours supérieurs les plus courts. Donc, dans l'analyse statistique il n'est pas possible de traiter les tambours comme s'ils formaient qu'une seule classe; pour déterminer la hauteur minimale et maximale du fût, il est nécessaire de calculer des intervalles de confiance qui sont individuels pour chaque classe de tambours. Pour les tambours inférieurs, l'intervalle de confiance au niveau 95% est de 1,19 à 1,20 m, pour les deuxièmes de 1,11 à 1,14 m, pour les troisièmes de 1,05 à 1,08 m et pour les tambours supérieurs de 0,93 à 1,01 m. La hauteur minimale du fût est de 4,28 m et la hauteur maximale de 4,44 m; la hauteur totale de la colonne avec le chapiteau est de 4,53 m à 4,69 m.[15] La hauteur précise de la colonne doit être déterminée se basant sur la hauteur du mur de la cella. La hauteur d'un mur avec treize et quinze assises de 0,33 m (4,29 m et 4,95 m respectivement) tombe en dehors de l'intervalle de confiance de la hauteur de la colonne. Il s'ensuit que si le fût était composé de quatre tambours, le mur de la cella compterait quatorze assises

Fig. 2. Le profil du fût avec cinq tambours.

et la hauteur du mur et de la colonne auraient été 4,62 m, suivant la suggestion de Will.[16]

La possibilité que le fût se composait de cinq tambours ne peut pas être aussi facilement rejeté comme le donne à croire Will.[17] L'état de conservation d'une partie des deuxièmes tambours est si mauvais qu'on pourrait diviser le groupe en deux sous-groupes.[18] L'intervalle de confiance au niveau 95% de la hauteur du fût avec cinq tambours est de 5,25 à 5,72 m et de la hauteur totale de 5,50 à 5,97 m. L'intervalle est plus grand que dans le cas où le fût comprend quatre tambours; cela s'explique par le nombre réduit de tambours dans le deuxième sous-groupe.[19] La hauteur du mur avec dix-sept (5.61 m) et dix-huit assises (5.94 m) est dans les deux cas dans l'intervalle défini. Il est donc nécessaire d'analyser le profil du fût et les proportions de la colonne pour déterminer si l'on doit considérer le fût avec cinq tambours comme une possibilité correcte.

La figure 2 présente le profil du fût avec cinq tambours qui correspond à une hauteur du mur de 5,61 m – la hauteur de 5,36 m dans le graphique donne la hauteur du fût sans le chapiteau. Sur la figure l'axe des *x* et l'axe des *y* sont sur des échelles différentes pour faciliter l'observation de la courbe d'entasis : l'échelle de l'axe des *x* est dix fois plus grande que celle de l'axe des *y*. Les trois points du bas représentés comme des cercles sur la figure 2 sont calculés à partir des mesures des premiers et deuxièmes tambours de Will et la coordonnée de *x* le plus haut est dérivée du diamètre connu.[20] La jointure du premier et du deuxième tambour est un peu à gauche de la ligne droite qui relie le pied et le sommet du fût, et le haut du deuxième tambour est à droite de la ligne, mais il est possible que ces divergences sont causées par des inexactitudes légères des dimensions des tambours. La comparaison des proportions fournie un meilleur argument pour rejeter cette restitution du fût: le fût avec cinq

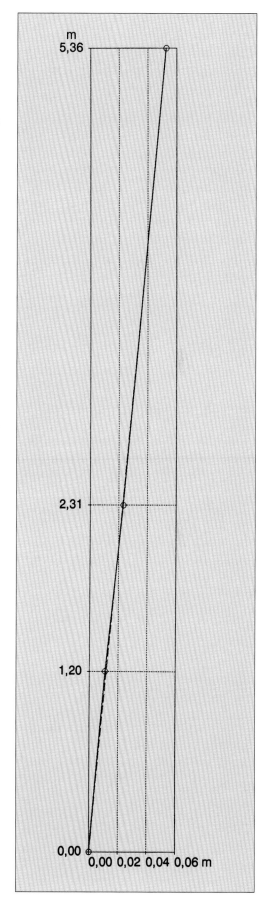

tambours a une hauteur de 8.1 fois son diamètre,[21] une hauteur qui n'a aucun parallèle dans architecture dorique contemporaine – à l'exception des colonnes exceptionnellement hautes de 7.4 diamètres utilisées dans la Stoa d'Attale à Delphes, les colonnes les plus élancées du IIIᵉ siècle que je connais sont celles de la Stoa Nord-Ouest à Thasos et celles du péristyle de l'Hérôon à Pergame, qui sont 7.0 diamètres.[22]

La figure 3 montre le profil du fût avec quatre tambours. Les coordonnées du profil pour les deux tambours du bas sont les mêmes que sur la figure 2, mais parce que le fût est plus court, le point le plus haut est placé à 4,37 m. La courbe d'entasis est tracée par rechercher le polynôme du troisième degré qui donne la meilleure taille aux coordonnées connues.[23] Le profil montre que le fût avait un galbe peu sensible avec à peu près au milieu du fût une projection maximale de 5 mm.[24] On ne dispose pas d'assez de données pour déterminer la formule mathématique utilisée pour la conception du profil du fût.[25] Les parallèles les plus proches de ce profil se trouvent dans l'architecture péloponnésienne du IVᵉ siècle et dans la Stoa à Lindos datant du IIIᵉ siècle.[26] La hauteur de la colonne du Dôdékathéon de 6.7 diamètres a des parallèles dans l'architecture classique tardive et hellénistique.[27] C'est très probable que cette restitution du fût est correcte. La figure 4 présente la colonne avec quatre tambours et une entasis légère.

Fig. 3. Le profil du fût avec quatre tambours.

Fig. 4. La restitution de la colonne.

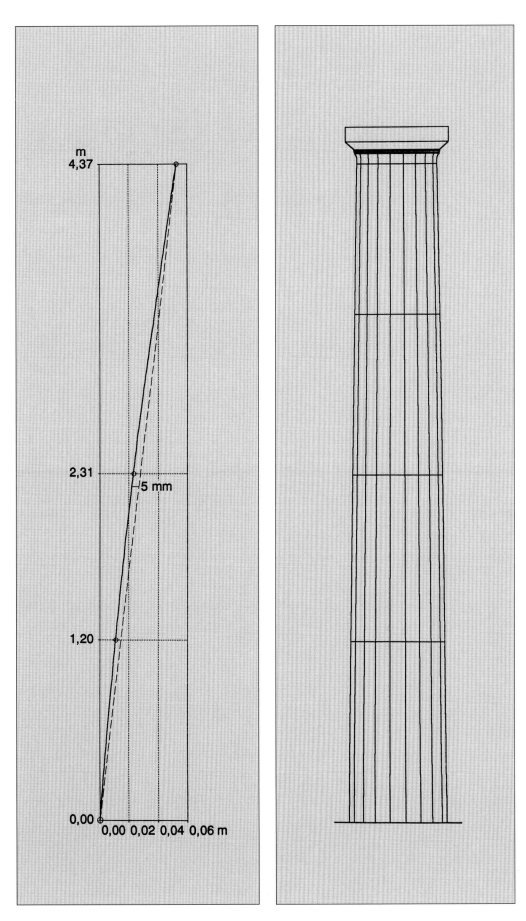

Notes

NOTE 1
Je suis reconnaissant à Anne Destrooper d'avoir lu le texte français et à Richard Tomlinson de ses remarques.

NOTE 2
Vallois 1929, 225–249.

NOTE 3
Le *terminus ante quem* du temple est 282 av. J.-C. (le bâtiment est mentionné dans *IG* XI2 158A, 65); ses caractéristiques architecturales datent d'après la periode classique; voir Will 1955, 166–167.

NOTE 4
Will 1955, 12, pl. B.

NOTE 5
Will 1955, 26.

NOTE 6
Vallois 1966, 112.

NOTE 7
Voir par ex. Bundgaard 1955, 133–136 (sur les colonnes du Parthénon).

NOTE 8
Will 1955, 26 n. 1.

NOTE 9
Si la krépis du bâtiment est courbée, il est possible que les lits sont non parallèles pour annuler l'effect du stylobate courbé et faire les colonnes verticales, comme dans le temple d'Aléa Athéna à Tégée; voir Pakkanen 1996b, 164.

NOTE 10
«L'absence d'entasis se vérifie sur les tambours I», Will 1955, 26 n. 1.

NOTE 11
Sur l'entasis qui n'est pas observable dans les tambours individuels, voir par ex. Pakkanen 1997, 332 et Pakkanen 1998, 152 n. 39.

NOTE 12
Will 1955, 28.

NOTE 13
Will 1955, 67–131.

NOTE 14
Will 1955, 28.

NOTE 15
En utilisant l'intervalle de confiance au niveau 95%, il y a une probabilité de 95% que la hauteur du fût est située dans l'intervalle [4,28 m; 4,44 m]. La formule suivante est utilisée pour calculer l'intervalle de confiance: $\overline{X}_n \pm (t_{n-1}) \frac{S}{\sqrt{n}} \sqrt{1 - \frac{n}{N}}$, où $\overline{X}_n$ est la moyenne empirique, t_{n-1} le fractile t qui correspond à $n-1$ degrés de liberté, S l'écart-type d'échantillon, n la taille d'échantillon, et N le nombre total des tambours dans chaque niveau. Les valeurs pour les tambours inférieurs sont $\overline{X}_n = 1,196$, $t_{n-1} = 2,365$, $S = 0,01776$ et $n = 8$; pour les deuxièmes tambours $\overline{X}_n = 1,126$, $t_{n-1} = 2,262$, $S = 0,04399$ et $n = 10$; pour les troisièmes tambours: $\overline{X}_n = 1,065$, $t_{n-1} = 2,306$, $S = 0,04563$ et $n = 9$; pour les tambours supérieurs: $\overline{X}_n = 0,9715$, $t_{n-1} = 3,182$, $S = 0,03316$ et $n = 4$; N est dans chaque cas 12. Sur l'intervalle de confiance, voir par ex. Siegel & Morgan 1996, 321-330, 590 (table C.3); Shennan 1997, 363–365.

NOTE 16
Will 1955, 28.

NOTE 17
Will 1955, 28.

NOTE 18
Groupes II et II^A dans la table de Will 1955, 27.

NOTE 19
Les intervalles de confiance au niveau 95% des deux sous-groupes des deuxièmes tambours sont de 1,10 à 1,15 m et de 0,98 à 1,27 m ; on peut calculer l'intervalle du fût avec cinq tambours sans tenir compte des deuxièmes tambours dans le calcul du fût avec quatre tambours (voir n. 14) et substituer ces deux intervalles dans l'addition. Parce qu'il y a seulement trois tambours dans l'autre sous-groupe, l'intervalle de confiance est très grand. Les valeurs pour le premier sous-groupe sont $\overline{X}_n = 1,125$, $t_{n-1} = 2,447$, $S = 0,03676$ et $n = 7$, et pour le deuxième $\overline{X}_n = 1,128$, $t_{n-1} = 4,302$, $S = 0,06817$ et $n = 3$.

NOTE 20
Les dimensions moyennes du tambour inférieur sont calculées sur l'ensemble de sept tambours bien préservés (n°s 1, 2, 3, 4, 35, 36 et 41 dans Will 1955, 27) – tous les diamètres sont mesurés au fond des cannelures: diamètre inférieur 0,630 m; hauteur 1,197 m; diamètre supérieur 0,607 m. Les dimensions du deuxième tambour sont fondées sur cinq tambours (n°s 5, 6, 8, 32 et 33): diamètre inférieur 0,609 m; hauteur 1,115 m; diamètre supérieur 0,583 m. Le diamètre supérieur du tambour inférieur et le diamètre inférieur du deuxième tambour devraient être les mêmes; par conséquent, j'utilise la moyenne de 0,608 m dans les figures 2 et 3. Un tambour supérieur (n° 10) et un chapiteau (fig. 7) sont suffisamment conservés pour permettre la restitution du diamètre de 0,524 m au sommet du fût; Will 1955, 27, 29, fig. 7 et 8.

NOTE 21
5,61 m / 0,69 m ≈ 8.1 (pour le diamètre inférieur, voir Will 1955, 26).

NOTE 22
Delphes: 6,6m / 0,886 m ≈ 7.4 (Roux & Callot 1987, 57–58. La hauteur correcte de la colonne est de 7,4 diamètres, non de 7,67 comme Roux propose); Thasos: 5,16 m / 0,74 m ≈ 7.0 (Martin 1959, 14, 17); 4,66 m / 0,666 m ≈ 7,00 (Boehringer & Krauss 1937, 60–64, fig. 7, 13). Pour les proportions des colonnes dans l'architecture dorique hellénistique en général, voir table 1 dans l'appendice de Pakkanen 1998, 222–223.

NOTE 23
Sur les courbes et l'entasis, voir Pakkanen 1996a et 1997, 336–341. Les points tracés sur la fig. 3 sont (0 ; 0), (0,011 ; 1,20), (0,024 ; 2, 31), (0,053 ; 4,37), et la formule de la courbe est $y = 121,5x - 1125,2x^2 + 7377,2x^3$ quand $x \in [0 ; 0,053]$. La différence entre les échelles de l'axe des x et des y fausse l'angle entre la ligne d'entasis maximale et la ligne droite; les lignes sont perpendiculaires bien qu'elles s'en donnent pas l'impression.

NOTE 24
L'entasis maximale est à 2,22 m du pied du fût. On peut calculer l'accent proportionnel d'entasis en divisant la longueur d'entasis par la hauteur du fût : $100\% \times 0,005$ m / 4,37 m $\approx 0.11\%$. La position proportionnelle d'entasis maximale dans le fût est calculée en divisant la hauteur d'entasis maximale par la hauteur du fût : 2,22 m / 4,37 m $\approx 0,508$. Ces valeurs ont été publiées dans l'appendice de Pakkanen 1998, 155 n. 57, 156, mais le fût du Dôdékathéon n'y est pas examiné en détail.

NOTE 25
L'emploi d'une formule mathématique n'est pas certain; voir Pakkanen 1997, 336–341.

NOTE 26
La Tholos à Epidaure, le temple d'Athéna Aléa à Tégée et la colonne du pronaos du temple de Zeus à Némée ont tous des profils à peu près similaires; voir Pakkanen 1997, 342, table 3. Sur la Stoa à Lindos, voir Pakkanen 1998, 156–157, table 1.

NOTE 27
4,62 m / 0,69 m $\approx 6,7$. Pour les références, voir n. 21.

Bibliographie

Pour les abréviations de la bibliographie, voir *American Journal of Archaeology* 95 (1991), 4–16.

Boehringer E. & Krauss, Fr. 1937
Der Temenos für den Herrscherkult. AvP 9. Berlin.

Bundgaard, J. A. 1957
Mnesicles. A Greek Architect at Work. Copenhagen.

Martin, R. 1959
L'Agora. Études Thasiennes 6. Paris.

Pakkanen, J. 1996a
The *Entasis* of Greek Doric Columns and Curve Fitting: a Case Study Based on the Peristyle Column of the Temple of Athena Alea at Tegea, *Archeologia e Calcolatori* 7, 693–702.

Pakkanen, J. 1996b
The Height and Reconstructions of the Interior Corinthian Columns in Greek Classical Buildings, *Arctos* 30, 139–166.

Pakkanen, J. 1997
Entasis in Fourth Century BC Doric Buildings in the Peloponnese and at Delphi, *BSA* 92, 323–344.

Pakkanen, J. 1998
The Column Shafts of the Propylaia and Stoa in the Sanctuary of Athena at Lindos, *Proceedings of the Danish Institute at Athens* 2, 146–159.

Roux R. & Callot, O. 1987
La terrasse d'Attale I à Delphes. FdD II. Paris.

Shennan, S. 1997[2]
Quantifying Archaeology. Edinburgh.

Siegel, A. F. & Morgan, C. J. 1996[2]
Statistics and Data Analysis. An Introduction. New York.

Vallois, R. 1929
Topographie délienne, II, *BCH* 53, 185–315.

Vallois, R. 1966
L'Architecture hellénique et hellénistique à Délos jusqu'à l'éviction des Déliens (166 av. J.-C.), vol. 2.1. BEFAR 157. Paris.

Will, E. 1955
Le Dôdékathéon. Délos 22. Paris.

The Greek–Danish Excavations in Aetolian Chalkis 1997–1998. Second Preliminary Report

Edited by Søren Dietz, Lazaros Kolonas, Sanne Houby-Nielsen and Ioannis Moschos

Contents

Acknowledgements

*Søren Dietz and
Lazaros Kolonas*

The field project in ancient Chalkis, Aetolia near the small, present-day fishing village of Kato Vassiliki, is being carried out under the auspices of the 6th Ephoria of Prehistoric and Classical Antiquities in Patras and the Danish Institute at Athens. In 1997 Denmark was represented by the National Museum of Denmark, while the actual responsibility for the field work done in 1998 was divided between this museum and the Ny Carlsberg Glyptotek, Copenhagen. We are most grateful to the Greek Ministry of Culture for permission to carry out work in Chalkis and to the Consul General Gösta Enbom Foundation which, as during previous campaigns, covered the expenses of the Danish participatation. Further support was provided by the Carlsberg Foundation. The community and the Mayor of Gavrolimni kindly made the old school in Kato Vassiliki available for storage and study rooms for the expedition.

Preface

Søren Dietz and Lazaros Kolonas

The first preliminary report on the Greek-Danish surveys and excavations in Chalkis, Aetolia, was published in 1998 (PDIA II, 1998, 233-317) and covered the work done by the joint expedition during the years 1995 and 1996. It is from now on referred to as FPR. In that report we gave a brief introduction to the geographical setting, and the history of the Aetolian coastland on the Gulf of Patras, and presented some general considerations which determined the choice of the site.

During the first two campaigns, an intensive survey was accomplished on both sites under examination: Pangali on the east slope of Mount Varassova, and the small mound of Haghia Triadha on the coast in the central part of the valley, to the east of the village of Kato Vassiliki. In addition, cleaning of the visible walls was carried out.

The architectural remains on the surface were measured and drawn on a plan. Finally, a grid system was introduced on both sites in 1995. In 1996 excavations were carried out at strategic points on the Haghia Triadha hill in order to gain an impression of the architectural remains. A geological study was initiated in order to trace the history of the changing shoreline from Antiquity to the present day. Finally, a small trench, 2 metres square was opened at the Final Neolithic site at Pangali in order to gain an impression of the stratigraphical situation on the site.

In 1997 and 1998, research was carried out on the Haghia Triadha hill only. An intensive cleaning in 1997, on the eastern side of the hill, of stone concentrations fallen from the upper part of the Byzantine fortification wall, created the oppor-

tunity to excavate the ancient strata in this part of the site. Two trenches were opened in the southeastern part of the middle terrace, and a trial trench, around the middle part of the eastern wall, which extended from the Byzantine wall to the border of the plateau. A second trial trench further north extended from the Byzantine wall to the slopes below the middle terrace testing the construction and stratigraphical position of the stone walls running peripherical to the oval mound in this part of the hill. The trial trenches were continued on the Acropolis, but except for Byzantine foundations and layers close to the defence wall, the layers above bedrock were modest.

The existence of marine deposits has been demonstrated during the geological survey to the west of the mound towards the village of Kato Vassiliki proving the existence of a bay in ancient times. AMS-datings of sediments show the existence of such a bay during the transition to the early Bronze Age (3310-2930 BC) and during the transition between Middle Helladic and Late Helladic (1750-1630 BC). Both periods are well represented in the archaeological material excavated on the hill. More research is necessary in order to estimate the extension of the bay at different periods and the character of the harbour of Chalkis mentioned in ancient literary sources. The geological survey thus unambiguously stated that the harbour has to be found on the west side of the hill.

In 1998, the excavation continued in the trenches opened on the middle terrace in 1997. In addition, two trial trenches were opened on the west side of the mound, in

Fig. 1. Participants in the campaign 1997.

order to establish documentation of habitation, and eventually harbour installations, at the waterfront in the small bay. Only one of these trenches was excavated extensively. In one area bedrock was reached 3.75 m below surface.

The participants in the two campaigns were the following (Figs. 1-2):

1997:
Project leaders: Søren Dietz and Lazaros Kolonas
Field directors: Sanne Houby-Nielsen and Ioannis Moschos
Archaeologists: Michalis Gazis and Konstantina Soura
Surveying: Charalambos Marinopoulos and Christos Kolonas
Pottery registration: Jonas Eiring
Geology: Kaj Strand Petersen

Photography: Hans Henrik Frost
Conservation: Leonidas Pavlatos
Technicians: Augerinos Anastasopoulos, Dimitrios Evangeliou, Spyros Pittas, Eugenios Tsamis and Apostolis Zarkadoulas
Students: Søren Fredslund Andersen, Craig Barker, Elizabeth Bollen, Jesper Jensen, Sine Toft Jensen, Kim Jessen, Louise Mejer, Kirsten Kvist Hansen, Heidi von Wettstein, Trine Eltang, Theophanis Mavridis.

1998:
Project leaders: Søren Dietz and Lazaros Kolonas
Field directors: Sanne Houby-Nielsen and Ioannis Moschos
Archaeologists: Michalis Gazis and Konstantina Soura
Surveying: Charalambos Marinopoulos and Christos Kolonas
Pottery registration: Jonas Eiring, Elisabeth

Fig. 2. Participants in the campaign 1998.

Bollen, Kirsten Kvist Hansen and Hildegunn Borup
Geology: Kaj Strand Petersen
Tiles: Claus Grønne
Photography: Hans Henrik Frost
Conservation: Leonidas Pavlatos
Technicians: Augerinos Anastasopoulos, Dimitrios Evangeliou, Spyros Pittas, Eugenios Tsamis and Apostolis Zarkadoulas
Students: Annette Højen Nielsen, Mette

Hvelplund, Dorthe Blaabjerg Nissen, Anna Høher Kiil Jørgensen, Christine Lorentzen Nielsen, Peter Rose, Søren Skriver Tillich, Julie Maria E.F. Mortensen, Marina Thomatos, Hege Alisøy, Theophanis Mavridis, Panagiota Galiatsatou, Marianna Demopoulou, Nancy Katsaiti, Vlacia Michalis, Chara Skarmea, Paraskevi Staikou, Panagiota Tsakalou, Antonia Sidiropoulou
Logistics: Ann Thomas

Excavations on the Hill of Haghia Triadha

Sanne Houby-Nielsen, Ioannis Moschos and Michalis Gazis

Introduction

During five weeks in the summer of 1997 and 1998, the Greek–Danish archaeological project continued its investigations in the area of Kato Vassiliki. In both seasons the investigations were concentrated on the hill of Haghia Triadha east of the village.

Five long trial trenches and three excavation-units were excavated. The total length of the excavated trial trenches, four of which were 1 m wide and one 2 m wide, came to just under 140 m, and the excavation units to approximately 160 m² (Fig. 3). Most of these trial trenches and the majority of the excavation units were excavated down to bedrock. The depth of the trial trenches ranged from about 0. 10 m to 3.75 m, and the character of the stratigraphy varied from floating layers and deposits to fairly well-defined cultural layers. All trenches and units produced architectural remains, which were surveyed. The excavation results are presented preliminarily in more detail below.

With regard to the registration of finds from the 1997-98 excavations these amounted to approximately 60.–70.000 potsherds, approximately 4000 kgs of tile, and 500 small-finds (see the report by J. Eiring). Among the small-finds, the coins have been given preliminary treatment by G. Alexopoulou in this report. Apart from the excavations, registration of finds and surveys of architectural remains, the investigations comprised geological studies, study of the pottery from the Final Neolithic site on Pangali and work on the tiles from collapsed roofs found in situ was

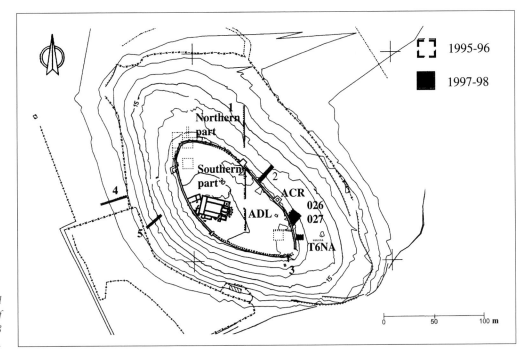

Fig. 3. The trial trenches and units excavated on the hill of Haghia Triadha 1997-1998 (Charalambos Marinopoulos).

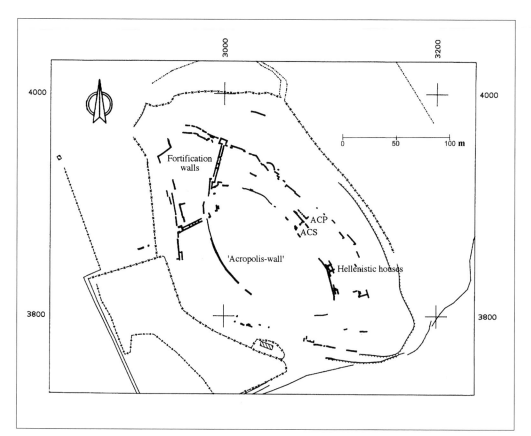

Fig. 4. Classical-Hellenistic Chalkis. Map showing the Classical-Hellenistic remains excavated and cleared during the campaigns 1995-1998 (Charalambos Marinopoulos 1998).

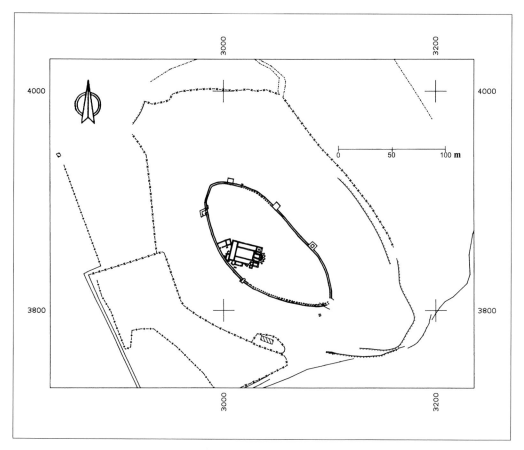

Fig. 5. Byzantine Chalkis, later the episkepsis Baresobés. Map showing the Byzantine fortification wall excavated and cleared during the 1995-1998 campaigns in relation to the Byzantine basilica excavated by A.D. Paliouras (Charalambos Marinopoulos 1998).

Fig. 6. Byzantine tower ACR. (Photo: Henrik Frost).

begun (see the reports by K. Strand Pedersen, T. Mavridis and C. Grønne).

It should also be mentioned that a couple of ancient limestone blocks similar to those used in the classical fortification on Pangali and Haghia Triadha were observed in one place in the western part of Kato Vassiliki and close to the road leading towards Gavrolimni about 2 km from the sea. Finally, the 6th Ephoria carried out emergency excavations of Hellenistic tombs along this road during the autumn and reinvestigated two grave reliefs in the Museum of Agrinion which were said to come from the region of Kato Vassiliki (see the report by I. Moschos).

All in all the archaeological investigations in 1997-98 have considerably increased our knowledge of the prehistory and early history of Chalkis and of the Classical-Hellenistic town (Fig. 4) as well furthered our understanding of the Byzantine fortification and its relation to the Early Christian basilica (Fig. 5).

Surveys of the Byzantine fortification wall and the Classical 'acropolis wall'

Surveys of the Byzantine fortification-wall and the Classical circuit-wall – from now on referred to as the 'acropolis wall' – began back in 1995 and were continued in 1996. During those campaigns long sections of both walls and part of two towers belonging to the Byzantine wall had appeared.[1] In 1997-98 the surveys continued and a third, well-preserved tower (ACR) came to light (Figs. 3, 6). Tower and wall were constructed as a single unit and thus clearly built at the same time. The bottom part of a large pithos was found embedded in clayish soil in the Byzantine wall just behind the tower indicating that this level had once served as a floor level. Among the finds in the debris of the tower, a fragment of a Classical terracotta sima from a gable deserves mention. It is decorated with a band of 'running palmette' and 'bead-and –reel' paint-

ed in red and black on a white slipped surface (Fig. 7).[2] The Archaic or Early Classical bronze handle from a cauldron or basin shown in Fig. 8 was likewise found close to the tower [3].

Long sections of the Classical 'acropolis wall' could be traced almost all the way around the hill sometimes under or directly in front of the Byzantine wall,[4] sometimes running parallel to the Byzantine wall at a distance of up to about two metres (compare Figs. 4–5). As far as can be judged from the present state of excavation and surveyings, the 'acropolis wall' is constructed of a single row of large, cut sandstone blocks which are sometimes built up against the rock and sometimes against an earth- or stonefill (Fig. 9). This is described in more detail in the section dealing with the excavation–units O26, O27 and T6NA.

Trial trenches

In order to gain an overview of the stratigraphy of the hill, long trial trenches were laid out at five different locations (Fig. 3).

Trench 1 (Tx30-35, Tx4-7)

One 1 m wide trial trench was opened out over a distance of 100 m in a N-S direction, 80 m of which was excavated. The southern part of the trench cut across an upper plateau of the hill running

northwards towards the Byzantine wall. The northern part of this trench, to the north of the Byzantine wall, started at the edge of the middle terrace and ran from here down the lowermost slope of the hill across a series of parallel walls which had appeared at different levels during the clearing in 1995-96 (Figs. 3-4).

In the southern part of the trench, bedrock was in most places reached very soon, and finds were of mixed date. The main exception was a pit (ADL in Tx33) which contained solely Early Helladic pottery (Figs. 3 and 10). The foundation trench for the Byzantine wall was excavat-

Fig. 7. Fragment of a Late Classical terracotta gable-sima (F97-7) decorated with a band of 'running palmette' and 'bead-and-reel' found during clearing near tower AQR (Photo: Henrik Frost).

Fig. 8. Archaic or Early Classical bronze handle (F97-24) from a cauldron or basin found during clearing near tower ACR (Photo: Henrik Frost).

Fig. 9. A view of excavation-unit T6NA in 1998 from the East showing the Byzantine wall in the background with the 'acropolis-wall' in front. In the foreground, room I and II (Photo: Henrik Frost).

ed to a depth of about 2 m. It contained mainly stones and enormous masses of tiles but few sherds: all were of mixed date (Archaic, Classical, Hellenistic, Byzantine). Excavation reached what seemed to be ancient deposits below the stonefill.

In the southern sections of the northern part of the trench (in Tx7 and Tx4), bedrock was reached at a depth varying from about 0,75 m to 1, 25 m below the surface. In the following sections towards the north (Tx5-6), bedrock was reached at a depth of about 0, 50 m below surface level. A couple of floating-layers covered the aforementioned series of parallel dry-stone walls and also some secondary deposited stonepackings which mainly contained prehistoric pottery (in Tx7 and 4). The Late Classical female head of a terracotta figurine, the neck of a Hellenistic unguentarium and the Late Classical loom weight with gem impression and stamped decoration[5] shown in Figs. 11-13 may serve as examples of the mixed finds and the remarkably large number of different types of loom weights from these layers.

No floors were connected with the parallel-running walls which crossed the

Fig. 10. Fragments of a rim and base (bag 555) from Early Helladic coarse ware bowls found in a pit (ADL) in the southern part of trench 1 (Photo: Henrik Frost).

Fig. 11. Late Classical female head of a terracotta figurine (F97-1019) found in floating layer in the northern part of trial trench 1. (Photo: Henrik Frost).

Fig. 12. Neck of a Hellenistic unguentarium (bag 47:1; T x4/2 N) found in floating-layer in the northern part of trial trench 1 (Photo: Henrik Frost).

trench at different levels and in some cases were supported by a stonefill. Initially the suggestion was made that the walls were those of terraces and not part of a fortification system. Ancient mixed deposits had accumulated in between the walls, the finds of which generally ranged from the Geometric/Archaic to the Hellenistic periods (Fig. 14). However, at the northernmost end of the trench where the slope terminates on the plain, part of a floor, consisting of small, irregular stones packed with mortar was found just below the surface and immediately above bedrock.

Fig. 14. Rim sherd with part of handle (bag 268) from archaic louterion found in a mixed deposit (ADA) in between walls in the northern part of trial trench 1 (Photo: Henrik Frost).

Fig. 13. Late Classical pyramidal loom weight (F97-1031) with two holes, gem impression and stamped decoration from floating-layer in the northern part of trial trench 1 (Photo: Henrik Frost).

Fig. 15. General view of trial trench 2 from NE towards SW showing the long wall ACP in the foreground, the Byzantine wall in the background and in between these a series of housewalls.

Trench 2 (Tx20-22 and Tx41-43)

A second trial trench, 1 x 20 m, was laid out at right angles to the Byzantine wall on the Northern side of the hill extending down the slope and terminating in the natural terrace on this side of the hill. In

Fig. 16. Classical-Hellenistic pyramidal loom weight (F98-2002) carrying the same stamped decoration on all four sides, from the huge stone-packing in trench 2 (Photo: Henrik Frost).

1998, the trench was widened with a parallel-running 2 m wide trench (Figs. 3, 15). The trench was in most of its parts excavated down to bedrock which was reached at a depth of about 2 m. below the surface level at the Byzantine wall and at a depth of less 0. 50 m in its north-easternmost part.

The upper – that is the southwestern – part of the trench was characterized by a huge stonepacking below the surface layer consisting of smaller and medium-sized rubble-stones, some tiles and sherds, and several loom weights one of which bore the same stamp on all four sides (Fig. 16). The stonepacking formed a characteristic slope being thickest at the Byzantine wall and thinning out towards the northeast. None of the finds from this stonepacking were later than the Classical-Hellenistic period, and not a single piece of mortar – characteristic of the stonefill stemming from the Byzantine wall – was in evidence. The stone packing therefore seems likely to have been part of a large stonefill originally from the upper part of the hill. Accordingly, the Byzantine wall appears to have been built from the SW up against the ancient stonefill in the area of this trench.

A series of ancient walls crossed the trench, the construction of which varied greatly. Starting from the SW, the first four of these walls appeared below the 'ancient' stonefill. The first among these, ACS – still counting from the SW – was built of large sandstone blocks which had partly slid due to the pressure of the stonefill (Fig. 3 and visible in Fig. 15 in front of the Byzantine wall). A wall built of much smaller stones, visible in the NE baulk line, ran up towards ACS at a right angle. The three following walls were drystone walls built of irregular rock-stones, one of which, however, was covered with plaster on the side facing the NE. The fifth and sixth walls appeared below the surface-layer and were built of large blocks of rock and sandstone, one of which (ACP) could be traced in the surface for at least 20 m (Fig. 3 and visible in Fig. 15). Finally, a drystone wall was visible in the baulk line in the most north-easterly section of the trench (in Tx22).

A few disturbed, thin layers were excavated in between the walls below the "ancient" stonepacking and surface-layer. The upper one of these thin layers contained sherds from the Bronze Age, Classical, Hellenistic as well as Byzantine periods indicating that the "ancient" stonefill above them in this area was redeposited in Byzantine times. Among the better preserved pieces is a stamped amphora handle saying ΝΙΚΟΣΤΡΑΤΟΣ ΕΝΛΥΜΑΙ, a Late Classical plate and a discoid, probably Late Classical loom weight[6] (Figs.17-19). Sherds from the lowermost layers were tiny and very worn, but seemed mainly to range in date from the Archaic to the Classical period. Excavation reached a floor of hardstamped earth, pebbles and small sherds NE of ACP (Fig. 15).

Below the "ancient" stonepacking in between the Byzantine wall and the sandstone wall (ACS), an extremely hard-packed layer characterized by pebbles, medium-sized stones and disintegrated bedrock was excavated just above the bedrock, and contained only Bronze Age pottery, most of which was Early Helladic

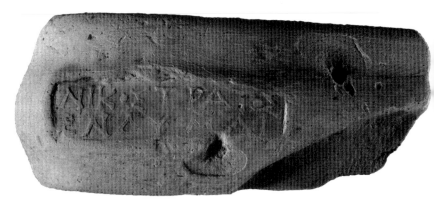

(Fig. 20). Underneath, red, porous sandstone intermixed with charcoal and a few pieces of Early Helladic pottery was excavated directly on the bedrock at the level of the lowermost course of the Byzantine wall (Fig. 21).

Thus, the general impression of the stratigraphy of the trench at the time of writing is that the ancient walls date from the Archaic-Classical Period and partly rest on material stemming from prehistoric clearings. The walls must already have been demolished when they were covered by the "Classical-Hellenistic" stone-fill stemming from the top of the hill. The masons who constructed the Byzantine

Fig. 17. Stamped amphora handle (bag 673; Tx21/3) from mixed deposits in between the house walls in trench 2 (Photo: Henrik Frost).

Fig. 18. Part of Late Classical plate with stamped decoration and rouletting (F97-4027) from mixed deposits in between house walls in trench 2 (Tx21) (Photo: Henrik Frost).

Fig. 19. Late Classical discoid
loom weight with two holes
(bag 648; Tx21/3 NW);
from mixed deposits in
between house walls in trench
2 (Photo: Henrik Frost).

Fig. 20. Fragment from large Early Helladic coarse ware
jar with band of impressed decoration (bag 1260:3;
Tx43/3a); from a bronze age deposit below the 'ancient'
stonefill in trench 2 (Photo: Henrik Frost).

Fig. 21. Bottom of Bronze
Age deposit (ADD) and
lowermost course of the
Byzantine wall situated on
the bedrock in trench 2.

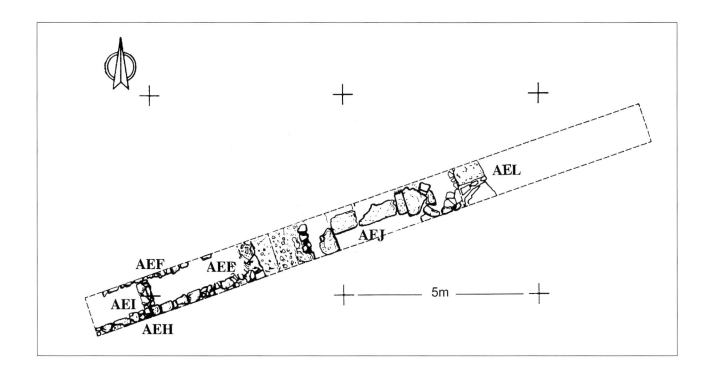

fortification wall utilized the 'ancient' stone-packing as support for the wall.

Trial trench 3 (Tx40)

This was a 1 x 3.50 m large trench which extended southwards from the Byzantine wall on the southern side of the hill. It was excavated to a depth of about 0.50 m. Below the mortar-mixed rubble layer stemming from the Byzantine wall, the familiar 'ancient' stone packing (see description of trench 2) was found. The bottom of the lowermost course of the Byzantine wall lay exactly at the dividing line between the surface layer and the stonepacking showing that in this area the wall had been built on top of the 'ancient' stone-packing.

Trench 4 (Tx70-74)

On the western side of the hill of Haghia Triadha, a 1 x 25 m trench was opened out, 20 m of which was excavated. It was oriented NE-SW starting on the lowermost part of the slope and terminating on the plain itself. The excavated depth down to bedrock ranged from about 0.50 m in the NE to about 3.75 m in the SW.

Below a couple of floating layers three structures came to light of varying dates (ancient-post antique) (Fig. 22). The first of these structures, starting from the highest point of the trench in the NE, was a compact mortar-floor constructed partly upon the rock, partly upon earlier clearings and stone-packings. Quite a number of Middle Helladic-Late Helladic I polychrome sherds (poorly preserved) come from these last-mentioned deposits. Among the later pottery, the base of a black-glazed Attic skyphos with a graffito inscription is worth mentioning (Fig. 23).

The second of these structures was found further down the hill and consisted

Fig. 22. Architectural structures in trial trench 4 (section Tx71-72) (measured by Charalambos Marinopoulos).

Fig. 23. Base of Attic black-glazed skyphos with a graffito inscription (F98-3009) from mixed deposit in the upper, north-eastern part of trench 4 (Photo: Henrik Frost).

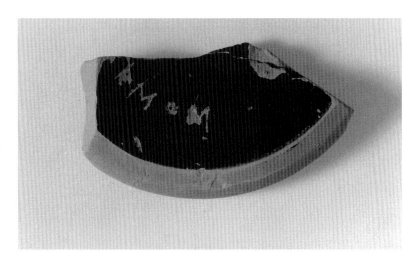

Fig. 24. Stonepacking underneath pebble floor in trench 4 seen from the North-East. Behind it, the belonging wall AEE. In the background, drystone wall AEF is visible in the trench-profile (Photo: Henrik Frost).

of a simple drystone wall (AEE) initially dated to the Classical-Hellenistic period (Fig. 22) which crossed the trench and appeared to be connected with a pebble floor resting on a packing of medium-sized stones (Fig. 24). The third structure was a drystone wall which crossed the trench below the aforementioned pebble floor and may have formed a corner with a long drystone wall (AEF) visible in the northern profile further towards the West (Figs. 22, 24).

Several other structures were found which are provisionally dated to the Archaic and Classical period. Starting again in the upper eastern end of the trench, the first of these structures consisted of two large, flattish and irregular rock stones (AEL) (Fig. 22). Somewhat further down the slope, excavation reached the surface of a structure built of finely cut ashlar blocks (AFJ) (Figs. 22, 25). West of this structure, that is on the plain itself, a succession of nine layers was excavated below wall AEF (in Tx72) before bedrock was reached 0. 25 m above sea level. Below AEF, another long drystone wall (AEH) came to light. It was visible in the Southern profile and lay on a lower level than the above-mentioned structure (AFJ). AEH was covered by a thick, clayish layer, characterized by only a few sherds, a loom weight, several large pieces of charcoal, several fragmentary iron objects (so far unidentified), and other small-finds among which a small spindle whorl, probably Iron Age, is shown (Fig. 26). The wall rested upon a dark, fattish layer the finds from which mainly appeared to be Archaic, among which was a tiny loom weight or spindle whorl, probably Protocorinthian[7] (Fig. 27). At a slightly lower level, a third drystone wall (AEI) crossed the trench and partly touched AEH. It rested upon a thin, hard-packed layer, possibly a floor, containing tiny pieces of pottery, many sherds and smaller stones. The datable sherds from this stratum have so far been seen to

Fig. 25. Structure of finely cut ashlar blokcs (AFJ) found in the middle part of trench 4 (Photo: Henrik Frost).

Fig. 27. Terracotta spindle whorl, possibly Protocorinthian (F98-3505); found in culture layer below wall AEH in trench 4 (Photo: Henrik Frost).

Fig. 26. Terrocatta spindle whorl, possibly Iron Age, found in a thick culture layer below wall AEF and above wall AEH in trench 4 (Photo: Henrik Frost).

made prehistoric pottery. Among the wheel-made pottery, both burnished (yellow and red minyan) and matt-painted wares (black on white) were represented. At the very bottom, pottery reminiscent of the Final Neolithic site on Pangali was found.

range from the Early Bronze Age to the Protocorinthian period.

No more structures were found in the trench, but below the last-mentioned wall (AEI), a couple of thick layers were excavated characterized by the presence of charcoal, seashells, obsidian-, and flint tools and a mixture of hand-made and wheel-

Trial trench 5 (Tx60-61)

The 14 m long trial trench oriented NE-SW was opened on the western side of the hill on its lower slope. Bedrock was hit very soon throughout the trench below a couple of floating layers.

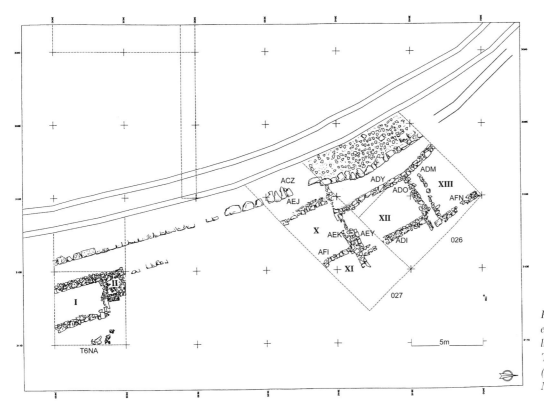

Fig. 28. Hellenistic rooms excavated outside the 'acropolis wall' in excavation units T6NA, O26 and 027 (measured by Charalambos Marinopoulos).

Fig. 29. General view from the NE of room X with tile-spill and room XI in unit O27. To the right wall AEK of room X is seen running parallel to wall AEY of room XII; in the foreground, wall AFI separating room X and XI; in the background wall AEJ of room X and the 'acropolis wall' (ACZ) is visible both resting on bedrock (Photo: Henrik Frost).

Excavation units: T6NA, O26, O27

Due to the finds made in 1996 of Archaic-Hellenistic architectural remains immediately outside the 'acropolis wall' in the northwest, it was decided in 1997 to open up two large excavation units located entirely outside this wall (T6NA and O26). The two units, measuring c. 5. 00 x 7.50 m and c. 7. 50 x 10. 00 m, were located at the Southern end of the middle terrace in order to gain an impression of the extension of the settlement (Fig. 3). Both units were largely excavated down to bedrock. A neighbouring unit of equal size (O27) was opened in 1998, the surface layer and stonefill of which were excavated.

In the three excavation units, part of six or possibly more rooms were excavated which lay along an 'alley' running parallel to and outside the 'acropolis wal' (Fig. 28).

Stratigraphy and Architecture

Common to all three excavation units was a huge stonefill rather similar to the one found in trenches 2 and 3. It consisted of medium-sized rubble-stones, often with one flattish side, ancient tiles, some pottery of mixed date (Prehistoric-Hellenistic), quite a number of poorly preserved fragments of terracotta roof-decoration (possible metopes and triglyphs), small fragments of plaster and pebble floors, some

Fig. 30. Tilespill between the 'acropolis wall' and wall ADY of room XII in unit 026 seen from the NW (Photo: Henrik Frost).

coins and an abundance of loom weights (compare Fig. 44). The stonefill was found below the rubble and mortar-mixed soil from the superstructure of the Byzantine wall. In the two northernmost units, O26 and O27, the stone-packing was enormous, hard-packed and extremely rich in tiles, while less so in unit T6NA. It covered both the 'acropolis wall' and the complex of rooms described below.

Fig. 31. Water canal (ADM) in room XIII in unit 026 seen from the NE (Photo: Henrik Frost).

Another remarkable feature in all three units was a layer of tiles in the Laconian system below the stonefill which in several places still formed a distinct tile-spill and accordingly belonged to the complex of house walls (Figs. 29-30). Below the tile-layer from a thick layer was excavated characterised by a very homogeneous, yellowish, and soft soil containing some sherds, and a few stones and tiles. This stratum covered pits and structures and continued down to bedrock. At its very bottom, often lying directly on bedrock, appeared a large number of well-preserved finds to which we will return below.

In unit 026, the 'acropolis wall' was still standing to a height of six courses (H: 1, 60 m). It was seen here to consist of a single wall built of large, fairly well-cut blocks of sandstone (maximum L c.1 m and maximum H c. 0. 50 m) which rested directly on the bedrock. Its lowest course was seen to protrude to form a base and the following five courses alternated between rectangular ashlar blocks and courses of large, more squarish boulders with smaller stones in between (Fig. 30). The wall leaned against a compact stone-fill mixed with tile which has not yet been excavated. In unit 027, the 'acropolis wall' ran on a much higher level than in 026 (Figs. F28, 29: ACZ). In this area, the 'acropolis wall' had collapsed so that only its lowermost course was preserved. Large boulders from its upper courses had tumbled down and destroyed part of wall AEJ of room X, and the stonefill behind the 'acropolis wall' had accordingly spilled out into the interior of this room as is visible to the left in Fig. 30.

Along the 'acropolis wall' on the outside, part of six rooms or possibly more was excavated to which reference has already been made several times above. Five of these rooms lie in a row (though separated by a strip of unexcavated land) parallel to the 'acropolis wall' at a distance of c. 1. 50 m creating a small 'alley' in between the 'acropolis wall' and the rooms (Fig. 28).

Fig. 32. Reversible lid of lekanis decorated in 'West Slope' technique found in room I in unit T6NA (Photo: Henrik Frost).

The small room II is likely to have been an annex to room I, since two doorsteps were found which gave access to the room either directly from room I or from the surroundings of rooms I. Room XII and XIII have a common 'end wall' (ADY) while wall AEJ, as already mentioned, of room X was situated on a much higher level and more towards the west. In room XI a water canal (ADM) had been cut into the bedrock, the walls of which were lined with flat stones. The canal ran under wall ADY channelling water from the 'alley', through the room in a north-easterly direction (Fig. 31). In room XII, a pit in the south-western corner went below wall ADY.

All the walls of the rooms were dry-stone walls built of medium-sized rock-stones, roughly cut and smoothed in places (maximum W: c. 0. 50 m).

The Finds

Below the tile-level in units T6NA and O26, a large number of objects appeared as already stated above. Noteworthy among these was a considerable number of coins (31), the majority of which were Aetolian League bronze coins. In addition, three silver coins were found originally from Mykalessus, Sikyon and Chalkis in Euboea (compare Figs. 46-47 and the contribution by G. Alexopoulou). Moreover, more or less whole pots had in several cases broken into many pieces, the scatter pattern of which suggested that they had fallen from an upper floor, shelf or similar. For instance, in Room I the

reversible lid of a lekanis decorated in the characteristic 'West Slope' technique (Fig. 32) was found broken into about twenty pieces which lay scattered over an area of approximately 4m². Fragments of an amphora with repairs in lead and fragments of a Hellenistic cooking-ware lid were found scattered over a similarly large area. During the excavation of a tilespill in the doorway between Room I and II, a large number of objects were found, such as a concentration of bronze coins, fragments of yet another Hellenistic cooking-ware lid (Fig. 33), terracotta fragments of drapery stemming from a large figurine (Fig. 34), the bottom of a Hellenistic

black-glazed plate with graffito inscription, part of a Hellenistic bowl with black slip on the inside (Fig. 35), shells, unidentifiable fragments of lead and bronze objects, iron nails, a bronze fishing hook, and a large number of potsherds from different types of vessels. Big pieces of charcoal were a common feature, especially in the soil among the tiles in Room II.

In Room XII, an unfinished marble lamp with three spouts was found so close to the northern wall of Room XII (ADO) that it may have been built into this wall (Fig. 36). On the whole, finds (registered as F98-1006-1037 and F98-1082-1091, F98-1093-1094, F98-1096-

Fig. 35. Hellenistic bowl, black slipped on the inside (F97-2014), found in tilespill between room I and II in unit T6NA (Photo: Henrik Frost).

1097) were especially concentrated in the north-western half of this room, either

Fig. 34. Terracotta fragment of drapery from a large figurine (F97-2055), found in tilespill between room I and II in unit T6NA (Photo: Henrik Frost).

lying at the same level as the tiles or below the tile-level, and often directly on the bedrock. Thus, from this area alone came a considerable number of fragments of fine table-ware, household ware, a simple handle of bronze sheet, several unidentifiable metal objects, large lead nails – often with traces of charcoal – bronze nails, loom weights, and the following items most of which are visible in Fig. 37: a characteristic Hellenistic lamp (F98-1010), the possible neck of a loutrophoros (F98-1009), two silver coins from Sikyon (F98-1018, F98-1020; Alexopoulou n.s 25-26), nine bronze coins (F98-1016-1017, F98-1024-25, F98-1080, F98-1087-88, F98-1094-1095) seven of which can be identified as Aetolian League coins (Alexopoulou n.s 5, 9, 13, 18-21) (Figs. 47a-b), while one had been minted in Oiniadai (Alexopoulou n. 2) (Fig. 47:2)

and a pedestal of a Hellenistic thymiaterion (Fig. 37).[8] In the north-eastern part of
the room, more loom weights, fragments
of bronze sheet, another bronze coin
issued by the Aetolian League (Fig.
47a:12) (F98-1110 and Alexopoulou n.
12) and a polished bone bead as well as
more pottery came to light. Along the
south-eastern profile of O26, a large, compact pile of clay mixed with tiny pieces of
crushed pottery and tile was found.

In Room XIII, many loom weights,
iron nails, poorly-preserved fragments of
terracottas, five much corroded bronze
coins (F98-1038, F98-1042-1043, F98-
1115-1116; Alexopoulou n.s 28-31), four
Aetolian League bronze coins (F98-1074,
F98-1107-08, F98-1130, Alexopoulou n.s
3-4, 17, 22), one silver coin from Chalkis
in Euboea (F98-1114, Alexopoulou n. 24)
(Figs. 47a-b) and fragments of tableware
and household ware were found. East of
wall ADI of Room XII, five Aetolian
League bronze coins lay scattered over an
area of approximately 2m[2] near large fragments of a pithos (F98-1133, F98-1135,

F98-1138-39; F98-1150 and Alexopoulos
n.s 8, 10, 11, 14, 16). East of Room XIII a
loomweight, a terracotta object and unidentifiable bronze objects came to light.

Excavation in O27 in 1998 revealed as
mentioned above a huge tile-level stemming from a collapsed roof which covered
most of Room X (Fig. 29) (see the report
by C. Grønne).

Re-excavation in unit F15

In connection with a re-excavation
beneath wall ACC in unit F15 (see FPR
fig. 15), part of an early 5th century black-
glazed Attic lamp came to light indicating
a terminus post quem for the wall (Fig.
38).[9]

Conclusion

Altogether the 1997-98 campaigns have
enabled us to further significantly our
understanding of the character and development of Aetolian Chalkis. It is now certain that a large-scale settlement began on

the hill of Haghia Triadha in the Late Neolithic/Early Helladic period. This settlement should probably be understood as a continuation of the Final Neolithic site on Pangali and is therefore likely to provide important new information on settlement patterns and movements in this period. Judging by the many finds from the Bronze Age, Geometric, Archaic and Classical-Hellenistic Periods in floating layers in most of the trenches, the upper plateau was inhabited throughout most of these periods. Probably, to judge from the fragments of fine terracotta roof decoration from the upper plateau, one or more temples once stood here, presumably on the site of the present basilica. No 'exotics' have so far been found. The imported pottery points to Corinth, Athens and not least the cities of Achaea and Elis as the main trading and contact partners while coin circulation points to contacts with

Central Greece, Acarnania and cities along the Corinthian Gulf. A basic idea was obtained of the architectural layout and cultural identity of Classical-Hellenistic Chalkis, and no less important, an undisturbed part of the Archaic city was located on the western side of the hill close to the harbour. These results constitute an important step towards the understanding of the significance and development of Chalkis not only in relation to the surrounding landscapes but also in relation to the many other small harbour towns which lie like a string of pearls on the northern coast of the Corinthian Gulf all the way up to the Ambrakian Gulf. Similarly, the construction of the Byzantine fortification and its relation to the large basilica and ancient remains became more fully understood and made it possible to link Chalkis to sites as far away as Duel and Teurnia in Austria.[10]

Fig. 37. Concentration of finds below the tile-level in the southwestern part of room XII in unit 026. From the East. Visible are first and foremost a Hellenistic lamp (F98-1010), a possible neck of a loutrophoros (F98-1009), a pedestal of a Hellenistic thymiaterion (F98-1013) and several Aetolian League coins (Photo: Henrik Frost).

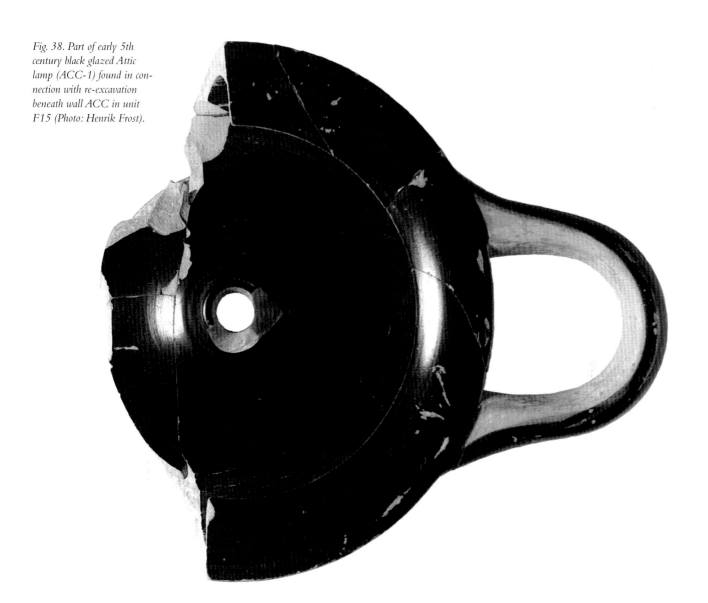

Fig. 38. Part of early 5th century black glazed Attic lamp (ACC-1) found in connection with re-excavation beneath wall ACC in unit F15 (Photo: Henrik Frost).

The Registration Process of Finds from Haghia Triadha

Jonas Eiring

In what follows, the working procedures in the pot-shed will be described in summary. The registration process during an ongoing campaign cannot be more than preliminary: the overriding aim is to register all the material so that, once it has gone through our hands, it will be possible to find it again during future study seasons. This sounds self-evident and simple, but is in reality a fairly complicated matter.

As the finds arrive at the end of the day's excavation, they have already been tagged with a unique number, here called bag number. A 'bag' can be a bag of pottery, tile or other material, but objects recovered as single finds also receive a tag with a pre-printed number. This procedure minimises the risk of misunderstandings due to unclear or wrong labelling, lost labels, and other possible mishaps. A concordance is drawn up day by day, so that the context can be established from the bag number. The objects are marked

with the specific number. To use a single, unique number in this way has the advantage of speed, a four digit number being easier to write on a sherd than a context denomination, which would have to include year, trench, level, and in many cases structure and find number.

When washed and marked, each bag of pottery is sorted by the students. The sherds are divided by ware. At Chalkis the terms used are 'fine ware' (few visible inclusions, generally table ware), 'medium ware' (main inclusions up to 1mm in diameter, typically household vessels and transport amphorae), 'cooking pot ware' (hard-fired fabric, appropriate for use over fire, with abundant, often large, inclusions and much sand), and 'coarse ware' (inclusions larger than 1mm, often storage pithoi). Tiles are generally bagged separately on site. Sherds are counted and weighed; rims, handles, bases and decorated sherds are counted in each category. The information is entered on a report

Fig. 41. The frequency of dated material from the Northern part of Trench 1 (Tx4-7).

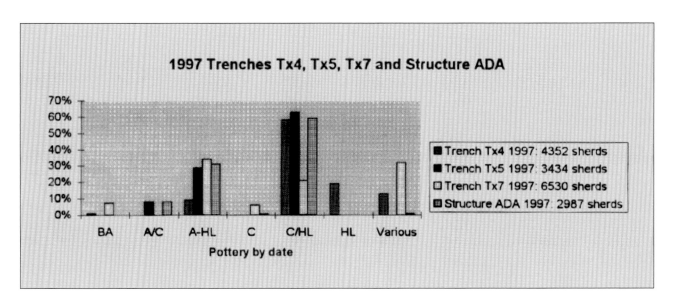

1997 Trenches Tx4, Tx5, Tx7 and Structure ADA

Pottery by date

- ■ Trench Tx4 1997: 4352 sherds
- ■ Trench Tx5 1997: 3434 sherds
- □ Trench Tx7 1997: 6530 sherds
- ▨ Structure ADA 1997: 2987 sherds

form, with any additional comments which can help to form a general impression of the contents. Pieces are selected for drawing and photography, and detailed descriptions of these are entered on a separate form.

It is always desirable to be able to provide a date for each find as early as possible in the registration process. This task is difficult on many counts. First of all little is known about the pottery of Aetolia and the local pottery sequence has yet to be established. Secondly, the site of Haghia Triadha has been exposed to heavy erosion, which means that many contexts are of mixed date, and, finally, the soil conditions are such that in many trenches the sherds are poorly preserved. The character of local Early Iron Age, Geometric and Archaic pottery is particularly ill-defined at the site. This, and the relative scarcity of imports during these periods make the dating difficult. There is, however, no doubt that the periods are well represented at the site, especially Late Geometric and Archaic. Classical pottery is present in all trenches, and there is conspicious abundance of material datable to the late

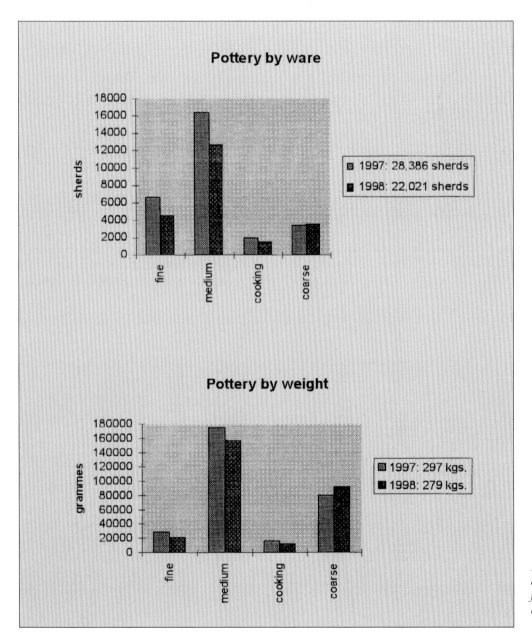

Figs. 39-40. The total amount of registered pottery from Haghia Triadha by ware and by weight in 1997 and 1998.

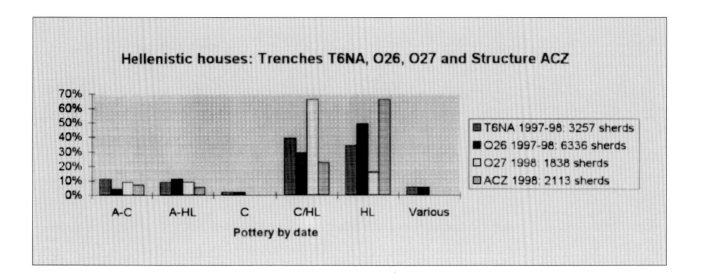

Fig. 42. The frequency of
dated material from the
excavation units T6NA, 026,
and 027 including the
structure ACZ.

fourth or early third century B.C., here
labelled Classical/Hellenistic.

In spite of the difficulties of dating the
excavated pottery, we try to give an indication of the date of each bag. This is giv-
en in broad terms by period. 'C/HL' on a
report may either reveal a presence of
badly-preserved body sherds with black
gloss, impossible to date more closely, or
fragments close in date to the watershed
of 323 B.C. This happens frequently, since
fourth to third century pottery is abundant on the site. 'EH + C + HL' would
mean that the context is mixed with
sherds which can be confidently dated to
each of three periods. It should be stressed
that the trench charts in this preliminary
report do not attempt to give a date for
each sherd, but the aggregate by date

group: undiagnostic sherds are assumed to
follow the date of diagnostic sherds. Once
a local pottery sequence has been established, revisions in the dating will have to
be done and, hopefully, much of hitherto
undatable material will be identified.

Objects other than pottery are described separately. Bone, shell and stone
material are set aside for specialist study.
Coins and other metal finds are sent to
Patras for conservation, whereas a good
deal of cleaning and mending of the pottery is done by the conservator at the
ephoria on location.

The information is filed by excavated
context, i.e. by trench or structure, unless
the object is classified as a 'find', in which
case it is sorted by find number. A 'find' is
defined as any object whose exact find

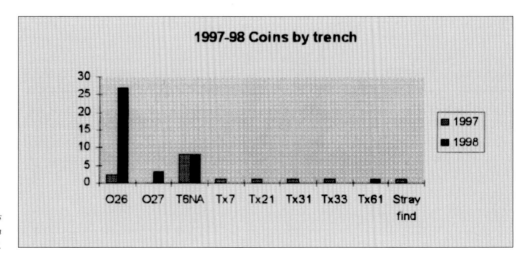

Fig. 43. The frequency of coins
in relation to trenches in
respectively 1997 and 1998.

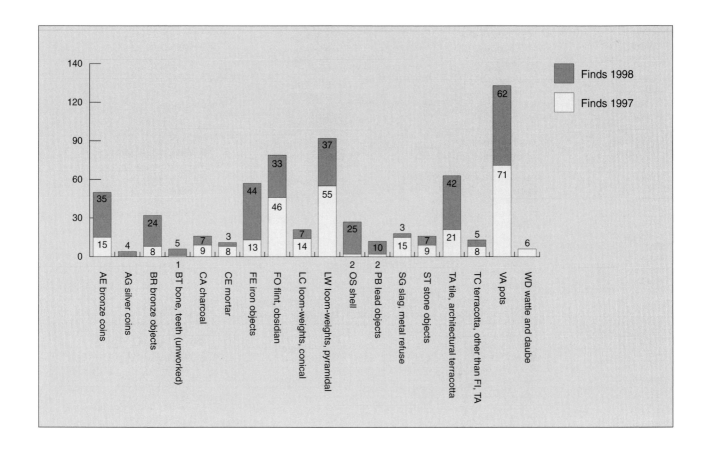

Fig. 44. The frequency of 'finds' by object type in respectively 1997 and 1998.

spot has been measured: it often has intrinsic interest, such as a coin or a complete pot, but it can also be a collection of tiles or sherds, whose location is stratigraphically significant.

With the help of a database, an overview over the excavated material can easily be obtained. At the time of writing, data from the two last years have been entered: the information concerning the year 1997 is complete, whereas the material excavated during the last few days in 1998 has yet to be registered.

Thus, in 1997 a total of 31,842 sherds were registered, their total weight being nearly 300 kgs. If the weight of registered tile fragments is included, the sum increases nearly ten-fold to 2,679 kgs. For the 1998 season, 22,201 sherds have so far been registered, representing 280 kgs (Figs.39-40). The figures for the two years correspond remarkably well, both numerically and by weight. The fine ware accounts for nearly a quarter of the sherds, representing less than a tenth of the total weight; medium ware accounts for nearly 60 per cent of the pottery, both numerically and by weight; cooking pot ware, at seven per cent of total sherds for both years, has a four to five per cent share of the total weight, whereas coarse ware, at 12 and 16 percent of sherds for 1997 and 1998 respectively, has twice as large a share of the total weight.

Below, charts describing the distribution by date group for selected trenches and structures are presented. As mentioned, the statistics are to be taken as an indication only. Revisions in the dating are inevitable, but such as they are, the figures give an idea of the quantities involved. Fig. 41 gives an impression of the mixed character of the strata of the northern part of Trench 1 (Tx4-7) containing a few large, secondary deposits of Bronze Age material. The abundance of material from the Classical-Hellenistic destruction layers of the houses in the excavation units T6NA, O26 and O27 is well reflected in Fig. 42, as is the way these destruction layers were covered by mixed layers containing earlier pottery.

Code	Type of object	1997	1998
AE	bronze coins	15	35
AG	silver coins	-	4
AS	stamped amphorae	1	-
BO	bone objects, worked	3	1
BR	bronze objects	8	24
BT	bone, teeth (unworked)	1	5
CA	charcoal	9	7
CE	mortar	8	3
FE	iron objects	13	44
FI	terracotta figurines	2	-
FO	flint, obsidian	46	33
IN	inscriptions (stone, sherds)	-	1
LA	lamps	-	1
LC	loom weights, conical	14	7
LW	loom weights, pyramidal	55	37
MB	mud brick	1	2
OS	shell	2	25
PB	lead	2	10
SG	slag, metal refuse	15	3
SP	stucco, plaster	1	3
ST	stone	9	7
TA	tile, architectural	21	42
TC	terracotta objects other	8	5
VA	pots	71	62
VE	glass	-	1
WD	wattle and daube	6	-
WE	weights other than LC,	1	-

A chart showing the distribution of coins by context is shown in Fig. 43. As appears from this, the majority of the coins have been found in the Hellenistic houses in units O26, O27, and T6NA.

Finally, charts showing the types of objects, registered as 'finds' are included (Figs. 44-45). It would require too much space to show the distribution of all kinds of objects by context, so the charts given here only give a rough idea of what kind of objects are found on the site. Further, the charts include only such objects as are registered as 'finds' with a known exact find spot. The greater part of stone, bone and shell material is registered as part of the context only. Each object category will be the subject of specialist study.

The Roof Tiles from Haghia Triadha

Claus Grønne

During the excavations in 1997-98 on the hill of Haghia Triadha, an abundance of roof tiles was excavated. Apart from a few fragments of Corinthian type, the majority of the tiles so far studied are of Laconian type. Below follows a short description of the types.

The Laconian tiles

No complete Laconian tile has hitherto been found. However, since the studied examples stem from collapsed roofs excavated *in situ* in T6NA, 026 and 027, many fragments can be reassembled and the original shape and dimensions be established (compare Figs. 29-30).

There are two types of Laconian tiles (type I and II), similar in shape and size but differing in firing and clay composition. Since both types have been found side by side where the roofs have collapsed it would be reasonable to suggest that one type was used as pan-tile (στρωτηρ) and the other as cover-tile (καλυπτηρ). The find context, as well as the resemblance in shape and size of the two types, indicates that each type served both purposes.

The pan-tiles were placed with their *wide* end pointing upwards towards the ridge, while the cover tiles have their *narrow* end pointing upwards in order to achieve the right overlap. Many fragments of both types have a flange along the upper edge, on the concave side, to support the lower edge of the tile above, which indicates that they were used both as pan- and as cover-tiles. On some tiles the flange is reduced to a groove which cannot have given much support. This suggests that the inclination of the roof was rather low, and since no ridge tiles have been found so far we may assume that the buildings on the slopes of the hill had only slanting roofs and not hipped roofs.

Both Laconian types have a red/brown slip only on the concave side.

Laconian I.

Form: trapezoidal, curved with an upturned rim on the long sides with a very sharp and well defined edge.

Dimensions: Lower width c. 37- 40 cm; upper width c. 49 cm; th. min.1. 5; th. max. 2. 5 cm; estimated length c. 100 cm.

Clay: very fine to medium coarse with some inclusions.

Estimated weight 12-14 kg.

Firing: homogeneous and rather hard (clings when struck).

Slipped only on the concave side.

Colour: core 10R 6/8 – 10R 7/8. Surface on convex side and under slip 7.5 Y/R 7/6 – 10 R 7/8. Slip 10R 4/6 – 2.5 YR 5/8

Laconian II.

Form: curved, trapezoidal, with rounded edges on the long sides.

Dimensions: Lower width c. 40 cm; upper width. c. 49 cm; th. min. 2,2; th. max. 2.8 cm; estimated length c. 100 cm.

Clay: medium coarse to coarse with many black and red particles. Not as compact as tp I.

Estimated weight 12-14 kg

Firing: homogeneous, but not as hard as tp. I

Slipped only on the concave side.

Colour: core 10R 6/8 – 2.5 YR 6/8;

surface under slip and on convex side 2.5 Y/R 7/8 – 5YR 6/8. Slip 10R 4/6 – 10R 5/6.

Judging by the closest parallels for the tiles so far discussed, the roof system of the houses outside the Acropolis wall points to a date in the Classical /Hellenistic period.

The Corinthian tiles

Two different types of Corinthian combination tiles were recognised among the tiles studied so far. These appear to be represented in far smaller quantities than the Laconian type. The older of these two Corinthian systems comes from the stone-fill in trench 2 described above and is made of a rather coarse, buff clay with many inclusions (Munsell 7.5YR 8/4) and is covered by a cream-coloured slip (Munsell 10YR 8/4). Both clay and slip are very similar to those of the sima-fragment with painted palmette decoration in Fig. 7. It is difficult to establish the precise dimensions of the Corinthian combination tiles, but to judge from the preserved fragments they were of a rather large and heavy type. The date of this system probably falls within the second half of the 6th. cent. BC.

The second and younger type of Corinthian combination tile appears in a yellow and a red variety of more or less the same fabric.

Form: combination tile.

Dimensions: th. 5. 5 cm on edge, 3. 2 cm in centre. Original length and width cannot be established.

Clay: coarse with many large particles Firing: homogenous

Colour in core red type: 5YR 6/6 (reddish yellow); yellow type: 2.5 YR 8/4 (pale yellow) to 10YR 7/3 (very pale brown).

The Coins from Haghia Triadha[11]

Georgia Z. Alexopoulou

The coins from the hill of Haghia Triadha discussed in this presentation come from various regions of Greece (Fig. 46). As can be seen in Table I relatively few coins originate from Greek cities outside Aetolia compared to the large number from the Aetolian League (BMC: Thessaly to Aetolia, 194-200; Scheu 1960; Λιάμπη 1996; Arnold-Biucchi 1981 a-b). The coinage of the Aetolian League is in bronze as well as there being a bronze coin from Eccara (Phthiotis?) and another from Oiniadai of Acarnania. Three cities, Mykalessus, Chalkis (Euboea) and Sikyon are represented in the excavations of Aetolian Chalkis by silver coinage. Even generally speaking, the majority of the coins issued by the Aetolian League are of bronze. This fact suggests that the transactions within the limits of the 'koinon'[12] covering local financial needs must have been conducted with coins of this material. The fourth century is represented in the excavations on the Haghia Triadha hill by silver and bronze coinage from mints situated in the east and south-east of the Aetolian territory and by one specimen from a western mint (Oiniadai).

As far as the coins of the Aetolian League are concerned, it is possible to identify the following five numismatic types:

1) Head of Aetolia or Atalante with causia r. / Calydonian Boar at bay (two pattern)
2) Young male head, laureate, r. / trophy (one pattern)
3) Young male head, laureate, r. / spearhead and jaw-bone and the legend ΑΙΤΩLΩN (seven patterns)
4) Young male head, laureate, r. / spearhead, ΑΙΤΩ and monogram (one pattern)
5) Head of Athena in Corinthian helmet, r. / Heracles standing and the legend ΑΙΤΩLΩN (nine patterns)

Type 1) presents similarities with the silver issues. Therefore, despite their poor condition, these coins, if carefully examined, prompt us to conclude that whoever was responsible for the matrix must have had the archetypes of the silver ones in mind (Κραβαρτόγιαννος 1993, 77). There appears also to have existed another type which represents Atalante or Aetolia with *causia* on the obverse and a spearhead with the legend ΑΙΤΩLΩN on the reverse (SNG.: Copenhagen nos. 22-25; BMC: Thessaly to Aetolia, 197 nos. 34-37). This type has however not yet appeared in our excavations (Κραβαρτόγιαννος 1993, 78).

Types 3) and 4) can be considered as two variants of the same type (Κραβαρτόγιαννος 1993, 78). According to F. Scheu, type 5) does not show the national symbols of the Aetolians, such as the *causia*, the boar, the spearhead, and the jaw-bone. It may therefore have been the issue of a regime favourable to Rome (Scheu 1960, 50-51). Type 3) and 5) are the most frequently represented, by respectively seven and nine specimens. The weight of the lighter one varies by 2.1 to 2.5 g. And the weight of the heavier one is around 6.8 g. This weight variation suggests that we maybe are dealing with *chalkoi* and double *chalkoi* (Picard 1984, 285).

The rarity of the silver coins can be explained by the high inflation of the Aetolian economy or by the scarcity of suitable metals (Scheu 1960, 50).

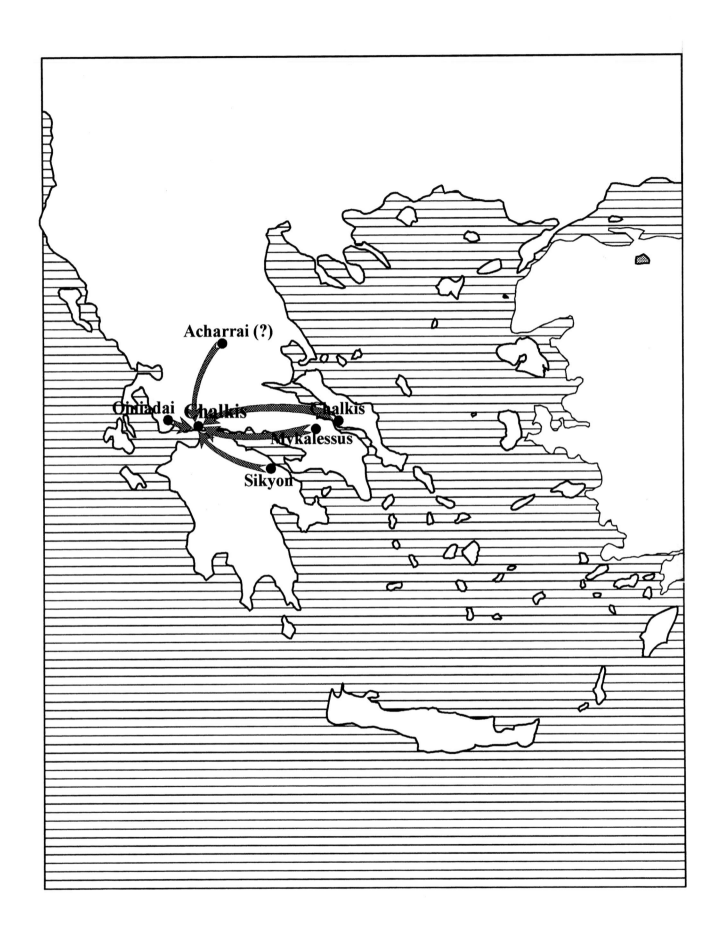

Fig. 46. Map showing the
origin of coins found in
Rooms XII-XIII below the
tile-level.

The coins of the 'koinon' have the legend
ΑΙΤΩΛΩΝ and exhibit a general federal
character, while the issuing city is not
known (Gardner in BMC: Thessaly to
Aetolia, lviii).[13] The issue of the bronze
coins is likely to have begun immediately
after the invasion of the Gauls in 279 B.C.
when the Aetolians took control of Delphi, and it continued throughout the
whole third century until the Battle of
Pydna in 168 B.C. (Gardner in BMC:
Thessaly to Aetolia, lvii; HN, 334-355;
Scheu 1960, 49). On the whole, the
majority of these bronze coins seem to be
the product of a prospering society
(Λιάμπη 1996, 163), which continued to
flourish during the second and first century B.C., according to archaeological finds
(Πετρόπουλος 1991, 122). We can deduce
that the transactions between the cities
were based on the silver issues, while the
bronze coinage was used on a local level.
During the third century the Aetolians,
apart from the silver issues, present a noteworthy bronze coinage which merits a
thorough study. We therefore hope that
future excavations in Aetolian Chalkis will
bring to light examples of this coinage.

The coins included in the catalogue
below and depicted in Figs. 47a-b have
been classified according to issuing cities
and, as far as the coins of the Aetolian
League are concerned, according to their
iconography as described in the SNG:
Copehagen and the BMC: Thessaly to
Aetolia. For every specimen we have indicated the denomination, the diameter, the
weight and the inventory number. After
the catalogue there follows additional
information on the excavation data and
further observations on the coins.

Catalogue

Eccara (Phthiotis?), c. 350-300 B.C.

1. Head of Zeus laureate, l.
   Artemis is shown standing frontally looking l. and resting on a spear; on the l. of the camp the legend EKKAP and on the r. PEΩN.
   AE; h 2; 13 mm; 1.3 g.; N.I.1
   SNG: Copenhagen n. 47.

Oiniadae, c. 219-211 B.C.

2. Head of Zeus laureate, r.
   Head of man-headed bull, r. (probably Achelous); above trident; on the l. of the camp the legend OINIAΛAN.
   AE; h c. 12; 23 mm; 5.3 g.; N.I.14
   SNG: Copenhagen n. 403.

Aetolia: Aetolian League, c. 279-168 B.C.

3. Head of Aetolia wearing *causia*, r.
   Calydonian Boar at bay (?). l.
   AE; h 12; 18 mm (obverse); 1.2 g.; N.I.24
   SNG: Copenhagen n. 21

4. As n.3.
   AE; h 9; 15 mm; 2.5 g.; N.I.28
   SNG: Copenhagen n. 21.

5. Young male head laureate, r.
   trophy consisting of helmet, cuirass, spear and shield; on the r. of the camp AITΩ and on the l. LΩN.
   AE; h 11; 15 mm; 3.1g.; N.I.9.
   SNG: Copenhagen n. 26; BMC: Thessaly to Aetolia, 197, n. 38.

6. Young male head laureate, r.
   Spear head and jaw-bone of Calydonian Boar; the legend AI[TΩ]ΛΩN
   AE; h 9; 16 mm; 2.5 g.; N.I.3
   SNG: Copenhagen n.31.

7. As n.6.
   AE; h 12; 14 mm (obverse); 2.4 g.; N.I.5
   SNG: Copenhagen n. 32.

8. As n.6.
   Obliterated
   AE; h 12; 16 mm (obverse); 3.3 g.; N.I.22
   SNG: Copenhagen n.32.

9. As n.6.
   AE; h 8; 17 mm; 4.2 g.; N.I.13
   SNG: Copenhagen n. 28.

10. As n.6.
    AE; h 12; 20 mm; 4.5 g.; N.I.2
    SNG: Copenhagen n. 28; BMC: Thessaly to Aetolia, 198, n. 43.

11. As n.6.
    AE; h: 6; 18 mm, 4.5 g.; N.I.26
    SNG: Copenhagen n. 28.

12. Young male head laureate, r.
    Spearhead and jaw-bone of a boar; traces of monogram.
    AE; h 9; 17 mm; 5.0 g.; N.I.19
    SNG: Copenhagen n. 29.

13. Similar to n.12 (obverse).
    Spearhead r.; above the legend [AI]TΩ; in the middle the monogram ⚡; on the r. of the camp, below, traces of symbol.
    AE; h 10; 17 mm; 4.0 g.; N.I.10
    BMC: Thessaly to Aetolia, 197, n. 41.

14. Head of Athena in Corinthian helmet r.
    Heracles standing with club and lion´s skin.
    AE; h 3; 16 mm; 2.1 g.; N.I.7
    SNG: Copenhagen n. 39.

15. Similar to n.14.
    AE; h 3; 18 mm; 2.9 g.; N.I.21
    SNG: Copenhagen n. 37 and ff.

16. Similar to n.14.
    AE; h 6; 16 mm; 4.3 g; N.I.6
    SNG: Copenhagen n. 37; BMC: Thessaly to Aetolia, 199, n. 64.

17. Similar to n.14, but on the reverse the legend AITΩΛΩN is visible.

AE; h 10; 17 mm; 4.3 g.; N.I.18
SNG: Copenhagen n. 37.
18. Similar to n.17.
AE; h 9; 18 mm; 4.6 g.; N.I.17
SNG: Copenhagen n. 35 and ff.
19. Similar to n.17.
AE; h 9; 17 mm; 4.9 g.; N.I.8
SNG: Copenhagen n.35 and n. 37;
BMC: Thessaly to Aetolia, 199, n. 64.
20. Similar to n.14.
AE; h 9; 18 mm; 5.0 g.; N.I.23
SNG: Copenhagen n. 35 and ff.
21. Similar to n.14.
AE; h 10; 16 mm; 5.6 g; N.I.27
SNG: Copenhagen n. 35 and ff.
22. Similar to n.14.
AE; h 5; 18 mm; 6.8 g.; N.I.16
SNG: Copenhagen n. 35.

Mykalessus, c. 387-374 B.C.
23. Boeotian shield.
Thunderbolt; MY
AR; h 3; 10 mm; 0.5 g.; N.I.4
SNG: Copenhagen n. 190; HN, 346.

Chalkis, c. 369-313 B.C. and later.
24. Female head r.
Flying eagle holding serpent.
AR; h 12; 16 mm; 2.3 g.; N.I.31

SNG: Copenhagen n. 432 and ff.
Picard 1979, pl. IV, n° 8F.

Sikyon, 4th cent. B.C.
25. Chimaera l.
Flying dove l.
AR; h 9; 15 mm; 2.0 g.; N.I.11
SNG: Copenhagen 57 and *ff.*; BMC:
Peloponnese 42, n. 69.
26. Head of Apollo laureate, r.
Flying dove r.
AR; h 3; 10 mm; 0.3 g.; N.I.12
SNG: Copenhagen n.s 67 and 68.

The following coins are so disintegrated
and oxidated as to be illegible for which
reason we will cite only their inventory
number, diameter and weight. Also due to
the oxidated state of the coins and to their
normal wear and tear through handling,
the weight cited cannot be taken to represent their original one.

27. AE, h; 18 mm; 1.3 g; N.I.15
28. AE, h; 15 mm; 1.5 g; N.I.20
29. AE, h; 13 mm;1.6 g; N.I.29
30. AE, h; 18 mm; 1.6 g; N.I.25
31. AE, h; 18 mm; 3.4 g; N.I.30.

	Mint	Number of specimens	Date
		TABLE I	
1.	Eccara (Phthiotis?)	1 (AE)	c.350-300 B.C.
2.	Oeniadai	1 (AE)	c.219-211 B.C.
3.	Aetolia: Aetolian League	20 (AE)	c.279-168 B.C.
4.	Mykalessus	1 (AR)	c.387-374 B.C.
5.	Chalkis (Euboea)	1 (AR)	c.369-313 B.C. and later
6.	Sikyon	2 (AR)	4th cent. B.C.

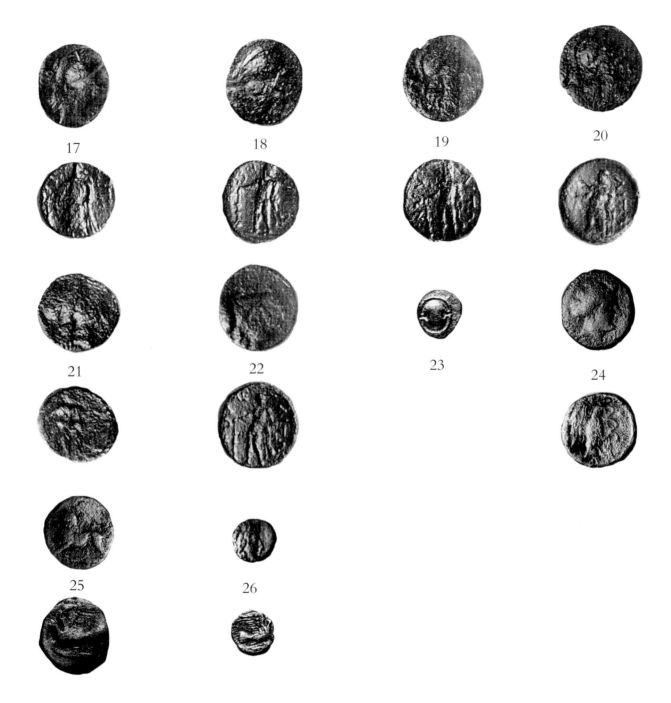

17   18   19   20

21   22   23   24

25   26

Figs. 47 a-b Coins from room
XII-XIII.

Additional Information on the Coins in the Catalogue

1. Found 21-1-1997 in trench O26 S.E, stratum 5b, F97-2044. The attribution of the coin, which is very well preserved, to Eccara according to the SNG: Copenhagen remains uncertain. The name of the city in the 'Ethnika' by Stephanus Byzantius is Akarra. Compared to an example from the SNG: Copenhagen dated to c. 350-300 B.C. its weight is approximately the same (1. 44 g.) B.V. Head dates a similar specimen to the later half of the 4th century B.C. (HN, 294).

2. Found 13-7-1998 in trench 026, stratum 3, F98-1017. Related to a specimen from the SNG, Cop., weighs less (7.55 g.), while a similar coin from the BMC is dated to c. 230-168 B.C and has a symbol on the obverse. Good state of preservation.

3-4. Coin n. 3 was found 16-7-1998 in trench 026, stratum 3, registrered as F98-1074, n. 4 on the 21-7-1998 in the same trench and stratum, registered as F98-1130. Both of them are in poor condition. Numismatists have identified the head on the obverse of both coins as either Aetolia or Atalante. N.3 is lighter than an example from the SNG: Copenhagen (2.85 g.) while n. 4 weighs approximately the same.

5. Found 17-7-1998 in trench 026, registered as F98-1087: The coin is in good condition and is similar to one from the SNG: Copenhagen which weighs 3.61 g.

6. Found 25-7-1997 in trench O26 SE. The coin, a small part of which is missing, is related to a specimen from the SNG: Copenhagen (4.59 g.). According to P.A. Pantos, the national symbol of the Aetolians was the spearhead, alone or accompanied by a boar or a jaw-bone of a boar (Παντός 1985, 147).

7. Found 25-7-1997 in trench O26 SE. The reverse has greatly deteriorated and it is only with great difficulty that it is possible to make out a spearhead and on the r. of the camp. only the letter W of the legend is visible.

8. Found 22-7-1998 in trench 026, stratum 3, registrered as F98-1133. Also the reverse of the coin is thoroughly damaged; weighs the same as the one from the SNG: Copenhagen.

9. Found 13-7-1998, in trench O26, stratum 3, registered as F98-1024. Due to its poor condition, only a part of the legend is visible (ΛΩN). It weighs approximately the same as the one from the SNG: Copenhagen (4.85 g.)

10. Found 22-7-1998 in trench 026, stratum 3, registered as F98-1135. Weighs approximately the same as the one of the SNG: Copenhagen (4.85 g.).

11. Found 23-7-1998 in trench 026, stratum 3, registered as F98-1150. It is badly preserved and weighs approximately the same as the one from the SNG: Copenhagen (4.85 g.)

12. Found 20-7-1998 at the trench 026, stratum 3, registered as F98-1110. The second part of the legend ΛΩN is not visible, while there are traces of a monogram between the spearhead and the jaw-bone of the boar. Related to a specimen from the SNG: Copenhagen (5.62 g.), though it is slightly lighter.

13. Found 17-7-1998 in trench 026, registered as F98-1088. A similar coin from Thessaly has the same monogram on the reverse as well as the spearhead and the jaw-bone of a boar (BMC: Thessaly

to Aetolia, 198, n. 51). Another specimen from the SNG: Copenhagen (n. 23) has the whole legend (–ΑΙΤΩΛΩΝ) on the reverse, but on the obverse Aetolia or Atalante with causia is represented, as well as bounch of grapes.

14. Found 22-7-1998 in trench 026, registered as F98-1138. On the reverse the legend ΑΙΤΩΛΩΝ is not visible and the coin, which is in very poor state of preservation but with only a small part missing, is lighter than a similar specimen from the SNG: Copenhagen (4.07 g.)

15. Found 23-7-1998 in trench 026, stratum 3, registered as F98-1149. On the reverse the legend is not visible due to the poor condition of the coin.

16. Found 22-7-1998 in trench 026, registered as F98-1139. Weighs the same as the one from the SNG: Copenhagen (4.26 g.) and this type of coin is also related to the BMC: Thessaly to Aetolia and HN. On the reverse the legend is illegible due to the poor condition of the coin.

17. Found 20-7-1998 in trench 026, stratum 3, registered as F98-1108. Relatively good state of preservation.

18. Found 13-7-1998 in trench 026, stratum 3, F98-1025. It is lighter than a similar specimen from the SNG: Copenhagen (5.9 g.) and is well preserved.

19. Found 17-7-1998 in trench 026, registered as F98-1094. It has been related to two similar specimens from the SNG: Copenhagen which weigh 5.9 g. and 4.39 g. respectively. The coin is in very good condition.

20. Found 17-7-1998 in trench 026, stratum 3, registered as F98-1080. Because of its poor condition the part LWN of the legend is not visible. It is lighter than a similar coin from the SNG: Copenhagen (5.90 g.)

21. Found 17-7-1998 in trench 026, stratum 3, registered as F98-1095. Weighs slightly less than a similar coin from the SNG: Copenhagen (5.90 g.) Due to the poor condition of the coin, the legend is not visible on the reverse.

22. Found 20-7-1998 in trench 026, stratum 3, F98-1107. Weighs more than a similar coin from the SNG: Copenhagen (5.90 g.) and on the l. of the camp appears ΛΕ, which also appears on silver issues (Scheu 1960,46).

23. Found 26-7-1997 in trench 026. Slightly lighter than the one from the SNG: Copenhagen (0.82 g.) and is in excellent condition. Also B.V. Head gives the same date (HN, 346).

24. Found 21-7-1998 in trench 026 NW, stratum 3, F98-1114. Related to a specimen from the SNG, Cop. (3.18 g) which, however, is lighter. B.V. Head says that "The Eagle devouring a Serpent seems to be an emblem of the Olympian Zeus, as on the coins of Elis, for at Chalcis one of the chief shrines was that of Zeus Olympios" and this dates this type of the specimen to c. 369-336 B.C. (HN 1960, 359). Due to damage on the l. side of the camp it is only with difficulty that we can distinguish traces of the letters ΧΑΛ (see also Picard 1979, 28-30)

25-26. Registered as F98-1018 and F98-1020 respectively. N. 25 is lighter than a similar coin of the SNG: Copenhagen (2. 80 g.) and n.26 is also lighter than two similar specimens from the SNG: Copenhagen, weighing 0.79 g. and 0.74 g. respectively.

27. Found 15-7-1998 in trench O26 NW, stratum 3, and registered as F98-1043.

28. Found 21-7-1998 in trench O26 NW, stratum 3, and registered as F98-1116.

29. Found 21-7-1998 in trench O26 NW, stratum 3, and registered as F98-1115.

30. Found 14-7-1998 in trench O26 NW, stratum 3, and registered as F98-1038.

31. Found 15-7-1998 in trench O26 NW, stratum 3, and registered as F98-1043.

Geological Investigations in the Area of Haghia Triadha

Kaj Strand Petersen

The bay of Kato Vassiliki

The small fishing town of Kato Vassiliki is situated on the bay of Patras on the western side of a delta which was formed between the mountains Varassova (914 m) and Klokova (1037 m). The small bay of Kato Vassiliki is very shallow even at a distance of 1-2 km from the shore and in the eastern part of the bay of Patras, the depth never exceeds 80 m. Accordingly, during the periods of low sea level during the last glaciation most of the bay of Kato Vassiliki was land.

The karstic limestone and the site of Haghia Triadha

According to the Geological Map of Greece (Mettos & Karfakis, 1991), the high NNW-SSE-running crest of Varassova in the west consists of strongly karstic limestone with marine gastropods and bivalves and dates from the Upper Cretaceous period (Cenomanian – Senonian). Conformable with the Upper Cretaceous limestone one passes through younger limestone beds from the Paleocene – Middle Eocene period into cohesive conglomerates, shales and sandstones again of Upper Eocene date belonging to the Flysch. As is also visible on the Geological Map of Greece, the hill of Haghia Triadha forms a small 'island' in the delta, as it consists of conglomerates alternating with thin layers of sandstone and shale. These layers constitute the youngest part of the more than 1000 m thick Tertiary sequence overlaying the Mesozoic limestone (Mettos & Karfakis, 1991). To the east of Haghia Triadha, Flysch series are visible in a low ridge (287 m), and further towards the east the limestone of Palaeocene – Middle Eocene age reappears overlaying the upper Cretaceous limestone in Mt. Klokova.

The geological character of the valley of Kato Vassiliki was found to be a syncline. Thus, the older sediments visible along the lower flanks of the Varassova and Klokova mountains lie beneath the delta at varying depth depending on the dip of the synclinal axis.

The changing face of the landscape around Haghia Triadha

The strongly karstic limestone from the Upper Cretaceous period, decribed above, forms one of the most conspicious geological features of the valley of Kato Vassiliki. Moreover, it is characterised by a multitude of caves which are of archaeological and historic interest, since caves of this kind were often used for habitation in the Paleolithic period and in more recent times the caves of the Varassova were inhabited by monks. It was therefore important to obtain a fuller picture of the karstic limestone in the area. For this reason, strike and dips were measured of the strata in four areas covering the delta up towards Gavrolimni and the slopes of Varrasova and Klokova (hatched areas marked A-D in Fig.48). As appears from Fig. 48, 81 strike and dips were used resulting in an orientation best-fit-great-circle 162/76 (dip/direction) which gives a fold axis orientation 342/14. The crest zone of the fold can then be estimated to dip 14° towards north-north-west. This observation is highly important for our under-

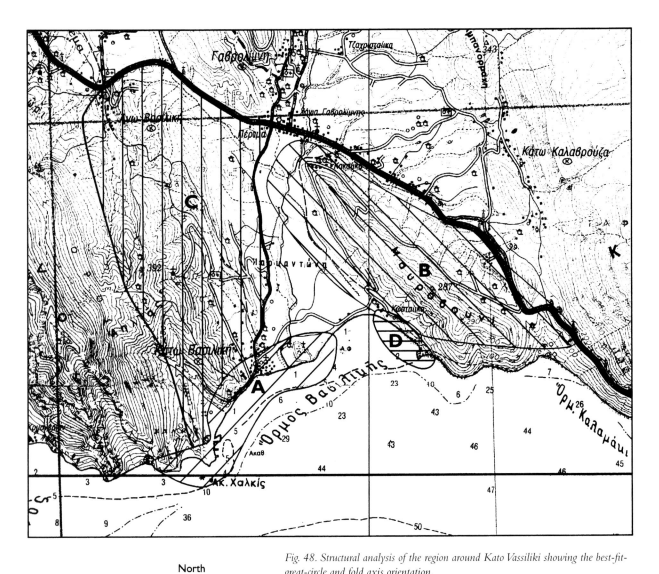

Fig. 48. Structural analysis of the region around Kato Vassiliki showing the best-fit-great-circle and fold axis orientation.

Equal Area
(Schmidt)

North

Kato A   ●

Kato B   +

Kato C   ▶

Kato D   ★

Foldaxis ○

Orientation best fit great
circle 162/76 (dip/direction)

Fold axis orientation: 342/14

Axial

N = 81

shoreline

Fig. 49. Sketch drawn from the hill of Haghia Triadha towards the east showing a crescent shaped island in the sea which was revealed to be part of the Flysch.

standing of the profound ways in which the landscape around the hill of Haghia Triadha has changed during the last approximately 25,000 years. The structural analysis implies that during the Late Weichselian period when the sea level was around 120 m below the present sea level, karstic limestone formed part of a vast landscape which extended far towards the south of the Haghia Triadha hill into what is today the bay of Kato Vassiliki. Thus, karstic limestone might appear less than two km from the coast of the hill of Haghia Triadha in a south-south-east direction at a depth of approx. 50 m.

A small crescent shaped island which is visible in the sea close to the coast on the eastern side of the Haghia Triadha hill must also have formed part of this land-scape (Fig. 49). This island was first con-sidered to be a beach ridge, but was revealed to be part of the Flysch. It might be the trace in the horizontal plane of the syncline dipping north-north-west.

Marine deposits

Marine deposits were not located on the eastern side of the hill of Haghia Triadha, but only on the western side. Here marine strata were found in three places proving the existence of a small bay. These marine sediments were characterised by molluscs such as *Conus, Bittium* and *Gibbula* which facilitated AMS-datings of the sediments. According to the datings so far obtained by this method, the small bay existed in 3310-2930 BC (AAR-4348) and in 1750-1630 BC (AAR-4347).

Diet of the people in ancient Chalkis

A considerable quantity of molluscs were found during the excavations on the hill of Haghia Triadha which gives a valuable insight into the diet of the people who once lived here. So far, as many as 25 marine species have been identified, all of which no doubt once served as an impor-tant food-supply. To judge by its frequen-cy, the *Cerastoderma glaucum* (Poiret, 1789) was by far the most popular (Fig. 50) and

among the gastropods the *Cerithium vulgatum* (Bruguiére, 1792) (Fig. 51). In addition, ten terrestrial gastropods were recorded. Among these, only the *Helix pomatia* (L., 1758) is likely to have been eaten.

With regard to shellfish, the find of fragments of the *Pinna nobilis* L., 1758 (Fig. 52) and the large predatory gastropod *Tonna galea* (L., 1758) (Fig. 53), both spectacular molluscs occur still on the sandy bottoms along the coast of Haghia Triadha.

The samples of molluscs from the oldest layers of trench 4 (compare Fig. 3), near the area now known to have been a small bay, have also been dated by the AMS method. All of these datings point to the Bronze Age: 1890-1740 BC (AAR-4586), 1740-1620 BC (AAR-4588), and 1520-1430 BC (AAR-4587). In other words they stem from a period in which the area southwest of the trench formed a small bay.

Fig. 50. Cerastoderma glaucum (Poiret, 1789).

Fig. 51. *Cerithium vulgatum*
(Bruguiére, 1792).

Rise of sealevel

Most of the molluscs have a habitat of sandy shores as found off the hill of Haghia Triadha today. It is therefore also interesting that epifauna elements can be found on the solid rock of the hill of Haghia Triadha, as well as to the east and west of this site. Thus, heavy bioerosion occurs on outcrops of limestone to the west of the hill and the forming of such notches is a well-known effect of bioero-

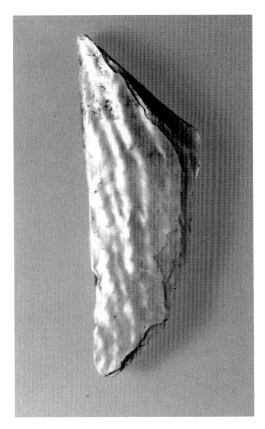

Fig. 52. Pinna nobilis L., 1758.

sion. Of particular interest are the exposures in the western part of the bay of Kato Vassiliki immediately below the site of Pangali. In this area it appears that from a depth of around 2 m below the present sea level the limestone has been substantially bioeroded as seen on Fig. 54. This might show a constant rise of sea level up to the present position. However, the former levels have not been dated.

Summary

Up till now the geological studies including records of recent and subfossil molluscs have depicted the geological setting of the strongly karstic limestone with the potential of palaeolithic settlements in caves like the finds of caves in the Marseilles area below present day sea level. The demonstration of the existence of a former bay west of the site of Haghia Triadha might suggest a possible place for anchorage. Moreover an overlap of the dates from the marine deposits of the former bay and the dates of the shellfish from the excavation – both falling within the Helladic period – was demonstrated.

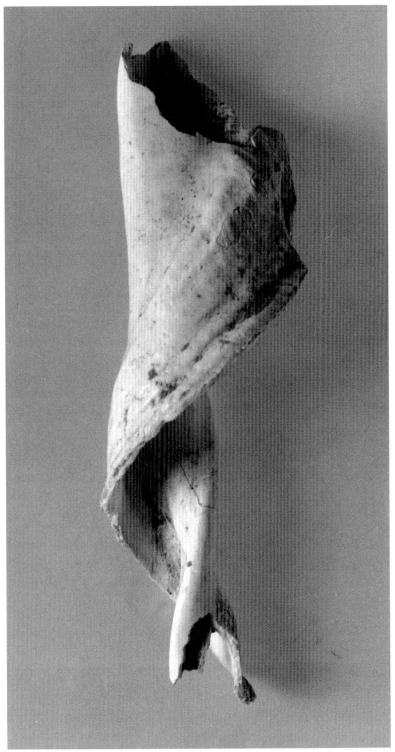

Fig. 53. Tonna galea (L., 1758).

In giving an account of the recorded molluscs from the site it should be kept in

Fig. 54. Underwater photo off the site at Pangali showing the substantial bioerosion up to present-day sea level.

mind that the many vertebrate remains have not been given a closer study. Therefore the main part of the diet is still unknown. The progradation of the delta seems to indicate rising sea level and the studies of bioerosion from under the water (no traces were observed above sea level) may support the idea of rising sea level in the last part of the Holocene. So far no age can be established for the older sea level.

The Final Neolithic Pottery from the Excavation at Pangali in 1996

Theophanis Mavridis[14]

In 1995 a rich Neolithic site was discovered during a systematic survey at the location called Pangali on the eastern slope of Mt. Varassova. The following year, a test trench was opened under the supervision of M. Gazis in order to examine the character and chronology of this site (FPR 1998, 255-258, 280-281).[15]

The pottery in this report has been selected with a view to giving some clue to the dating of the site in the absence of radiocarbon dates and detailed stratigraphic information. It is, however, important to stress that the presentation is preliminary and that further study is required in order to obtain a fuller picture.

Fabric

The fabric of the Pangali pottery ranges from coarse to semi-coarse with many inclusions. Fine fabric is very uncommon and only thin-walled vessels contain fewer inclusions. Thus, the size as well as the quantity of inclusions varies according to the size of vessels and thickness of walls, a characteristic which is likely to be functionally dictated (Coleman 1977, 9; Immerwahr 1971, 4).

Moreover, the non-plastics contained in the clay are angular to sub-rounded and range greatly in size according to the estimation charts in Orton et al. (1993, figs. A5, A6). Mica seldom appears.

Technique

The Pangali pottery provides valuable information on firing techniques which is worth mentioning. Thus, certain white inclusions were identified as calcium carbonate with the use of hydrochloric acid following the procedure described by K. Vitelli (1993, 5). The presence of calcium carbonate gives some clues to the firing temperature since it begins to decompose above 750(C (Rye 1981, 33). Further attempts to identify tempering agents will, however, have to await a petrographic analysis (see also Pullen 1995, 8).

With regard to the pottery from Pangali, it has to be remembered that the surface colour reflects the mineralogical content of clay as modified by firing treatment, coatings and finishing techniques. Thus, the surface of the pottery from Pangali ranges from a clear orange red to darker shades of red, brown and buff to grey. Moreover, it is known that the subsurface colour of fired pots is also dependent on mineralogy and firing treatment and can be thought of as the natural fired colour of the clay body (Rice 1987). For this reason, the clay body of the pottery from Pangali seems to be homogeneous and a dark brown/reddish clay was used. As is the case for other final Neolithic sites, the varying thickness of the blackened core of the Pangali pottery is due to uncontrolled firing (Spitaels 1982, 14).

The same conclusion can be drawn regarding sherds with mottled areas. Such mottling is the result of localized differences in the firing atmosphere and temperature probably owing to the fact that the pots from which the sherds stem were fired in direct contact with fuel and thus without the use of true kilns (Vitelli 1993, 5).

Other manufacturing processes can also be deduced from the Pangali pottery. Some of the bases from Pangali belonging to large vessels had clearly been built up from a rather thick clay disc and a coil had been added around it (on this technique, see Kotsakis 1996, 245). Moreover, several sherds have fine striations on the exterior which indicate smoothing and bear traces of dry-burnishing (compare Rice 1987). On the interior of several sherds from closed vessels, traces of trimming or scraping are present. This procedure was probably conducted while the pots were still wet.

With regard to incised decoration on the Pangali pottery, the thrown up edges of several incised patterns indicate a plastic condition of the clay during the decoration procedure while decoration consisting of shallow and 'clean' lines indicates a leather hard stage of the clay. The varying depth and width of the incised lines point to the use of different tools. However, the appearance of the lines, whether uniform or irregular, most likely depended on factors such as the degree of pressure, the angle of the tool and the dryness of the clay (Rye 1981, 67).

Regarding plastic decoration, the applied clay must have had a plastic consistency in most of the cases and have been applied to the pot when this had reached a leather hard stage. Lugs and handles were added separately.

Wares and shapes

Generally, the Pangali-pottery is monochrome or slipped and burnished or just smoothed, but the categories are not always distinct due to the «self slip» effect of the finishing techniques (compare Rye 1981, 57).

With regard to shapes, open shapes – mostly bowls – are by far the most frequent. This estimation is based on a consideration of the fact that smaller and thinner pots break more easily than larger and thicker vessels (for the statistical procedure, see Cullen 1985, 174; Rice 1987, 223).

Burnished ware (Fig. 55)

Most burnished vessels are open shapes,

the rim-diameter of which ranges from about 10 to 30 cm (Fig. 55: 3, 10-11). Coarser pots with thick walls were usually larger. These pots have straight, out- or inside turned walls and rims, and thin or thicker walls which range from 0, 2 to about 0, 8 cm. They also have different types of lugs and handles and knob-decoration. Examples are raised buttons (Fig. 55: 7), a combination of buttons (Fig. 55 : 6), single or double buttons (Fig. 55: 4, 10, 11) and small vertical strap handles usually below the rim (Fig. 55: 8, 9). Unperforated, horizontal or vertical lugs are also found (Fig. 55: 5). Bases of open pots are flat, but in a few cases low ring bases are also attested (Fig. 55: 1, 2).

Incised ware (Fig. 56)

Another characteristic category of the assemblage is incised ware. Shapes of this ware are open, usually thin-walled and small or medium-sized. Decoration is confined to a frieze which is either narrow or wide, vertical or horizontal and which may be divided into panels and is usually placed near the rim (Fig. 56: 12, 15). Margin lines (Fig. 56: 14, 16), parallel groups of oblique lines (Fig. 56: 13, 16, 18) as well as more complicated arrangements of lines (Fig. 56: 13, 16, 18), filled bands (Fig. 56: 12, 15), and triangles (Fig. 56: 17, 19, 20) are also present.

Pots with this kind of incised decoration are usually well burnished and dark coloured. The incisions are normally shallow and fine. On bowls with thick walls, however, they are deep and have thrown up edges. Moreover, lugs are not unusual. This is remarkable since lugs are highly unusual on pots of similar ware from Kastria in Achaia and Prosymna in Argolis (Sampson 1997, 245; Blegen 1937, fig. 633: 1, 2 are much coarser pots with thick walls).

The large amount of sherds of this ware and its presence in the whole sequence of the trench (though especially stratum 2) indicate that its production was not confined to the Peloponnesos, as has so far been believed (Sampson 1997, 326).

Red slipped and burnished ware (Fig. 57)

A few sherds stem from red slipped, rather well burnished bowls, which are usually decorated with thin ridges (Fig. 57: 21) or buttons (Fig. 57: 22). They were found in stratum 2. Probably some black or dark grey sherds from open pots of good fabric and burnish should be considered here. However, the few sherds from Pangali which belong to shouldered or carinated open shapes may belong to the burnished category identified at Kastria and other Aegean sites (Sampson 1997, 90) but further study of the Pangali-sherds is needed.

Coarse ware (Fig. 57)

Most coarse ware sherds belong to undecorated pots. The exception to this rule are jars which are often decorated with ridges and occasionally with unperforated flat lugs (Fig. 57: 23) and may carry relief bands combined with impressed dots (Fig. 57: 32) or bands with rope decoration (Fig. 57: 31). The wall-thickness of coarse ware sherds varies. Several sherds with a wall-thickness exceeding 1 cm belong to large pithoid jars. Large strap handles (Fig. 57: 24), biconical handles Fig. 57: 25) and unperforated lugs (Fig. 57: 26) may also belong to such jars. Coarse ware vessels with thinner walls are decorated with horizontal straight ridges (Fig. 57: 29), angular bands (Fig. 57: 30), or ridges with pointillé decoration (Fig. 57: 27, 28).

Chronology

The pottery excavated in the trial-trench at Pangali must belong to an "early Final Neolithic" phase for several reasons. Firstly, the fabric and technique of the pottery is very homogeneous in all four strata. A similar homogeneity characterizes many Final Neolithic sites (Coleman 1977, 9; Spitaels 1982, 34). Secondly, only a few sherds from the trial trench (not included in this report) find parallels to representative later material from sites such as Plaka-ri in Euboea and the Agora of Athens (Spitaels 1982; Immerwahr 1971; see also Phelps 1975, 297; Sampson 1981; Pullen 1995). The fact that these sherds were especially characteristic of stratum 1 is of little significance since wares common in the lower strata were also found in this stratum. Thirdly, there were no significant differences among the ware-groups and shapes between strata 2 and 3. Finally, and most importantly, the Pangali-pottery is closely parallelled at several "early Final Neolithic" sites in Greece which – just like Pangali – lack matt-painted, pattern-burnished and crusted wares as well as rolled rim bowls. An especially close parallel is Kastria phase III termed transitional Late Neolithic Ib-IIa by the excavator (Sampson 1997, 324). Here matt-painted wares were no longer produced and pattern-burnished and crusted ware and rolled rim bowls had not yet appeared while incised ware similar to that at Pangali was found in great quantity. Moreover, a Final Neolithic (LN Ib) phase with the chronological characteristics described above has previously been indentified in the Peloponnesos (Phelps 1975, 301) as well as in Euboea (Sampson 1993, 89) and elswhere. Also, the pottery from Pangali has close parallels to the material excavated at the site of Aghios Demetrios in Triphylia, SW Peloponnesos, but the presence at the latter site of sherds with crusted and pattern burnished decoration implies a rather later date (see Zachos 1987, 123-124).

In view of the little we know about pottery sequence and cultural development in Aetolia-Akarnania in the crucial transitional period between the Late Neolithic period and the Early Bronze Age, the importance of the site of Pangali cannot be overestimated. Especially promising is its relation to the nearby site of Haghia Triadha where Early Helladic finds are coming to light (see this report, 232-240). Future Excavation at Pangali may, however, add even further to our understanding of the transition between Final Neolithic-Early Bronze Age in western Greece,

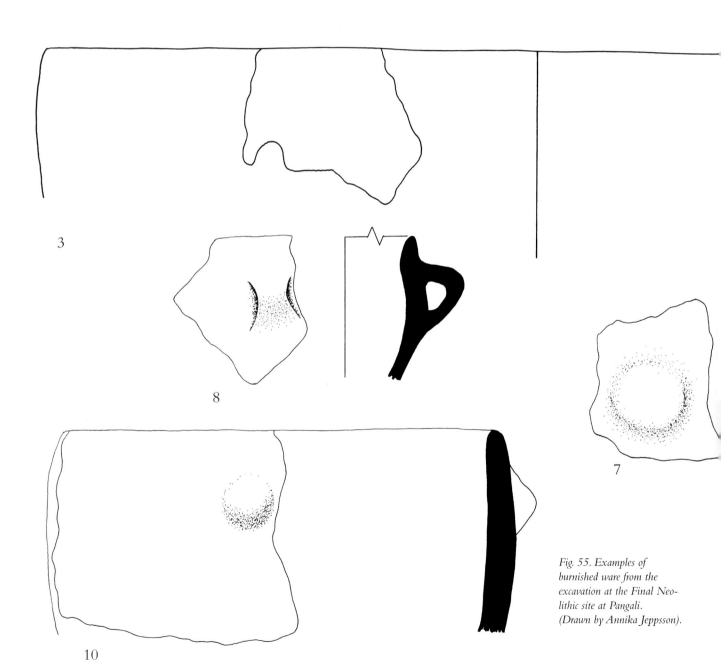

Fig. 55. Examples of burnished ware from the excavation at the Final Neolithic site at Pangali. (Drawn by Annika Jeppsson).

2

4

5

9

6

11

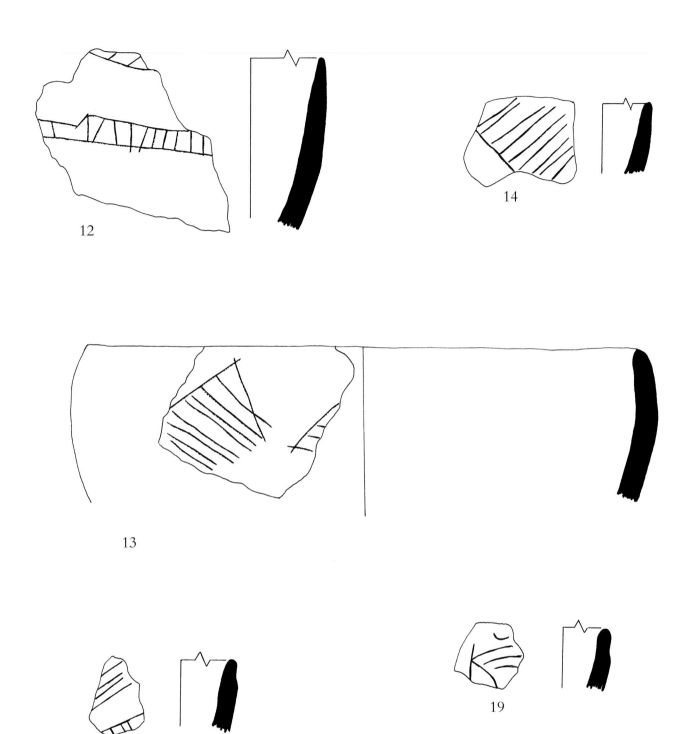

Fig. 56. Examples of incised ware from the excavation at the Final Neolithic site at Pangali. (Drawn by Annika Jeppsson).

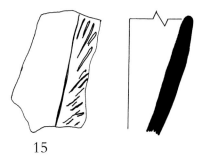

15

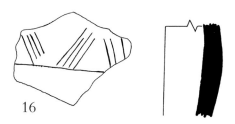

16

especially in relation to the evidence from other sites such as the cave of Drakaina on the island of Kephalonia visible from Pangali on clear days (for this cave: Stratouli, pers.com, in press).

Key to catalogue

The diagnostic sherds from the trial Excavation amounted to about 200, all of which were drawn and registered. Since no major chronological differences were observed the material was treated as a single entity. It should therefore be pointed out that the numbering of the sherds in the catalogue has no stratigraphic significance but represents the order in which the sherds were studied. Stratigraphic information is, however, given for each sherd. Colour descriptions follow the Munsell system and the measurements are given in centimeters unless stated otherwise. According to the estimation of the rim diameter, pots were divided into three categories : a) 0-15 small, b) 16-25 medium and c) 26- large.

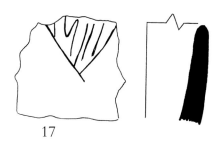

17

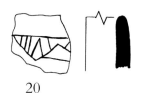

20

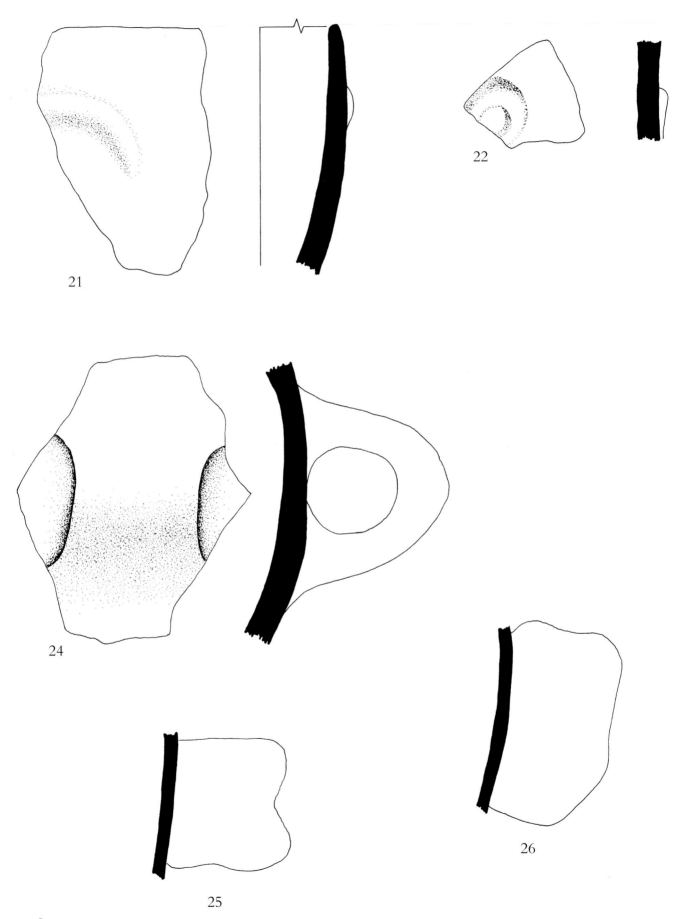

21

22

24

25

26

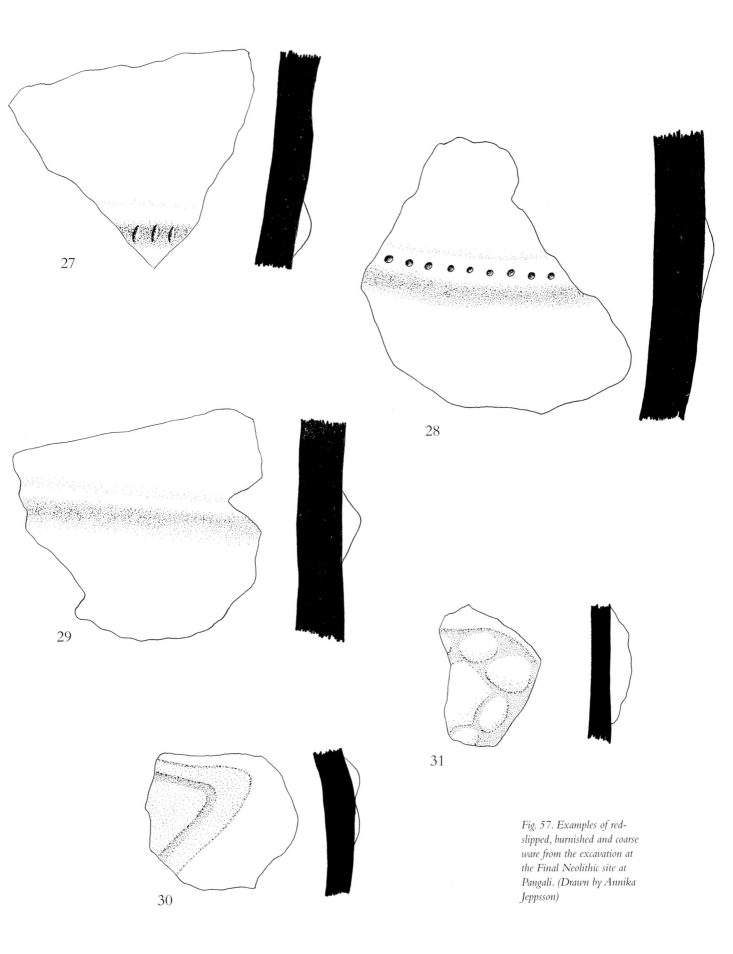

27

28

29

31

30

Fig. 57. Examples of red-slipped, burnished and coarse ware from the excavation at the Final Neolithic site at Pangali. (Drawn by Annika Jeppsson)

Catalogue

1. T1/Σ2/Π4: 202. Fragment of a ring base. Coarse fabric with large inclusions. Smoothed out, rough in (4/4 7.5 YR brown). Grey core. Diam:13, H:5,5, Th:0,8-1.2.

2. T1/Σ3/Π5: 193. Fragment of a ring base. Coarse fabric. Smoothed out, rough in (4/6 7.5 YR strong brown).Red to brown core (4/6 10 R red-4/4 5YR reddish brown). Diam: 14 ; H:4 ; Th:0,7-1,1.

3. T1/Σ1/Π3: 74. Rim and body of a medium-sized bowl with fairly straight walls. Plain, rounded rim. Semi-coarse fabric with some silver mica, yellowish to reddish brown. Slipped and polished (2.5/2 very dark brown out, 7.5 YR, 3/1 5YR very dark grey in). Grey core. Mending hole on the lower part. Diam: 22; H: 5;Th: 0,5.

4. ΠΦ1/54. Body fragment of a convex bowl. Double mastoid projection on the lower part. Fabric semi-coarse (4.8 dark red, 2.5 YR) with few inclusions and mica. Slipped and burnished (4.8 red, 2.5 YR out, 5.2 greyish brown, 10 YR in). Grey core. Diam.: -; H: 6; W: 6; Th: 0,5.

5. T1: 203. Rim and body of a convex bowl. Plain, rounded rim. Unperforated, flat, ear-shaped lug below rim. Semi-coarse fabric. Burnished (3.1, 7.5 YR very dark gray out, 4/4 7.5 YR brown in). Grey core. Diam.:-, H: 5; W: 6;Th: 0,7.

6. T1/Σ2/Π3: 182. Body fragment of a convex walled, open pot. Decorated with double buttons. Semi-coarse fabric. Slipped and burnished (5/4 reddish brown 5YR). Grey core. H: 3; W: 4,5;Th: 0,5.

7. T1/Σ2/Π3: 121. Body fragment with a raised knob. Semi-coarse fabric with some mica. Slipped and polished (4/8 dark red, 2.5 YR). H: 5; W: 4,5;Th: 0,6.

8. T1/Σ2/Π3: 95. Rim and body of a medium, convex-walled, rather closed bowl. In diagonal position, below rim a small strap handle. Slipped and smoothed (3/1, 7.5YR very dark grey). Grey core. Diam: 22; H: 4;Th: 0,5.

9. T1/Σ2/Π3: Small strap handle from a bowl or cup. Thickened at both ends. Semi-coarse fabric. Plain, slightly smoothed (3/4, 7.5 YR dark brown). Black core. H:2,4; W: 1; T: 0,6.

10. ΠΦ1/54. Rim and body of a small, convex-walled, closed bowl. Plain, rounded rim. Semi-coarse fabric. Mastoid projection below rim. Slipped and smoothed (5/2, 10 YR greyish brown). Grey core. Diam.: 13; H: 6,2; T: 0,7.

11. T1/Σ2/Π3: 97.Rim and body of a medium, convex-walled bowl. Plain, rounded rim. Mastoid projection on the body. Semi-coarse fabric. Slipped and burnished (4/8, 2.5 YR, red). Grey core. Diam: 18; H: 5; T: 0,4.

12. T1/Σ2/Π3: 190. Rim and body of a slightly convex-walled bowl. Plain, pointed rim. Incised decoration of two parallel zones filled with oblique lines. Semi-coarse fabric with small inclusions. Slipped and very well burnished (2.5/1, 2.5 Y reddish black). Black core, red near surface. D:-; H: 4,5;W:6; T: 0,5.

13. ΠΦ1:70. Rim and body of a medium, convex-walled bowl. Plain, rounded rim. Systems of intersecting

and joining, oblique lines below rim. Semi-coarse fabric with mostly small inclusions and mica. Slipped and smoothed (4/4 reddish brown, 5YR). Grey core. Diam.: 17; H:4,4; Th:O, 6.

14. Τl/Σ2/Π3: 109. Rim and body of a convex- walled bowl. Plain, rather pointed rim. Incised decoration of one marginal and several oblique lines. Semi-coarse fabric with few small inclusions. Slipped and smoothed (4/3 brown 7.5 YR out, 3/3 dark reddish brown 5YR in). Grey core. Diam.:-; H: 2,3; W: 2,5; Th: 0,5.

15. Τl/Σ2/Π3: 108. Rim and body of a slightly convex-walled bowl. Rim plain, rounded. Vertical zone filled with oblique incisions. Fabric fine to semi-coarse with few sporadic inclusions. Slipped and burnished (4/3 brown 7.5 YR). Grey core. Diam:-; H: 3,3; W: 2,1; T: 0, 4.

16. Τl/Σ2/Π3: 149. Body fragment of a convex- walled bowl. Incised decoration with horizontal margin line and systems of oblique lines. Semi-coarse fabric. Slipped and smoothed (3/3 dark brown 7.5 YR out, 2.5/2 very dark brown in). Grey core. Unevenly fired. Diam:-; H: 3; W: 3,5; Th: 0,4.

17. Τl/Σ1/Π3: 73. Rim and body of a rather straight-walled bowl. Plain, rounded rim. Incised lines forming a triangle, filled with asymmetrical incisions. Semi-coarse fabric with few small inclusions. Slipped and smoothed (5/4, 7.5 YR brown). Grey core. Diam:-; H: 3,1; W: 3,4; T: 0,5.

18. Τl/Σ2/Π3: 165. Rim of a straight-walled bowl. Plain, rounded rim. Systems of oblique lines below rim. Semi-coarse fabric with few inclusions and mica. Slipped and burnished (4/8, 2.5 YR red). Brown core. Diam.:-; H: 2,2; W: 1,4; T: 0,4.

19. Τl/Σ1/Π3: 137. Rim of a convex walled bowl. Plain, rounded rim. Decorated with very shallow incised lines, one vertical (marginal), two which form an angle and inside two oblique. Semi-coarse fabric with few

small inclusions and mica. Slipped and burnished (4/6, 5YR yellowish red out, 3/1, 5YR very dark gray in). Grey core. Diam.:-; H: 1,7; W: 2; T: 0,3.

20. ΠΦ1. Rim of a straight-walled bowl. Plain, rounded rim. Very fine incisions below rim forming a horizontal zone filled with incisions and plain opposed triangles. Semi-fine fabric with few inclusions. Slipped and burnished (6.4, 7.5 YR light brown). Brown core. Diam.:-; H: 1,7; W: 1,8; T: 0,4.

21. Τl/Σ2/Π3: 94. Rim and body of a large, hemispherical bowl. Plain, rounded rim. Thin curved ridge below rim. Semi-coarse fabric with few small inclusions and mica. Slipped and very well burnished (3/3, 2.5 YR dark reddish brown out, 4/6, 2.5 YR red in). Grey core. Diam.: 28; W: 4,5; Th: 0,6.

22. Τl/Σ2/Π3: 80. Fragment of the body of a well burnished and slipped bowl (4/6, 2.5 YR red). Raised button with a deep symmetrical deepening in the middle. Coarse fabric with small inclusions and mica. Grey core. H: 3, W: 2,5, Th: 0,5.

23. Τl/Σ2/Π4(not depicted): 99. Body fragment of a large storage jar. Several plastic bands, some of which curved, combined with impressed dots and an unperforated, vertical, oval shaped lug. Fabric stone gritted with small and bigger inclusions. Traces of finished procedures on the outside. Smoothed (4/8, 2.5 YR dark red out, 2.5/1 5YR black in). Black core. H: 12, W: 14; Th: 1,5.

24. Τl/Σ2/Π3: 98. Vertical strap handle of a large vessel. Semi-coarse fabric with mostly small inclusions and mica. Smoothed (4/8, 2.5 YR red). Grey core. H: 8,5, W: 8, Th: 0,6.

25. Τl/Σ3/Π5: Large biconical handle. Coarse fabric with small and bigger inclusions. Smoothed (4/4, 2.5 YR reddish brown). Grey core. H: 3,5; W: 3,7; Th: 1,5.

26. Τl/Σ3/Π4: 194. Unperforated, flat

elongated lug. Stone gritted fabric with smaller, bigger inclusions and mica. Smoothed (4/4, 2.5 YR reddish brown). Grey core. H: 5,5; W: 3,2.

27. T1/Σ2/Π3: 146. Body fragment of a coarse vessel with a plastic band decorated with three vertical grooves. Coarse fabric with small, bigger inclusions and mica. Smoothed (5/6, 5 YR yellowish red out, 3/6, 2.5 YR dark red in). Grey core. H: 7; W: 7,5; Th: 1.

28. T1/Σ3/Π5: 188. Body fragment of a jar with a cordon decorated with impressed dots. Coarse fabric with small and bigger inclusions. Smoothed (4/4, 5 YR reddish yellow). Grey core. H: 7,5; W: 8,5; Th: 1,3.

29. T1/Σ1/Π3: 76. Body fragment of jar with a plain horizontal ridge. Semi-coarse fabric with mostly small inclusions. Smoothed (6/3, 7.5 YR light brown out, 3/1, 7.5 YR very dark gray in). Brown core. H: 6,8; W: 7,5; Th: 1,4.

30. ΠΦ1: 183. Body fragment of a jar ? with an angular band. Coarse fabric with big and smaller inclusions. Smoothed (5/4 reddish brown 5 YR). Grey core. H: 4,2; W: 4; Th: 0,9.

31. T1/Σ3/Π5: 185. Body fragment of a coarse vessel with a curved raised band with finger impressions. Coarse fabric with small, bigger inclusions and mica. Rough surfaces (4/4, 7.5 YR brown). Grey core. H: 4; W: 3; Th: O,5.

32. Body fragment of a large jar. System of vertical and horizontal bands which enclose area with impressed dots. Coarse fabric with small, bigger inclusions and mica. Slightly smoothed (3/6, 2.5 YR dark red). Black core H: 16; W: 12; Th: 2.

The Cemetery of Ancient Chalkis. Recent Rescue Excavation[16]

Ioannis Moschos

In 1916 the late K. A. Rhomaios identified ancient Chalkis in the ruins on the Haghia Triadha hill, near the village of Kato Vassiliki (Rhomaios 1916, 46-47; see also Houby-Nielsen in FPR, 253). To support his thesis he also referred to the nearby extensive cemetery. This was the first mention of the necropolis. According to his report "... a number of tombs are seen half an hour north-west of the acropolis, on both sides of the road to Kalydon. It was the disastrous circumstances of tomb robbing that brought them to light".

Some thirty years ago the late E. Mastrokostas reported the discovery of two grave steles of limestone from this region, now housed in the Agrinion Museum (Mastrokostas 1963, 148). The first one, AMS 158 (Fig. 58), is partly preserved and measures 0.50 x 0.37 x 0.09m. The inscription ΚΛΕΥΜΕΝΗΣ is clearly visible below the *kymation* on the top. From the second one, AMS 159 (Fig. 59), only the uppermost part has survived, which measures 0.505 x 0.525-0.575 x 0.12-0.15 m. Probably due to misunderstanding it was reported again by F. Zafeiropoulou (AMS 242), a few years later (Zafeiropoulou 1973-74, 539, pl. 362b). This is an elaborate example[17] as it has a pediment top with a relief bowl in a tympanum. On the lower part there are waves and the partly preserved inscription [E]ΥΡΥΛΑΜΟ[Υ]. The exact provenance of these two grave steles is unknown. The catalogue of Agrinion Museum has merely reproduced the report: "They were handed over by P. V. Vasilakopoulos and transferred from Aitolian Chalkis, beside Kato Vasiliki". Mastrokostas also mentions an amphora, AMP 154 (Fig. 60) with two bands below the handles, as coming from a grave beside the road that leads from Kato Vassiliki to Gavrolimni (Mastrokostas 1965, 344). Although it is not stated, we know without doubt that this was a looted cist grave.[18]

Of course, the presence of the cemetery was better known to peasants who, until

Fig. 58. Grave stele AMS 158 from the cemetery of Chalkis.

Fig. 59. Grave stele AMS 159/242 from the cemetery of Chalkis.

Fig. 60. Amphora AMP 154 from the cemetery of Chalkis.

recently, have engaged in active land cultivation with traditional implements. Farmers today remember a big inscribed limestone slab, which was removed from a tomb at the time of World War II. They say it was reused as building material in a modern house a few years later. This possibly-inscribed limestone slab might have been transferred to the cemetery and re-used as a cover slab.

The rescue Excavation

During the building work for the installation of a new water supply network in progress at Kato Vassiliki, two cist graves were accidentally revealed (Gr1, Gr2), within the bounds of Konstantinos Panagiotopoulos' property. Although a long trench was dug across the foot of the hill by the workers, nothing else was unearthed. This is likely to indicate that the cemetery extended to the valley, rather than that there was only a small number of tombs in this area. The small river to the east, known as "Rema", probably served as the border. But the possibility that other tombs also exist on the low hill to the west or in the valley extending east of the river, cannot be excluded.[19] Some sherds and small fragments of Laconian-type tiles are visible in the hill and traces of two tumuli of unknown date are also visible east of the river. Without any doubt, the Classical – Hellenistic cemetery

must be situated on both sides of the modern road which leads from Kato Vassiliki to the state highway.

Until now only cist graves have been excavated in Chalkis' cemetery, but there is a strong possibility that other types have also been preserved. Traces of tile-covered graves as well as several disturbed cist graves can be seen at the side of the road.[20] We have already mentioned the two tumuli which are shield-like mounds of earth. They were probably first constructed in the prehistoric period, but their use must also have continued in historic times, as is clear from the sparsely scattered pottery. The location of the Mycenaean cemetery is also unknown, although soft white rock has been spotted in various neighbouring sites. This rock is suitable for chamber tombs. Furthermore, inside the Classical – Hellenistic cemetery there are mounds of limestone or sandstone, which probably came from constructions with funerary purposes. Across these "monuments" an ancient road must have led inland from Chalkis' harbour.

The rescue Excavation was carried out by the 6th Ephorate of Prehistoric and Classical Antiquities in September 1998. It was very brief because of the almost complete lack of finds, but now we have the

Fig. 61. The empty Gr1.

first Excavation element from Chalkis' cemetery. Of course, the two graves are not representative samples.

Grave 1 (Figs. 61-62)

It is located at the western end of the field, some 50 m west of the road that leads to the village of Kato Vassiliki and about 730 m from the coast. Its orientation is east-west and it is constructed of two upright standing slabs of sandstone. At the ends of these slabs, two smaller flat stones have been set up. The one on the eastern narrow side has collapsed outwards. The inner dimensions of the grave

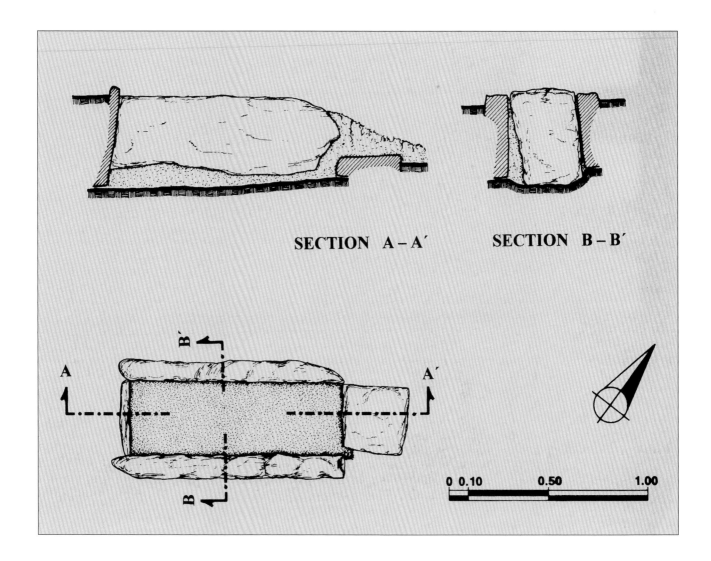

SECTION A–A′ SECTION B–B′

which are very close to Grave 2, are 1.06 x 0.36 x 0.48 m. The thickness of the slabs is 0.10-0.11 m, while that of the narrow stones is 0,05 m. It was found uncovered and full of brownish earth. In the earth-fill a few small tile fragments were found, presumably not associated with the tomb. The grave was found empty, probably looted.

Grave 2 (Figs. 63-64)

About 27 m SE a second grave was found. Its orientation is north – south and it is constructed of pieces of flat and square sandstone of various sizes. One covering flat stone had been recently partly removed from the grave due to the working activity, while another one, larger and broken had been moved nearby, probably during cultivation in the recent past. The

inner dimensions are 1.69-1.79 x 0.67-0.72 x 0.81-0.95 m. The grave was full of brownish earth. It contained a partly disturbed primary burial (Gr 2.A). The body was lying on its back, with the skull towards the south, facing west. The right hand was preserved parallel to the body, but the left had vanished. The legs were also placed at full length, the left thigh bone partly under the right one.

The burial was accompanied by pottery and a silver ring. A trefoil-mouthed oinochoe (Gr2.1) was found west of the skull, fallen horizontally with the neck towards the NW. Near the left hand-side a small echinus bowl (Gr2.2) had fallen horizontally with the mouth towards the SE. In its original position near the left wrist was a silver ring (Gr2.3). In contact with the western inner wall of the grave a saucer

Fig. 62. Plan and sections of Gr1.

Fig. 63. Gr2 during the excavation

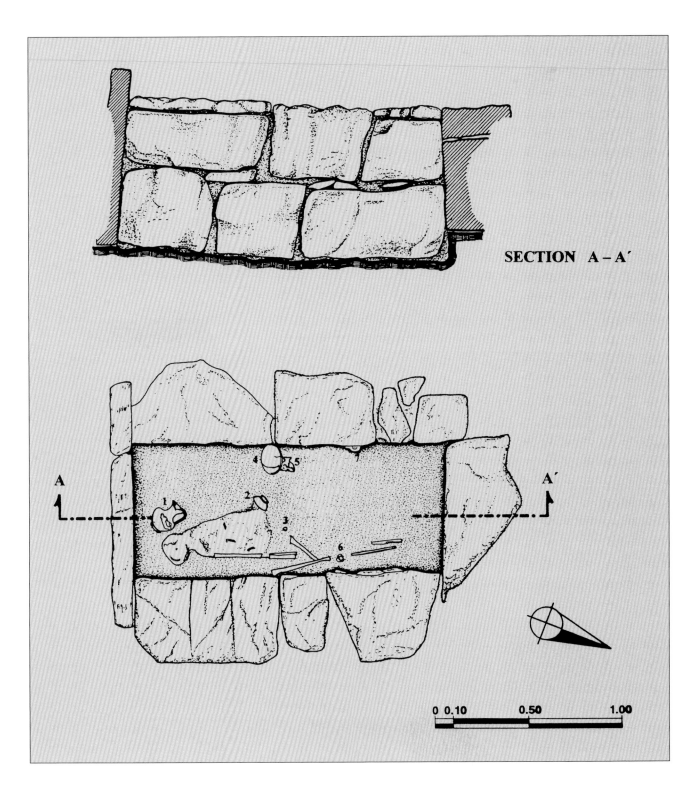

SECTION A – A'

plate (Gr2.4) was found in a slanting position. Partly under the previous one, a skyphos (Gr2.5) was found fallen horizontally with the mouth towards the east. A miniature, handled, trefoil-mouthed oinochoe (Gr2.6) was at knee level, facing north. Finally, an oil-lamp (Gr2.7) was found in contact with the west inner-wall, near the northern narrow side of the grave.

Fig. 64. Plan and section of Gr2.

Catalogue

Gr2.1:

Figs. 65, 72. Trefoil-mouthed oinochoe, reassembled from many fragments and restored at shoulder. Soft, reddish yellow (5YR 6/6) fabric. Twisted handle from opposite rim to shoulder, squat body, off-set ring foot. Thin, matt black "glaze" outside, reserved zone above foot. Pairs of horizontal grooves on neck and shoulder. H. 19.7. D.rim 7.5. D.max. 13.3. D.foot 7.3. Paramythiá : Vokotopoulou 1971, 333, pl. 308b.

Gr2.2:

Figs. 66, 72. Small echinus bowl, reassembled from several fragments. One chip off rim. Porous, reddish yellow (5YR 6/6) fabric. Rim with strong inward curve, concave base. Fully brownish black painted. H. 3.4. D.rim 5.5. D.max. 6.5. D.foot

Fig. 66. Gr2.2: Small echinus bowl.

3.6. Cf. Corinth VII, III, 32 (no 55), pls. 2, 44. Chalkis: Dietz 1998, 303, fig. 31:21. Lamia: Pantos 1981, 206, pl. 128c. The concave base might be a local characteristic. For similar bases see some specimens in Agrinion Museum: AMP 69 from Stratos, see Mastrokostas 1961/2, 184 (not on plates); AMP 1342 from Agrinion; AMP 1346 from Stratos or Lepenou.

Gr2.3:

Figs. 67, 72. Silver ring, partly damaged in the sling. The link is roughly rectangular in section, the sling almost elliptical and plain. Thick shallow engravings on the sling, presumably from use rather than decoration. D. 2.1. Th. 0.2. Dim. of the sling 1.9 X 0.2 m. Cf. Orsi 1906, 539, fig. 371. Ori 1985, 288, no 206. Themelis & Touratsoglou 1997, 90 (B 134), 128 (Z 9), pl. 102, 144. Kaltsas 1998, 277, plan 37 (661a).

Fig. 65. Gr2.1: Trefoil-mouthed oinochoe.

Fig. 67. Gr2.3: Silver ring.

Fig. 68. Gr2.4: Saucer plate.

Gr2.4:

Figs. 68, 72. Saucer plate, reassembled from several fragments. Soft, reddish-yellow (7.5YR 7/6) fabric. Gently in-turned rim, broadly-curved wall, plain ring foot. Traces of brown-black glaze on both surfaces. Five stamped palmette patterns on bottom inside, slightly visible. H. 3.9. D.rim 0.15. D.foot 7.2. Cf. Corinth VII, III, 43 (no 158), pls. 5, 46. Similar from Stratos in Agrinion Museum (AMP 40), see Mastrokostas 1961/2, 184 (not on plates).

Gr2.5:

Figs. 69, 72. Skyphos of "Corinthian" type, reassembled from many fragments and partly-restored at rim, body and handle. Fine, reddish-yellow (5YR 7/6) fabric. Plain rim, round horizontal handles below rim, thin walls with slightly in-curving profile, pedestal foot with conical recession under base. Brownish-black glaze, partly worn off. Wholly glazed inside, from rim to below body outside. A thin line is added on lower body. Glaze under foot except the hollow part, where a punt decorates the top of recession. H. 8.6. D.rim 6.2. D.max 6.9. D.foot 3.8. Cf. Andreou 1994, 202, pls. 146a, 150a. Aggeli 1993, 277 (tomb III), pl. 90 (for the

Fig. 69. Gr2.5: Skyphos.

298

Fig. 70. Gr2.6: One handled miniature trefoil-mouthed oinochoe.

system of decoration). Similar base in a specimen from Naupaktos (AMP 1387), see Mastrokostas 1961/2, 183 (not on plates).

Gr2.6:

Figs. 70, 72. One-handled miniature trefoil-mouthed oinochoe, restored at handle. Slightly porous, reddish-yellow (5YR 6/6) fabric with a few very small white inclusions. Tightly-pinched trefoil mouth, vertical strap handle from rim to shoulder,

squat body, low ring base. Fully brownish-black paint – the base included, mostly worn off. H. 3.7. D.max 3.4. D.foot 2. Chalkis: Dietz 1998, 294, fig. 27:13,15. Miniature vases are common in Amvrakia, see Vokotopoulou 1972, 443. Also see two miniature vases from a tomb in Calydon, Papapostolou 1972, 435 (no 7), pl. 366a.

Gr2.7:

Figs. 71–72. Oil-lamp, reassembled from several fragments. Soft, very pale brown (10YR 7/4) fabric. Attachments of horizontal strap handle. Traces of use on nozzle. Fully black paint, entirely worn off. D. filling hole 2.8. Pres. H. 3.2. Pres. L. 7.9. D.foot 3.1. Cf. Agora IV, 72-73, type 25B. Schreibler 1976, 26-30, type RSL4. Olympia Bericht III, 59, fig. 62. From Aitolian sites: Alikirna, see Dekoulakou 1971, 325 (no 4), pl. 301e-st. Kalydon, see Papapostolou 1972, 434 (no 7), 435 (no 9), pl. 365a.

Gr.2 is very important as it offers a closed pottery assemblage which probably dates to the late 4th – first quarter of 3rd cent.

Fig. 71. Gr2.7: Oil-lamp.

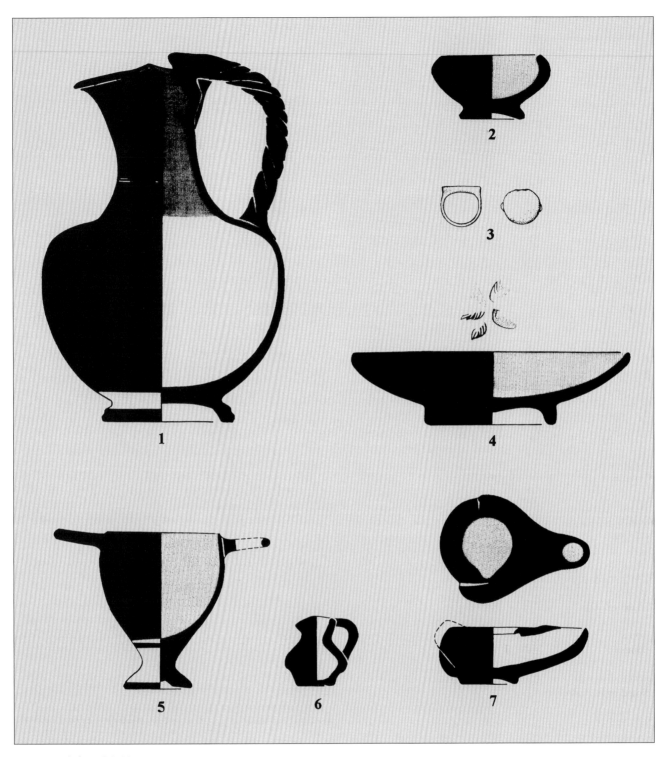

Fig. 72. Finds from Gr2.21

Notes

NOTE 1
Compare figs. 8 and 15 in FPR.

NOTE 2
For similar sima-profiles and decoration, though of Early Classical date, see OF XXIV, pl. 9:3, 10:1, and 11:1.

NOTE 3
Compare OF XX, le 404-9 (especially le 409), Taf. 26.

NOTE 4
See figs. 15, 17 and 18 in FPR.

NOTE 5
Compare Corinth XII, nos. 1196 and 1201, pl. 76-77.

NOTE 6
Compare Corinth XII, no. 1205, pl. 77.

NOTE 7
Compare Corinth XII, nos. 1213-15, pl. 77 and Corinth VII:II, An 348, pl. 85.

NOTE 8
Compare Agora XXII, nos. 1437-1441; Αδαμ-Βελενη 1997, pl. 112:a; in particular Κομβου-Ραλλη 1997, pl.164 a-b.

NOTE 9
Compare Athenian Agora IV, pl. 33: 145.

NOTE 10
Noted by A. Andrén.

NOTE 11
I wish to express my thanks and appreciation to Dr. Lazaros Kolonas, head of the 6th Ephoria of Prehistoric and Classical Antiquities in Patras who authorised me to make a preliminary presentation of the coins of the excavation in Aetolian Chalkis which is being conducted in collaraboration with Ny Carlsberg Glyptothek in Copenhagen and the Danish Institute Athens. I would also like to thank the conservators of the 6th Ephoria, D. Marinopoulou and G. Bubuca, as well as the surveyor C. Marinopoulos who produced Fig. 46 and I cannot omit thanking the philologist Miss G. Gaitanidou who was kind enough to check the fluency of the English text.

NOTE 12
The first information about 'koinon' of Aetolia is given by Diodor (29.66.2) who refers to the events of 314 B.C. and more information is given by an Athenian decree of 367/6 B.C. concerning the Aetolian League: Schweigert 1939, Bousquet 1957. The earlier 'koinon', of the fifth century B.C., seems not to have consisted of cities (poleis) since Thucydides states that the Aetolians lived in unfortified villages (Thuc. 3.94). See also Παντος 1985.

NOTE 13
Only two cities of the Aetolian League, Apollonia and Potidania, issued coins for a brief period (see Λιάμπη 1996).

NOTE 14
I am most grateful to Dr. Kolonas for his permission to make the following brief presentation of characteristic pottery categories and to Dr. Dietz for having encouraged me in this work.
I would also like to thank S. Houby-Nielsen, J. Eiring and H.A. Alisoy for stimulating discussion and help during the study of the material.

NOTE 15
For the stratigraphy and other finds from the excavation see FPR 1998, 280.

NOTE 16
The head of the personnel of workers has been the experienced chief craftsman D. Evangeliou. The archaeologist K. Soura has also taken part in the excavation and has drawn the architectural sketches. They have been inked by T. Stamatopoulou, while K. Iliogamvrou has sketched the vases. Ephor Dr. L. Kolonas gave the permission to study the old material from Chalkis in the Agrinion Museum. To all of them I express my warmest appreciation.

NOTE 17
For the types of these two grave *stelae*, see Mela-Preka-Strauch 1998, 281-282 (types I and II).

NOTE 18
The information was provided by the retired watchman of antiquities I. Manthos, who was present at this excavation. The amphora AMP 154 had been handed to the Ephorate by Chr. Paganias before the excavation, which did not uncover any other finds.

NOTE 19
K. Stergiopoulos mentioned many ancient tombs on and around the Haghia Triadha hill (Στεργιόπουλος 1939, 40). Up to the present time there has been no signs of tombs outside the walls of Chalkis. Some cist graves which have been excavated by A. Paliouras in the area of the Early Christian church are dated to Middle Byzantine Period and seem unlikely to have been visible for Stergiopoulos.

NOTE 20
See also the brief report in Bommelje & Doorn 1987, 112.

Περίληψη

Τα έτη 1997 και 1998 συνεχίστηκαν οι ανασκαφές στο λόφο της Αγ. Τριάδας στην Κάτω Βασιλική Αιτωλίας (Αρχαία Χαλκίδα), με τη συνεργασία της ΣΤ΄ Εφορείας Προϊστορικών και Κλασσικών Αρχαιοτήτων Πάτρας και του Ινστιτούτου της Δανίας στην Αθήνα. Στη δεύτερη προκαταρκτική έκθεση παρουσιάζεται το χρονικό των ανασκαφών, μια στατιστική προσέγγιση στα ευρήματα, τα πρώτα αποτελέσματα των γεωλογικών ερευνών στην περιοχή της Αγ. Τριάδας καθώς και τα πρώτα ευρήματα από το νεκροταφείο της αρχαίας πόλης, που ήρθαν στο φως από σωστική ανασκαφή της Εφορείας. Στην έκθεση αυτή παρουσιάζονται επίσης νομίσματα που βρέθηκαν στην ανασκαφή καθώς και η τυπολογία των κεραμίδων που χρησιμοποιήθηκαν στις κατοικίες. Τέλος, δημοσιεύεται αντιπροσωπευτική κεραμεική της εγκατάστασης στη θέση Πάγκαλη, η οποία ανήκει στην Τελική Νεολιθική περίοδο.

Η ανασκαφή στο λόφο της Αγ. Τριάδας κατά τα παραπάνω έτη είχε διερευνητικό χαρακτήρα για τον έλεγχο της στρωματογραφίας σε διαφορετικά σημεία του λόφου. Για το λόγο αυτό ορίστηκαν πέντε δοκιμαστικές τομές συνολικού μήκους 140 μέτρων και πλάτους 1 μ. και 2μ., που στην πλειοψηφία τους ερευνήθηκαν έως το φυσικό βράχο. Το βάθος της στωματογραφίας ποικίλει από 0,10 μ. έως 3,75 μ. Επίσης ερευνήθηκαν κατάλοιπα κλασσικών-ελληνιστικών οικιών σε τρεις ακόμα τομές, συνολικής επιφάνειας 160 μ². Από την έρευνα προέκυψαν 60-70.000 όστρακα, 4.000 κιλά κεραμίδων και 500 περίπου κινητά ευρήματα (αγγεία, νομίσματα, μεταλλικά, πήλινα και λίθινα μικροαντικείμενα).

Οι έως τώρα έρευνες στο λόφο της Αγ. Τριάδας επιτρέπουν με σχετική ασφάλεια να κατανοήσουμε την εγκατάσταση στην Αρχαία Χαλκίδα. Είμαστε πλέον βέβαιοι στρωματογραφικά ότι η κατοίκηση στο λόφο ξεκινά από την Τελική Νεολιθική / Πρωτοελλαδική περίοδο. Τα διάφορα ευρήματα από την Εποχή του Χαλκού, τη Γεωμετρική, την Αρχαϊκή και την Κλασσική-Ελληνιστική περίοδο που βρέθηκαν κυρίως σε μεικτά στρώματα, μας οδηγούν στο συμπέρασμα πως το κορυφαίο τμήμα του λόφου κατοικήθηκε για μεγάλα χρονικά διαστήματα. Επιπλέον γνωρίζουμε βασικά στοιχεία του αρχιτεκτονικού σχεδίου του κλασσικού-ελληνιστικού οικισμού, ενώ διαπιστώσαμε την παρουσία αδιατάραχτου τμήματος της αρχαϊκής πόλης στη δυτική πλαγιά του λόφου, κοντά στο χώρο όπου οι γεωλογικές έρευνες τοποθετούν το αρχαίο λιμάνι. Διάφορα πήλινα θραύσματα (σίμες, μετόπες) στοιχειοθετούν την παρουσία ενός ή περισσοτέρων ναών στην κορυφή του λόφου, πιθανώς στο χώρο που κατέλαβε η Παλαιοχριστιανική βασιλική. Η εισηγμένη κεραμεική από την Αθήνα, την Κόρινθο, την Αχαΐα και την Ηλεία φανερώνει τις σχέσεις και επαφές, ενώ από την μελέτη των νομισμάτων προκύπτουν επαφές με την κεντρική Ελλάδα, την Ακαρνανία και πόλεις του Κορινθιακού Κόλπου.

Τα αποτελέσματα των τελευταίων ανασκαφών συνιστούν το πρώτο βήμα στην κατανόηση του χαρακτήρα και της σημασίας της Αρχαίας Χαλκίδας, όχι μόνο στην ευρύτερη περιοχή της αλλά και σε σχέση με τα άλλα μικρά λιμάνια στην περιοχή του Κορινθιακού και στην έξοδο προς το Ιόνιο.

Bibliography

Αδαμ-Βελένη, Π. 1997
Πέτρες Φλώρινας. Πρώτη προσέγγιση στην τοπική κεραμική παραγωγή, in: Δ'Επιστημονική Συνάντηση για την Ελληνιστική Κεραμική. Αθήνα. 138-154.

Aggeli, A. 1993
Arta. Odos Kommenou, *ADelt* 48, B1 Chron., 275-278.

Ανδρέου, Ι. 1994
Σύνολα ελληνιστικής κεραμικής από τα νεκροταφεία της αρχαίας Λευκάδος, in: Γ' Επιστημονική Συνάντηση για την Ελληνιστική Κεραμική. Αθήνα. 196-204.

Arnold-Biucchi, C. 1991a
Aitolia, in *LIMC*. I, 432.

Arnol-Biucchi, C. 1991b
Aitolos, in *LIMC* I, 433.

Blegen, C. 1937
Prosymna. The Helladic Settlement preceding the Argive Heraeum. Cambridge.

Bommeljé, S. & P.K. Doorn (eds.)1987
Aitolia and the Aitolians. Towards the Interdisciplinary Study of a Greek region. Studia Aitolica 1, Utrecht.

Bousquet, J. 1957
Les Aetoliens a Delphes au IVe siècle, *BCH*, 81, 485-495.

Coleman, J. 1977
Keos I : Kephala. A Late Neolithic Settlement and Cemetery. Princeton.

Cullen, T. 1985
A Measure of Interaction among Neolithic Communities: Design Elements of Greek Urfirnis Pottery. PhD thesis, Indiana University.

Dekoulakou, I. 1971
Alikirna, *ADelt* 26, B2 Chron., 325-326.

Dietz, S. 1998
A Catalogue of Selected Finds from the Excavations at Hagia Triadha, 1996, in *FPR*, 287-311.

Houby-Nielsen, S. 1998
Chalkis in Aetolia in Ancient Written Sources and Early Modern Travel Accounts. A Survey, in *FPR*, 238-254.

Immerwahr, S. 1971
The Athenian Agora. Results of Excavations conducted by the American School of Classical Studies at Athens. Volume XIII. The Neolithic and Bronze Ages. Princeton, New Jersey.

Καλτσας, Ν. Ε. 1998.
Ακανθος Ι. Η ανασκαφή στο νεκροταφείο κατά το 1979. Αθήνα.

Κομβου, Μ. - Ευτ. Ραλλη, 1997
Αγγεία καθημερινής χρήσης από το πηγάδι της οδού Νικομηδείας στην Επάνω Σκάλα Μυτιλήνης, in: Δ'Επιστημονική Συνάντηση για την Ελληνιστική Κεραμική. Αθήνα. 241-246.

Kotsakis, K. 1996
Ceramic Technology, in: *Papathanasopoulos* 1996, 245.

Κραβαρτόγιαννος, Δ. 1993
Εύρημα Αμφίσσης του Β αι. π. Χ χιλίων περίπου νομισμάτων, *Φωκικά Χρονικά*, Ε, 77.

Λιάμπη, Κ. 1996
Η νομισματική παραγωγή της Ποτιδανίας, πόλεως των Αποδωτών, in: Χαρακτήρ.Αφιέρωμα στη Μάντω Οικονομίδου, Αθήνα, 157.

Mastrokostas, E. 1961/2
Archaeotites ke mnemeia Aetoloakarnanias, *ADelt* 17, B Chron., 182-185.

Mastrokostas, E. 1963
Chalkis, *ADelt* 18, B1 Chron., 148.

Mastrokostas, E. 1965
Perisylogi Archaeon, *ADelt* 20, B1 Chron., 343-344.

Mela P., K. Preka, D. Strauch 1998
Die Grabstelen vom Grundstück Andrioti auf Korkyra, *AA*, 281-303.

Mettos, A & Karfakis, I. 1991
Geological Map of Greece
1:50.000. Evinokhorion Sheet.
Institute of Geology and Mineral
Exploration.

Orsi P. 1906
Gela. Scavi del 1900-1905, *MonAnt*
17, 539.

Παλιούρας, Α. Δ. 1985
Έκθεση για την ανασκαφή του
πανεπιστημίου Ιωαννίνων στην
Κάτω Βασιλική Αιτωλίας.Ιωάννινα.

Pantos, P.A. 1981
Lamia. Odos Metsovou 18, *ADelt*
36, B1 Chron., 206.

Πάντος, Π.Α. 1985
Τα σφραγίσματα της Αιτωλικής
Καλλιπόλεως, Διδακτόλεως
Διατριβή, Athens.

Papapostolou, I.A. 1972
Kalydon, *ADelt* 27, B2 Chron.,
434-436.

Papathanasopoulos, G. 1996 (ed.)
Neolithic Civilization in Greece. Gou-
landris Foundation. Athens.

Πετρόπουλος, Μ. 1991
Η Αιτωλοακαρνανία κατα τη
ρωμαική περίοδο, in: Πρακτικά Α
Αρχαιολογικού και Ιστορικού
Συνέδριου Αιτωλοακαρνανιας,
Αγρίνιο, 21-22-23 Οκτωβρίου
1988, 93-125.

Phelps, W. 1975
*The Neolithic Pottery Sequence in
Southern Greece*. Ph.D. thesis, Uni-
versity of London.

Picard, O. 1979
Chalcis et la confédération
Eubéenne. Étude de numismatique
et d´historie (IVᶜ – Ier siècle).
Paris.

Picard, O. 1984
Monnaies, in: L´Antre Corycien II,
BCH supplement IX, 281-306.

Pullen, D. 1995
The Pottery of the Neolithic, Early
Helladic I and II, in *Runnels et
al.(eds.)* 1995, 6-42.

Rice, P. 1987
Pottery Analysis. A Source Book.
Chicago.

Rhomaios, K. 1916
Chalkis, *ArchDelt* 2, 46-47.

Runnel, C. et al. (eds.) 1995
*Artefact and Assemblage. The Finds
from a Regional Survey of the Southern Argolid, Greece*, I, Stanford.

Rye, O.S. 1981
Pottery Technology (Manuals in
Archaeology 4). Washington.

Sampson, A. 1993
*Skoteini Tharrounion: the Cave, the
Settlement, the Cemetery*. Athens.

Sampson, A. 1997
*The Cave of Lakes at Kastria of
Kalavryta*. Athens.

Scheibler, I. 1976
*Griechische Lampen. Kerameikos.
Ergebnisse der Ausgrabungen,* Band
XI, Berlin.

Schweigert, E. 1939
Greek Inscriptions (1-13), Hesperia, 8, 1-47.

Scheu, F. 1960
Coinage Sytems of Aetolia, *NC*,
37-51.

Spitaels, P. 1982
Final Neolithic Pottery from Thorikos, in *Spitaels (ed.)* 1982, 9-45.

Spitaels, P. 1982
Studies in South Attica. (Miscellanea
Graeca 5). Gent.

Στεργιόπουλος, Κ. 1939
Η Αρχαία Αιτωλία, Αθήναι.

Stratouli, G. et al. in press
*Towards Understanding the Late Neo-
lithic and the Chalcolithic in the Ionian
Islands, Western Greece: C14 Evidence
from the Cave of Drakaina, Poros,
Cephalonia.* (Proceedings of the 3ʳᵈ
International Congress: C14 and
Archaeology). Lyon, France, 6-10
April, 1992.

Θέμελις, Π. Γ. - Ι. Π.
Τουρατσόγλου 1997
Οι τάφοι του Δερβενίου. Αθήνα.

Vitelli, K. 1993
Franchthi Neolithic Pottery I. Bloom-
ington/Indianapolis.

Vokotopoulou, I. 1971
Gardikion Paramythiá, *ADelt* 26,
B2 Chron., 332-333.

Vokotopoulou I. 1972
Arta, *ADelt* 27, B2 Chron., 442-
443.

Zapheiropoulou, F. 1973-74
Phokis – Aetoloakarnania, *ADelt*
29, B2 Chron., 539.

Zachos, K. 1987
*Ayios Demetrios. A Prehistoric Settle-
ment in the South-Western Peloponnesos: The Neolithic and Early Helladic
periods.* Ph.D. thesis, Boston University.

Abbreviations used in this report

AMP
Agrinion Museum Catalogue of Pottery

AMS
Agrinion Museum Catalogue of Stone
Finds

The Athenian Agora IV
The Athenian Agora. Results of Excavations conducted by the American School of Classical Studies at Athens. Volume IV. Greek Lamps and their Survivals, by Richard Hubbard Howland. Princeton, New Jersey. 1958.

The Athenian Agora XXIX: 1-2
The Athenian Agora. Results of Excavations conducted by the American School of Classical Studies at Athens. Volume XXIX. Hellenistic Pottery. Athenian and Imported Wheelmade Table ware and related Material, by Susan I. Rotroff. Princeton, New Jersey 1997.

BMC: Thessaly to Aetolia
R. St. Poole (edt.), The British Museum, London: Catalogue of Greek Coins. Thessaly to Aetolia. Bologna. 1963. (Reprint)

Corinth VII, I-II
Corinth. Results of Excavations conducted by the American School of Classical Studies at Athens. Volume VII, I-II. Archaic Corinthian Pottery and the Anaploga Well, by D.A. Amyx and Patricia Lawrence, Princeton New Jersey 1975.

Corinth VII, III
Results of Excavations conducted by the American School of Classical Studies at Athens.
Volume VII, III. Corinthian Hellenistic Pottery, by Edwards R.G., Princeton University, 1975.

Corinth XII
Corinth. Results of Excavations conducted by the American School of Classical Studies at Athens. Volume XII. The Minor Objects, by Gladys R. Davidson. 1952.

FPR 1998
Dietz, S., Kolonas, L., Moschos, I. And S. Houby-Nielsen (eds.), Surveys and excavations in Chalkis, Aetolias, 1995-1996. First preliminary report. *Proceedings of the Danish Institute at Athens*, II, 233-317.

HN
Head, B.V. 1911 (1963)
Historia Numorum. A Manual of Greek Numismatics. New and Enlarged Edition. Oxford, 1911.(Reprint: 1963)

OF XX
W. Gauer, Die Bronzegefässe von Olympia I, Olympische Forschungen XX. Berlin – New York. 1991.

OF XXIV
J. Heiden, Die Tondächer von Olympia, Olympische Forschungen XXIV, Berlin – New York, 1995.

Ori 1985
Gli ori di Taranto in eta ellenistica, Milano. 1985.

SNG: Copenhagen
Sylloge Nummorum Graecorum, The Royal Collection of Coins and Medals, Danish National Museum, Copenhagen, III, Greece: Thessaly to Aegean Islands. New Jersey. 1982. (Reprint).